Access to Mental Health Care in South Asia

S. M. Yasir Arafat · Sujita Kumar Kar
Editors

Access to Mental Health Care in South Asia

Current Status, Potential Challenges, and Ways Out

Editors
S. M. Yasir Arafat ⓘ
Department of Psychiatry
Enam Medical College and Hospital
Dhaka, Bangladesh

Sujita Kumar Kar
Department of Psychiatry
King George's Medical University
Lucknow, Uttar Pradesh, India

ISBN 978-981-99-9152-5   ISBN 978-981-99-9153-2 (eBook)
https://doi.org/10.1007/978-981-99-9153-2

© The Editor(s) (if applicable) and The Author(s), under exclusive license to Springer Nature Singapore Pte Ltd. 2024

This work is subject to copyright. All rights are solely and exclusively licensed by the Publisher, whether the whole or part of the material is concerned, specifically the rights of translation, reprinting, reuse of illustrations, recitation, broadcasting, reproduction on microfilms or in any other physical way, and transmission or information storage and retrieval, electronic adaptation, computer software, or by similar or dissimilar methodology now known or hereafter developed.
The use of general descriptive names, registered names, trademarks, service marks, etc. in this publication does not imply, even in the absence of a specific statement, that such names are exempt from the relevant protective laws and regulations and therefore free for general use.
The publisher, the authors, and the editors are safe to assume that the advice and information in this book are believed to be true and accurate at the date of publication. Neither the publisher nor the authors or the editors give a warranty, expressed or implied, with respect to the material contained herein or for any errors or omissions that may have been made. The publisher remains neutral with regard to jurisdictional claims in published maps and institutional affiliations.

This Springer imprint is published by the registered company Springer Nature Singapore Pte Ltd.
The registered company address is: 152 Beach Road, #21-01/04 Gateway East, Singapore 189721, Singapore

Paper in this product is recyclable.

To Asma Khatun
Sarvodaya Tripathy

Preface

South Asia consists of eight countries (Afghanistan, Bangladesh, Bhutan, India, Maldives, Nepal, Pakistan, and Sri Lanka) with low- and middle-income backgrounds. The people of this region share common cultures, beliefs, and behavioral patterns regarding physical and mental health and health care seeking. At the same time, there are some variations based on the local culture, language, and religion of the country. The region contains about 2 billion populations making up about a quarter of the global population. Among them, more than 200 million people have been suffering from common mental disorders. Historically, there are persisting high treatment gaps for mental illness in the countries of the region. Despite having a mental illness, only a small proportion of the population is able to avail essential mental healthcare due to the treatment gaps and existing challenges. Though the sector is gradually improving by improvising mental health policies and programs, it still stands as a major challenge in delivering mental healthcare to all people in need due to the pattern of disease burden, income category of the country, and mental health care delivery system. The basic mental health services structure was laid down during the British regime which is supposed to overlook the enduring cultural barriers like help-seeking patterns and non-medical management of mental disorders (religious healers, herbalists, Kabiraz, Homeopathy and alternate medicine, and Samans). Additionally, due to the income category and dual disease burden of the countries, there are some enduring challenges like poor funding and research, inadequate and inequitable manpower, huge out-of-pocket expenses, poor mental health literacy, income disparity, and high stigma. Furthermore, poor attention is noted to the above-mentioned issues and the provision of standard mental health care. We did not find any previous attempt focusing on the challenges and possible ways out of access to mental health care in South Asia highlighting the similarities and dissimilarities of the countries along with regional help-seeking behavior. We aimed to highlight the issues related to mental health services access in a densely populated low- and middle-income setting, i.e. South Asia. This book is the first of its kind of approach contrasting the mental health services delivery status of South Asian countries. We focus on the practical challenges of access to mental health services in the regions along with our speculations suggesting the possible ways out.

At the beginning, we highlighted the epidemiology of mental illness and an overview of access to mental health care in South Asia, and subsequently, we discussed the country-wise chapter for Afghanistan, Bangladesh, Bhutan, India, Nepal, Pakistan, and Sri Lanka. For an individual chapter, we highlighted historical aspects of mental health services development in a country, epidemiology and burden of mental illness in a country, available mental health services, new avenues (telepsychiatry), challenges of mental care (poor fund and research, inadequate and inequitable manpower, huge out-of-pocket expense, poor mental health literacy, low income and income disparity, high stigma, help-seeking patterns, non-judicious prescribing [poly pharmacy], and non-medical management of mental disorders [religious healers, herbalist, kabiraz, Homeopathy and alternate medicine, and samans]), and finally potential country-specific ways out. Subsequently, we looked at the variations of challenges and ways out of access to mental health care among the countries in South Asia. We highlight the research, innovations, and ideas to facilitate mental healthcare delivery in South Asia, public mental health aspects, and research innovations for better service delivery in the region.

This book will be useful for researchers, academics, and professionals in the fields of mental health, public health, public mental health, public health administration, mass media and communication, behavioral science, and social science. A good understanding of the challenges of access to mental health services and adopting its remedies would be a focus for health science as it is useful for the development of behavior change communication and human psychology.

Dhaka, Bangladesh S. M. Yasir Arafat
Lucknow, Uttar Pradesh, India Sujia Kumar Kar

Contents

Epidemiology of Psychiatric Disorders and Overview of Access to Mental Health Care in South Asia 1
S. M. Yasir Arafat and Sujita Kumar Kar

Mental Healthcare in Afghanistan 17
Sheikh Shoib, Syed Sameer Hussaini, Sardar Khan Nazari, and Fahimeh Saeed

Access to Mental Health Care in Bangladesh—Current Status, Potential Challenges, and Ways Out 29
S. M. Yasir Arafat, Noor Ahmed Giasuddin, and Atiqul Haq Mazumder

Access to Mental Health Care in Bhutan: Current Status, Potential Challenges, and Ways Out 57
Pawan Sharma and Devavrat Joshi

Mental Healthcare Access in India: Models, Trends, and Challenges ... 71
Sujita Kumar Kar and Vikas Menon

Access to Mental Health Care in Nepal: Current Status, Potential Challenges, and Ways Out 91
Pawan Sharma, Kamal Gautam, and Kedar Marahatta

Mental Health Care in Pakistan 113
Aisha Noorullah, Nargis Asad, Shahina Pirani, Samiya Iqbal, and Murad M. Khan

Psychiatric Morbidity and Mental Health Services in Sri Lanka 137
Sajeewana C. Amarasinghe and Thilini N. Rajapakse

Access to Mental Health Care in South Asia: Variations of Challenges and Ways Forward 155
Ravi Philip Rajkumar

Research, Innovations, and Ideas to Facilitate Mental Healthcare Delivery in South Asia 197
Nilamadhab Kar

Public Mental Health and Access to Mental Health Services in South Asia 229
Russell Kabir, Sharon Shivuli Isigi, and Catharina Candussi

About the Editors

Dr. S. M. Yasir Arafat is currently working as Assistant Professor of Psychiatry at Enam Medical College and Hospital, Dhaka, Bangladesh. He completed his MD in Psychiatry from Bangabandhu Sheikh Mujib Medical University, Dhaka and MBBS from the Dhaka Medical College, Dhaka, Bangladesh. He also did an MPH in Health Economics and an MBA in Marketing. Dr. Arafat has (co)authored more than 300 peer-reviewed articles and book chapters, and (co)edited several books with Springer. He has been included in the global 2% researcher list in 2021 and 2022. He is acting as an editorial member in more than 10 leading journals in mental health published by Frontiers, Wiley, Hindawi, Springer, Taylor, and Francis. He focuses on the epidemiological aspects of mental disorders and human behaviors.

Dr. Sujita Kumar Kar is currently working as Additional Professor of Psychiatry at King George's Medical University, Lucknow, Uttar Pradesh, India. He is the editor-in-chief of the Indian Journal of Health, Sexuality and Culture. He is also the editorial board member and reviewer of various national and international journals. He has written 62 book chapters and more than 450 articles in various national & international journals and made 70 presentations at various national and international conferences. He has been included in the global 2% researcher list released by Stanford University in 2021 and 2022. His research interests include brain stimulation, neuropsychiatry, and suicide prevention.

List of Figures

Epidemiology of Psychiatric Disorders and Overview of Access to Mental Health Care in South Asia

Fig. 1	Major health care challenges in South Asia	6

Access to Mental Health Care in Bangladesh—Current Status, Potential Challenges, and Ways Out

Fig. 1	Map of Bangladesh	31
Fig. 2	Health services delivery care levels in Bangladesh. Adapted from Facility Registry (2023), Government of the People's Republic of Bangladesh (2022)	36
Fig. 3	Potential help-seeking pathway for mental disorders in Bangladesh	38

Mental Healthcare Access in India: Models, Trends, and Challenges

Fig. 1	Visions of National Mental Health Policy of India. *Source* National Mental Health Policy, Ministry of health and family welfare, Government of India	77

Access to Mental Health Care in South Asia: Variations of Challenges and Ways Forward

Fig. 1	Illustration of the typical course of events in a person with mental illness	175

Research, Innovations, and Ideas to Facilitate Mental Healthcare Delivery in South Asia

Fig. 1	Patient-centric care provision	218

List of Tables

Access to Mental Health Care in Bhutan: Current Status, Potential Challenges, and Ways Out

Table 1   Mental Health Resources of Bhutan (Addressing Mental Health in Bhutan, WHO, 2022) 65

Mental Healthcare Access in India: Models, Trends, and Challenges

Table 1   Number of mental health facilities/establishments engaged in provision of mental healthcare in India by 2017 (World Health Organization, 2017) 75

Access to Mental Health Care in Nepal: Current Status, Potential Challenges, and Ways Out

Table 1   Historical landmarks in mental health in Nepal (Shyangwa & Jha, 2008; Upadhyaya, 2015) 92

Table 2   Findings of National Mental Health Survey, 2019/20 (Dhimal et al., 2022) 94

Table 3   Mental health resources of Nepal in 2023 (*WHO*, 2021; Rai et al., 2021) 98

Mental Health Care in Pakistan

Table 1   Demonstrates varying levels of anxiety and depression being reported by various studies 117

Access to Mental Health Care in South Asia: Variations of Challenges and Ways Forward

Table 1   Other specific challenges related to mental health care in South Asian countries 170

Table 2	Principles and objectives of the WHO's comprehensive mental health action plan (World Health Organization, 2021c)	174
Table 3	Proposed initiatives, innovations and "ways forward" to improve mental health in South Asian countries	176

Research, Innovations, and Ideas to Facilitate Mental Healthcare Delivery in South Asia

Table 1	Summary of the level, roles, and actions in the process of facilitating mental health care	216

Public Mental Health and Access to Mental Health Services in South Asia

Table 1	Mental health programmes according to WHO mental health atlas (WHO, 2021b)	233
Table 2	Status of mental health programmes in South Asian countries	237

Epidemiology of Psychiatric Disorders and Overview of Access to Mental Health Care in South Asia

S. M. Yasir Arafat and Sujita Kumar Kar

Abstract South Asia is a densely populated area consisting of eight countries with low- and middle-income backgrounds. The region shares some common cultural beliefs, distribution of psychiatric disorders, care-seeking patterns, and enduring treatment gaps. At the same time, there are some variations among the countries based on religion, local culture, languages, and sociocultural aspects. This chapter discusses an overview of the epidemiology of mental disorders in South Asian countries along with potential challenges, including treatment gaps, help-seeking patterns, and out-of-pocket expenses to provide mental health services in South Asia. It also highlights the influence of non-medical management of psychiatric disorders, like traditional healers and religious persons, in help-seeking for mental health in the region.

Keywords Epidemiology · Psychiatric disorders · South Asia · Mental health care · Mental health services · Challenges of mental health care

1 Introduction

Afghanistan, Bangladesh, Bhutan, India, Maldives, Nepal, Pakistan, and Sri Lanka are the eight countries with low- and middle-income country (LMIC) backgrounds make South Asia (World Bank, 2023a, 2023b). These are also called the *South Asian Association for Regional Cooperation (SAARC)* countries. The SAARC was initially started in 1985 with seven South Asian countries (Bangladesh, Bhutan, India, Maldives, Nepal, Pakistan, and Sri Lanka). Later, in 2005, Afghanistan joined the regional network (Trivedi et al., 2007). Afghanistan, Bangladesh, the Maldives, and Pakistan are Muslim-majority countries, India and Nepal are Hindu majorities, and Bhutan and Sri Lanka are Buddhist-majority countries. Afghanistan and Pakistan

S. M. Y. Arafat (✉)
Department of Psychiatry, Enam Medical College and Hospital, Dhaka, Bangladesh
e-mail: arafatdmc62@gmail.com

S. K. Kar
Department of Psychiatry, King George's Medical University, Uttar Pradesh, Lucknow, India

© The Author(s), under exclusive license to Springer Nature Singapore Pte Ltd. 2024
S. M. Y. Arafat and S. K. Kar (eds.), *Access to Mental Health Care in South Asia*,
https://doi.org/10.1007/978-981-99-9153-2_1

are the Islamic Republic, Bhutan has a constitutional monarchy, and the rest five countries are parliamentary democracies (Isaac, 2011). Among them, Afghanistan is a low-income country, the Maldives is an upper-middle-income country, and the rest six are lower-middle-income countries (World Bank, 2023a). The region has 1.92 billion population in 2022, covering about one-fourth (24.15%) of global populations representing different ethnicities, cultures, languages, and religions (Grover, 2023; Trivedi et al., 2007; World Bank, 2023b). Among the South Asian countries, the majority of the population lives in India (1.4 billion), Pakistan (235 million), and Bangladesh (171 million) (World Bank, 2023b), covering about 95% of the South Asian population. Sri Lanka was facing violence and civil war till 2009, with a war of more than two and half decades; Afghanistan has also faced extreme violence for US invasions till 2021 over the past decades; and Pakistan has been facing political instability for decades. The region faces several forms of manmade disasters and natural calamities. There are crises over the transition of power, money laundering, and political oppression in Bangladesh. There are conflicts among religious minorities in India. The South Asian countries have been sharing similar characteristics like less developed industrial sector, agro-based economy, poor living standards, poverty, inadequate resources for mental health, and fragile public health systems (Grover, 2023). When we look into the development of mental health services in the region, we see that mental asylums are found in India (see Kar & Menon, 2024), Bangladesh (see Arafat et al., 2024), Pakistan (see Noorullah et al., 2024), and Sri Lanka (Amarasinghe & Rajapakse, 2024); whereas no asylum was established in Nepal (Sharma et al., 2024).

While South Asia has significantly improved health care services in recent years; however, the region still faces unique health care challenges that require urgent attention (Grover, 2023). Efforts to address mental health disorders in South Asia have been limited and inadequate. There are persisting high treatment gaps for mental illness in the countries of the region. Despite having a mental illness, only a small chunk of the population avail essential mental health care due to the treatment gaps and existing challenges. Though governments are trying to bridge the gap by improvising mental health policies and programs, it still stands as a major challenge in delivering mental health care to all people in need due to the pattern of disease burden and income category of the country. In this chapter, we highlighted the epidemiology of mental illness and an overview of access to mental health care in South Asia.

2 Epidemiology of Psychiatric Disorders in South Asia

Psychiatric disorders worldwide, including in South Asia, are a major public health concern. South Asia holds about one-fifth of the mentally ill patients in the world (Trivedi et al., 2007). Due to the lack of adequate health care infrastructure and resources, psychiatric disorders remain poorly recognized, diagnosed, and treated in this region. Mental health disorders are associated with a substantial burden of disease and disability-adjusted life years (DALYs) in South Asia, leading to increased health care costs, poor quality of life, and reduced productivity.

According to the Global Burden of Disease (GBD) study, the prevalence of mental health disorders in South Asia ranged from 4.4 to 13.4%, with depression being the most common disorder, followed by anxiety disorders, substance abuse, and schizophrenia (GBD, 2017). The burden of mental health disorders is higher among women, with a higher prevalence of depression, anxiety, and somatic symptoms.

Other reviews found that the prevalence of psychiatric disorders ranges from 12.2 to 14.2% with country-wise variations where depression and anxiety disorders are the prominent disorders (Neveed et al., 2020; Ranjan & Asthana, 2017; Hossain et al., 2020). Considering the prevalence rate, the total number of psychiatric patients is more than 200 million in this region (Trivedi et al., 2007).

In Bangladesh, it was found 18.7% from a nationwide study, ranging from 6.5 to 31% from a systematic review (see Arafat et al., 2024; Hossain et al., 2020). The lifetime prevalence of psychiatric disorders was 13.7%, and the current prevalence was 10.6% in India, obtained from the recent national mental health survey (Grover, 2023). The lifetime prevalence of psychiatric disorders was 10% among adults, and the current prevalence was 4.3% in Nepal, obtained from the recent national mental health survey (Grover, 2023). There is a scarcity of studies assessing the nationwide prevalence of psychiatric disorders in Pakistan. However, available studies revealed a high prevalence of common mental disorders (see Noorullah et al., 2024).

The region is a suicide-dense area. According to the World Health Organization (WHO) report of 2021, about 30% ($n = 205{,}847$) of total suicides happened in 2019 in South Asia where about 25% of the total population live. Among the eight countries, India shared the major burden (one quarter) followed by Pakistan and Sri Lanka (World Health Organization, 2021). Suicide is not considered a criminal offense in Afghanistan and Bhutan, and it is never considered a criminal offense in Nepal. It was decriminalized in Sri Lanka in 1998, in India in 2017, and in Pakistan in 2022 (Lew et al., 2022; Piracha, 2023). In South Asia, Bangladesh and the Maldives are the countries where suicide is considered a criminal offense (World Health Organization, 2023a).

3 Changing Trends of Psychiatric Disorder

The past century witnessed a revolutionary change in psychiatric care, globally. After the development of newer pharmacological, somatic treatments, and more structured psychotherapeutic interventions, the outcome of psychiatric disorders is changing rapidly. Now, the majority of psychiatric disorders have evidence-based treatments, which are effective enough in changing the quality of life, and disability and enable patients with psychiatric disorders to lead a productive life. At the same time, the burden on the caregivers is also reduced. A recent systematic review and meta-regression analysis revealed that there is a high prevalence of common mental illnesses in the South Asian population (Naveed et al., 2020). As per the GBD study, the prevalence of psychiatric disorders increased globally from 1990 to 2019, as well as the disabilities due to mental illnesses during this period (GBD 2019 Mental Disorders Collaborators, 2022).

Various factors contribute to change in the epidemiology of psychiatric disorders. The major factors that attribute to change in psychiatric disorder epidemiology are:

1. Agent-related factors
   a. Stress
   b. Substance use (there is a changing trend of substance use and as substance use is a major risk factor for other mental illnesses, the risk of development of other mental illnesses)
   c. Infections (systemic infections, particularly those with a high propensity to involve the central nervous system, are more likely to produce psychiatric symptoms)
   d. Nutritional factors
   e. Ecological adversities

2. Host-related factors (Population characteristics)
   a. Resilience
   b. Beliefs
   c. Literacy
   d. Attitude toward mental health
   e. Addiction

3. Environment-related factors
   a. The time frame of study
   b. Geographic region (war and disaster-prone zones may have a high prevalence of stress-related disorders)
   c. Cultural beliefs (changing cultural beliefs, geographical variations in cultural beliefs)
   d. Changing family dynamics (Resolution of joint family and more of nuclear family)
   e. Education
   f. Poverty
   g. Access to mental health care facilities
   h. Stigma
   i. Migration

4. Research design-related factors
   a. Tools used for estimating the epidemiology
   b. Nature of assessment (self-reported versus interview by a trained lay person versus interview by experts)
   c. The setting of assessment (community-based or clinic-based).

The above-mentioned factors keep on changing from time to time and region to region, resulting in changing trends in psychiatric disorder epidemiology.

Earlier there was a gross lack of structure in mental health care, which has changed significantly over the past several decades. To protect the rights of people with mental illnesses, legislation has been implemented in most South Asian countries, though the coverage of mental health legislation, policy, and program in South Asian countries is not at par with that of Western countries (Trivedi et al., 2015; World Health Organization, 2017). Gradually most of the countries are trying to abide by the international norms and standards by having a country-specific mental health legislation, policy, action plan, and program.

4 Health Care Challenges in South Asia

South Asia is a heavily populated region of the globe. It has several health care challenges, that adversely affect the population's well-being. The common health care challenges in South Asia are (Fig. 1).

4.1 High Burden of Communicable Diseases Including HIV/AIDS

South Asia has a high burden of communicable diseases, such as tuberculosis, malaria, and HIV/AIDS. According to the WHO, by 2018, 3.8 million people were living with HIV/AIDS in eleven Southeast Asian countries (World Health Organization, 2023b). Similarly, South Asia harbors 40% of the global cases of tuberculosis and approximately 38% of global deaths due to tuberculosis (Basnyat et al., 2018). When it comes to South East Asia, it accounts for 26% of the global burden of tuberculosis in 2021 and more than 505 of global deaths due to tuberculosis (World Health Organization, 2022b). South Asia is a major contributor to the global burden of malaria. India is the country that is most responsible for the prevalence of malaria in Southeast Asia, followed by Indonesia, Myanmar, and Thailand (Kumar et al., 2012). The spread of these diseases is facilitated by poverty, poor sanitation, and overcrowding, making it challenging to control them.

4.2 Rise of Non-communicable Diseases

While communicable diseases remain a significant problem in South Asia, the region is also experiencing a rapid rise in non-communicable diseases (NCDs), such as diabetes, cardiovascular diseases, and cancer. These diseases are now the leading

Fig. 1 Major health care challenges in South Asia

cause of death in the region, and the trend is expected to continue. According to the WHO, NCDs account for 62% of deaths in Southeast Asia (World Health Organization, 2023c). Hypertension is the most common non-communicable disease that increases the risk of cardiovascular mortality and morbidity and renal diseases in LMICs (Rahut et al., 2023). NCDs like diabetes, hypertension, other cardiovascular & metabolic disorders, and mental health issues are the major burden in South Asian countries, which are in a rising trend (Siegel et al., 2014).

4.3 Limited Access to Health Care

Access to health care is a significant challenge in South Asia, particularly in rural areas. Many people in the region do not have access to basic health care services, such as clean water, sanitation, and primary health care. Inadequate infrastructure, a shortage of health care workers, and limited funding are major obstacles to improving health care access in the region. Moreso there is an inequitable distribution of health care with most of the health care facilities being centered in and around urban areas (van Weel et al., 2016).

4.4 Malnutrition

Malnutrition is a significant health problem in South Asia, particularly among children (Global Nutrition Report, 2022). The prevalence of stunting and wasting are 30.7% and 14.1%, respectively, in South Asia (Global Nutrition Report, 2022). More than one-fourth (26.4%) of children in South Asia have low birth weight and approximately half (48.4%) of the women of reproductive age have anemia (Global Nutrition Report, 2022). The adult population in South Asia is also not spared from malnutrition. In South Asia, 11% of men and 10.1% of women live with diabetes, whereas 8.4% of women and 4.8% of women live with obesity (Global Nutrition Report, 2022). Malnutrition is responsible for reduced cognitive function and productivity (Akhtar, 2016). Several factors have been identified that attributes to malnutrition. These factors are—poverty, unavailability of food, micronutrient deficiency, illiteracy, low income, scarcity of health care resources, high cost of health care, poor hygiene, and low standard of living (Akhtar, 2016).

4.5 Gender-Based Violence

Gender-based violence, including domestic violence, sexual violence, and child marriage, is prevalent in South Asia. These forms of violence significantly impact women's physical and mental health, leading to long-term health problems. South Asian countries with patriarchal societies have witnessed extreme degrees of gender-based violence for centuries (Niaz, 2003). The recent COVID-19 pandemic-related lockdown has increased gender-based violence (domestic violence, intimate partner violence) significantly across the globe, including South Asia (Dlamini, 2021).

4.6 Inadequate Mental Health Care

Mental health care is often neglected in South Asia, with limited resources and funding allocated to mental health services. The stigma associated with mental illness is a significant barrier to seeking help, and there is a shortage of trained mental health professionals in the region (Kakuma et al, 2011; Meshvara, 2002).

4.7 Other Major Factors

Other major factors, that may stand as health care challenges in South Asia are—stigma, unawareness, poverty, political instabilities, war & terrorism, and natural calamities and disasters. Poverty, lack of education leading to poor health literacy and awareness, and stigma are closely related factors that may result in poor help-seeking for health care ailments. South Asia is having long-standing conflicts, wars, and terrorism (which is more evident in Afghanistan, Pakistan, Sri Lanka, Nepal, and India [more in the Kashmir belt]) that affected the development of health infrastructure and providing health care facilities. Disasters & calamities like floods, earthquakes, cyclones, and famines are common in South Asia and also affect access to health care.

5 Access to Mental Health Care in South Asia

Access to mental health care in South Asia is influenced by various factors, including socioeconomic status, cultural beliefs and stigma, inadequate mental health infrastructure, and inadequate numbers of mental health professionals. Below are some of the key factors affecting access to mental health care in South Asia.

5.1 High Treatment Gap

Historically, there are persisting high treatment gaps for mental illness in the countries of the region. According to a study published in The Lancet Psychiatry, in LMICs, including those in South Asia, the treatment gap for mental disorders is as high as 85%, with only a small proportion of individuals receiving any kind of mental health care (Kakuma et al., 2011). It was found 91% in Bangladesh (Arafat et al., 2024), 85–95% in India (Grover, 2023; Sagar et al., 2017), and 70% in Afghanistan (Sadat et al., 2023).

5.2 Unregulated Help-Seeking Pattern and Non-medical Management of Mental Disorders

Since the early days, there have been many popular traditional, religious, and alternate methods of treatment like Ayurveda, Homeopathy, and herbal medicine; Alternative medicine was available and chosen by the inhabitants of this region (Isaac, 2011; Trivedi et al., 2007). Mental illness has been considered to be associated with supernatural powers like Jinn among Muslims are prevailed. Therefore, remedial measures have been sought from religious persons. Community people can choose any treatment modality based on their will.

5.3 Poor Fund and Research

Overall, health has received a low priority in the region, evidenced by meager governmental spending on health (Isaac, 2011; Trivedi et al., 2007). The governments in all South Asian countries except Afghanistan have less than 1% budgetary allocation for mental health (Grover, 2023). And the majority of this allocation is directed toward mental hospitals. Additionally, we found in the Mental Health Atlas 2020 data the region produces a minuscule of research on mental health (Grover, 2023). There are only three indexed journals in India from the region, and researchers from this region face plenty of publishing challenges (Arafat et al., 2022a). Many countries in South Asia have limited mental health infrastructure, with few facilities dedicated to mental health care. Additionally, there is often a lack of funding for mental health services and research, resulting in inadequate mental health care resources.

5.4 Inadequate and Inequitable Manpower

There is a shortage of mental health professionals in South Asia, with few psychiatrists, psychologists, and other mental health professionals per capita (Grover, 2023; Isaac, 2011; Trivedi et al., 2007). This shortage is further compounded by inadequate training and a lack of access to continuing education for mental health professionals. Additionally, the distribution of manpower in mental health is centralized and inequitable, as most of the psychiatrists practice in the cities (Trivedi et al., 2007). The number of psychiatrists per 100,000 population ranges from 0.14 (Pakistan) to 3.2 in Maldives (World Health Organization, 2022a). It was 0.34 in Afghanistan, 0.17 in Bangladesh, 0.39 in Bhutan, 0.29 in India (2017 data), 0.64 in Nepal, and 0.58 in Sri Lanka (World Health Organization, 2017, 2022a). The number of mental health nurses per 100,000 population ranges from 0 (Maldives) to 2.93 in Sri Lanka. It was 0.07 in Afghanistan, 0.43 in Bangladesh and Nepal, 1.18 in Bhutan, 0.80 in India, and 0.09 in Pakistan (World Health Organization, 2022a). The number of psychologists per 100,000 population ranges from 0 (Bhutan) to 1.32 in Maldives (World Health Organization, 2022a). The number of social workers per 100,000 population ranges from 0 (Bhutan and Nepal) to 0.38 in Maldives (World Health Organization, 2022a).

5.5 Huge Out-of-Pocket Expense

Insurance services for the treatment of psychiatric disorders are technically absent in the region. Therefore, out-of-pocket expense is the primary source of funds available for the treatment of mental disorders in South Asia (Isaac, 2011). Based on the chronic nature of psychiatric disorders and enduring management services create challenges in meeting out-of-pocket expenses.

5.6 Malfunctioning Referral System

Based on the existing health services structure, the referral system works poorly in the region. There is literally a non-existence of a referral system in Bangladesh (Arafat et al., 2024). Additionally, it is affected by peculiar help-seeking behavior from non-medical treatment providers.

5.7 Lower-Middle Income and Income Disparity

Poverty is a significant barrier to accessing mental health care in South Asia. People struggle to meet their livelihoods, residence, physical health, and education while treatment of psychiatric disorders is neglected. Low-income individuals may struggle to afford treatment or transportation to mental health facilities. In addition, mental health services are often concentrated in urban areas, where they may be inaccessible to rural populations.

5.8 High Stigma and Poor Mental Health Literacy

Cultural beliefs and stigma surrounding mental illness can prevent individuals from seeking care. In South Asia, mental illness is often viewed as a sign of weakness or as a punishment for past actions. There is a high prevalence of stigma toward psychiatric disorders (Grover, 2023). This can lead to discrimination and social exclusion, causing individuals to avoid seeking help for fear of being ostracized or discriminated against (Thornicroft et al., 2022). Mental health literacy is untapped in South Asia, and it is expected to be lower due to high stigma and few or no education programs.

6 Future Directions

6.1 Augmented Research and Funds

There is no alternative to augmented research in the mental health of South Asian countries (Trivedi et al., 2007; Isaac, 2011; Grover, 2023). There is a need for cultural adaptation of psychometric tools in local languages to foster further research (Grover, 2023). The development of an improved research system and supportive research environment is essential for local researchers and females in leadership positions (Arafat et al., 2022a, 2022b; Isaac, 2011). Adequate funds and a separate budget for mental health problems are immediate priorities in the region.

6.2 Insurance for Mental Health

Insurance coverage for the treatment of mental disorders in South Asia is an immediate need to increase mental health access and reduce out-of-pocket expenses and poverty. Certainly, it will improve the functional activity of persons with mental illness and quality of life.

6.3 Mental Health Services at Primary Care

To reduce the huge treatment gap, mental health services should be available in primary care settings in the countries of South Asia. Mental health services should be readily available to community populations (Isaac, 2011).

6.4 Multi-lateral Collaboration

As there are similarities and dissimilarities among the South Asian countries, multi-lateral collaboration is needed to enhance mental health services in the region. The *SAARC Psychiatric Federation (SPF)*, which was started in 2005, should play the deciding role in organizing the collaboration (Grover, 2023). Additionally, collaboration with the World Psychiatric Association (WPA) would bolster the efforts (Trivedi et al., 2007).

6.5 Mass Media Promotion

Careful promotion of mental health issues targeting the reduction of stigma and promotion of mental health literacy could be considered a universal strategy (Trivedi et al., 2007). Such efforts would like to improve the access to mental health services.

6.6 Academic Reformations

Changes in the undergraduate psychiatry curriculum could be targeted to ensure homogeneity in SAARC countries as well as to prepare dedicated and skillful mental health professionals (Grover, 2023; Arafat et al., 2021). Regular training programs and exchanges of faculty/trainees among the SAARC countries would potentiate skilled manpower development and regional cooperation (Trivedi et al., 2007). Adequate manpower for the growing mental health burden in South Asian countries should be prioritized. Proper country-specific or region-specific strategies could be planned and implemented.

7 Conclusion

Despite progress in health care, there are still significant gaps in access to mental health care that require urgent attention. To address these challenges, South Asian countries need to invest in mental health care infrastructure, improve access to mental health care, and increase funding for mental health research. Addressing these challenges will require a coordinated effort from governments, non-governmental organizations, and international organizations to improve the health outcomes of people in the region.

References

Akhtar, S. (2016). Malnutrition in South Asia-A critical reappraisal. *Critical Reviews in Food Science and Nutrition, 56*(14), 2320–2330.

Amarasinghe, S., & Rajapakse, T. (2024). Psychiatric morbidity and mental health services: The way forward for Sri Lanka. In S. M. Y. Arafat, & S. K. Kar (Eds.), Access to Mental Health Care in South Asia—Current status, potential challenges, and ways out. Springer Nature Singapore. https://doi.org/10.1007/978-981-99-9153-2_8

Arafat, S. Y., Ali, S. A. E. Z., Saleem, T., Banerjee, D., Singh, R., Baminiwatta, A., & Shoib, S. (2022a). Academic psychiatry journals in South Asian countries: Most from India, none from Afghanistan, Bhutan and the Maldives. *Global Psychiatry Achieves, 5*, 1–9. https://doi.org/10.52095/gp.2021.4395.1036

Arafat, S. M. Y., Amin, R., Baminiwatta, A., Hussain, F., Singh, R., Kar, S. K., & Mubashir, A. S. (2022b). Gender distribution of editors in psychiatry journals of South Asia. *Psychiatry Research, 317*, 114819. https://doi.org/10.1016/j.psychres.2022.114819

Arafat, S. M. Y., Giasuddin, N. A., Mazumder, A. H. (2024). Access to Mental Health Care in Bangladesh—Current status, potential challenges, and ways out. In S. M. Y. Arafat, S. K. Kar (Eds.), Access to Mental Health Care in South Asia—Current status, potential challenges, and ways out. Springer Nature Singapore. https://doi.org/10.1007/978-981-99-9153-2_3

Arafat, S. M. Y., Kar, S. K., Sharma, P., Marahatta, K., & Baminiwatta, A. K. A. B. (2021). A comparative analysis of psychiatry curriculum at the undergraduate level of Bangladesh, India, Nepal, and Sri Lanka. *Indian Journal of Psychiatry, 63*(2), 184–188. https://doi.org/10.4103/psychiatry.IndianJPsychiatry_615_20

Basnyat, B., Caws, M., & Udwadia, Z. (2018). Tuberculosis in South Asia: A tide in the affairs of men. *Multidisciplinary Respiratory Medicine, 13*, 10. https://doi.org/10.1186/s40248-018-0122-y

Dlamini, N. J. (2021). Gender-based violence, twin pandemic to COVID-19. *Critical Sociology, 47*(4–5), 583–590. https://doi.org/10.1177/0896920520975465

GBD 2017 Disease and Injury Incidence and Prevalence Collaborators. (2018). Global, regional, and national incidence, prevalence, and years lived with disability for 354 diseases and injuries for 195 countries and territories, 1990–2017: A systematic analysis for the Global Burden of Disease Study 2017. *The Lancet, 392*(10159), 1789–1858.

GBD 2019 Mental Disorders Collaborators. (2022). Global, regional, and national burden of 12 mental disorders in 204 countries and territories, 1990–2019: A systematic analysis for the Global Burden of Disease Study 2019. *The Lancet Psychiatry, 9*(2), 137–150.

Global Nutrition Report. (2022). Country nutrition profiles: Southern Asia. The burden of malnutrition at a glance. Retrieved July 09, 2023 from https://globalnutritionreport.org/resources/nutrition-profiles/asia/southern-asia/#:~:text=The%20Southern%20Asia%20subregion's%20adult,of%20men%20live%20with%20obesity

Grover, S. (2023). Status of mental health in South Asian countries. *Journal of SAARC Psychiatric Federation, 1*(1), 1–5. https://doi.org/10.4103/jspf.JSPF_15_23

Hossain, M. M., Purohit, N., Sultana, A., Ma, P., McKyer, E. L. J., & Ahmed, H. U. (2020). Prevalence of mental disorders in South Asia: An umbrella review of systematic reviews and meta-analyses. *Asian Journal of Psychiatry, 51*, 102041. https://doi.org/10.1016/j.ajp.2020.102041

Isaac, M. (2011). Mental health services in South Asia: Past, present and future. *South Asian Journal of Psychiatry, 2*(1), 4–12.; Kakuma, R., Minas, H., van Ginneken, N., Dal Poz, M. R., Desiraju, K., Morris, J. E., & Saxena, S. (2011). Human resources for mental health care: current situation and strategies for action. *The Lancet Psychiatry, 378*(9803), 1654–1663.

Kakuma, R., Minas, H., Van Ginneken, N., Dal Poz, M. R., Desiraju, K., Morris, J. E., et al. (2011). Human resources for mental health care: current situation and strategies for action. *The Lancet, 378*(9803), 1654–1663.

Kar, S. K., & Menon, V. (2024). Mental Healthcare Access in India: Models, trends, and challenges. In S. M. Y. Arafat, & S. K. Kar (Eds.), Access to Mental Health Care in South Asia—Current status, potential challenges, and ways out. Springer Nature Singapore. https://doi.org/10.1007/978-981-99-9153-2_5

Kumar, A., Chery, L., Biswas, C., Dubhashi, N., Dutta, P., Dua, V. K., Kacchap, M., Kakati, S., Khandeparkar, A., Kour, D., Mahajan, S. N., Maji, A., Majumder, P., Mohanta, J., Mohapatra, P. K., Narayanasamy, K., Roy, K., Shastri, J., Valecha, N., Vikash, R., et al. (2012). Malaria in South Asia: prevalence and control. *Acta Tropica, 121*(3), 246–255.

Lew, B., Lester, D., Mustapha, F. I., Yip, P., Chen, Y. Y., Panirselvam, R. R., Hassan, A. S., In, S., Chan, L. F., Ibrahim, N., Chan, C. M. H., & Siau, C. S. (2022). Decriminalizing suicide attempt in the 21st century: An examination of suicide rates in countries that penalize suicide, a critical review. *BMC Psychiatry, 22*(1), 424. https://doi.org/10.1186/s12888-022-04060-5

Meshvara, D. (2002). Mental health and mental health care in Asia. *World Psychiatry, 1*(2), 118.

Naveed, S., Waqas, A., Chaudhary, A. M. D., Kumar, S., Abbas, N., Amin, R., Jamil, N., & Saleem, S. (2020). Prevalence of common mental disorders in South Asia: A systematic review and meta-regression analysis. *Frontiers in Psychiatry, 11*, 573150. https://doi.org/10.3389/fpsyt.2020.573150

Niaz, U. (2003). Violence against women in South Asian countries. *Archives of Women's Mental Health, 6*(3), 173–184. https://doi.org/10.1007/s00737-003-0171-9

Noorullah, A., Asad, N., Pirani, S., Iqbal, S., & Khan, M.M. (2024). Mental Health Care in Pakistan. In S. M. Y. Arafat, & S. K. Kar (Eds.), Access to Mental Health Care in South Asia—Current status, potential challenges, and ways out. Springer Nature Singapore. https://doi.org/10.1007/978-981-99-9153-2_7

Piracha, R. (2023). Suicide attempts finally decriminalised in Pakistan. Retrieved January 01, 2023, from https://voicepk.net/2022/12/suicide-attempts-finally-decriminalised-in-pakistan/

Rahut, D. B., Mishra, R., Sonobe, T., & Timilsina, R. R. (2023). Prevalence of prehypertension and hypertension among the adults in South Asia: A multinomial logit model. *Frontiers in Public Health, 10*, 1006457.

Ranjan, J. K., & Asthana, H. S. (2017). Prevalence of mental disorders in India and other South Asian Countries. *Asian Journal of Epidemiology, 10*, 45–53. https://doi.org/10.3923/aje.2017.45.53

Sadat, S. J., Rasuli, M., Ahmadzadeh, E. A., Hassanzadah, A., Faqireyan, H., Alekozay, M., et al. (2023). Depression and anxiety cases in Herat, Afghanistan: Awareness, accessibility to Mental Health Services and treatment gap. *Health Care Current Review, 11*, 335.

Sagar, R., Pattanayak, R. D., Chandrasekaran, R., Chaudhury, P. K., Deswal, B. S., Lenin Singh, R. K., Malhotra, S., Nizamie, S. H., Panchal, B. N., Sudhakar, T. P., Trivedi, J. K., Varghese, M., Prasad, J., & Chatterji, S. (2017). Twelve-month prevalence and treatment gap for common mental disorders: Findings from a large-scale epidemiological survey in India. *Indian Journal of Psychiatry, 59*(1), 46–55. https://doi.org/10.4103/psychiatry.IndianJPsychiatry_333_16

Sharma, P., Gautam, K., & Marahatta, K. (2024). Access to Mental Health Care in Nepal: Current status, potential challenges, and ways out. In S. M. Y. Arafat, S. K. Kar (Eds.), Access to Mental Health Care in South Asia—Current status, potential challenges, and ways out. Springer Nature Singapore. https://doi.org/10.1007/978-981-99-9153-2_6

Siegel, K. R., Patel, S. A., & Ali, M. K. (2014). Non-communicable diseases in South Asia: Contemporary perspectives. *British Medical Bulletin, 111*(1), 31–44.; Thornicroft, G., Sunkel, C., Alikhon Aliev, A., Baker, S., Brohan, E., El Chammay, R., Davies, K., Demissie, M., Duncan, J., Fekadu, W., Gronholm, P. C., Guerrero, Z., Gurung, D., Habtamu, K., Hanlon, C., Heim, E., Henderson, C., Hijazi, Z., Hoffman, C., Hosny, N., et al. (2022). The lancet commission on ending stigma and discrimination in mental health. *Lancet (London, England), 400*(10361), 1438–1480.

Trivedi, J. K., Goel, D., Kallivayalil, R. A., Isaac, M., Shrestha, D. M., & Gambheera, H. C. (2007). Regional cooperation in South Asia in the field of mental health. *World Psychiatry: Official Journal of the World Psychiatric Association (WPA), 6*(1), 57–59.

Trivedi, J. K., Triapthi, A., & Kar, S. K. (2015). Mental Health Legislation: Comparison of South Asian and Western countries. In: *Mental Health in South Asia: Ethics, resources, programs and legislation* (pp. 343–362).

van Weel, C., Kassai, R., Qidwai, W., Kumar, R., Bala, K., Gupta, P. P., et al. (2016). Primary health care policy implementation in South Asia. *BMJ Global Health, 1*(2), e000057.

World Bank. (2023a). World Bank Country and Lending Groups. Retrieved from June, 20, 2023, https://datahelpdesk.worldbank.org/knowledgebase/articles/906519-world-bank-country-and-lending-groups

World Bank. (2023b). Population, total—South Asia. Retrieved from June 20, 2023, https://data.worldbank.org/indicator/SP.POP.TOTL?locations=8S

World Health Organization. (2022a). Mental Health Atlas 2020 Country Profile.

World Health Organization. (2022b). Tuberculosis in South-East Asia Region. Retrieved from July 08, 2023, https://www.who.int/southeastasia/health-topics/tuberculosis#:~:text=Tuberculosis%20in%20South%2DEast%20Asia,WHO%20Global%20TB%20Report%202021

World Health Organization. (2017). Mental Health Atlas 2017 Country Profile: India. Retrieved from July 03, 2023, https://www.who.int/publications/m/item/mental-health-atlas-2017-country-profile-india

World Health Organization. (2021). *Suicide Worldwide in 2019: Global Health Estimates.* WHO. Retrieved from September 15, 2021 https://www.who.int/publications/i/item/9789240026643

World Health Organization. (2023a). WHO Policy Brief on the health aspects of decriminalization of suicide and suicide attempts. Retrieved from September 13, 2023, https://www.who.int/southeastasia/publications/i/item/9789240078796

World Health Organization. (2023b). HIV/AIDS in the South-East Asia. Retrieved from July 08, 2023, https://www.who.int/southeastasia/health-topics/hiv-aids

World Health Organization. (2023c). Non-communicable diseases in the South-East Asia. Retrieved from July 08, 2023, https://www.who.int/southeastasia/health-topics/noncommunicable-diseases

Mental Healthcare in Afghanistan

Sheikh Shoib , Syed Sameer Hussaini, Sardar Khan Nazari, and Fahimeh Saeed

Abstract Since the late 1970s, Afghanistan has experienced political unrest, civil conflict, and crippling Taliban-led administrations. The destructive effects of war have been harmful to the mental health of a population. Almost half of the population suffers from mental illnesses such as depression, anxiety disorders, post-traumatic stress disorder, suicide, drug misuse, and other conditions. It has been difficult to provide proper mental healthcare as the nation attempts to rebuild its foundation. The mentally ill have few possibilities to seek adequate support in a nation where mental health treatment has historically been stigmatized and where mental health services are in bad shape. The Afghan government aims to enhance the nation's mental health infrastructure in conjunction with Non-Governmental Organizations and international organizations.

Keywords Mental healthcare · Afghanistan · Pathway of mental healthcare · Mental health services · Challenges of mental healthcare

---

S. Shoib (✉)
Department of Health Services, Srinagar 190001, India
e-mail: Sheikhshoib22@gmail.com

Sharda University (SSh), Greater Noida, India

S. Shoib · F. Saeed
Psychosis Research Center, University of Social Welfare and Rehabilitation Sciences, Tehran, Iran
e-mail: Fa.saeed@uswr.ac.ir

S. Shoib
Healing Mind and Wellness Initiative Nawab Bazaar, Srinagar, India

S. S. Hussaini
M. S. Ramaiah Medical College, Bengaluru, Karnataka, India

S. K. Nazari
Kabul University of Medical Sciences-PGD Psychiatry (Kabul Mental Health Hospital, Fellowship Psychiatry (VIMHANS)), Kabul, Afghanistan

© The Author(s), under exclusive license to Springer Nature Singapore Pte Ltd. 2024
S. M. Y. Arafat and S. K. Kar (eds.), *Access to Mental Health Care in South Asia*,
https://doi.org/10.1007/978-981-99-9153-2_2

1 Introduction

Years of armed conflict, violence, and political upheaval have left an entire country shattered to its core. Multiple generations have experienced the detrimental consequences of war. Many who were born during this humanitarian crisis have never known a time of peace. The people of Afghanistan have suffered war injuries, witnessed the deaths of family members, been forcefully displaced from their homes, served in combat, turned into refugees, and were torn from their communities. Afghanistan has been strained by its social and cultural infrastructure, leading to unemployment, economic deprivation, and domestic violence, leading to a hugely negative impact on the livelihood of its people. This long-lasting, intergenerational trauma has had pervasive impacts on the population's mental health. The Institute of Health Metrics and Evaluation, Global Burden of Disease, in 2019 revealed that approximately 1.5 million people in Afghanistan suffered from depression and 1.7 million suffered from anxiety (Our World In Data, 2023). Substance abuse, drug trafficking, and the production of opium in Afghanistan have been making headlines among media outlets around the world (Stanikzai & Wahidi, 2023). Four decades of war inevitably impacted the mental health of those experiencing this turmoil. This chapter reviews the current state of mental healthcare in Afghanistan. A focus on the various challenges faced by the people of Afghanistan and the opportunities to provide sufficient support and treatment to those with mental illnesses in the country is explored. Additionally, this chapter will discuss the existing mental health infrastructure, initiatives, and recommendations for the improvement of mental healthcare services in Afghanistan.

2 Historical Perspectives on Mental Health in Afghanistan

In 1933, the Ali Abad Hospital introduced a custodial in-patient care unit for psychiatric care. Along with providing psychiatric care, this unit also served as a teaching facility for medical students. The hospital trained many neuropsychiatrists and also trained students at Kabul Medical University. As the unit became popular, it also attracted stigma among the general population. It was widely believed that the patients admitted to this unit were especially dangerous and should be kept away from other patients, especially children. Eventually, the patients in these wards were kept behind locked doors and some behind bars as well. After an incident, which involved an escaped patient from this unit who incidentally jumped in front of the car of the country's prime minister, the patients were all transferred out of the city to the suburbs. The facilities in these suburbs were extremely poor, and most patients were kept in chains. It wasn't until 1985 when the Department of Mental Health was opened in the Ministry of Public Health, which introduced community psychiatric services with its open-door policy. With the help of Dr. Burna-Asefi, a UK-trained psychiatrist and her team, mental health services quickly developed to a high standard. Other psychiatric services such as "day hospitals", group psychotherapy, detoxification centres, mental health acts, and the recruitment of mental health workers, were all achieved in a short period. A close co-operative relationship with the World Health Organization (WHO) was also collaborated by the department (Rahimi & Azimi, 2012).

Mental health services in Afghanistan faced difficulties before the 1980s but the issues became particularly difficult during the occupation of the country by the Soviets in 1979. However, mental health services' progress suddenly collapsed when the Mujahideen took control of Kabul. Lawless armed groups had taken over the country and criminal activities ran rampant. Most of the health centres, including mental health centres, were completely ruined due to internal fighting. Most of the mental healthcare workers fled the country, leaving the nation void of most mental health services. The situation further deteriorated during the Taliban era, when most public health services were abandoned.

After the fall of the Taliban, mental health services slowly began to reopen. The Department of Mental Health reopened at the Ministry of Public Health in 2005. In the coming decades, the number of mental healthcare services and workers has progressively increased in attempts to meet the demands of the current populations suffering from mental health conditions and substance abuse (Rahimi & Azimi, 2012).

As is the case with many societies, the stigmatization of mental healthcare influences the cultural barriers to seeking psychiatric care. The misunderstanding and lack of awareness of mental illness have interfered with the perception of the seriousness of psychological/psychiatric problems. Many people suffering from mental illnesses were reported only to share their symptoms with close family members (Nine et al., 2022). In some areas of the country, people suffering from mental illnesses were taken to religious shrines in an attempt to seek a cure for their symptoms. It was a common practice to take the mentally ill to a mullah, a person learned in Islamic theology, rather than a mental health specialist. Not surprisingly, their illnesses were incorrectly treated or unrecognized completely. But in a country where the population is largely religious believers, questioning a shrine's recommendations may have been seen as unreligious. About 30 kms from Jalalabad, a city in Afghanistan, there is a place called Samachel, there is a traditional healing centre where people bring the more severe cases of the mentally ill. In Samachel, there are members of a clan who are the descendants of a special healer and have been caring for the mentally ill for generations. The compound of this centre consists of destroyed buildings, a graveyard, and a shrine at the centre of it. Small rooms with mud flooring and no doors or furniture exist among these destroyed buildings. On average, four male patients are chained by the ankles to the walls of each room. Some are even chained to the trees outside. The clan leader explains that the patients' mental illness is caused by a "Jinn" or some supernatural power. The only way to get rid of these spirits is by a 40-day treatment in which the patient is kept on a strict diet, limited water, and holy verses are blown on the patient. They claim this method calms the patient and rids them of any illness-causing entity (Van De Put, 2002).

3 Epidemiology and Burden of Mental Illness

The people of Afghanistan have been facing continuous conflict, turmoil, and violence for two decades. This has led to a build-up of serious mental health problems. The mental health issues are profoundly greater in populations who were exposed to traumatizing events such as bombardment, mass killings, violence, and living in a war zone (Ullah et al., 2023). Anxiety disorders, post-traumatic stress disorder (PTSD), and depression are particularly common among people in such regions. For many who have experienced war, reliving the event through memory can feel as threatening as inciting trauma (Inoue et al., 2023). Yet, those living in such dangerous zones have the lowest access to healthcare services. A significant amount of evidence has shown that low social support leads to an increase in the rate of psychological problems (Ullah et al., 2023). Poverty, displacement, homelessness, debt, and a loss of self-esteem and confidence are some of the burdens suffered by war refugees. Consistent with pertinent literature, unemployed individuals report much higher rates of psychological problems than those who are employed. Substance use is also common in refugee camps. For refugees, their displacement usually occurs after a period of violence in their native areas. This resettlement can cause stress among people of all ages. Many children in Afghanistan have experienced high levels of trauma before being forcefully displaced from their homes. Studies have shown that childhood traumas are broadly linked to negative health outcomes across a lifetime (Javanbakht et al., 2021).

During the Taliban period (1996–2001), 81% of women reported a decline in their mental health, 97% reported major depression, 86% reported significant anxiety symptoms, and 21% reported suicidal ideations. The prevalence of PTSD was 48% for women and 32% for men. In 2010, the Afghan government announced that nearly 66% of its population suffered from some form of psychological problem (CW4WAfghan, 2014). The use of synthetic drugs, like methamphetamine, opium, cannabis, and heroin, has been increasingly observed during assessments and treatment of drug use disorders. In a 2020 survey, it was reported that 12% of boys and nearly 8% of girls were using illicit drugs or alcohol (Alemi et al., 2023).

It is essential to recognize that the mental disturbances of war weren't just limited to the general population but were noted in war veterans who served in Afghanistan. It has been estimated that nearly 15% of American soldiers who returned from Afghanistan suffered from PTSD and/or depression (Inoue et al., 2023).

4 The Current State of Mental Healthcare Services in Afghanistan

Low and middle-income countries struggle to bear the burdens of war and population morbidity. Providing adequate healthcare, including mental health services, has been a challenge in Afghanistan for decades. Armed conflicts and violence have rendered the healthcare systems completely disorganized, disproportionately affecting the mental health system. Low funding, inadequate government resources, and lack of awareness have all negatively contributed to the current state of the healthcare system.

Afghanistan has only a few specialized mental health resources. Only a few psychiatrists are in the region, with an estimated 0.34 per 100,000 people. In the entire country, there are only 133 psychologists (World Health Organization, 2022). The total number of mental health nurses and psychologists is also very low compared to the population. There is only one mental hospital and only four units in general hospitals among the community outpatient facilities. The mental hospital is known for being unhygienic and dilapidated and only offers 60 beds, where 300 are needed. It has also been criticized for its lack of patient follow-up and relapse of drug addiction among its patients (CW4WAfghan, 2014).

With funding from the European Union, the Ministry of Health operates a mental health training program. The aim is to increase the number of qualified personnel at various mental healthcare facilities. In 2005, the Afghan government introduced a "Basic Package of Health Services", which included mental health education, awareness, case detection, and identification and treatment of mental illnesses.

Many non-government organizations (NGOs) operate in the country under the supervision of the health ministry. These organizations provide mental health services around the country but generally serve the more urban centres. For example, Canadian Women for Women in Afghanistan (CW4WAfghan) has partner organizations that provide psychological counselling services to women and girls who have suffered through violence and war. The aim is to help women regain their independence and improve their quality of life. Another partner organization is Physiotherapy and Rehabilitation Support for Afghanistan (PARSA), which provides counselling services to women's mental healthcare facilities in Kabul. Various other NGOs exist to help tackle mental health problems, including suicide prevention (CW4WAfghan, 2014).

The United Nations Office on Drugs and Crime (UNODOC) is one of the global leaders in the fight against the use of illicit drugs, organized crime, corruption, and terrorism. The agency provides evidence-based policy advice and guidelines on how to effectively counter-narcotics and criminal interventions to the Afghanistan government. At a local level, UNDOC promotes the rollout of services to the provinces. At a national level, UNDOC supports national institutes and line ministries by providing international standards for policymaking on drug and crime issues. UNDOC has a strong presence and partnership with the government of Afghanistan and continuously aims to enhance operational planning. Today, the UNDOC has its country office in Kabul and 5 key provinces, including Balkh, Badakshan, Herat, Kandahar, and Nangarhar (UNODC, n.d.).

5   Stigma and Social Barriers to Mental Healthcare

People living with mental illness in Afghanistan are often victims of the stigmatization of mental health treatment. Seeking treatment for mental problems isn't entirely accepted by general populations and sometimes even results in social exclusion. Stigma is a barrier when it comes to mental healthcare. While it may be a consequence of misinformation or ignorance, the fact of the matter is that many people suffering often go untreated or end up self-medicating. The unregulated pharmaceutical industries in Afghanistan only play a catalyst in self-medication, drug misuse, and high rates of addiction to medications such as benzodiazepines.

During the civil war, led by the Mujahideen during 1996–2001, attitudes towards women were conservative and regressive. This limited the opportunities for women to seek employment. In many areas, women were banned from getting an education or working altogether. This denial of education and work led to many women's mental health deterioration. Many women reported that they attributed their depression and anxiety to these restrictions and feared for their children's futures, specifically their girl children. In one study, nearly 81% of women reported a decline in their mental condition during the Taliban period. What is interesting to note is that Afghanistan is possibly one of the only countries in the world where suicide rates among women are higher than among men (CW4WAfghan, 2014).

In one study, respondents admitted that receiving the label of "mental illness" was stigmatizing and thus would report most mental health problems to family and friends rather than having the "officially" reported to a mental healthcare provider. It was also found that the general view on mental healthcare was positively associated with higher socioeconomic status (Nine et al., 2022). It is important to understand content-specific stigmas against mental health in Afghanistan to design appropriate interventions to address mental health. Using culturally appropriate, non-stigmatizing language while communicating with people on a family level may help to lessen stigmas and misconceptions.

6   Community-Based Interventions

Intervening in a deteriorated environment requires a tailored approach. Providing adequate healthcare in such populations is a challenge in itself. Mental health awareness campaigns hosted by local government appointees to inform the community about the different behavioural problems and the available treatments may help educate people about the risks of not seeking care and the benefits of psychiatric treatments. These awareness campaigns can be presented in a culturally sensitive manner and be presented in local languages. The government should instruct local healthcare workers to make appropriate and timely referrals to mental healthcare workers. The improvement of psychiatric education in medical schools will improve the training of graduates. Adding to the number of mental healthcare workers would be ideal, but at the same time, it can be a slow process. Primary care workers, including nurses, midwives, and doctors, can enhance their training in the fundamentals of mental health support. Training these providers will facilitate them to further provide support to patients and community members within their facilities (HRW.ORG). NGOs may also contribute by improving access to quality mental healthcare services.

7 Mental Health Initiatives and Programs

Afghanistan's national mental health legislation has been in use ever since it was enacted in 1987. This includes developing a mental health program within primary healthcare, downsizing large mental health hospitals, advocacy, more accessible access to mental health services, promotion, financing, and overall quality improvement and monitoring. In 1997, the policies were revised and components were added, such as less restrictive care, rights of patients and families, voluntary and involuntary treatment, judicial treatment for those suffering mental illness, and further accreditation of mental health professionals and facilities (WHO, 2006).

The Ministry of Public Health (MOPH) introduced a basic package of health services in 2005. This was one of the first health service packages offered to the people of Afghanistan, which included mental health services and enhancements. The package is known as "The Six Elements of the Basic Package of Health Services". Of the six, the mental health-specific element included mental health education and awareness, case detection, and treatment of mental illness. A recent survey suggests that modest but meaningful gain was achieved during the early stages of this program (Silove & Ventevogel, 2022).

Afghanistan's mental health policy was enacted in 1987. The plan contained developing more community mental health services, downsizing large mental hospitals, developing human resource/advocacy programs, incorporating mental health services into primary care, and financing the overall improvement of quality. The Ministry of Public Health aims to revise the current legislation and policies to include disaster/emergency preparedness, law enforcement for people with mental health issues, and further mechanisms to implement the provisions of mental health legislation (WHO-AIMS).

Small groups of NGOs provide women and girls with mental health services in urban areas. Providing vulnerable women with the right psychosocial support aims to lower the prevalence of mental health issues among this population and help them regain their independence and quality of life. Many other organizations offer vulnerable populations counselling, rehabilitation, physiotherapy, and psychotherapy (CW4WAfghan, 2014).

Strengthening mental health services in Afghanistan by using technological innovations, such as telemedicine and E-Health (electronic health), can enhance the capacity of healthcare providers and improve access to specialists. Training healthcare workers to utilize interactive platforms can positively affect the utilization of services by technologically aware individuals who may not be able to attend appointments in person for one reason or another (Khoja et al., 2015).

Partnerships with international organizations, such as Health Net International, International Medical Corps, and the International Assistance Mission, have all launched mental health programs in Afghanistan over the last two decades, which have had an impact on the improvement of mental health services in the region (CW4WAfghan, 2014).

8 Challenges and Roadblocks

Afghanistan is commonly referred to as a "graveyard" of empires. This label is likely due to the past and ongoing crisis. A label like this generates pessimism about supporting developments in the area. Still, even in these conditions, international mental health agencies have been working under adverse conditions, upholding the principle that sound mental health is integral to building a strong and resilient society. Social upheaval and armed conflict have limited the establishment efforts by mental health agencies in the country. These establishments appoint hundreds of psychosocial workers around the country. These agencies need to ensure the safety of their workers, and as one might imagine, doing so in such environments can be challenging. A concern for public safety encompasses not just the population at risk but also the workers who migrate to the regions to provide care. Even after overcoming such obstacles, the lack of public awareness, stigmas, and geographical constraints continue to interfere with the equitable utilization of available services (Silove & Ventevogel, 2022).

Host governments should proactively enhance funding to service providers to meet Afghanistan's inevitable increase in mental health needs. Strategic support should also be given to the various community agencies led by the Afghan people involved with resetting newly arrived refugees. Local governments should support the contributions of local and international agencies, assisting them in delivering their intended services without hindrances and disruption from local factors.

Efforts and strategies by local and international agencies continue to face unprecedented circumstances that interrupt their goals' processes. Afghan refugees' resettlement policies produce protracted insecurities, prolonging their mental and psychosocial problems. Simultaneous efforts to rapidly resettle refugees and provide early support with culturally relevant mental health services can benefit these displaced individuals (Silove & Ventevogel, 2022).

9 Recommendations for Improving Mental Healthcare

Strengthening mental health policies and legislation requires interventions at various levels from community-based to group and individual-focused interventions. In Afghanistan's collective traditional culture, the majority of its people mention the word "Allah" (God) as a resource for emotional support during times of worry, sadness, or tension. Many gather in places of worship and perform rituals such as meditation and relaxation exercises. An effective response to this by mental health agencies would be to take this into account and work with the "Department of Islam and Health". This may prove to be an effective way of promoting an entire community's mental well-being (Syed, 2011).

To ensure proper implementation of reforms, health agencies can work together to optimize mental healthcare delivery. NGOs, government agencies, and international organizations can work alongside each other to gain insight into the challenges and susceptibilities of the local community. Spreading awareness among the population, especially those at increased risk, will positively affect service utilization.

Strategies to enhance mental healthcare workforce capacities should also be given priority. Apart from bringing in psychiatrists, psychologists, nurses, and other mental healthcare workers, funds should be allotted to enhance already trained professionals within the country with the skills to recognize and treat various mental health conditions at their facilities. In 2011, the International Medical Corps announced its plans to work with the Ministries of Higher Education and Public Health to improve psychiatric education at medical universities around Afghanistan (CW4WAfghan, 2014). Supplying healthcare workers with training materials in their mother tongue, such as Pashto, can also help to optimize training in crucial mental healthcare. Supporting existing mental health hospitals will enable an increase in inpatient admissions and consults, thereby increasing access to quality care.

Improving coordination and collaboration between the government, NGOs, and international organizations would be beneficial to the program's functioning. Using culturally tailored approaches, these organizations can share techniques to battle stigmas, recognize challenges, and connect with the public (CW4WAfghan, 2014). A joint effort between mental health organizations will help not only facilitate a program's objectives but it will also create an organized process for the people of Afghanistan to gain access to mental healthcare.

Creating public awareness and subsequent advocacy can be a complicated ordeal. Battling stigmas and challenging long-time misconceptions must be handled with utmost care and consideration towards local cultures. Recognizing groups more vulnerable to psychological burdens and offering them help may give them hope for a better life. As more and more individuals accept mental health treatments, it may influence others who may be suffering in private to reach out and accept help.

10 Conclusion

The effects of war have detrimental consequences on a country and its people. Decades of civil unrest, violence, and agony have left the people of Afghanistan with burdens that may take a lifetime to overcome. As this country rebuilds itself, special attention must be given to the mental health of its people. The prevalence of depression, anxiety, PTSD, substance abuse, suicidal ideations, and other psychiatric conditions must be recognized and addressed. Organizations around the world have shown generosity towards building a better infrastructure of mental health services in the region. Local governments and communities are also working hard to deliver healthcare, including mental health services. But the challenges are ongoing. Structural, societal, and economic hurdles continue to threaten this progress.

Even during these challenging times, the people of Afghanistan have shown resilience through unprecedented circumstances. They have demonstrated the ability to strengthen their communities and the communities where they sought asylum through their indomitable spirit. But even among this kind of strength, the prevalence of mental illness soars and demands serious efforts and a coordinated effort to assist all men, women, and children suffering from psychological disturbances and mental illness. Mental health continues to be one of the most overlooked aspects of healthcare in the country and among the international donor communities. To rebuild lives after a war requires reducing poverty and supporting the people of Afghanistan, and to do this, one requires not just a healthy body but also a healthy mind.

References

Alemi Q, Panter-Brick C, Oriya S, Ahmady M, Alimi AQ, Faiz H, Hakim N, Sami Hashemi SA, Manaly MA, Naseri R, Parwiz K, Sadat SJ, Sharifi MZ, Shinwari Z, Ahmadi SJ, Amin R, Azimi S, Hewad A, Musavi Z, Siddiqi AM, et al (2023) Afghan mental health and psychosocial well-being: thematic review of four decades of research and interventions. BJPsych Open 9(4):e125. https://doi.org/10.1192/bjo.2023.502

CW4WAfghan (2014) https://www.cw4wafghan.ca/sites/default/files/attachments/pages/3.1_women-and-mental-health.pdf

Inoue C, Shawler E, Jordan CH, Jackson, CA (2023) Veteran and military mental health issues. In: StatPearls [Internet]. Treasure Island (FL). StatPearls Publishing. PMID: 34283458

Javanbakht A, Stenson A, Nugent N, Smith A, Rosenberg D, Jovanovic T (2021) Biological and environmental factors affecting risk and resilience among Syrian Refugee children. Journal of Psychiatry and Brain Science 6:e210003. https://doi.org/10.20900/jpbs.20210003

Khoja S, Khan MA, Husyin N, Scott R, Yousafzai AW, Durrani H, Mohbatali F, Khan D (2015) Improving mental health care for young adults in Badakshan province of Afghanistan using eHealth. Studies in Health Technology and Informatics 209:46–50 PMID: 25980704

Nine SB, Najm AF, Allan EB, Gronholm PC (2022) Mental health stigma among community members in Afghanistan: a cross-sectional survey. Int J Soc Psy 68(7):1470–1485 https://doi.org/10.1177/00207640211036169

Our World In Data. Number of people with depression. https://ourworldindata.org/grapher/number-with-depression-by-country?tab=chart&country=AFG. Retrieved from Feburary 1, 2023

Rahimi YA, Azimi S (2012) War and the crisis of mental health in Afghanistan. Int Psy 9(3):55–57. https://www.ncbi.nlm.nih.gov/pmc/articles/PMC6735073/

Silove D, Ventevogel P (2022) Living through interminable adversity: the mental health of the Afghan people. World Psyc 21(1):55–56. https://doi.org/10.1002/wps.20955

Syed G (2011) The International Bank for Reconstruction and Development/The World Bank 1818 H Street, NW Washington, DC 20433

Ullah H, Ahmad H, Tharwani ZH, Shaeen SK, Rahmat ZS, Essar MY (2023) Intergenerational trauma: a silent contributor to mental health deterioration in Afghanistan. Brain Behav 13(4):e2905. https://doi.org/10.1002/brb3.2905

Van de Put W (2002) Addressing mental health in Afghanistan. Lancet 360(Suppl):s41–s42. https://doi.org/10.1016/s0140-6736(02)11816-2

World Health Organization (2006) WHO-aims report on mental health system in Afghanistan. https://cdn.who.int/media/docs/default-source/mental-health/who-aims-country-reports/afghanistan_who_aims_report.pdf?sfvrsn=2a61bfbc_3&download=true#:~:text=Afghanistan%20has%20had%20a%20national,not%20exist%20for%20mental%20health

World Health Organization (2022) Mental Health Atlas 2020 country profile: Afghanistan. Retrieved from September 11, 2023. https://www.who.int/publications/m/item/mental-health-atlas-afg-2020-country-profile

Stanikzai MH, Wahidi MW (2023) Bio-psycho-social profile of people with substance use disorders treated in locally assigned treatment facilities in Kandahar, Afghanistan. Substance Abuse and Rehabilitation, 89–98

UNODC (n.d.) Afghanistan. UNODC. https://www.unodc.org/unodc/en/alternative-development/afganistan.html

Access to Mental Health Care in Bangladesh—Current Status, Potential Challenges, and Ways Out

S. M. Yasir Arafat, Noor Ahmed Giasuddin, and Atiqul Haq Mazumder

Abstract Bangladesh is an emerging economy in South Asia with the potential double burden of both communicable and non-communicable diseases. Mental illness is one of the top fifth burdensome non-communicable diseases in the country. Historically, there is more than 90% of services gaps for mental health disorders. This chapter aims to discuss the current status, potential challenges, and ways out of mental health care access in Bangladesh. In the beginning, we discussed the historical aspect of mental health services in Bangladesh followed by a discussion on the epidemiology and services burden in the country. We discussed the potential challenges of access to mental health care like poor funds and inadequate research, inadequate and inequitable manpower, huge out-of-pocket expenses, poor mental health literacy, low income and income disparity, high stigma, enduring disorganized help-seeking patterns, non-judicious prescribing (poly-pharmacy) as the potential challenges. Finally, we speculated on the potential ways to cope with the challenges for better mental health care in Bangladesh.

Keywords Mental health care · Bangladesh · Pathway of mental health care · Mental health services · Challenges of mental health care

S. M. Y. Arafat (✉)
Department of Psychiatry, Enam Medical College and Hospital, Dhaka, Bangladesh
e-mail: arafatdmc62@gmail.com

N. A. Giasuddin
Department of Psychiatry, Shaheed Tajuddin Ahmad Medical College, Gazipur, Bangladesh

A. H. Mazumder
Ministry of Health and Family Welfare, Government of Bangladesh, Dhaka, Bangladesh

1 Introduction

1.1 Country Profile

Bangladesh is a densely populated country in South Asia with over 170 million population and an area of 1,47,570 km^2 (World Population Review, 2023). It is surrounded by the border of India on its North, East, and West, and its South is occupied by the Bay of Bengal (Fig. 1). As a part of the Indian subcontinent, it was ruled by the British regime till 14 August 1947 and by the Pakistanis till 16 December 1971 as East Pakistan. After its independence, the country achieved tremendous economic growth and currently, it lies under the lower middle-income bracket (World Bank, 2022). The country is enjoying a demographic dividend due to its proportions of young populations. Bangladesh is a Muslim-majority country where more than 90% of the population is Muslim (World Population Review, 2023). Although it is a democratic country several times it went under Military rulers and a stable peaceful transition of power is yet to be established. Despite its economic growth, there is an inequitable distribution of wealth among the citizens. During recent years, an extreme inflation of necessary livelihoods has been noted perhaps due to the COVID-19 pandemic, the Russia-Ukraine war, money laundering, and financial and political corruption. Since the early days, there have been strong influences of Indian culture due to its location and long-term political relationship. It is found that more than 54% of Indian medical tourists visited from Bangladesh; about 2.5 million people from Bangladesh visited India for treatment purposes which incurred about 500 million USD in 2020 (Amin, 2023). It can be easily speculated that the real number would be much higher than the reported data.

1.2 Evolution of Psychiatric Services in Bangladesh

1.2.1 Asylum Period

Before the British period, no traceable mental health services care setting was found. The asylum set up for isolating mentally ill patients was found during the British administrative period. The administrative persons of the British East India Company built separate infrastructure to seclude the insane in 1815, at Muralibazar (Murli Bazar) in Dhaka (Arafat, 2019a; Bandyopadhyay et al., 2018; Varma, 1953). Initially, it was established to isolate the European patients who were living in the sub-continent at that time which was used for the native people later. The asylum was situated at the backside of the former central jail which is currently located at Bakshi Bazar under Chawkbazar Thana, Dhaka 1211 (Bandyopadhyay et al., 2018; Varma, 1953). The asylum shared the same boundary as the central jail with a partition between these two. There were two separate gates, one had been used to enter the jail and another to enter the asylum. Inside the asylum, the arrangement included

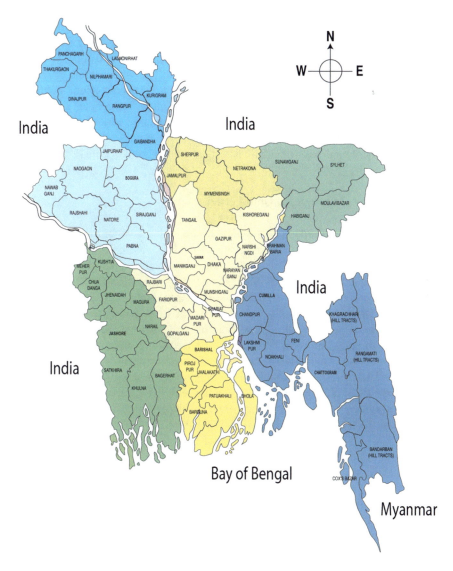

Fig. 1 Map of Bangladesh

two tile sheds along with three single-story buildings. As far as the evidence was traced, a distribution of 323 patients was found, among them, 278 were male and the rest 45 were females (Arafat, 2019a). The people of Dhaka and Chattogram (former Chittagong) divisions (Fig. 1), and the people of Rangpur and Pabna districts were supposed to be shifted here (Bandyopadhyay et al., 2018; Basu, 2004; Varma, 1953). Patients from some parts of Bangladesh were being shifted to the asylums outside of the country (according to the current boundary). For example, patients from the

Rajshahi division (except the Rangpur and Pabna districts) were being shifted to the Berhampore (currently part of India) lunatic asylum (Varma, 1953). Due to space constraints, the lodging of Dhaka lunatic asylum was increased by 40 in 1913 (Varma, 1953). A 10-year report of Dhaka asylum from 1827 to 1837 showed that there were 757 patients lodged during that tenure. Another report of Dhaka asylum, published in 1878 revealed a remarkable recovery in comparison with the other asylums of the Indian subcontinent. Nevertheless, no rational explanation was found supporting better recovery in the Dhaka asylum. Furthermore, the report did not disclose any specific treatment methods or modalities responsible for the outcome (Basu, 2004).

1.2.2 Evolution Through Pakistan Period

In the Pakistan period (1947–1971) mental health services shifted from asylum to hospital settings. The Pabna Mental Hospital (PMH) was the first infrastructure developed for specialized as well as separate services for mentally ill patients in Bangladesh. At first, it was started in 1957 under the supervision of a Civil Surgeon in a rented area (local landlord's abandoned residence) named *Sitlai House* (Arafat et al., 2020; Karim et al., 2006). Subsequently, in 1959, it was transferred to its current location at Hemayetpur, 8 kms away from the district, Pabna, in an area of 111.25 acres of land. The PMH was started with the arrangement of 60 indoor beds which was increased gradually and currently, the establishment has an arrangement of 500 beds (Arafat, 2019a). No other important specialized services establishment could be identified during the Pakistan regime. However, during that period, the necessity of further establishments for mental health services was considered taking into account the patient load, distance of PMH from the capital city (Dhaka), and transport facility (Morning News, 1970). At that time, it was thought that there should have been four hospitals like PHM in East Pakistan to cope with the mental health patient load (Morning News, 1970). According to a newspaper report of a seminar on mental health, in 1970, the 400-bed PMH had treated about 9000 inpatients and 6000 out-patients. Among them, 60% were patients with schizophrenia. The president of that seminar Prof. M U Ahmed stressed the need for a mental health institute for the training of psychiatrists and research in the province.

1.2.3 Bangladesh Period

Along with the PMH, the development of further specialized establishments for mentally ill patients was started in the month of February 1981 with the initiative of establishing the national services centre. The *National Institute of Mental Health* (NIMH), was started as an *organization in training in mental health* in February 1981 at Suhrawardy Hospital premises at Sher-e-Bangla Nagor, Dhaka-1207. In 1984, it was scheduled to be established as a separate complex in a separate area of Sher-e-Bangla Nagor. However, in 1988 it was shifted to *Sir Salimullah Medical College* (SSMC) premises with a 50-bed indoor facility as the *Institute of Mental*

Health and Research (IMHR). In 1993, it was shifted to *Dhaka Medical College Hospital* (DMCH). The label of the project was modified to the NIMH on October 19, 1992, and eventually, it got a separate area at Sher-e-Bangla Nagor. During the initial period, it was started with the facility of 100 inpatient admissions along with regular outpatient services (*National Institute of Mental Health and Hospital*, n.d.).

In addition to the PMH in Pabna and the NIMH in Dhaka as specialized hospitals, psychiatric services have been allocated at the government medical college hospitals by departments of psychiatry. The psychiatric services were started at DMCH in 1974. The services were expanded to the *Institute of Postgraduate Medicine and Research* (IPJMR) (now *Bangabandhu Sheikh Mujib Medical University*, BSMMU) (Karim et al., 2006). However, dedicated indoor admission for psychiatric patients is still not available in several public medical college hospitals in the country. Some private medical colleges and hospitals have also functional departments of psychiatry. BSMMU, the oldest medical university of Bangladesh, has also run outpatient and inpatient services for mental health services in the country. In addition to that, there are 72 outpatient care services and 64 in-patient services across the country that are attached to a hospital (World Health Organization, 2022a).

Currently, there are 500 inpatient beds in PMH, and 400 inpatient beds in NIMH (World Health Organization, 2022b). In addition to that, there are other 195 beds in general hospitals, medical college hospitals and medical universities and 15 inpatient beds for the forensic psychiatry unit (World Health Organization, 2022b).

1.2.4 Private Clinics and Psychiatric Services in Bangladesh

The private sector plays a significant role in psychiatric services in Bangladesh as there are inadequate and inequitable services in the public sector. The first private clinic for mental health services was established in Dhaka named the *Dhaka Monorog Clinic*. It was initiated in 1980 by Professor Hidayetul Islam and received its formal registration in 1984 (Arafat et al., 2020). At the contemporary time, *Zaman's Clinic* by Dr. A K M Kamaruzzaman was also established as another private sector setting for mental health care in Dhaka. Later, this sector has been expanding gradually to extend the services in different parts of the country.

Many of the core mental health services have not been developed adequately, to be more precise, community psychiatric services, and community mental health teams are yet to be started.

1.2.5 Major Advocacy Group

Bangladesh Association of Psychiatrists (BAP): As an organization, BAP was started in 1975 with the objectives of promoting mental health and advancing the speciality of psychiatry across the country. The BAP has been moving for almost all mental health issues and negotiations with other stakeholders actively (Arafat, 2019a).

1.2.6 Mental Health Act

A fresh mental health act was enacted on November 14, 2018, which inactivates the previously practiced the *Lunacy Act*, 1912 (Mental Health Act, 2018). The *National Mental Health Policy* and the *National Mental Health Strategic Plan 2020–2030* were approved in 2022 (World Health Organization, 2022b).

2 Epidemiology and Burden of Mental Illness in Bangladesh

Over the last three decades, Bangladesh made significant improvements in several aspects of health indicators, especially in maternal and child health. At the same time, it is experiencing a double burden of diseases (both communicable and non-communicable). About 60% of the disease burden is incurred by non-communicable diseases (Ahmed, 2018). Among the non-communicable diseases, mental illness was noted as one of the top fifth burdensome conditions in Bangladesh (Ahmed, 2018).

There is a dearth of studies assessing the prevalence of mental disorders in Bangladesh. One systematic review identified that the prevalence of psychiatric disorders among adults was 6.5–31% and among children 13.4–22.9% (Hossain et al., 2014). The prevalence of psychiatric disorders in Bangladesh has increased by more than 2% from the initial study conducted in 2003–2005 (Ministry of Health & Family Welfare, 2021). The recent nationwide mental health survey conducted by the *Ministry of Health & Family Welfare* in 2018–2019 revealed the prevalence of mental disorders among the adult populations (18 years and above) was 18.7% (95% CI 17.4–20%) which was 16.1% in the earlier national survey conducted in 2003–2005 (Ministry of Health & Family Welfare, 2021). The rate was higher in females (21.5%) than males (15.7%), and among persons with 60 years and above aged (28.1%). Depression was the commonest disorder (6.7%) followed by anxiety disorders (4.7%). The prevalence of other notable diagnoses was 2.3% for somatic symptom disorder, 1% for psychoses, 0.6% for obsessive-compulsive disorder (OCD), and 0.5% for bipolar disorder. The prevalence of psychiatric disorders is almost equal in rural and urban settings. The prevalence of psychiatric disorders among children and adolescents (7–17 years) was 12.6%, higher in boys (13.7%) than girls (11.5%). Among the disorders, neurodevelopment disorder (NDD, 5.1%) was the most common diagnosis, followed by anxiety disorders (4.7%), disruptive disorder (1.7%), and depression (0.4%) (Ministry of Health & Family Welfare, 2021).

Suicide is yet to get attention as a public health problem in Bangladesh. A suicide attempt is a criminal offence in the country (Arafat, 2023). There are variations in rate according to different sources and reports. People are dying at young ages (<30 years); females, housewives, and students are dying more; hanging and poisoning are the leading methods; psychiatric disorders, life events, social isolation, and unemployment are prominent risk factors (Arafat, 2019a, 2019b, 2019c). There are two suicide prevention clinics in Bangladesh (Arafat, 2023). Various studies are coming out which is essential for formulating a national suicide prevention strategy. For a detailed discussion, we refer to a recently published book *Suicide in Bangladesh* (Arafat & Khan, 2023).

3 Mental Health Services in Bangladesh

3.1 Conventional Services

Based on the disease burden, mental illnesses are one of the top ten health priorities. As a pluralistic system, the health sector of Bangladesh has four main components, i.e. government services, services from private organizations, nongovernmental organizations (NGOs), and donor agencies (World Health Organization, 2015). In Bangladesh, the people receive mental health care through the government, private, and NGO-sponsored health service providers, and health facilities. There are formal and informal mental health services in the country. The formal mental health services in the country include outpatient clinics, inpatient units, residential facilities, mental hospitals, forensic psychiatric units, primary health care centres, and other facilities. Most of the service users attend outpatient services, and a far lower number of users utilize the inpatient units of tertiary-level hospitals, mental hospitals, and other residential facilities (World Health Organization, 2007).

The government health system of Bangladesh provides services in three distinct levels i.e. primary, secondary, and tertiary (Fig. 2). Primary care extends services through community clinics (end-stage services point), union sub-centres (next to community clinic), and upazila (sub-district) health complexes. District hospitals are considered a secondary level of care. Medical college hospitals and specialized hospitals are considered tertiary care services level (Government of The People's Republic of Bangladesh, 2022). As per the organogram, there is no post of psychiatrist in the primary and secondary care services level of the government. There are allocated posts for psychiatrists at the tertiary care services level in the country (Government of The People's Republic of Bangladesh, 2022). In government health services, along with Western (Allopathic) medicine, there are services from Alternative Medicine doctors (Naher, 2022). The uniqueness of care-seeking is that people can choose to see primary, secondary, or tertiary-level settings at their own will. There is no system to prohibit their freedom in this respect (Giasuddin et al., 2012).

The second important sector in health services in Bangladesh is the private sector. It also comprises of formal and informal services. The formal services cover both Western and alternative medicine (Unani, Ayurvedic, Homeopathic) services through a range of facilities such as diagnostic centres, chamber complexes, hospitals, clinics, laboratories, and pharmacies (World Health Organization, 2015). The informal section is largely dominated by unqualified practitioners of Western medicine (polli cikitsok/village doctor), homeopathy, and local (kobiraji) medicine (World Health

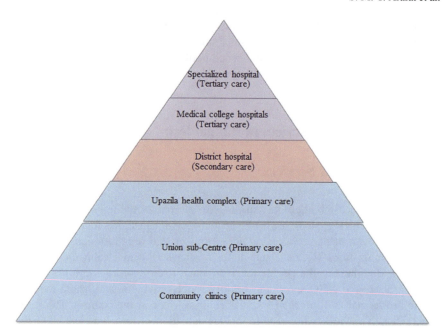

Fig. 2 Health services delivery care levels in Bangladesh. Adapted from Facility Registry (2023), Government of the People's Republic of Bangladesh (2022)

Organization, 2015). The formal section of private services is more developed in city areas whereas the informal section is more practiced in rural areas (World Health Organization, 2015). This sector is poorly regulated by the regulatory bodies. Among the informal services providers, religious and/or traditional healers serve as a prominent source of psychosocial support for psychiatric problems in the country (Kemp et al., 2022). There is no epidemiological catchment area services design in Bangladesh. Also, the referral system of the country is not well-functioning in any way (Andalib & Arafat, 2016; Arafat, 2019b; World Health Organization, 2015).

Doctors in Bangladesh working in government health services, private organizations, and without any institutional affiliation provide consultations to patients at their private chambers outside their office time. Generally, there are large chamber complexes built by different corporate bodies (Labaid, Popular, Ibn Sina, Medinova etc.) for availing of this practice. Usually, this practice is unregulated, and practically nobody sets the standard of service in this section. The evening is the popular time for private chamber practice in the country. Additionally, as psychiatrists mostly live in the cities, on the weekend they travel to the peripheral districts to see patients every week (Andalib & Arafat, 2016).

The third prominent sector is NGOs. NGOs and donor agencies predominantly focuses on the deprived, marginalized section of society and the rural parts of the country (World Health Organization, 2015). In Bangladesh, non-governmental organizations provide substantial *mental health and psychosocial support* (MHPSS) services specifically for refugees and other displaced people (Kemp et al., 2022).

In general, people with mental disorders are likely to have five levels and four filters in case of utilizing psychiatric services throughout the world (Goldberg & Huxley, 1980). The first level seems to be the presence of mental illness in the community; the second level is the presence of mental disorders in persons attending the general physician for any reason; the third level in the number of mental disorders correctly identified by the general physician; the fourth level is the number of persons with psychiatric disorders referred to specialist mental health care services; and the fifth level is the persons with mental disorders who are admitted to the hospital. The first filter in this pathway is the service-seeking behavior of the patients. The second filter is the capability of the general physician to identify someone with a mental disorder efficiently. The third filter seems to be the referral to psychiatric services. The fourth filter is the decision of the mental health service to hospitalize the patient (Goldberg & Huxley, 1992).

Due to the low mental health literacy, the enduring culture of availing non-medical (non-qualified) care, and the belief in supernatural causation of psychiatric disorders (the help-seeking of community persons (first filter) is grossly chaotic (see Fig. 3). Mental health training is scarce and the undergraduate (MBBS) curriculum covers inadequate content to identify the common psychiatric disorder at the community level (Arafat et al., 2021). Therefore, the second filter is automatically malfunctioning. There is a non-functional referral system (discussed later) which indicates the total failure of the third filter. As there are posts of psychiatrists available at the tertiary care level, the fourth filter is supposed to be functioning. It is expected that the majority of the patients are dealt with by others before reaching tertiary care services. Community people can consult any level (primary, secondary, or tertiary) of government services delivery, private services delivery, or other care like NGOs, non-medical healers, or traditional healers based on their literacy, motivation, financial affordability, the distance of their residence from the service centre, and social influence. Referral norms, the relationship between mental health services with other health services, availability and accessibility of mental health services and other services, etc. influence the decision to take help from mental health services (Gater et al., 1991). People of Bangladesh go to different levels of services for their mental and physical health requirements. The usual persons they go to for informal care include their friends and family, native or religious healers. These informal healers have seemed to bring relief to mental illness through their rituals or sacred verses. They equate mental illness as the possession of bad spirits, 'Jinn", and black magic (Giasuddin et al., 2012). Usually, patients who want to consult medical practitioners prefer to consult renowned practitioners, and professor-level physicians in their chamber setting as their first-level services encounter. At the same time, there is a good proportion of persons with mental illness visit non-medical practitioners, and traditional healers as their first services encounter. We postulate the possible consultation pathways in Fig. 3. In Bangladesh, any patient can consult with any consultant at their chamber by providing consultation fees. For considering help-seeking for

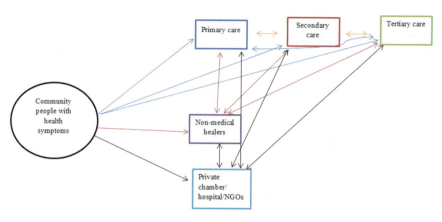

Fig. 3 Potential help-seeking pathway for mental disorders in Bangladesh

Western medicine, in cities, persons with symptoms usually visit specialized hospitals, their family physicians, or private chambers of the physicians. Generally, in most of the rural and suburban areas persons with symptoms visit village doctors, pharmacy men (drug vendors), and governmental primary care services. From these initial encounters, they are referred mostly to specialist private practitioners practicing in different consultation centres owned by several corporate businesses and local clinics where they perform laboratory investigations. At this point, there are various malicious efforts to divert referrals to a specific physician or a consultation centre. Generally, there are no justified price margins for laboratory investigations in the private sector. Also, based on the marketing principle, the referred physician and/or chemists/persons get referral fees from the diagnostic centres. A small proportion of patients are referred to specialized hospitals and tertiary care centres. There are ample examples of performing unnecessary laboratory investigations and improper referral of patients to different specialities. Referral to mental health services is affected in various ways in the private sector. In one end specialist physicians are reluctant to refer patients to the psychiatrist due to a lack of judicious professional practice and accountability, and for the fear of losing the particular patient and income. On the other hand, patients are reluctant to visit psychiatrists despite repeated referrals from multiple physicians due to a high stigma towards mental health and low mental health literacy. It is important to note that there is an extreme dearth of studies assessing the aspects of mental health services in Bangladesh. We mention here the aspects of our clinical experience.

3.2 New Developments-Tele-Psychiatry

With the expansion of the internet, smartphones, and electronic gadgets, telemedicine has opened a new dimension of health services in Bangladesh. Nowadays, almost all practitioners provide their *WhatsApp* details to their patients and respond to their queries. Although the services started in 1999 (Khan, 2022) they got real momentum during the COVID-19 pandemic when the government and several NGOs initiated and promoted the services. In the case of mental health services, tele-psychiatry has been practiced in various forms like providing psychiatric treatment through *Skype, WhatsApp, Messenger, IMO, FaceTime*, etc., video/audio calls, and providing psychotherapy and counselling. Psychiatrists from the capital city or district levels provide services to rural patients whilst sometimes mentioning the mediation names in Bangla in their prescriptions. There is another telepsychiatry service where the local psychiatrist provides consultations for Bangladeshi expatriates. In that case, the family members or relatives visit the psychiatrists' chambers, explain the problems, make video calls to discuss with the patients, and receive prescriptions. Then they send the prescriptions and medications to the overseas expatriates.

Currently, there are multiple tele-psychiatry services in the private sector. Based on personal communication, it revealed that the government started a project on tele-psychiatry at the NIMH, Dhaka which was stopped later. The project has been continued by *International Centre for Diarrhoeal Disease Research, Bangladesh* (ICDDR, B) for selected sub-districts. As an emerging niche private sector healthcare service, tele-psychiatry is practically unregulated in Bangladesh.

4 Challenges of Mental Health Care

4.1 High Treatment Gap

Historically, mental health care is neglected in Bangladesh. People usually seek care when there is severe functional impairment or social nuisance. Additionally, because of the belief of the supernatural causation of mental illness and enduring coverage by traditional healers, the majority of persons with mental disorders remain outside the mental health care. The latest national mental health survey 2018–19 identified the treatment gap for psychiatric disorders among the adult population was 91% which was more in males (92%) than females (90.4%) (Ministry of Health & Family Welfare, 2021). This gap is higher among children and adolescents. The overall treatment gap for child psychiatric disorders was 94.3% which was 98.4% among boys and 89.7% among girls. The findings indicate that less than 10% of persons reach mental health care services in Bangladesh.

4.2 Unregulated Help Seeking Pattern

Based on the non-existence of a functioning referral system, pluralistic health services, service structure, and service availability, one individual can seek help from any point of services. Here, people follow various help-seeking methods for mental health care. Our national survey identified that only 20% of the patients with psychiatric disorders visited public hospitals, only 3% visited specialized mental health services, about one-fourth of the patients visited the chamber of the psychiatrist, about 19% visited private hospitals, 22% visited the chambers of other specialist physicians, and about 2% visited homoeopathy, Unani, and ayurvedic practitioners. We can extrapolate that only 23% of patients received services provided by the Government, and 28% of patients received specialist mental health services. Therefore, 77% of mental health patients took services other than Government services and 72% received other than specialist mental health services at their first encounter (Ministry of Health & Family Welfare, 2021). For child mental disorders, the highest number of first consultations was made at homeopathy, unani, and ayurveda practitioners (30.6%) whilst only 16.5% of children visited psychiatrists. One systematic review found that a significant proportion of mental health patients visited religious and traditional healers (Hossain et al., 2014).

Giasuddin and his colleagues (2012) found that 84% of psychiatric patients visited other outlets before consulting mental health services providers, 44% first consulted non-psychiatric general practitioners, 22% first attended native or religious healers and 12% attended rural medical practitioners/polli cikisak. They identified four main pathways of psychiatric care in Bangladesh i.e. direct consultations, and referrals from private practitioners, general hospitals and traditional healers whilst family members were found to have the dominant role in care seeking (Giasuddin et al., 2012). Another study assessing the pathway of psychiatric care also revealed a similar role of family members for care-seeking (Nuri et al., 2018). The study identified that 27.5% of the psychiatric patients attended mental health professionals, 30% non-medical persons, and 42.5% attended non-psychiatric medical care professionals (Nuri et al., 2018) as their first contact services point. The study also identified that the psychiatrists in their private chambers were the most frequently consulted persons (30%) followed by traditional healers (22.5%).

4.3 Poor Fund and Research

Bangladesh has a budget of 0.5% of the total health budget on mental health and mental health expenditure per person is 0.1 USD in a year (World Health Organization, 2022a). We extrapolate the information that a person has only about 10 Taka for his/her mental health in a year. Along with the poor expenditure, the WHO-ATLAS country profile (1987) of Bangladesh revealed that only 35 peer-reviewed articles were published on mental health in 2020 which indicates an extreme dearth of research in the country (World Health Organization, 2022a). These also indicate poor political and academic interest in mental health in the country which can be either be the cause or effect of poor funding and research.

4.4 Inadequate and Inequitable Manpower

The manpower for services needed in mental health care in Bangladesh is scarce. A recent WHO report found that there are 270 psychiatrists for 170 million populations (World Health Organization, 2022a). It has been noticed that about 10–20 specialists are coming out yearly (Arafat, 2023). There are 0.17 psychiatrists, 0.43 psychiatric nurses, and 0.35 psychologists per 100,000 population in Bangladesh (World Health Organization, 2022a). A simple calculation revealed that one psychiatrist is assigned to 110,000 psychiatric patients considering the prevalence of psychiatric disorders among adults (18.7%) and the availability of psychiatrists (0.17 per 100,000). The situation is more complex due to the inequitable distribution of mental health professionals. The majority of psychiatrists live in the urban areas specialty in the capital city (Dhaka). There are districts where no psychiatrist is available for the whole population and there are no mental health professionals at the *Upazila* (sub-district) level. Except for the capital city, the other mental health professional concentrated cities are Chattogram, Sylhet, and Rajshahi (Government of The People's Republic of Bangladesh, 2022). In Bangladesh, the distribution of mental health professionals is uneven, with a concentration of professionals in urban areas and a severe shortage in rural areas (Faruk, 2022).

The number of psychiatric beds is greater in or around the capital of the country as well as other large cities, but the opposite scenario exists in the case of smaller districts. Inequality of access to mental health care for linguistic, ethnic, or religious minorities may raise concerns. It is important to mention again that there is no allocated post for psychiatrists in the primary and secondary levels of government health services.

Mental health service is hospital-centred, community approach is limited. Although, the community mental health facilities are expanding gradually, the available services are quite inadequate.

4.5 Huge Out-of-Pocket Expense

There is no available insurance facility in Bangladesh to cover mental health care expenses and risks (Government of The People's Republic of Bangladesh, 2022; Giasuddin et al., 2012; Nuri et al., 2018). At the same time, there is an extreme dearth of studies assessing the out-of-pocket expense of psychiatric care in the country (Arafat, 2023). We could not find any empirical studies assessing out-of-pocket expenses for any specific psychiatric disorders. The World Bank report indicated that overall out-of-pocket expense is more than 70% in the health sector of Bangladesh (World Bank, 2023a). We speculate that the scenario would not be better in mental health care in Bangladesh.

4.6 Malfunctioning Referral System

People can visit any level of services and psychiatrists for any sort of symptoms. We speculate the possible pathways of approaching mental health care for community people in Fig. 3. In Bangladesh, practically there is a nonexistence of referral systems in any sector of health services and mental health care is not an exception (Arafat, 2019b; World Health Organization, 2015). Additionally, there is no specific catchment area for mental health services in the country.

4.7 Poor Mental Health Literacy

Mental health literacy is a newer academic focus in Bangladesh. Studies are coming out assessing the literacy of specific disorders like depression (Arafat, et al., 2019). However, we could not find any empirical study assessing the overall mental health literacy in the country. One important assessment of science books of primary and secondary schools (up to grade 10) and found that content on mental health was almost absent (Uddin, 2020). We speculate that mental health literacy would be poor in the country. However, further studies are warranted to explore the issues.

4.8 Lower-Middle Income Status and Income Disparity

Since its independence, Bangladesh gained significant economic growth. As a country, Bangladesh is one of the fastest growing economies in the world and recently it has been promoted to the lower-middle income group from the low-income group. The World Bank report revealed, in 2021 the per capita income was 2158 USD (World Bank, 2023b). At the same time, income and wealth inequality are also rising. It is revealed from the latest (2022) *Household Income and Expenditure Survey* that the poorest 24% had contributed 0.23% of income which was 0.78% in 2010 whilst the top 5% of people contributed to 28% of the total income which was 20% in 2010 (Haque, 2022; TBS Report, 2023). This income disparity affects mental health care and the expenses allocated for it.

4.9 High Stigma

Mental health is a stigmatized topic in the country (Hossain et al., 2014; Ministry of Health & Family Welfare, 2021; Hasan & Thornicroft, 2018). Rural people as well as urban people hold some degree of misconception about mental illness. Even MBBS medical students in the country showed increasing stigma in their upper medical school years (Giasuddin et al., 2015). Also among the doctors of other specialties, there is some prejudice against this subject.

4.10 Non-judicious Prescribing (Poly Pharmacy)

There is a dearth of studies assessing the prescribing pattern of psychotropic medication in Bangladesh. One study identified that more than 45% of patients with schizophrenia received polypharmacy in the country (Yang et al., 2018). From our personal experience, we speculate that a good proportion of psychiatrists practice rampant poly-pharmacy with multiple antipsychotics. Some of them justify their poly-pharmacy with the concern that there is a lower proportion of active ingredients in the medications available in Bangladesh. There is a common notion among laypersons that psychiatrists only give hypnotics to make the patients calm. Therefore, persons with minor psychiatric problems avoid psychiatric consultations. This notion can partially be attributed to such rampant poly-pharmacy practice.

4.11 Administrative Difficulties

A separate and dedicated authority for mental health is yet to be established in Bangladesh. There is no separate mental health wing in the health ministry. There is a limitation of human resources, logistics and financial support. The organization of mental health services does not follow the aspects of catchment/service areas. The coordination system with other ministries, professional & consumer groups is insufficient. There is lack of harmonious collaboration among different sectors of the country like education, legal system, social welfare and others.

4.12 Scarcity of Medications

The *National Mental Health Strategic Plan*, 2020–2030 considered some psychotropics as national essential medicines in Bangladesh. These are; antidepressants (Fluoxetine and Amitriptyline), antipsychotics (Haloperidol, Risperidone, Chlorpromazine, and Fluphenazine), Anticholinergics (Biperiden and Trihexyphenidyl), mood stabilizers (Lithium, Sodium valproate, and Carbamazepine), and anti-dementics (Cholinesterase inhibitors-Donepezil, Galantamine, and Memantine) (Government of The People's Republic of Bangladesh, 2022). Essential psychotropic medicines are available in PMH and the NIMH, but not widely available in general hospital psychiatry units or Upazila level pharmacy stores.

5 Non-medical Management of Mental Disorders in Bangladesh

In Bangladesh, a large portion of mental health care providers practices non-medical/non-western treatments. They are unqualified allopathic practitioners (e.g. community health workers, health assistants, chemists or pharmacy men or drug sellers, *Palli cikitsak* or village doctors), alternate medicine practitioners, and traditional healers (World Health Organization, 2015). Traditional healers include "Ojha", "Kabiraz", "Baba", "Pirr", "Sufi", "Fakir", "Huzur", "Samans", "Homeopathy", "and alternate medicine" (Giasuddin et al., 2012; Nuri et al., 2018). The study conducted by Giasuddin and his colleagues (2012) found that 22% first attended native or religious healers and 12% attended rural medical practitioners/*polli cikitsak*. Whereas a study conducted by Nuri et al. (2018) found that 30% of psychiatric patients attended non-medical persons as their first contact service point. As we previously mentioned our national mental health survey found that about 2% of adult psychiatric patients and 30% of children with mental illness visited homeopathy, Unani, and ayurveda practitioners for treatment as a first encounter (Ministry of Health & Family Welfare, 2021). One study identified that 26.3% of mentally ill patients preferred religious and traditional healers including herbalists (Islam et al., 2001). From the available studies, we extrapolate that about one in four to half of the patients seek help from non-medical caregivers at their first encounter and this scenario usually persists for subsequent encounters also. The encounters affect care-seeking in various ways depicted in Fig. 3. Even though these services are not a part of the mainstream health service, a considerable portion of community populations seek their help, especially in the poor rural segment of society and hard-to-reach areas (World Health Organization, 2015). This pattern is attributable by considering the belief about supernatural causation of mental illness, especially the belief about being possessed by jinn, harm by others through black magic (Tabiz) which is considered an overvalued idea in Bangladesh (Selim & Satalkar, 2008; Mullick et al., 2013).

A study assessed the perception of Jinn, black magic, and the evil eye among 320 respondents in a large tertiary care hospital revealed that 61% believe in revealed Jinn possession, 50% believe in black magic, and 44% believe in the evil eye (Mullick et al., 2013). Lower educational attainment was found to be an associated factor for holding these beliefs.

6 Potential Ways Out

6.1 Augmented Research and Funding

One of the key challenges in mental health services in Bangladesh is the limited funding and resources for mental health care (World Health Organization, 2022a). To address this challenge, it is essential to increase funding for large-scale mental health epidemiologic research in Bangladesh. This can be done by establishing dedicated mental health research funding agencies or by integrating mental health research into existing national and international research funding agencies. Augmented funding is also necessary to invest in mental health training and capacity building for researchers, clinicians, and other mental health professionals by providing scholarships and fellowships.

6.2 Country-Wide Distribution of Mental Health Professionals

Previously, we mentioned the inequitable and concentrated distribution of mental health professionals in the country where there is no allocated post for psychiatrists at primary and secondary care levels. Equal and equitable distribution and utilization of resources are necessary. Without closing the gap among different social strata we cannot ensure better mental health. Mental health services need to be readily available through the existing health services. Adequate measures are warranted to secure psychiatrists at the secondary level of government health services and special training should be initiated so that at least one person, who will be trained in mental health issues, is available in every primary health care service point. These strategies will help increase the number of mental health professionals and improve the accessibility and availability of mental health services in Bangladesh. We need to allocate resources evenly to make the services available to people of all geographical, socio-economic, racial, ethnic, or gender groups. Mental health professionals should get accustomed to the community care approach. They should be offered an adequate remuneration package for their job. They also have to be ideologically motivated to work for the community.

6.3 Health Insurance

We mentioned earlier that in Bangladesh there is no national health insurance scheme in place that covers explicitly mental health services (Giasuddin et al., 2012; Nuri et al., 2018). The *Bangladesh National Mental Health Strategic Plan* (2020–2030) emphasizes the importance of promoting advocacy for mental health coverage in all health insurance schemes, both in the government and private sectors. This includes coverage for evidence-based treatments for mental health conditions, both medical and non-medical. Direct Project Aid, Reimbursable Project Aid, and Government funding will be used for this (Government of The People's Republic of Bangladesh, 2022). Additionally, some private health insurance providers in the country may offer coverage for mental health services as part of their policies. To increase mental health insurance coverage in the country, it is essential to raise awareness about mental health insurance and develop mental health-specific insurance plans that cover a range of mental health services, including psychotherapy, medication, and hospitalization. The government can provide incentives like tax breaks, subsidies, or other financial incentives to insurance providers to encourage them to offer mental health insurance.

6.4 Awareness Creation Targeting Mental Health Literacy

Awareness creation targeting the general population, health professionals, policy-makers, mental health professionals and organizations, and community leaders can be an effective strategy for improving mental health literacy (Nejati et al., 2023; Stuart et al., 2023; Petersen et al., 2023). Long-term digital media mental health campaigns can have a positive effect on mental health awareness, help-seeking behaviors, and stigma reduction (Curran et al., 2023). Increasing public awareness, especially through the young generation can increase the use of modern digital health technologies to access mental health care and to remove mental health-related stigma in Bangladesh (Sifat et al., 2022a).

6.4.1 Social Media Campaigns

Utilizing the widely used social media platforms like *Facebook, Instagram, Twitter, and TikTok* to create and share content that raises awareness about mental health issues, promotes mental health literacy, encourages conversation on the topic and reduces stigma (Koly et al., 2022; Hasan & Thornicroft, 2018).

6.4.2 Educational Workshops

Organize workshops in schools, colleges, and workplaces to educate people about different aspects of mental health, its importance, and how to recognize and address mental health challenges.

6.4.3 Celebrity Endorsements

Collaborate with well-known personalities or influencers to promote mental health literacy and help break the stigma associated with mental health issues.

6.4.4 Public Service Announcements (PSAs)

Partner with local radio and television stations to broadcast PSAs related to mental health literacy and the importance of seeking help when needed (Sauda et al., 2023; Chen et al., 2022).

6.4.5 Community Events

Organize community events like mental health awareness walks, concerts, and art exhibitions to bring people together and spread the message of mental health literacy.

6.4.6 Mental Health Apps

Develop user-friendly mental health apps that provide resources, tips, and self-assessment tools to raise mental health literacy and encourage help-seeking behavior (Sifat et al., 2022b; Koly et al., 2022).

6.4.7 Print Media

Publish articles, infographics, and opinion pieces in newspapers and magazines to educate readers about mental health issues and promote mental health literacy.

6.4.8 Collaboration with Mental Health Organizations

Partner with established mental health organizations to share resources, expertise, and knowledge with the aim of promoting mental health literacy on a broader scale (Hasan et al., 2021).

6.5 Dedicated Programs for Non-medical Responders

As a good portion of the services is encountered by non-medical responders, dedicated programs for non-medical responders should be implemented utilizing various resources. The ultimate goal of this campaign will be to raise mental health literacy, decrease stigma, and reinforce help-seeking behavior. The 3rd *Health, Nutrition and Population Strategic Investment Plan* (HPNSP) 2011–2016 and the ongoing 4th HPNSP 2017–2022 both include the establishment and circulation of mental health social and behavior change communication details and television advertisement spots, as well as awareness activities on drug abuse and detrimental consumption of alcohol, as part of their strategies for improving mental health outcomes (Government of The People's Republic of Bangladesh, 2022).

6.6 Functioning Referral System

The *Bangladesh National Mental Health Strategic Plan* (2020–2030) includes a policy and plan that calls for the integration of psychiatric services at all levels of the public healthcare system (Government of The People's Republic of Bangladesh, 2022). The plan emphasizes the integration of mental health services into primary healthcare, which will be achieved by strengthening the existing healthcare delivery system by improving the capacity of healthcare providers at all levels to identify and manage mental health conditions. The strategy also emphasizes the importance of developing referral pathways and protocols to ensure that patients receive appropriate care at the right level of the healthcare system. Furthermore, the plan aims to decentralize mental health services by extending them to divisions, districts, and Upazilas/Thanas (Sub-district) in both rural and urban areas. This will ensure that mental health services are available and accessible to all people across the country. The World Health Organization (WHO) developed the *Mental Health Gap Action Programme* (mhGAP) to help scale up services for mental, neurological, and substance use disorders, particularly in low and middle-income countries which have been implemented in Bangladesh (Momotaz et al., 2019). However, the initiative has not yet been fully implemented in Bangladesh, except for the people of forcibly displaced Rohingya (Hasan et al., 2021).

6.7 Good Governance

Good governance requires strong leadership and accountability mechanisms that ensure mental health services are delivered in an ethical and transparent manner (Cheong Chi Mo et al., 2023). This includes effective regulation, monitoring, and evaluation of mental health services to ensure they meet international standards and best practices. The Directorate General of Health Services (DGHS) is responsible for overseeing mental healthcare services in Bangladesh, including the management of primary and secondary care services at district hospitals and Upazila health centres and clinics (World Health Organization, 2015).

In recent years, the government of Bangladesh has made efforts to improve the quality and accessibility of mental healthcare services in the country. *Bangladesh National Mental Health Strategic Plan* (2020–2030) has been developed to guide the development and implementation of mental health services across the country

(Government of The People's Republic of Bangladesh, 2022). Clinical audits, supervision to reduce poly-pharmacy, maintaining transparency, equity, and indiscriminating distribution of government resources can set a culture of good governance.

6.8 Availability of Psychotropic Medications

There are listed essential psychotropics consisted of psycholeptics, anti-anxiety drugs, antidepressants, mood stabilizers, and antiepileptic medications (Government of The People's Republic of Bangladesh, 2022). We need to ensure the regular supply of these medications from tertiary centres to the root level so that community mental health services and primary health care teams and the clients do not face difficulty in getting the required medication. Updating the essential medicine list could be a potential attempt as some generics like biperedine are not available in the country and olanzapine is a cheap generic that could be included in the list.

6.9 Involvement of the Clients and Their Families in the Service Delivery Process

At present, there is no available consumer association in our country. There is one family association consisted of that has 40 family representatives. There is lack of funding for the association to continue the activities. The association has no role in policy formulation or implementation in the country in previous days. There is also lack of collaboration between psychiatric services and the associations. We need to break this cycle and improve the situation. We need to encourage the formation of different consumer groups. At the time of preparing the mental health policy, plan, and programs we need to consider their views and include these views in the outcome.

6.10 Inter-Sectoral Collaboration

We need to have enduring multisectoral collaborations among the government departments responsible for psychiatric services in Bangladesh.

6.11 Protection of Human Rights

Currently, Bangladesh has no human rights review body in the country to supervise inspections of psychiatric services. We need to consider these while making the policy, plan, and programs and include these in our agenda.

6.12 Disaster Preparedness

Natural disasters like floods, cyclones, earthquakes, river erosion, and accidental disasters like accidents, fire burns, and building collapse are common in Bangladesh. Some of them have acute effects like acute stress disorder, PTSD, depression, and anxiety, and some have enduring effects like migration, poverty, and adjustment disorder. Currently, we do not see any specialized trauma-focused services in the country. Bangladesh needs a specialized disaster-focused approach considering the biopsychosocial approach as selected and indicated prevention strategy. As Bangladesh is a disaster-prone country, a disaster preparedness plan for mental health is an utmost importance in the mental health policy, plan and programs (Alam et al., 2021; Choudhury et al., 2006).

6.13 Human Resources Development

A significant portion of the policy should devote consideration to the development of trained qualified professionals in the mental health field. Considering the low number of trained staff, short and long-term nation-wide training programs should be taken to increase the qualified staff. The undergraduate course curriculum, ward time and examinations should have adequate exposure to mental disorders and treatment. To increase competence among primary health care physicians and primary care health workers we need to take training programs with continued educational programs. A sufficient number of nursing staff should be trained in mental health.

6.14 Administrative Reform

We need to create a separate mental health wing in the health ministry which will coordinate the mental health activity in the country. We need to divide the country according to service areas. The individual areas should be given a separate budget to perform their function.

6.15 Clinical Audits

Formal clinical audits are warranted to reduce the rampant poly-pharmacy of psychotropic medications. Appointment of clinical psycho-pharmacologists in indoor services could be a gate-keeper initiative.

6.16 Decriminalization of Suicide Attempt

Criminalized legal status hinders access to mental health care for suicidal behavior. In Bangladesh decriminalization of suicide is warranted to measure the problem, increase access to care, and to formulate the national suicide prevention strategy (Arafat, 2019a, 2019b, 2019c).

7 Conclusions

Although Bangladesh has significant achievements in maternal and child health, access to mental health services is poor and inequitable. More than nine out of ten individuals are out of mental health services even though psychiatric illness is one of the top fifth burdensome non-communicable diseases in the country. There are an inadequate number of mental health professionals with inequitable distribution between rural and urban settings and negligible budgetary allocation for mental health. Services positions for psychiatrists are only available in the tertiary care level of government health services. Functionally, the private sector is poorly regulated resulting in unethical practices like polypharmacy. There is no functional referral system or insurance coverage for mental illness. Low mental health literacy, a perception of supernatural causation of mental illness creates challenges for help-seeking in the country. Immediate initiatives are warranted to reduce the huge treatment gap. Augmented research and funding in mental health services, country-wide distribution of mental health professionals, initiation of health insurance, raising awareness targeting mental health literacy, dedicated programs for non-medical responders, the establishment of a functioning referral system, and good governance in mental health services including clinical audits and supervision are potential ways out to improve the mental health services in Bangladesh.

References

Ahmed. (2018). Non-communicable diseases and their prevention: A global, regional and Bangladesh perspective. *National Bulletin of Public Health (NBPH), 1*(3), 2–4.

Alam, F., Hossain, R., Ahmed, H. U., Alam, M. T., Sarkar, M., & Halbreich, U. (2021). Stressors and mental health in Bangladesh: current situation and future hopes. *Bjpsych International, 18*(4), 91–94. https://doi.org/10.1192/bji.2020.57

Amin, Z. A. (2023). Outbound medical tourism from Bangladesh. Daily Sun. Retrieved from March 29, 2023. https://www.daily-sun.com/post/670262/Outbound-Medical-Tourism-from-Bangladesh#:~:text=About%2054%25%20of%20all%20foreign,not%20in%20the%20official%20list

Andalib, A., & Arafat, S. Y. (2016). Practicing pattern of physicians in Bangladesh. *International Journal of Perceptions in Public Health, 1*(1), 9–13.

Arafat, S. Y., & Khan, M. M. (Eds.). (2023). *Suicide in Bangladesh: Epidemiology, risk factors, and prevention*. Springer Nature. https://doi.org/10.1007/978-981-99-0289-7

Arafat, S. Y. (2019a). Current challenges of suicide and future directions of management in Bangladesh: A systematic review. *Global Psychiatry, 2*(1), 09–20. https://doi.org/10.2478/gp-2019-0001

Arafat, S. M. Y. (2023). Mental Health and Suicide in Bangladesh. In Arafat, S. M. Y., Khan, M. M. (Eds.), *Suicide in Bangladesh. New perspectives in behavioral & health sciences*. Springer. https://doi.org/10.1007/978-981-99-0289-7_3

Arafat, S. M. Y., Kar, S. K., Sharma, P., Marahatta, K., & Baminiwatta, A. K. A. B. (2021). A comparative analysis of psychiatry curriculum at undergraduate level of Bangladesh, India, Nepal, and Sri Lanka. *Indian Journal of Psychiatry, 63*(2), 184–188. https://doi.org/10.4103/psychiatry.IndianJPsychiatry_615_20

Arafat, S. Y., Al Mamun, M. A., & Uddin, M. S. (2019). Depression literacy among first-year university students: A cross-sectional study in Bangladesh. *Global Psychiatry, 2*(1), 31–36. https://doi.org/10.2478/gp-2019-0002

Arafat, S. M. Y. (2019b). History of psychiatry in Bangladesh. *Asian Journal of Psychiatry, 46*, 11–12. https://doi.org/10.1016/j.ajp.2019.09.024

Arafat, S. M. Y. (2019b). Poor Health Literacy, dilapidated referral system, step-wise commission business and huge out of pocket expense: The Hardcore challenges of Private Health Services in Bangladesh. *ARC Journal of Public Health and Community Medicine, 4*(3), 29–30. https://doi.org/10.20431/2456-0596.0403003

Arafat, S. M. Y., Mullick, M. S. I., & Islam, H. (2020). Development of psychiatric services in Bangladesh. *Asian Journal of Psychiatry, 47*, 101870. https://doi.org/10.1016/j.ajp.2019.101870

Bandyopadhyay, G. K., Ghoshal, M., Saha, G., & Singh, O. P. (2018). History of psychiatry in Bengal. *Indian Journal of Psychiatry, 60*(Suppl 2), S192–S197. https://doi.org/10.4103/0019-5545.224323

Basu, A. R. (2004). A new knowledge of madness-nineteenth century asylum psychiatry in Bengal. *Indian Journal of History of Science, 39*(3), 247–277.

Chen, J. L., VanRiel, Y., & Patel, F. (2022). Creating Mental Health Public Service Announcements. *Nurse Educator, 47*(4), 207. https://doi.org/10.1097/NNE.0000000000001185

Cheong Chi Mo, J., Shah, A., Downey, C., Genay-Diliautas, S., Saikat, S., Mustafa, S., Meru, N., Dalil, S., Schmets, G., & Porignon, D. (2023). Developing technical support and strategic dialogue at the country level to achieve Primary Health Care-based health systems beyond the COVID-19 era. *Frontiers in public health, 11*, 1102325. https://doi.org/10.3389/fpubh.2023.1102325

Choudhury, W. A., Quraishi, F. A., & Haque, Z. (2006). Mental health and psychosocial aspects of disaster preparedness in Bangladesh. *International Review of Psychiatry (Abingdon, England), 18*(6), 529–535. https://doi.org/10.1080/09540260601037896

Curran, T., Ito-Jaeger, S., Perez Vallejos, E., & Crawford, P. (2023). What's up with everyone?': The effectiveness of a digital media mental health literacy campaign for young people. *Journal of mental health (Abingdon, England)*, 1–7. https://doi.org/10.1080/09638237.2023.2182412

Faruk, M. O. (2022). Community-Based Mental Health Services in Bangladesh: Prospects and challenges. *World Social Psychiatry, 4*(3), 187.

Facility Registry. (2023). Ministry of Health and Family Welfare, Government of People's Republic of Bangladesh. Retrieved from April 04, 2023, http://facilityregistry.dghs.gov.bd/index.php

Government of The People's Republic of Bangladesh. (2022). National Mental Health Strategic Plan, 2020–2030. Retrieved from May 02, 2023, https://dghs.gov.bd/sites/default/files/files/dghs.portal.gov.bd/notices/e27171cb_a80b_42d4_99ad_40095adef31b/2022-08-16-08-42-af8622e2c4936593dd45601b84f4920f.pdf

Goldberg, D., & Huxley, P. (1980). *Mental illness in the community*. London: Tavistock.

Goldberg, D., & Huxley, P. (1992). *Common mental disorders: A bio-social model*. London: Routledge.

Gater, R., de Almeida e Sousa, B., Barrientos, G., et al. (1991). The pathways to psychiatric care: a cross-cultural study. *Psychological Medicine, 21*(3), 761–774.

Giasuddin, N. A., Chowdhury, N. F., Hashimoto, N., Fujisawa, D., &Waheed, S. (2012). Pathways to psychiatric care in Bangladesh. *Social Psychiatry and Psychiatric Epidemiology, 47*(1), 129–136. https://doi.org/10.1007/s00127-010-0315-y

Giasuddin, N. A., Levav, I., & Gal, G. (2015). Mental health stigma and attitudes to psychiatry among Bangladeshi medical students. *International Journal of Social Psychiatry, 61*(2), 137–147. https://doi.org/10.1177/0020764014537237

Haque, S. R. (2022). Income inequality: The Bangladesh scenario. The Daily Sun. Retrieved from May 10, 2023, https://www.daily-sun.com/printversion/details/651770/Income-Inequality:-the-Bangladesh-Scenario

Hossain, M. D., Ahmed, H. U., Chowdhury, W. A., Niessen, L. W., & Alam, D. S. (2014). Mental disorders in Bangladesh: A systematic review. *BMC Psychiatry, 14*, 216. https://doi.org/10.1186/s12888-014-0216-9

Hasan, M. T., Anwar, T., Christopher, E., Hossain, S., Hossain, M. M., Koly, K. N., Saif-Ur-Rahman, K. M., Ahmed, H. U., Arman, N., & Hossain, S. W. (2021). The current state of mental healthcare in Bangladesh: Part 2—Setting priorities. *BJPsych International, 18*(4), 82–85. https://doi.org/10.1192/bji.2021.42

Hasan, M. T., & Thornicroft, G. (2018). Mass media campaigns to reduce mental health stigma in Bangladesh. *The Lancet Psychiatry, 5*(8), 616. https://doi.org/10.1016/S2215-0366(18)30219-0

Islam, M. M., Ali, M., & Fenonia, P. (2001). Care seeking behavior of mentally ill: A qualitative and quantitative approach. *Bangladesh Journal of Psychiatry, 15*, 13–18.

Karim, M. R., Shaheed, F., & Paul, S. (2006). Psychiatry in Bangladesh. *International Psychiatry, 3*(3), 16–18.

Khan, N. H. (2022). Telemedicine in Bangladesh: Prospects and challenges. The New Nation. . Retrieved from May 08, 2023, https://thedailynewnation.com/news/331276/Telemedicine-in-Bangladesh:-Prospects-and-challenges?fbclid=IwAR0GLKqoLWS5Oc1vkOuzivPshvYCJQdtbNj4FjmR40wMdsXY0cQtvyBh7rA

Kemp, C. G., Concepcion, T., Ahmed, H. U., Anwar, N., Baingana, F., Bennett, I. M., Bruni, A., Chisholm, D., Dawani, H., Erazo, M., Hossain, S. W., January, J., Ladyk-Bryzghalova, A., Momotaz, H., Munongo, E., Oliveira E Souza, R., Sala, G., Schafer, A., Sukhovii, O., Taboada, L., et al. (2022). Baseline situational analysis in Bangladesh, Jordan, Paraguay, the Philippines, Ukraine, and Zimbabwe for the WHO Special Initiative for Mental Health: Universal Health Coverage for Mental Health. *PloS one, 17*(3), e0265570. https://doi.org/10.1371/journal.pone.0265570

Koly, K. N., Saba, J., Muzaffar, R., Modasser, R. B., M, T. H., Colon-Cabrera, D., & Warren, N. (2022). Exploring the potential of delivering mental health care services using digital technologies in Bangladesh: A qualitative analysis. *Internet Interventions, 29*, 100544. https://doi.org/10.1016/j.invent.2022.100544

Momotaz, H., Ahmed, H. U., Uddin, M. J., Karim, R., Khan, M. A., Al-Amin, R., et al. (2019). Implementing the Mental health gap action programme in Cox's Bazar, Bangladesh. *Intervention, 17*(2), 243.

Ministry of Health & Family Welfare. (2021). National Mental Health Survey 2019. Retrieved from March 29, 2023, http://nimh.gov.bd/wp-content/uploads/2021/11/Mental-Health-Survey-Report.pdf

Morning News. (1970). Mental Health.

National Institute of Mental Health and Hospital. (n.d.). https://nimhbd.com/web/index.php/home

Mullick, M. S. I., Khalifa, N., Nahar, J. S., & Walker, D.-M. (2013). Beliefs about Jinn, black magic and evil eye in Bangladesh: The effects of gender and level of education. *Mental Health, Religion & Culture, 16*(7), 719–729. https://doi.org/10.1080/13674676.2012.717918

Naher, K. (2022). Alternative medical care still has its place. Here is why. Business Standard. Retrieved from May 03, 2023, https://www.tbsnews.net/features/panorama/alternative-medical-care-still-has-its-place-here-why-419434

Nejati, S., Törnbom, K., Hange, D., Björkelund, C., & Svenningsson, I. (2023). How can care managers strengthen health literacy among patients with common mental disorders? A qualitative study. *Scandinavian Journal of Caring Sciences*, https://doi.org/10.1111/scs.13170

Nuri, N. N., Sarker, M., Ahmed, H. U., Hossain, M. D., Beiersmann, C., & Jahn, A. (2018). Pathways to care of patients with mental health problems in Bangladesh. *International Journal of Mental Health Systems, 12*, 39. https://doi.org/10.1186/s13033-018-0218-y

Petersen, J. M., Drummond, M., Crossman, S., Elliott, S., Drummond, C., & Prichard, I. (2023). Mental health promotion in youth sporting clubs: Predictors of stakeholder participation. *BMC Public Health, 23*(1), 481. https://doi.org/10.1186/s12889-023-15377-5

Sauda, V. C., Bisher, P., & Nason, M. (2023). Using our voice: Supporting College Student Mental Health through radio outreach in a Mental Health Nursing Course. *Nursing education Perspectives*. https://doi.org/10.1097/01.NEP.0000000000001117

Selim, N., & Satalkar, P. (2008). Perceptions of mental illness in a Bangladesh village. *BRAC University Journal, V*, 47–57.

Sifat, M. S., Saperstein, S. L., Tasnim, N., & Green, K. M. (2022a). Motivations toward using digital health and exploring the possibility of using digital health for Mental Health in Bangladesh University Students: Cross-sectional questionnaire study. *JMIR Formative Research, 6*(3), e34901. https://doi.org/10.2196/34901

Sifat, M. S., Tasnim, N., Stoebenau, K., & Green, K. M. (2022b). A qualitative exploration of university student perspectives on mindfulness-based stress reduction exercises via smartphone app in Bangladesh. *International Journal of Qualitative Studies on Health and Well-Being, 17*(1), 2113015. https://doi.org/10.1080/17482631.2022.2113015

Stuart, R., Shah, P., Olive, R. R., Trevillion, K., & Henderson, C. (2023). Experiences of every mind matters, Public Health England's adult mental health literacy campaign: A qualitative interview study. *BMC Public Health, 23*(1), 398. https://doi.org/10.1186/s12889-023-15280-z

TBS Report. (2023). A slower decline in poverty rate, but a rise in inequality. The Business Standard. Retrieved from May 10, 2023, https://www.tbsnews.net/economy/incomes-grow-inequality-widens-615274

Uddin, M. S. (2020). Mental health content in school science textbooks in Bangladesh. *The Lancet Psychiatry, 7*(3), e10. https://doi.org/10.1016/S2215-0366(20)30008-0

Varma, L. P. (1953). History of Psychiatry in India and Pakistan. *Indian Journal of Neurology & Psychiatry, 4*(1 & 2), 26–53.

World Health Organization. (2015). Bangladesh health system review. *Health Systems in Transition, 5*, 1–214.

World Health Organization. (2022a). Mental Health Atlas 2020 Country Profile: Bangladesh. Retrieved from March 30, 2023, https://www.who.int/publications/m/item/mental-health-atlas-bgd-2020-country-profile

World Health Organization. (2022b). Addressing mental health in Bangladesh. Retrieved from May 03, 2023, https://www.who.int/publications-detail-redirect/9789290210146

World Health Organization. (1987). *Care for the mentally ill. Components of mental policies governing the provision of psychiatric services*. WHO Collaborating Centre for Research and Training in Mental Health, Montreal.

World Population Review. (2023). Muslim Majority Countries 2022. Retrieved from May 18, 2023, https://worldpopulationreview.com/country-rankings/muslim-majority-countries

World Bank. (2022). World Bank Country and Lending Groups. Retrieved from August 29, 2022, https://datahelpdesk.worldbank.org/knowledgebase/articles/906519-world-bank-country-and-lending-groups

World Health Organization. (2007). WHO-AIMS report on mental health system in Bangladesh. WHO Regional Office for South-East Asia. Retrieved from May 05, 2023, https://apps.who.int/iris/handle/10665/206149

World Bank. (2023a). Out-of-pocket expenditure (% of current health expenditure)—Bangladesh. Retrieved from April 04, 2023, https://data.worldbank.org/indicator/SH.XPD.OOPC.CH.ZS?locations=BD

World Bank. (2023b). GDP per capita (current US$)—Bangladesh. Retrieved from May 10, 2023, https://data.worldbank.org/indicator/NY.GDP.PCAP.CD?locations=BD

Yang, S. Y., Chen, L. Y., Najoan, E., Kallivayalil, R. A., Viboonma, K., Jamaluddin, R., Javed, A., Hoa, D. T. Q., Iida, H., Sim, K., Swe, T., He, Y. L., Park, Y., Ahmed, H. U., De Alwis, A., Chiu, H. F., Sartorius, N., Tan, C. H., Chong, M. Y., Shinfuku, N., et al. (2018). Polypharmacy and psychotropic drug loading in patients with schizophrenia in Asian countries: Fourth survey of Research on Asian Prescription Patterns on antipsychotics. *Psychiatry and clinical neurosciences, 72*(8), 572–579. https://doi.org/10.1111/pcn.12676

Access to Mental Health Care in Bhutan: Current Status, Potential Challenges, and Ways Out

Pawan Sharma and Devavrat Joshi

Abstract Bhutan is a landlocked country in South Asia and is known for its cultural heritage. Compared to the neighbouring nations, there has been a late start of mental health care and services in Bhutan. However, the principle of mental health care in Bhutan is guided by the policy of gross happiness index which includes psychological well-being. Though very little reliable data is available on the prevalence of mental illness in the country the full range of major mental illnesses exists in Bhutan. There has been a slow and steady improvement in mental health services, however, with the establishment of the Pema Centre, which will be a dedicated centre to address mental health problems in the country, the care for people with mental health problems is expected to improve in the coming years. There are many challenges in mental health care in Bhutan like stigma, lack of awareness, less manpower, centralized services, dearth of research and information management etc. In this chapter, we discuss the historical aspects of the mental health care system, and the current scenario in regard to the burden and services and challenges regarding the mental health care system of Bhutan. We also discuss country-specific ways forward.

Keywords Bhutan · Mental health care · Challenges · Stigma · Way forward

1 Introduction

The Kingdom of Bhutan is a landlocked country in South Asia and is locally known as "Druk Yul" or "Land of the Thunder Dragon", a name that reflects the cultural heritage of the country. It has an area of 38,394 km^2 and a population of 0.7 million approximately. The guide to Health Care in Bhutan is the developmental philosophy of Gross National Happiness (GNH) (Masaki & Tshering, 2021). The conceptual

P. Sharma (✉)
Department of Psychiatry, School of Medicine, Patan Academy of Health Sciences, Lalitpur, Nepal
e-mail: pawan60@gmail.com

D. Joshi
National Academy of Health Sciences, Mental Hospital Lagankhel, Patan, Nepal

© The Author(s), under exclusive license to Springer Nature Singapore Pte Ltd. 2024
S. M. Y. Arafat and S. K. Kar (eds.), *Access to Mental Health Care in South Asia*,
https://doi.org/10.1007/978-981-99-9153-2_4

framework of GNH is based on four pillars: sustainable and equitable socio-economic development, environmental conservation, preservation and promotion of culture, and good governance. There is a further expansion of these pillars into nine domains. They are psychological well-being, health, time use, education, cultural diversity and resilience, good governance, community vitality, ecological diversity and resilience, and living standards (Masaki & Tshering, 2021). As per the values and principles of GNH, these nine domains are representative of the well-being of the Bhutanese population. Even then, similar to any other country, many people in Bhutan suffer from a variety of mental health-related issues. However, until 1996, there were no specialized psychiatric services for people suffering from mental disorders in Bhutan. People used to be treated either by traditional healers with different rituals or by general physicians with limited knowledge of psychiatry. In addition, difficult cases were referred to India.

The National Mental Health Programme (NMHP) was launched for the first time in Bhutan in July 1997 to make sure that primary mental healthcare is available and accessible for all sectors of the population by integrating of mental health into general healthcare (Pelzang, 2012). For this purpose, a psychiatrist from Burma was hired to start the mental health services at the national referral hospital in Thimphu due to the unavailability of mental health workers in the country. The aim of NMHP was the integration of mental healthcare with the primary healthcare (PHC) system by training health personnel at PHC. The idea behind this integration was it would enable patients to receive both physical and mental health care in a single visit simultaneously. This would in turn reduce the stigma associated with mental disorders and help in raising awareness. However, even after the launch of this program there was lack of trained mental health workers at the primary health care level, patients had to be referred to higher centres i.e. district and referral hospitals (Pelzang, 2012).

The first psychiatrist of Bhutan graduated in 1999 from Sri Lanka. After coming back to the country, he helped in the implementation of a range of programmes to train medical doctors and health workers throughout the country to treat common mental disorders at the community level. All new cases of mental disorders have been formally registered since July 1999. The inpatient service in psychiatry was started in 2003 when a former boys' hostel belonging to the Royal Institute of Health Sciences was converted into an in-patient unit with eight beds (Naveed & Nirola, 2012). Before that people needing inpatient psychiatric treatment were admitted to the general medical ward of Jigme Dorji Wangchuck National Referral Hospital (JDWNRH). The country now has 4 psychiatrists. The total bed strength increased to 18 beds in 2012 and to 20 beds in 2018 due to the increased demand for services. In 2022, three bedded family wards within the 20-bed psychiatry ward were established for children and adolescents with mental health issues needing inpatient care. The Department of Psychiatry in JDWNRH is the only psychiatric unit providing specialized psychiatric treatment in Bhutan. Furthermore, Khesar Gyalpo University of Medical Sciences of Bhutan started a 4 years MD course in Psychiatry from 2018 and the first candidate graduated in 2022. As of 2023, 2 doctors are undergoing MD Psychiatry courses in the University.

2 Epidemiology and Burden of Mental Illness

The full range of major mental illnesses listed in the Diagnostic and Statistical Manual of Mental Disorders, 5th edition (DSM-5) or the International Classification of Disease, Tenth revision (ICD 10) exists in Bhutan, however, there is a dearth of reliable data available regarding the prevalence of mental disorders in the country. A community-based pilot survey conducted in 2002 on the prevalence of severe mental disorders in three districts of Bhutan with a sample population of 45000 identified 273 cases of severe illness: 83 cases of alcohol dependence, 69 cases of epilepsy, 49 cases of depression, 39 cases of intellectual disability, 17 cases of psychosis and 16 cases with suicidality (Dorji, 2004).

Data of 2008 showed more than 2846 new cases of mental disorders were treated at the National Referral Hospital (NRH). Of these cases, 29.3% had depression, 19.2% had anxiety disorder, 9.7% had psychosis and 41.5% of cases had alcohol and/substance abuse-related problems. Similarly, among the patients treated in the community mental health outpatient facilities mood disorders (32%); mental and behaviour disorders due to substance use including alcohol (27%); neurotic, stress-related and somatoform disorders (17%); and schizophrenia (19%) were the primary diagnosis (WHO, 2006). A study analyzing data from Bhutan's 2015 Gross National Happiness (GNH) Survey which was a multistage, cross-sectional nationwide household survey among 7041 respondents aged 15 years and above using a 12-item General Health Questionnaire showed the prevalence of Common Mental Disorders (CMD) to be 29.3%. The factors associated with symptoms of CMDs were: female gender, older age, illiteracy, low income, being divorced or widowed, having poor self-reported health and having co-morbid disability (Sithey et al., 2018).

Among the various conditions related to mental health, alcohol use disorder is a major problem in Bhutan. According to the National Statistics Bureau (Dorji & Bkod, 2012), deaths from alcohol-related liver disease had increased from 2003 to 2009 in a steady way. In 2009 alcohol use disorder became the top cause of death in JDWNRH. The majority of deaths related to alcohol-related liver disease occurred in the age group of 35–49 years (Dorji & Bkod, 2012).

A study using a dataset of the nationally representative Bhutan WHO STEP-wise approach to NCD risk factor surveillance (STEPS Survey) of 2014 showed that the prevalence of suicidal ideation to be 3.1% and suicide attempt to be 0.7% (Dendup et al., 2020). A secondary analysis of a nationally representative data from Global School-Based Student Health Survey in 2016 among 5809 students aged 13–17 years from 50 schools using a self-administered questionnaire showed that 11.6% of adolescents reported considering a suicide attempt and 11.3% of adolescents reported making an attempt of suicide in the past 12 months. Factors like food insecurity, female gender, sexual violence, physical violence, bullying, low parental engagement, feeling of loneliness, worry about lack of sleep and drug abuse were the factors associated with suicidal ideation and attempt (Dema et al., 2019).

Additionally, during COVID-19 pandemic there was a state of heightened mental health problems in Bhutan. There was an increase of mental health disorders in

Bhutan from 87 per 10,000 in 2016 to 156 per 10,000 population in 2021. When we look at the illness-specific data during the pandemic the prevalence of depression and anxiety showed an increasing trend unlike seen at any time previously. There was rise in cases of depression from an average prevalence of 9 per 10,000 between 2011 and 2019 to 16 per 10,000 in 2020. Similarly, anxiety had an average prevalence of 18 per 10,000 between 2011 and 2019 which then rose to 29 per 10,000 in 2020. In 2021 the average prevalence of depression and anxiety was 32 and 55 per 10,000 respectively. Depression among patients were more than twice as likely to have occurred in 2020 as compared to 2011 and it was four times as likely to have occurred in 2021 (Tsheten et al., 2023). Besides the pandemic, these increasing trends could probably be also due to increase in the advocacy regarding depression and anxiety and the increase in help seeking behavior of people with mood and anxiety disorder. A rapid survey was conducted by UNICEF in partnership with the Department of Youth and Sports under the Ministry of Education among adolescents aged 10–24 years in September 2021. This survey found that 30% of the adolescents were sad and stressed, and 7% of adolescents had depression (UNICEF South Asia, 2021).

Suicide ranks among the top six leading causes of death in Bhutan. For every four suicide deaths in the country only one attempted suicide is recorded due to poor record keeping (WHO, 2022). A five-year review of suicide cases from 2009 to 2013, the Royal Bhutan Police documented a total of 361 suicide deaths which is 73 suicide cases in a year or six suicide deaths in a month. The proportion of suicide deaths among all deaths was 4.5% which is higher than 1.4% in the low middle-income countries. 87% of deaths due to suicide occurred in the most productive age group of 15–40 years (Lhadon, 2014).

As per the annual health report of 2022, a total of 3056 new cases visited psychiatric Out Patient Department (OPD) for consultation. One-third of these new cases were patients with anxiety disorders. Other common psychiatric diagnoses included Alcohol and Substance use disorder, depression, and epilepsy. 891 new cases of children and adolescents visited psychiatric OPD in 2022. Also a total of 393 patients were admitted in the psychiatry ward in 2022. The most common reason for admission was Alcohol Use disorder and substance use disorder. Psychosis, bipolar affective disorder, and depression were the other common reasons for admission (Ministry of Health, 2022).

3 Available Mental Health Services and New Avenues

3.1 Governance

With the establishment of the Pema Center's under the Royal Command of her Majesty the Gyaltsuen, the mental health services in the country is expected to improve. The Pema Center will be a 60-bedded mental health hospital within the premise of the Jigme Dorji Wangchuck National Referral Hospital (JDWNRH) admission (Ministry of Health, 2022). It will be providing outpatient psychiatric consultations and counselling services, emergency services, treatment and procedure rooms, pharmacy, and inpatient wards, including child and family unit and separate detoxification unit. The Pema Center Secretariat was instituted on 16th June 2022. The Pema Center Secretariat would be the nodal agency for mental health services in the country, and for formulating plans and programmes regarding mental health in Bhutan. It also would implement them through the multisectoral and district administrative mechanism with an aim to reach to the district hospitals and the PHC.

The national policy has clear guidelines for integration of mental health services with primary care setting. The health workers including doctors at the PHC level are trained to identify, diagnose and manage common mental disorders like depression, anxiety, epilepsy and alcohol or drugs use with basic counselling and pharmacotherapy.

The constitution of Bhutan mandates the right to free access to essential health services. The government bears the expenditure for healthcare services including referrals to a third country. The healthcare system provides diagnostics and treatment of all diseases free of cost.

3.2 Services

The structure of the health system in Bhutan has three tiers. At the primary level there are 179 primary healthcare centres including three municipality centres, at the secondary level there are 49 general and district hospitals and there are three referral centres at the tertiary level as per data of 2021. Apart from this, there are 63 community-based psychiatric units with a total of 100 beds. The beds ratio is 14.9 per hundred thousand population. These are fully integrated with the general healthcare services (Dorji et al., 2023). However, there are no trained psychiatrists in the community mental health facilities. Psychiatrists are available only in the national referral hospital for now. The Department of Psychiatry in the national referral hospital is the only unit in the country which provides specialized psychiatry treatment. The multidisciplinary team providing specialized mental health care consists of Psychiatrists, Counselors, Occupational therapist, Speech and language therapists, Health assistants and Nurses.

The psychiatry department offers both in-patient and out-patient mental health services. The out-patient services include psychiatrist consultation, individual and group psychotherapy, family therapy, behavioral therapy, speech therapy, and various pharmacotherapies including medication-assisted treatment like opioid substitution therapy and disulfiram therapy. In the inpatient-unit, services such as psychiatric assessment and treatment (pharmacotherapy and psychotherapies), Electroconvulsive Therapy (ECT), detoxification of patients with substance use disorders, occupational therapy, speech therapy, and other behavioral therapy like laughter yoga, dancing and games are provided. Apart from these clinical services, the department also serves as a consultation and supervising team for the mental health and health professionals across the country. It also provides training to the resident doctors, medical interns, clinical counsellors, and nursing students from the Faculty of Nursing and Public Health (FNPH), Khesar Gyalpo University of Medical Sciences of Bhutan (KGUMSB) (Annual report JDWNRH, 2022).

Primary care physicians and community health workers manage the patients in their settings often by liaising with the psychiatrists through teleconsultation. Patient admission can be done both voluntarily and involuntarily. There is least one psychotropic medicine of each therapeutic class in all 63 facilities (antidepressant, antipsychotic, anxiolytic, and mood stabilizer) as per data of 2012. As of now there are no separate community mental hospitals, residential and forensic facilities (Pelzang, 2012).

The primary care physician and healthcare professionals like health assistants are working in primary healthcare and they receive training to provide psychoeducation, follow-up treatment and refill of psychiatric medicines. All 20 districts have a functional community-based psychiatric units with general health services, however, these facilities do not have psychiatrists except the Jigme Dorji Wangchuck National Referral Hospital (JDWNRH) in the capital. One of the important professions in the mental health team in Bhutan is clinical counselors. Clinical counsellors are graduates of bachelors in the clinical counselling program which is a 4-year course. The first batch of clinical counselors graduated in 2019. The country now has 8 clinical counselors placed in various districts. They assess patients with psychiatric issues, provide counselling and psychotherapy and follow up as required and are also engaged in mental health promotion activities. With the placement of clinical counselors in all the districts mental health services are expected to become better. Apart from this, schools, colleges and social service organizations have some trained counsellors who coordinate with the National Mental Health Program to manage mental health problems in their settings. Private mental healthcare facilities are not currently available in the country (Tsheten et al., 2023). Bhutan has seen significant growth in the development of counselling as a profession in recent years. The positive impact of helping people cope with social issues such as domestic violence, mental health problems and substance abuse have been realized (Doma & Dolkar, 2019).

3.3 Policies and Plans

As part of the country's 8th Five Year Plan of development the mental health policy of Bhutan was formulated in 1997 (WHO, 2006). The policy mandates providing community-based mental health services via integration of mental health services into the general health-care system, including primary health care (PHC).

The government of Bhutan has endorsed the National Suicide Prevention Action Plan. This action plan focuses on providing and strengthening mental health service delivery, suicide prevention strategy, and institutional and policy responses (Betts,

2020). The implementation of suicide prevention measures has been accelerated and activities like suicide-prevention actions in health, education, monastic communities and police sectors have been undertaken. The other activities are capacity building of gatekeepers, improvement of the suicide information system to inform policies and decision-making. The responsibility of suicide-prevention activities has been taken by local governments which would help pave the way for suicide prevention at the grass-root levels (Dorji et al., 2017). The 2018 Action Plan and Mental Health Programme was upscaled to a five-year project with a main focus on a multi-disciplinary approach for addressing mental health and suicide prevention throughout the country, providing services through a hotline, and capacity building of primary health care workers and counsellors (Pradhan & Lhamo, 2023).

There is no dedicated mental health law in Bhutan. However, some elements like rights and legal provisions of mental health treatment are covered in the Bhutan Penal Code and other laws. For example, there is provision for medical treatment instead of a prison sentence for people with mental disorders who commit crimes (WHO, 2022).

3.4 Newer Avenues

There has been recent advent of telemedicine service especially during the COVID-19 pandemic. This has become an important means to reach people with mental disorders who were previously unreached. The health workers and even the general practitioners can now seek specialist consultation through teleconsultation (Nirola, 2010).

4 Challenges of Mental Care

4.1 Lack of Awareness and Magico-Religious Beliefs

Mental illnesses are often unrecognized due to the lack of awareness about these conditions among the general population not only in rural areas but also in the cities. People are either unaware of concepts of mental disorders like bipolar disorder or panic attacks or they are in denial about having a problem. The traditional cultural beliefs have a strong influence in people's attitudes towards mental illness in Bhutan. The causal explanation for mental illness is given in the form of witchcraft, evil spirits, black magic, a curse, or 'karma' of previous life. These beliefs among general people contribute to the stigma about mental illness and discrimination against people with mental disorders. Further, there is also a belief among people that mental illness is largely incurable. As a result, most families and people with mental disorders resort to alternative healing practices, especially religious/faith healing. The majority of the people in Bhutan seek religious help when someone is physically or mentally ill.

In addition, depression is often synonymous with mental illness. This concept limits the conversation to a clinical approach to mental disorders. This is a very narrow focus and this prevents people from fully understanding the complexities of mental health often leading to further challenges in normalizing mental health and accessing mental health care. It further leaves out the wide range of mental health challenges, such as stress and anxiety allowing space for only stereotypical cases of mental disorders.

4.2 Stigma

The stigma surrounding dominates the challenge in understanding mental health. There is often an association of mental health with weakness or a lack of willpower among people. They further internalize the triggers and causes and have reluctance to seek help (Pradhan & Lhamo, 2023). People having severe forms of psychiatric disorder are usually marginalized and neglected in Bhutan. They are sometimes stigmatized with words like "choelo," or "psycho," especially if they have behavioural issues and their psychopathology make them act strangely (Calabrese & Dorji, 2013). These concepts seem to have a direct implication in their help-seeking behavior thereby rather than resorting to various rituals and shamanistic practices which strengthens their beliefs of disturbed deities causing various psychiatric illnesses and distancing themselves from mental health services. This vicious cycle is very difficult to address.

4.3 Lack of Manpower

While the numbers of psychiatrists and psychiatric nurses in Bhutan are minimal, other ancillary disciplines such as Psychiatrists subspecialized in various psychiatric fields, Clinical psychologists, social workers, specialized mental health nurses and sub-specialized Counselors are not available at all in Bhutan (Table 1). To cater for a need of the whole population current human resource numbers are not adequate.

4.4 Limited Specialty Services

The specialized psychiatric care is only provided by the national referral hospital. Clinical counselors are available in only 8 districts for now. There is uneven access to mental health services and facilities across the country. The services are available to only those who live in or near the capital city Thimphu.

Table 1 Mental Health Resources of Bhutan (Addressing Mental Health in Bhutan, WHO, 2022)

Health budget as a proportion of national budget 2023/24	11.6%
Government health expenditure as a % of GDP	4.5%
Estimated annual budget for mental health	Approx. 1%
Number of registered Psychiatrists	4
Number of child psychiatrists	None (One psychiatrist is undergoing fellowship)
Number of registered clinical psychologists	0
Number of social workers	0
Number of occupational therapists	7
Number of clinical counselors counsellors (4 years degree course in B.Sc. Clinical Counseling)	18
Number of school guidance counsellors	173
Number of psychiatric nurses	3

4.5 Lack of Mental Health Research

Generating empirical evidence as a basis for policy formulation is a challenge for Bhutan. Data related to mental illness are collected and compiled by healthcare facilities and an annual report is published by the Health Ministry through "Annual Health Bulletin". However, there has been limited research on mental health that have been published in indexed journals over the last five years. There is an obvious lack of academic development related to mental health as evidenced by lack of psychiatry journals in Bhutan (Arafat et al., 2022).

4.6 Lack of Mental Health Law

There is no mental health legislation to protect the rights of people with mental illness in Bhutan as of now. There are no clear policies and guidelines to prevent non-evidence-based therapies, coercive medications and inappropriate detention for psychiatric evaluation in the absence of gross psychotic symptoms.

5 Potential Ways Forward

5.1 Allocation of Fund

The allocation of adequate funds is necessary to provide the best standard of care to people with mental illness in Bhutan as evidence suggests the mental illnesses are increasing. For this, there is a need to take into consideration the cost–benefit analysis of treating people with mental illness. There is also a need to allocate sufficient funds for mental healthcare in order to make the healthcare services viable and sustainable.

5.2 Development of Organized Mental Health Care System

It is essential to develop an effective organized system for mental healthcare to provide quality services to the population. There is a lack of proper infrastructure, mental health professionals and an adequate supply of medicines in Bhutan that needs a prompt response. There is also a need to invest resources in community crisis centres, ambulance services and capacity building in the community. Further, the development of psychiatric services within district hospitals and at PHC levels is necessary in order to manage acute mental illnesses and rehabilitate people with chronic illnesses. The other possible steps forward could be training more mental health professionals and posting them in the community, increasing training of community health workers in mental health care, and making psychotropic medicines available at the community level.

5.3 Improve Training and Curricula

One of the ways the government policy could aim at improving the efficiency of PHC workers in mental healthcare is by providing adequate time for psychiatric training in medical education. It is also essential to train clinical psychologists, occupational therapists and social workers to provide standard mental healthcare to the people.

There is also a need to link mental health with other sectors like education, justice, transport, environment, housing and welfare. This can be done by considering mental health promotion in the policies and plans of all agencies of the government and intersectoral coordination.

5.4 Stigma Reduction and Improve Mental Health Literacy

Many aspects of mental healthcare require the active collaboration of the community. Hence, improving mental health literacy and awareness among the general public in the community should be given priority while developing mental health policies. The main reason for the negative attitude of the public leading to prejudice and discrimination is lack of mental health knowledge. This in turn leads to unjust treatment given to patients with mental illness. Therefore, it is necessary to develop a strategy to encourage the use of mass media in order to publicize knowledge regarding mental health.

5.5 Research and Good Health Information Management System

Considering the dearth of research, proper fund allocation to research activities is important. This can be achieved in collaboration with other countries and international organizations. Also, to ensure the real problem statement and burden, a health management system with an accurate diagnosis of mental disorders is a must. This would also help in further tracking the referrals. The contextualized intervention strategies could be developed with the data available and authorities could be informed for policy making. A reliable and valid database on the prevalence and burden of mental disorders in the community is essential for the successful integration of mental health services in the PHC system in Bhutan.

6 Conclusion

Bhutan is a small landlocked country in South Asia where mental health services is only around 25 years old. The health care in Bhutan is guided by the developmental philosophy of Gross National Happiness and psychological wellbeing is also a component of it. Though an accurate burden of disease is not available there is no denying the fact that mental disorders are on the rise in Bhutan. There are many challenges but steps such as proper allocation of funds, improvement in research, capacity building, promoting awareness, decentralization of manpower and improvement in training and curricula would help in building a proper mental health care system.

Acknowledgements We would like to thank Dr. Bikram Chhetri, Psychiatrist, Department of Psychiatry, Jigme Dorji Wangchuck National Referral Hospital, Bhutan for helping us to corroborate the information about mental health care in Bhutan.

References

Addressing mental health in Bhutan. WHO. (2022). Retrieved August 28, 2023, from https://www.who.int/publications-detail-redirect/9789290210153

Annual Reports | Ministry of Health. (2022). Retrieved August 31, 2023, from https://www.moh.gov.bt/about/program-profiles/national-suicide-prevention-program/plans-orders-activities/reports__trashed/annual-reports/

Arafat, S. M. Y., Ali, S. a. Z., Saleem, T., Banerjee, D., Singh, R., Baminiwatta, A., & Shoib, S. (2022). Academic psychiatry journals in South Asian countries: Most from India, none from Afghanistan, Bhutan and the Maldives. *Global Psychiatry Archives, 5*(1), 1–9. https://doi.org/10.52095/gp.2021.4395.1036.

Betts, L. (2020, December 1). Suicide Prevention in Bhutan. *IASP.* Retrieved from https://www.iasp.info/2020/12/01/suicide-prevention-in-bhutan/

Bhutan Case Study | UNICEF South Asia. (2021). Retrieved August 27, 2023, from https://www.unicef.org/rosa/documents/bhutan-case-study

Calabrese, J. D., & Dorji, C. (2013). *Traditional and modern understandings of mental illness in Bhutan: Preserving the benefits of each to support Gross National Happiness.*

Dema, T., Tripathy, J. P., Thinley, S., Rani, M., Dhendup, T., Laxmeshwar, C., Tenzin, K., Gurung, M. S., Tshering, T., Subba, D. K., Penjore, T., & Lhazeen, K. (2019). Suicidal ideation and attempt among school going adolescents in Bhutan—A secondary analysis of a global school-based student health survey in Bhutan 2016. *BMC Public Health, 19*(1), 1605. https://doi.org/10.1186/s12889-019-7791-0

Dendup, T., Zhao, Y., Dorji, T., & Phuntsho, S. (2020). Risk factors associated with suicidal ideation and suicide attempts in Bhutan: An analysis of the 2014 Bhutan STEPS survey data. *Plos One, 15*(1), e0225888. https://doi.org/10.1371/journal.pone.0225888

Doma D., & Dolkar T. (2019). Overview of Counseling in Bhutan. 淑徳大学大学院総合福祉研究科研究紀要, *26*, 149–160.

Dorji, C. (2004). *Achieving gross national happiness through community-based mental health services in Bhutan.* Centre for Bhutan Studies.

Dorji, G., Choki, S., Jamphel, K., Wangdi, Y., Chogyel, T., Dorji, C., & Nirola, D. K. (2017). Policy and governance to address depression and suicide in Bhutan: The national suicide-prevention strategy. *WHO South-East Asia Journal of Public Health, 6*(1), 39–44. https://doi.org/10.4103/2224-3151.206163

Dorji, L., & Bkod, B. R. R. (2012). Alcohol use and abuse in Bhutan. *(No Title).*

Dorji, T., Yangchen, Wangmo, S., Tenzin, K., Jamtsho, S., Pema, D., Chhetri, B., Nirola, D. K., & Dhakal, G. P. (2023). Challenges in epilepsy diagnosis and management in a low-resource setting: An experience from Bhutan. *Epilepsy Research, 192*, 107126. https://doi.org/10.1016/j.eplepsyres.2023.107126

Lhadon, K. (2014). Suicide trends in Bhutan from 2009 to 2013. *Journal of Bhutan Studies, 30*, 30–56.

Masaki, K., & Tshering, J. (2021). Exploring the origins of Bhutan's gross national happiness. *Journal of South Asian Devevelopment, 16*(2), 273–292. https://doi.org/10.1177/09731741211039049

Naveed, A., & Nirola, D. K. (2012). Mental health in Bhutan. *International Psychiatry, 9*(1), 11–12.

Nirola, D. K. (2010). Where psychiatrists are scarce: Bhutan. *Asia-Pacific Psychiatry, 2*(3), 126–126. https://doi.org/10.1111/j.1758-5872.2010.00073.x

Pelzang, R. (2012). Mental health care in Bhutan: Policy and issues. *WHO South-East Asia Journal of Public Health, 1*(3), 339–346. https://doi.org/10.4103/2224-3151.207030

Pradhan, S., & Lhamo, U. S. (2023). Global crisis, national commitment: Overcoming challenges to inclusive mental health in Bhutan. *The Druk Journal, 9*(1), 71–76.

Sithey, G., Li, M., Wen, L. M., Kelly, P. J., & Clarke, K. (2018). Socioeconomic, religious, spiritual and health factors associated with symptoms of common mental disorders: A cross-sectional secondary analysis of data from Bhutan's Gross National Happiness Study, 2015. *BMJ Open, 8*(2), e018202. https://doi.org/10.1136/bmjopen-2017-018202

Suicide prevention in Bhutan: Scaling-up during the pandemic WHO. (2022). Retrieved August 27, 2023, from https://www.who.int/news-room/feature-stories/detail/suicide-prevention-in-bhutan-scaling-up-during-the-pandemic

Tsheten, T., Chateau, D., Dorji, N., Pokhrel, H. P., Clements, A. C. A., Gray, D. J., & Wangdi, K. (2023). Impact of COVID-19 on mental health in Bhutan: A way forward for action. *The Lancet Regional Health—Southeast Asia, 11*, 100179. https://doi.org/10.1016/j.lansea.2023.100179

WHO, WHO-AIMS report on Mental Health System in Bhutan. (2006). Retrieved August 29, 2023, from https://extranet.who.int/mindbank/item/534

World Health Organization, W. H. (2006). Country Office for Bhutan. *WHO-AIMS Report on Mental Health System in Bhutan. Thimphu: WHO and Ministry of Health.*

Mental Healthcare Access in India: Models, Trends, and Challenges

Sujita Kumar Kar and Vikas Menon

Abstract Mental health issues are common health-related issues in India affecting approximately one in five people. Despite being a common health issue, there is a huge treatment gap (approximately 85%) which ultimately results in significant disability and impairment for the individual suffering from mental illness. Also, the burden on the caregivers is significant. Over the past several decades there has been a change in the mental health legislative framework, policy as well as program. The government has also taken initiatives to strengthen the workforce of mental health and the infrastructures. This chapter discusses the current mental health access scenario in India, changing trends in mental health delivery and the challenges faced.

Keywords Mental healthcare · Psychiatric disorders · India: Mental health · Health infrastructure · Health initiatives

1 Introduction

1.1 Indian Country Profile and Overview of Healthcare in India

India is the most populous country in the world (United Nations, 2023), well known for its culture and heritage. India is located in South Asia surrounded by the Bay of Bengal, the Indian ocean and the Arabian sea and the great Himalayan mountain range (Government of India, 2023). India is the largest democracy in the world. Recently (April 2023), India over took China to become the most populous country in the

S. K. Kar (✉)
Department of Psychiatry, King George's Medical University, Uttar Pradesh, Lucknow 226003, India
e-mail: drsujita@gmail.com

V. Menon
Department of Psychiatry, Jawaharlal Institute of Postgraduate Medical Education and Research, Puducherry 605006, India

world. The healthcare demands for such a huge population (more than 1400 million) is very high. It has been projected that the Indian population will rise significantly in the next few decades before a fall in population is anticipated (United Nations, 2023). However, the elderly population is expected to rise significantly in the coming decades in India and over next eight decades, 30% of the Indian population will be above 65 years. As per the World Health Statistics 2023 report, in India, the life expectancy at birth is 70.8 years and healthy life expectancy at birth was 60.3 years (World Health Organization, 2023b).

Since, ancient times India contributed significantly to the understanding about the disease and its treatment. Indian ancient medicine is still commonly practiced in the country and is also popular in the rest part of the world as *Ayurveda*. Till the invasion of the British to India, the mental health issues in India were dealt with by Indian indigenous systems of medicine like Ayurveda (Kumar, 2004). Also, traditional and religious healers were treating the patients with mental illness. The British people brought the modern system of medicine to India and established mental hospitals (so called asylums) for the treatment of patients with mental illness. The first mental hospital was established at Bombay (Now, Mumbai) in 1745 (Ganju, 2000). Subsequently, in the Modern India, the medical establishments and structure of the mental hospitals were laid down after the suggestions of Bhore Committee (Kumar, 2004). Several mental healthcare service delivery systems developed in the independent India to provide better access to mental healthcare, over past several decades.

Despite several adversities (wars, terrorism, natural calamities, political instabilities, poverty), India continued to excel in multiple domains, including the healthcare infrastructures. Despite advancements in health sectors, the investment in health in India is relatively less in comparison to developed countries and when it comes to mental health the investment is much less (Trivedi et al., 2015; World Health Organization, 2021b). Realizing the fact that workforce and infrastructure are highly essential components of the healthcare system, the government of India is focussing on strengthening the manpower in the recent years (World Health Organization, 2021b). Recently, the government of India had released the "The WHO India Country Cooperation Strategy 2019–2023", which gives a structure to the collaboration between World Health Organization (WHO) and Government of India to improve health of the Indian population by bringing healthcare transformation (World Health Organization, 2019). The Government of India, has taken initiatives like developing a scheme called Ayushman Bharat Pradhan Mantri Jan Arogya Yojana to avail healthcare to Indian citizens at an affordable price (World Health Organization, 2022). Wellness centres are developed in the community level, which aims to promote health and early identification of health ailments including common mental illnesses and providing linkage service with the mental health team (World Health Organization, 2023a).

1.2 Epidemiology of Mental Illnesses in India

Mental health issues are widely prevalent in India. As per the National Mental Health Survey (2015–16), the weighted lifetime prevalence of any mental illness is 13.67%; whereas the current prevalence of any mental illness is 10.56% (Gautham et al., 2020). The prevalence of any form of substance use disorder was found to be 22.44%, whereas that of mood disorders and neurotic & stress related disorders are 5.61% and 3.70%, respectively (Gautham et al., 2020). The report revealed that the current prevalence of common mental disorders to be 5.1%, which is highest among females and in the 5th and 6th decade of life (Jayasankar et al., 2022). Another large-scale mental health survey (World Mental Health Survey), that was conducted in 11 centres of India, prior to the National Mental Health Survey also estimated the prevalence of psychiatric morbidities in Indian population (Sagar et al., 2017). As per this survey the 12-month prevalence of common mental disorders was 5.52% and the prevalence of mood disorder, substance use disorder and anxiety disorder were 1.44%, 1.18% and 3.41%, respectively (Sagar et al., 2017). Prevalence of substance use disorders in India were estimated in many other large scale nationwide surveys, independent of the surveys on mental illness. As per the National Family Health Survey-4, the prevalence of any form of tobacco in Indian adult men was 45.5%, of which 24.6% use smoke form of tobacco, 29.1% use smokeless form of tobacco use and 8.4% use both smoke and smokeless form of tobacco (Islam et al., 2020). As per the Global Adult Tobacco Survey-2 (GATS-2) the prevalence of tobacco use among the youths (15–24 years) in India was 11.9% in 2016–17 (Grover et al., 2020). As per the report of National Drug Use Survey report (2019), 14.6% Indians between the age of 10 years and 75 years use alcohol (Ambekar et al., 2019). The ratio of male to female alcohol users in India is 17:1 (Ambekar et al., 2019). As per this survey report, the prevalence of cannabis, opioid and inhalant use in India is 2.8%, 2.1% and 0.7%, respectively (Ambekar et al., 2019). Suicide is a major public health problem. In India, every year the prevalence of suicide is published in a report released by the National Crime Records Bureau (NCRB) and as per the report of 2022, the prevalence was 12.0 per 100000 population (Menon et al., 2023; NCRB, 2022).

As per the WHO report the burden of psychiatric disorders in India is 2443 disability-adjusted life years (DALYs) per 100,000 population. As per the same report the age adjusted suicide rate is 21.1 per 100000 population (World Health Organization, 2023a). As per the global burden of diseases study, there is significant increase in contribution of mental illnesses to DALYs from 1990 to 2017 (Sagar et al., 2020). In 1990, mental illnesses contributed to 2.5% of the DALYs from all causes and by 2017, it has been increased to 4.7% (Sagar et al., 2020). In the Indian states, a significant association between prevalence of depression and suicide rate was found (Sagar et al., 2020). In the year 2017, it was found that depression alone was contributing to one third of DALYs due to mental illnesses and when anxiety disorders were also taken into account, the DALYs were more than 50% of DALYs due to any mental illness in India (Sagar et al., 2020). The burden of mental illness in India has been almost doubled between the period from 1990 to 2017 (Sagar et al., 2020).

1.3 Treatment Gap for Mental Illnesses in India

Treatment gap is a reflection of mental healthcare deprived population. As per the National Mental health survey (2015–16) report the treatment gap for any form of mental illness was 84.5% (Gautham et al., 2020). The treatment gap for common mental disorders was 80.4% (Jayasankar et al., 2022). However, the earlier conducted World Mental Health Survey, revealed a treatment gap of 95% for mental illnesses (Sagar et al., 2017).

In India, the existing evidences suggest that there is low service contact with mental health facilities for the treatment of common mental disorders including substance use disorders (Patel et al., 2016). For psychotic disorders the service contact is still lower. Inequity in distribution of mental health services in the country, resulted in variation in treatment gaps across the country. Rural areas are having higher treatment gap than the urban areas (Patel et al., 2016).

1.4 Mental Health Infrastructure and Resources in India

The mental health resources are undergoing rapid transformation in India. Medical colleges and postgraduate departments of psychiatry are the major infrastructures for training the psychiatrists (Kar, 2022). Many institutions in India are offering Diploma in Psychological medicine, Diplomate of National Board (DNB) in Psychiatry, fellowships and super-specialization courses to train mental health manpower (Kar, 2022).

Infrastructures and resources are required for mental health research. In India, adequate resources and infrastructures for good quality research, is limited to only few institutions (Ransing et al., 2022b). Lack of trained manpower, workload, inadequate funding and administrative hurdles stand as major challenges for carrying out mental health research in India.

As per the WHO report (updated till 2017), in India, there are 0.29 psychiatrists per 100000 population (World Health Organization, 2017). When it comes to the number of psychologists, psychiatric nurses and social workers per 100000 population, the numbers are 0.07, 0.80, and 0.06 respectively (World Health Organization, 2017). As per the 2017 data, the total number of workforce in mental health (both in government and non-government sectors) are 25,312, which roughly amounts to 1.93 mental health professionals per 100000 population (World Health Organization, 2017). The Table 1, summarizes the number of mental health facilities/establishments engaged in provision of mental healthcare by 2017 (World Health Organization, 2017).

Table 1 Number of mental health facilities/establishments engaged in provision of mental healthcare in India by 2017 (World Health Organization, 2017)

Mental health facilities/establishments in India (2017)	Number
Outpatient mental healthcare facilities (attached to a hospital)	952
Outpatient mental healthcare facilities that are Community based/non-hospital settings	1217
Mental hospitals	136
Mental health unit attached to a general hospital	389
Residential care facilities	223
Child & adolescent psychiatry outpatient facility	45
Inpatient facilities for medicolegal (forensic) patients	15

To combat the deficits of infrastructure and manpower various initiatives have been taken in the recent years by the government of India. Some of the notable initiatives are—opening new medical colleges, increasing undergraduate and postgraduate seats in medical education, opening online portals for teleconsultation and online counselling support (Agarwal et al., 2023; Bhatia, 2021; Kar & Tripathy, 2023). Similarly, to facilitate healthcare in the rural areas of the country by overcoming manpower deficits, the government has taken initiatives by implementing service bonds for the medical undergraduates and postgraduates (Chatterjee et al., 2022; Kar et al., 2023).

2 Mental Health Program, Policy, Legislation and Action Plan in India

2.1 Mental Health Program in India

In India, the national mental health program (NMHP) was introduced in 1982 with the objectives of making mental healthcare available and accessible to the vulnerable and deprived population, using knowledge on mental health for social development and promoting community participation in mental healthcare (Ministry of Health & Family Welfare, 2013; Wig & Murthy, 2015). Subsequently, the Government of India introduced district mental health program (DMHP) in 1996 under the ninth five year plan, which was based on Bellary Model (Ministry of Health & Family Welfare, 2013). The DMHP aimed at early identification and treatment of psychiatric disorders, training of the primary care physician for early identification of mental illnesses and their treatment, IEC activities related to mental illness (information, education and communication) and monitoring of the progress (Ministry of Health & Family Welfare, 2013; National Health Mission, 2023).

Subsequently, in due course of time the NMHP has been expanded by enrolment of more districts in the DMHP, manpower strengthening, upgradation of the psychiatric departments of the medical colleges and allocation of more fund for the provision of mental healthcare (Ministry of Health & Family Welfare, 2013). The NMHP aims at availing mental healthcare to people at need at the community level (World Health Organization, 2023a). During the COVID-19 pandemic there was significant disruption of mental healthcare. To facilitate the process of mental healthcare delivery, the government of India has introduced various online consultation facilities in the country (Agarwal et al., 2023; Bhatia, 2021; Das et al., 2020). Recently, an online counselling service (*teleMANAS*) for people at need has been operational in India to address the mental health issues, which is free of cost and works 24 * 7 in all the states of the country (Ahmed et al., 2022).

2.2 Mental Health Policy in India

The Government of India had formed an group of experts in April 2011, to develop a mental health policy for India and after rigorous discussions and deliberations a mental health policy was develop for India which was released on October 2014 (Ministry of Health & Family Welfare, 2014). The mental health policy is evidence and right based that is integrative and more participatory in nature. The policy emphasizes the importance of pharmacological as well as non-pharmacological management of mental illnesses and has also given importance to Indian indigenous methods and cultural aspects (Ministry of Health & Family Welfare, 2014). The policy focuses on strengthening of mental health infrastructure and also suggests to understand mental health holistically, by reaching to its social determinants (Ministry of Health & Family Welfare, 2014). The visions of national mental health policy are summarized in the Fig. 1.

The National Mental Health Policy not only limits its focus to patients with mental illness, it also gives importance to the needs of the caregivers of patients with mental illnesses and other marginalized population (Ministry of Health & Family Welfare, 2014). Other than the National mental health policy, India has independent policy for control of substances (Tandon & Collective, 2015) and prevention of suicide (National suicide prevention strategy) (Ransing et al., 2023; Vijayakumar et al., 2022).

2.3 Mental Health Legislation in India

In India, Mental health act (MHA), 1987, was implemented in most of the states since 1990s; however, due to several lacunae in the law, there was a felt need of new legislation nearly two decades of implementation of the MHA, 1987 (Kar & Tiwari, 2014). The new mental health legislation, i.e., mental health care act 2017 (MHCA, 2017) was launched in July 2018 and replaced the MHA 1987 (Chadda, 2020). This act has brought significant change in the mental health legislative framework

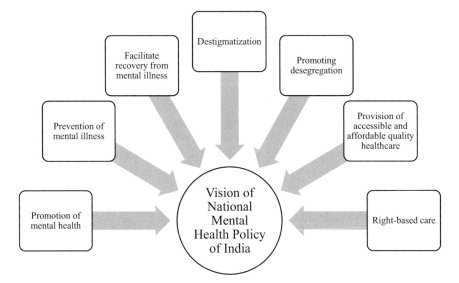

Fig. 1 Visions of National Mental Health Policy of India. *Source* National Mental Health Policy, Ministry of health and family welfare, Government of India

of India. The admission of a person with mental illness (voluntary admission and involuntary admission), rights of the patients with mental illness (nominated representative, advanced directive, refusal to treatment, choosing a treatment modality), restriction on certain treatment procedures (ban of electroconvulsive therapy without anaesthesia, restricting the use of electroconvulsive therapy in minors) and intense monitoring of the activity of the mental health practitioners and mental health establishments, licensing of the mental health establishments are some of the unique features and major highlights of the MHCA, 2017 (Chadda, 2020; Duffy & Kelly, 2019; Namboodiri et al., 2019).

After India became a signatory to the United Nation's Convention for Rights of Persons with Disabilities (CRPD), India has revised its legislations in this regard and developed Rights of Persons with Disabilities Act, 2016 (Duffy & Kelly, 2020). India, has legislations to control the use of substance in the country. The Narcotic and Psychotropic Substances Act is an Act was introduced in 1985 to keep a check on the Narcotic and Psychotropic Substances (Khanna & Garg, 2020). As per this act, production, possession, transport, marketing, storing and consuming any of the narcotic drugs are punishable (Khanna & Garg, 2020). The act has undergone amendment several times subsequently. To regulate the tobacco use, the government of India has introduced Cigarettes and Other Tobacco Products Act (COTPA) in 2003 (Kaur & Jain, 2011). The law restricts the free production, supply, and distribution of tobacco in India as well as the regulation of trade and commerce (Kaur & Jain, 2011).

2.4 Mental Health Action Plan in India

In India, there is no dedicated mental health action plan. However, at the global level, in 2013, at the 66th World Health Assembly, 194 member states of WHO had adopted the WHO's comprehensive mental health action plan 2013–2020 (World Health Organization, 2021a). Subsequent, world mental health assemblies endorsed updates to the action plan and various options of implementation. The WHO's comprehensive mental health action plan for 2013–2030 encompassed four primary goals: enhancing leadership and governance in mental health; delivering comprehensive, integrated mental health and social care services within community-based settings; executing strategies for mental health promotion and prevention; and reinforcing information systems, evidence, and research (World Health Organization, 2021a). This is an opportunity for all the countries including India, to ensure effectively adoption and implementation of the action plan to enhance the mental healthcare delivery (Singh, 2021).

3 Models of Mental Healthcare in India

In India, mental healthcare is provided by mental health professionals at government sectors, and private sectors. However, several other sources like traditional healers, doctors of alternative system of medicine, non-psychiatrist medical practitioners, yoga practitioners provide mental healthcare since long time. In India, the services are mostly centred around urban areas and big cities, depriving the rural areas form these essential care facilities (Chatterjee et al., 2022, 2023). In India, several models exist to provide mental healthcare in the community. Broadly, they can be collaborative models and non-collaborative models. Collaborative models operate independently; whereas the non-collaborative models work in partnership (Ginneken et al., 2017). In these Indian mental healthcare models at the primary care level, there is little specialist or professional involvement in comparison to the western countries (Ginneken et al., 2017). Patients with psychiatric illnesses in India, initially consult non-psychiatrist practitioners (ranging from traditional healers, to practitioners of alternative systems of medicine, primary care physicians, neurologists and doctors of various other specialities). Many of them are never referred or seldom referred to a psychiatrist. Poor referral system, unawareness and stigma often result in long pathway of care. Many studies from different corners of India, explored about the pathway of care of mental illnesses over past several decades and concluded that people with mental illnesses take consultation from multiple sources before reaching to a mental health professional (Jain et al., 2012; Jilani et al., 2018; Kar, 2008; Khemani et al., 2020; Lahariya et al., 2010; Prabhu et al., 2015; Singh et al., 2016; Trivedi & Jilani, 2011).

Excessive reliance on mental health specialists, like psychiatrists and psychologists, can hinder their ability to cater to a broader population. While these experts excel in treating severe mental disorders, they face challenges such as limited reach, resource constraints, scalability issues, and a potential neglect of prevention and early intervention strategies (Ginneken et al., 2017). Specialized treatments can lead to long waiting lists and restricted access to services for less severe cases. Moreover, these treatments are often costly and resource-intensive, making it difficult to allocate resources to a larger population. Specialists' availability and time limitations also impede scalability, creating bottlenecks in the system. Although specialists are crucial for targeted interventions in severe mental illnesses, comprehensive mental health care should involve preventive measures, early interventions, community-based support, and telehealth services (Ginneken et al., 2017). Integrating these approaches can improve mental health outcomes, reduce the burden on specialists, and ensure equitable access to care for all.

3.1 Mental Healthcare in Government Sectors

In the government sector, mental healthcare delivery occurs mostly through the tertiary care hospitals (psychiatric units of medical colleges, mental hospitals) and district hospitals. However, under the DMHP, the doctors working in primary care centres and community health centres are periodically trained to treat the common mental illnesses to facilitate the mental healthcare at the community level (Ministry of Health & Family Welfare, 2013; Singh, 2018). As per the updated information at National Medical Commission website, by 18th July 2023, in India, there are 706 medical colleges that offer the MBBS course (National Medical Commission, 2023). The psychiatric units of these medical collages offer mental health service. As per the source of Press Information Bureau (PIB), there are 43 mental hospitals (three are centrally run and rest 40 are run by the state government) in India (Press Information Bureau, 2014). These hospitals provide mental healthcare on out-patient basis as well as in inpatient settings. Most of the mental hospitals have long-stay facilities and rehabilitation facilities. There were a lot of challenges and facility deficits in the mental hospitals, which were identified by the national human rights commission from time to time and that helped in upgradation of the facilities and infrastructure of those settings (Murthy et al., 2017). UnTil 2022, in India, 704 districts are covered with DMHP facility with a team of mental health professionals, who provide the mental healthcare (Ministry of Health & Family Welfare, 2022).

3.2 Mental Healthcare in Private Sectors

Private sector is a big source of provision of mental healthcare in India. The national mental health survey 2015–16, mental health system assessment was done which attempted to explore the mental health infrastructures and resources in the surveyed 12 states of India (Arvind et al., 2020). In the private sector, private medical colleges, super-specialty and corporate hospitals, private hospitals, registered clinics and nursing homes provide mental healthcare services (Arvind et al., 2020). In the private sector, the consultation for mental illnesses is relatively costly than the government sector. Private clinics providing consultation for mental illnesses are very common and are mostly haphazard and not properly regulated by the state (Konar, 2016).

A study reported that significant number of doctors of other speciality treat psychiatric disorders despite of having no training or poor training in treating psychiatric disorders and less commonly the patients with psychiatric disorder are referred to the psychiatrist (Mishra & Kar, 2022). Another concern in the private sectors is due to unregulated practice, the cost of care goes very high. Evidences suggest there are over prescription of medications, excessive unreasonable investigations and over pricing in the private sector in India (Mathias et al., 2019).

3.3 Mental Healthcare by Other Sectors

Public-Private partnered services are some of the emerging facilities in India, engaged in providing the mental healthcare (Konar, 2016). Many states and even the central government is promoting this partnered health service model to facilitate mental healthcare and minimize the treatment gap. Several non-government organizations (NGOs) are also contributing significantly for the mental healthcare in India. Many of these NGOs are providing rehabilitation services for patients with mental illnesses (Balagopal & Kapanee, 2019). NGOs also play a key role in the conduct of mental health surveys in the community as well as implementation of mental health programs and some government mental health services in the community level (Balagopal & Kapanee, 2019; Kallivayalil & Enara, 2018). In India, another major source of provision of mental healthcare are practitioners of alternative systems of medicine (practitioners of Ayurveda, Homeopathy, Unani, Siddha) and traditional healers (Ransing et al., 2022a; Rudra et al., 2017). Despite of advancements in science, a large chunk of population with mental illnesses still visits the faith healers and religious healers. Stigma and unawareness are major attributing factors for seeking help from unauthentic sources.

4 Changing Trends of Mental Healthcare Services in India

Recent innovations in mental health care and service delivery in India can be divided into the following areas: 1. Service optimization and quality improvement initiatives; 2. Community-based mental health programs; 3. Initiatives to increase mental health workforce; 4. Digital service delivery initiatives. Below, we describe each of these, focussing on the opportunities and benefits they offer.

4.1 Service Optimization and Quality Improvement Initiatives

Using the WHOQR toolkit (*QualityRights Gujarat*, 2015) and WHO mhGAP framework (MhGAP Implementation in Kashmir, 2014) for training and capacity building of mental health professionals, investigators showed improvements in the quality of patient conditions through increased awareness and bridging of treatment gap in inaccessible areas. In Gujarat, an innovative Mental Health Support Program (MHSP), involving non-governmental and social organizations to create a pool of skilled manpower and organizational resources succeeded in improving access to mental health care and reducing treatment gap (Bhat et al., 2007). Integrated models that aimed to deliver specialist mental health services at the primary care level was effective in improving treatment adherence, facilitating rehabilitation of mentally ill, and reducing treatment gap (van Ginneken et al., 2017a).

4.2 Community-Based Mental Health Programs

These programs aim to increase the involvement of family and community in caring for the mentally ill and improving their outcomes. A good example of this is the "Dava-Dua" project in Gujarat (The Altruist, Ahmedabad and Action For Mental Illness, Bangalore, 2011) wherein anyone visiting a dargah in the service taluk was offered psychiatric treatment in collaboration with faith healers. Sensitization and training of faith healers preceded this phase. The program succeeded in making mental health services more accessible and less stigmatizing, apart from increasing awareness among religious faith healers whose services are sought after in rural areas. Similarly, a project that integrated mental health services within the broader context of participation in an income generating program for economically disadvantaged women found that the program resulted in lesser psychological distress, improvement in somatic symptoms, and increased perception of social support (Rao et al., 2011).

4.3 Initiatives to Increase Mental Health Workforce

Given the huge treatment gap in India and shortage of mental health professionals, training non-specialists to deliver mental health care interventions at the primary care level has been an important focus of research. In this regard, projects ESSENCE (ESSENCE Hub Project Summary, 2022) and EMPOWER (Nault, 2021), funded by National Institute of Mental health are important programs. Both the programs aim to leverage the power of digital technology to train non-specialist health workers to deliver brief psychological support interventions competently in primary care. They also seek to establish the necessary infrastructure at the primary care center to deliver these interventions at scale. Another example is the *Healthy Activity Program*

(Patel et al., 2017), a brief psychological intervention designed to be delivered by lay counsellors to persons with moderate to severe depression in primary care settings. The intervention was acceptable, effective, and cost-effective in this setting and merits further evaluation.

4.4 Digital Service Delivery Initiatives

Harnessing technology to deliver mental health services may have especial significance for low resource settings for two reasons. Firstly, they are likely to be perceived as less stigmatizing and, clearly, less burdensome compared to in person consultation for mental health issues. An important governmental initiative in this regard is the Tele-Mental Health Assistance and Nationally Actionable Plan through States (T-MANAS) which involves linking newly developed tele mental health centers with existing mental health care services and networks (Sagar & Singh, 2022). The goal is twofold: those in need of immediate help get it by dialing a number while the linkage to existing service networks facilitates referral and continuity of care.

The systematic medical appraisal, referral, and treatment (SMART) project by George Institute for Global Health (Tewari et al., 2017) is another pertinent example here. It uses a mobile phone-based electronic decision support system to enable screening, diagnosis and management by non-specialist health care workers. Preliminary indicators suggested that the intervention was acceptable and health service use increased significantly following the intervention.

5 Challenges in Access to Mental Healthcare in India

5.1 Major Hurdles to Access Mental Healthcare in India—Stigma, Lack of Awareness, Lack of Access to Care

A qualitative study involving adolescents and young adults, women, older adults, community leaders, and Anganwadi workers identified lack of awareness about mental health issues and treatment, perceived causes for mental illness, issues with accessibility, lack of multidisciplinary teams to deliver psychosocial treatments (considered less stigmatizing than medicines), lack of trained manpower leading to dissatisfaction and low degree of confidence in services, beliefs that mental illness is retribution for past life sins, and stigma as the major barriers to access mental health services (Lakshmana et al., 2022). Similar findings have been noted by other investigators (Shidhaye & Kermode, 2013). Interestingly, another qualitative study found that psychiatric symptoms and associated distress was connected to social and societal causes than medical reasons. This led to perceptions that clinical care could not help them, hindering service utilization (Weaver et al., 2023). Further, the relative lack of insurance coverage for mental illness vis-à-vis physical illness results in high out of pocket expenditure and considerable economic burden. This may deter people from seeking services in a timely manner (Mahashur et al., 2022).

5.2 Pathway of Care of Mental Illnesses in India

Knowing the pathway of care for mental illness may inform health system strengthening, organization and policy responses to delays in care seeking and poor service utilization. Two Indian facility-based studies, carried out more than a decade apart, showed that the proportion of patients in whom faith healers were the first point of contact for mental health symptoms had declined from more than two-thirds in 2004 (Lahariya et al., 2010) to just over a third in 2017 (Khemani et al., 2020). A subsequent study in 2019 (Joju et al., 2022) reported this proportion to be 12%. Correspondingly, the proportion of those visiting a psychiatrist increased from 9 to 33% and 40%, respectively. Help-seeking was most initiated on the advice of relatives or friends in all three studies. While these findings are encouraging, it also suggests that there is much more work to be done.

5.3 Recommendations to Improve Mental Health Care Access

Although significant gains have been made in reducing the treatment gap in Psychiatry in the last two decades, it continues to be unacceptably high, especially for common mental disorders (Sagar et al., 2017). As with other public health issues, this too requires a multipronged approach. First of all, there is a need to increase mental health workforce by training non-specialist health care workers and lay counsellors to effectively deliver brief psychological interventions. For this, they need to be trained effectively and periodically. As shown in project EMPOWER, this training can also be effectively done using digital platforms.

Next, there is a need to raise awareness about mental health issues to avoid delay in help-seeking. As explained earlier, myths and misconceptions about the origin of mental health symptoms abound. For this, mental health narratives must be included in school curricula and government programs on mental health should prioritize awareness and capacity building initiatives. Further, mental health professionals must partner with media to disseminate evidence-based information on mental health; this includes conventional and social media, both of which enjoy wide patronage among the public.

To reduce direct costs related to seeking specialist care for mental health issues, administrators must address low hanging fruit like cost of medicines and cost of travel. Simple solutions such as dispensing the medicines for a longer period of time and making the medicines available in the nearest district hospital would reduce the financial burden on the patient not only directly, but also indirectly because reduced time spent in travel translates to more work time and less income lost. More research on patient experiences and needs in this area will help the government frame evidence-based policies for disbursal of transportation and disability allowance and allow mentally ill to lead more productive lives.

Finally, health systems must be reorganized and strengthened for enhancing screening, diagnosis, and management of mental health issues. For this, a range of exciting initiatives have already been discussed in this chapter. There is promising evidence for use of technology to assist lay health care workers in screening, brief intervention, and referral of clients. Mental health screening must be incorporated into popular, successful health programs like maternal and child health program. This way, whenever a mother comes for her antenatal check up or postnatal immunization visits, a mental health screening can be conducted by public health nurses. Raising awareness of mental health and treatment issues among faith healers and traditional practitioners as well as horizontal and vertical integration of health care services may serve to further reduce delay in health care seeking.

6 Conclusion

Mental health issues affect one in five people in India, but the treatment gap remains wide, causing disability and putting a burden on caregivers. While progress has been made, challenges persist, including stigma, a shortage of mental health professionals, and limited access to care in rural areas. To address these challenges, education and awareness, investment in mental health services, capacity-building for professionals, and collaboration between stakeholders are needed. With these efforts, a more accessible, inclusive, and effective mental healthcare system for all in India, can be created.

References

Agarwal, A., Gupta, P. K., Singh, A., & Kar, S. K. (2023). Conceptual model of remotely accessed mobile application for psychiatric disorder screening (RoAdMAPS): A self-screening and referral aid for mental health in India. *The Lancet Regional Health—Southeast Asia, 8*,. https://doi.org/10.1016/j.lansea.2022.100100

Ahmed, T., Dumka, A., & Kotwal, A. (2022). Tele MANAS: India's first 24 × 7 tele mental health helpline brings new hope for millions. *Indian Journal of Mental Health, 9*(4), 403–406.

Ambekar, A., Chadda, R. K., Khandelwal, S. K., Rao, R., & Mishra, A. (2019). *Magnitude of substance use in India*. Ministry of Social Justice and Empowerment. Retrieved from http://www.ndusindia.in/report.html

Arvind, B. A., Gururaj, G., Rao, G. N., Pradeep, B. S., Mathew, V., Benegal, V., Gautham, M. S., Senthil, A., Kokane, A., Chavan, B. S., Dalal, P. K., Ram, D., Pathak, K., Lenin, S. R. K., Singh, L. K., Sharma, P., Saha, P. K., Ramasubramaniam, C., Mehta, R. Y., & Shibukumar, T. M. (2020). Framework and approach for measuring performance and progress of mental health systems and services in India: National Mental Health Survey 2015–2016. *International Journal of Mental Health Systems, 14*, 20. https://doi.org/10.1186/s13033-020-00349-8

Balagopal, G., & Kapanee, A. R. M. (2019). Lessons learnt from NGO approaches to Mental Healthcare provision in the community. In G. Balagopal & A. R. M. Kapanee (Eds.), *Mental Health Care Services in community settings: Discussions on NGO approaches in India* (pp. 185–204). Springer. https://doi.org/10.1007/978-981-13-9101-9_7

Bhat, R., Maheshwari, S. K., Rao, K., & Rushi Bakshi. (2007). *Mental Health Care Pilots in Gujarat: Processes, outcomes and learning.* https://doi.org/10.13140/RG.2.1.3353.1363

Bhatia, R. (2021). Telehealth and COVID-19: Using technology to accelerate the curve on access and quality healthcare for citizens in India. *Technology in Society, 64*, 101465. https://doi.org/10.1016/j.techsoc.2020.101465

Chadda, R. K. (2020). Influence of the new mental health legislation in India. *BJPsych International, 17*(1), 20–22. https://doi.org/10.1192/bji.2019.18

Chatterjee, S., Kar, S. K., & Singh, A. (2023). Solutions for health care enigma in Indian villages—Author's reply. *The Lancet Regional Health—Southeast Asia, 9*,. https://doi.org/10.1016/j.lansea.2022.100114

Chatterjee, S., Singh, A., & Kar, S. K. (2022). Service bonds in rural health care in India—Challenges and the way forward. *The Lancet Regional Health—Southeast Asia, 6*,. https://doi.org/10.1016/j.lansea.2022.100060

Das, S., Manjunatha, N., Kumar, C. N., Math, S. B., & Thirthalli, J. (2020). Tele-psychiatric after care clinic for the continuity of care: A pilot study from an academic hospital. *Asian Journal of Psychiatry, 48*, 101886. https://doi.org/10.1016/j.ajp.2019.101886

Duffy, R. M., & Kelly, B. D. (2019). India's Mental Healthcare Act, 2017: Content, context, controversy. *International Journal of Law and Psychiatry, 62*, 169–178. https://doi.org/10.1016/j.ijlp.2018.08.002

Duffy, R. M., & Kelly, B. D. (2020). History of Mental Health Legislation in India. In R. M. Duffy & B. D. Kelly (Eds.), *India's Mental Healthcare Act, 2017: Building laws, protecting rights* (pp. 51–59). Springer. https://doi.org/10.1007/978-981-15-5009-6_4

ESSENCE Hub Project Summary. (2022, August 22). National Institute of Mental Health (NIMH). Retrieved from https://www.nimh.nih.gov/news/media/2022/essence-hub-project-summary

Ganju, V. (2000). The Mental Health System in India: History, current system, and prospects. *International Journal of Law and Psychiatry, 23*(3), 393–402. https://doi.org/10.1016/S0160-2527(00)00044-3

Gautham, M. S., Gururaj, G., Varghese, M., Benegal, V., Rao, G. N., Kokane, A., Chavan, B. S., Dalal, P. K., Ram, D., & Pathak, K. (2020). The National Mental Health Survey of India (2016): Prevalence, socio-demographic correlates and treatment gap of mental morbidity. *International Journal of Social Psychiatry, 66*(4), 361–372.

Government of India. (2023). *Profile| National Portal of India*. Retrieved from https://www.india.gov.in/india-glance/profile

Grover, S., Anand, T., Kishore, J., Tripathy, J. P., & Sinha, D. N. (2020). Tobacco use among the Youth in India: Evidence from global adult Tobacco survey-2 (2016–2017). *Tobacco Use Insights, 13*, 1179173X20927397. https://doi.org/10.1177/1179173X20927397

Islam, M. S., Saif-Ur-Rahman, K. M., Bulbul, Md. M. I., & Singh, D. (2020). Prevalence and factors associated with tobacco use among men in India: Findings from a nationally representative data. *Environmental Health and Preventive Medicine, 25*(1), 62. https://doi.org/10.1186/s12199-020-00898-x

Jain, N., Gautam, S., Jain, S., Gupta, I. D., Batra, L., Sharma, R., & Singh, H. (2012). Pathway to psychiatric care in a tertiary mental health facility in Jaipur, India. *Asian Journal of Psychiatry, 5*(4), 303–308.

Jayasankar, P., Manjunatha, N., Rao, G. N., Gururaj, G., Varghese, M., & Benegal, V. (2022). Epidemiology of common mental disorders: Results from "National Mental Health Survey" of India, 2016. *Indian Journal of Psychiatry, 64*(1), 13–19. https://doi.org/10.4103/indianjpsychiatry.indianjpsychiatry_865_21

Jilani, A. Q., Saha, R., Dalal, P. K., Kallivayalil, R. A., Tiwari, A., & Kar, S. K. (2018). The impact of awareness of psychotic disorder on pathways to psychiatric care for first episode psychosis in India. *International Journal of Culture and Mental Health, 11*(3), 295–310.

Joju, S., Thilakan, P., Mani, M., & Simiyon, M. (2022). How lengthy and tortuous is the pathway to psychiatric care among patients visiting a tertiary care hospital in South India? A cross-sectional study. *Indian Journal of Private Psychiatry, 16*(1), 3–9. https://doi.org/10.5005/jp-journals-10067-0106

Kallivayalil, R. A., & Enara, A. (2018). Prioritizing rural and community Mental Health in India. *Indian Journal of Social Psychiatry, 34*(4), 285. https://doi.org/10.4103/ijsp.ijsp_74_18

Kar, N. (2008). Resort to faith-healing practices in the pathway to care for mental illness: A study on psychiatric inpatients in Orissa. *Mental Health, Religion and Culture, 11*(7), 720–740.

Kar, S. K. (2022). Post-graduate psychiatry teaching and training in India. *Indian Journal of Behavioural Sciences, 25*(02), Article 02. https://doi.org/10.55229/ijbs.v25i2.11

Kar, S. K., Chatterjee, S., & Singh, A. (2023). Service bond and Rural Mental Healthcare in India in the 21st Century: Why we stand here? *Indian Journal of Psychological Medicine, 02537176231154393,*. https://doi.org/10.1177/02537176231154393

Kar, S. K., & Tiwari, R. (2014). Impact of Mental Health Care Bill on caregivers of mentally ill: Boon or bane. *Asian Journal of Psychiatry, 12*, 3–6. https://doi.org/10.1016/j.ajp.2014.06.019

Kar, S. K., & Tripathy, S. (2023). Strategy to meet healthcare needs in India: Where should we focus? *Asian Journal of Psychiatry, 84*, 103565. https://doi.org/10.1016/j.ajp.2023.103565

Kaur, J., & Jain, D. C. (2011). Tobacco control policies in India: Implementation and challenges. *Indian Journal of Public Health, 55*(3), 220. https://doi.org/10.4103/0019-557X.89941

Khanna, M., & Garg, S. (2020). Narcotic drugs and psychotropic substances act (NDPS 1985): A critical analysis. *Nimitmai Review Journal, 3*(1), 28–32.

Khemani, M. C., Premarajan, K. C., Menon, V., Olickal, J. J., Vijayageetha, M., & Chinnakali, P. (2020). Pathways to care among patients with severe mental disorders attending a tertiary health-care facility in Puducherry, South India. *Indian Journal of Psychiatry, 62*(6), 664–669. https://doi.org/10.4103/psychiatry.IndianJPsychiatry_512_19

Konar, D. (2016). Private Sector and Public Mental Health in India. *Bengal Journal of Psychiatry*, 29–31.

Kumar, A. (2004). *History of Mental Health Services in India* (SSRN Scholarly Paper 1553597). Retrieved from https://papers.ssrn.com/abstract=1553597

Lahariya, C., Singhal, S., Gupta, S., & Mishra, A. (2010). Pathway of care among psychiatric patients attending a mental health institution in central India. *Indian Journal of Psychiatry, 52*(4), 333–338. https://doi.org/10.4103/0019-5545.74308

Lakshmana, G., Sangeetha, V., & Pandey, V. (2022). Community perception of accessibility and barriers to utilizing mental health services. *Journal of Education and Health Promotion, 11*, 56. https://doi.org/10.4103/jehp.jehp_342_21

Mahashur, S., Varma, A., & Fernandes, T. N. (2022). *Understanding costs associated with mental health care in India*. IMHO. Retrieved from https://cmhlp.org/wp-content/uploads/2022/06/Issue-Brief-Cost-of-Care.pdf

Mathias, K., Jacob, K. S., & Shukla, A. (2019). "We sold the buffalo to pay for a brain scan"—A qualitative study of rural experiences with private mental healthcare providers in Uttar Pradesh, India. *Indian Journal of Medical Ethics, 4*(4), 282–287.

Menon, V., Cherian, A. V., Gnanadas, J., Kar, S. K., & Vijayakumar, L. (2023). NCRB Indian suicide data 2021: The key trends and their implications. *Asian Journal of Psychiatry, 84*, 103568. https://doi.org/10.1016/j.ajp.2023.103568

MhGAP Implementation in Kashmir. (2014, October 19). Mental Health Innovation Network. Retrieved from https://www.mhinnovation.net/innovations/mhgap-implementation-kashmir

Ministry of health and family welfare. (2013). *National Mental Health Programme (NMHP)*. Ministry of health and family welfare, Government of India. Retrieved from https://main.mohfw.gov.in/sites/default/files/9903463892NMHP%20detail_0_2.pdf

Ministry of Health and Family Welfare. (2014). *New Pathways New Hope: National Mental Health Policy of India*. Ministry of Health and Family Welfare. Retrieved from https://nhm.gov.in/WriteReadData/l892s/6479141851472451026.pdf

Ministry of Health and Family Welfare. (2022, February 4). *Allocation of funds for mental health*. Retrieved from https://pib.gov.in/pib.gov.in/Pressreleaseshare.aspx?PRID=1795422

Mishra, S., & Kar, S. (2022). Patterns of practice and attitudes to referral for mental health needs among practitioners in Northern India. *Psychiatry, 85*(4), 433–434. https://doi.org/10.1080/00332747.2021.1989855

Murthy, P., Isaac, M., & Dabholkar, H. (2017). Mental Hospitals in India in the 21st century: Transformation and relevance. *Epidemiology and Psychiatric Sciences, 26*(1), 10–15. https://doi.org/10.1017/S2045796016000755

Namboodiri, V., George, S., & Singh, S. P. (2019). The Mental Healthcare Act 2017 of India: A challenge and an opportunity. *Asian Journal of Psychiatry, 44*, 25–28. https://doi.org/10.1016/j.ajp.2019.07.016

National Health Mission. (2023, June 19). *National Mental Health Programme (NMHP): National Health Mission*. Retrieved from https://nhm.gov.in/index1.php?lang=1&level=2&sublinkid=1043&lid=359

National Medical Commission. (2023, July 18). *List of College Teaching MBBS|NMC*. Retrieved from https://www.nmc.org.in/information-desk/for-students-to-study-in-india/list-of-college-teaching-mbbs/

Nault, K. (2021, April 14). *Project empower: Expanding mental health treatment in India via new digital platform the Lakshmi Mittal and Family South Asia Institute*. The Lakshmi Mittal and Family South Asia Institute. Retrieved from https://mittalsouthasiainstitute.harvard.edu/2021/04/project-empower/

NCRB. (2022). *Accidental Deaths & Suicides in India (ADSI)|National Crime Records Bureau*. Retrieved from https://ncrb.gov.in/en/accidental-deaths-suicides-india-adsi

Patel, V., Weobong, B., Weiss, H. A., Anand, A., Bhat, B., Katti, B., Dimidjian, S., Araya, R., Hollon, S. D., King, M., Vijayakumar, L., Park, A.-L., McDaid, D., Wilson, T., Velleman, R., Kirkwood, B. R., & Fairburn, C. G. (2017). The Healthy Activity Program (HAP), a lay counsellor-delivered brief psychological treatment for severe depression, in primary care in India: A randomised controlled trial. *Lancet (London, England), 389*(10065), 176–185. https://doi.org/10.1016/S0140-6736(16)31589-6

Patel, V., Xiao, S., Chen, H., Hanna, F., Jotheeswaran, A. T., Luo, D., Parikh, R., Sharma, E., Usmani, S., Yu, Y., Druss, B. G., & Saxena, S. (2016). The magnitude of and health system responses to the mental health treatment gap in adults in India and China. *The Lancet, 388*(10063), 3074–3084. https://doi.org/10.1016/S0140-6736(16)00160-4

Prabhu, A., Vardhan, G. V., & Pandit, L. V. (2015). Pathways to tertiary care adopted by individuals with psychiatric illness. *Asian Journal of Psychiatry, 16*, 32–35.

Press Information Bureau. (2014). *Mental Health Institutions in the Country*. Ministry of Health and Family Welfare, Government of India. Retrieved from https://pib.gov.in/newsite/PrintRelease.aspx?relid=112890

QualityRights Gujarat. (2015, June 15). Mental Health innovation network. Retrieved from https://www.mhinnovation.net/innovations/qualityrights-gujarat

Ransing, R., Arafat, S. M. Y., Menon, V., & Kar, S. K. (2023). National suicide prevention strategy of India: Implementation challenges and the way forward. *The Lancet Psychiatry, 10*(3), 163–165. https://doi.org/10.1016/S2215-0366(23)00027-5

Ransing, R., Kar, S. K., & Menon, V. (2022a). Alternative medicine under the Mental Health Care Act, 2017: Future implications and concerns. *Indian Journal of Medical Ethics, 1*, 1–9.

Ransing, R., Kar, S. K., & Menon, V. (2022b). Mental Health Research in India: New challenges and the way forward. *Indian Journal of Psychological Medicine, 44*(6), 612–614. https://doi.org/10.1177/02537176211016088

Rao, K., Vanguri, P., & Premchander, S. (2011). Community-based mental health intervention for underprivileged women in rural India: An experiential report. *International Journal of Family Medicine, 2011*, 621426. https://doi.org/10.1155/2011/621426

Rudra, S., Kalra, A., Kumar, A., & Joe, W. (2017). Utilization of alternative systems of medicine as health care services in India: Evidence on AYUSH care from NSS 2014. *Plos One, 12*(5), e0176916. https://doi.org/10.1371/journal.pone.0176916

Sagar, R., Pattanayak, R. D., Chandrasekaran, R., Chaudhury, P. K., Deswal, B. S., Lenin Singh, R. K., Malhotra, S., Nizamie, S. H., Panchal, B. N., Sudhakar, T. P., Trivedi, J. K., Varghese, M., Prasad, J., & Chatterji, S. (2017). Twelve-month prevalence and treatment gap for common mental disorders: Findings from a large-scale epidemiological survey in India. *Indian Journal of Psychiatry, 59*(1), 46. https://doi.org/10.4103/psychiatry.IndianJPsychiatry_333_16

Sagar, R., Dandona, R., Gururaj, G., Dhaliwal, R. S., Singh, A., Ferrari, A., Dua, T., Ganguli, A., Varghese, M., Chakma, J. K., Kumar, G. A., Shaji, K. S., Ambekar, A., Rangaswamy, T., Vijayakumar, L., Agarwal, V., Krishnankutty, R. P., Bhatia, R., Charlson, F., et al. (2020). The burden of mental disorders across the states of India: The global burden of disease study 1990–2017. *The Lancet Psychiatry, 7*(2), 148–161. https://doi.org/10.1016/S2215-0366(19)30475-4

Sagar, R., & Singh, S. (2022). National Tele-Mental Health Program in India: A step towards mental health care for all? *Indian Journal of Psychiatry, 64*(2), 117–119. https://doi.org/10.4103/indianjpsychiatry.indianjpsychiatry_145_22

Shidhaye, R., & Kermode, M. (2013). Stigma and discrimination as a barrier to mental health service utilization in India. *International Health, 5*(1), 6–8. https://doi.org/10.1093/inthealth/ihs011

Singh, A., Tripathi, A., Gupta, B., & Agarwal, V. (2016). Pathways to care for Dhat (Semen Loss Anxiety) syndrome: A study from North India. *International Journal of Mental Health, 45*(4), 253–261. https://doi.org/10.1080/00207411.2016.1238741

Singh, O. P. (2018). District Mental Health Program—Need to look into strategies in the era of Mental Health Care Act, 2017 and moving beyond Bellary model. *Indian Journal of Psychiatry, 60*(2), 163–164. https://doi.org/10.4103/psychiatry.IndianJPsychiatry_304_18

Singh, O. P. (2021). Comprehensive Mental Health Action Plan 2013–2030: We must rise to the challenge. *Indian Journal of Psychiatry, 63*(5), 415–417. https://doi.org/10.4103/indianjpsychiatry.indianjpsychiatry_811_21

Tandon, T., & Collective, L. (2015). Drug policy in India. In *IDPC Briefing Paper, February, International Drug Policy Consortium, London*. Retrieved from https://idhdp.com/media/400258/idpc-briefing-paper_drug-policy-in-india.pdf

Tewari, A., Kallakuri, S., Devarapalli, S., Jha, V., Patel, A., & Maulik, P. K. (2017). Process evaluation of the systematic medical appraisal, referral and treatment (SMART) mental health project in rural India. *BMC Psychiatry, 17*(1), 385. https://doi.org/10.1186/s12888-017-1525-6

The Altruist, Ahmedabad and Action For Mental Illness, Bangalore. (2011). *The Altruist and action for mental illness. Satisfaction-expectation rapid survey of District Mental Health Project in Banaskantha*. Retrieved from https://mhpolicy.files.wordpress.com/2011/05/seras-report.pdf

Trivedi, J. K., & Jilani, A. Q. (2011). Pathway of psychiatric care. *Indian Journal of Psychiatry, 53*(2), 97.

Trivedi, J. K., Triapthi, A., & Kar, S. K. (2015). Mental health legislation: Comparison of South Asian and Western Countries. In J. K. Trivedi & A. Tripathi (Eds.), *Mental Health in South Asia: Ethics, resources, programs and legislation* (pp. 343–362). Springer Netherlands. https://doi.org/10.1007/978-94-017-9017-8_20

United Nations. (2023, April 23). *UN DESA Policy Brief No. 153: India overtakes China as the world's most populous country | Department of Economic and Social Affairs*. Retrieved from https://www.un.org/development/desa/dpad/publication/un-desa-policy-brief-no-153-india-overtakes-china-as-the-worlds-most-populous-country/

van Ginneken, N., Maheedhariah, M. S., Ghani, S., Ramakrishna, J., Raja, A., & Patel, V. (2017a). Human resources and models of mental healthcare integration into primary and community care in India: Case studies of 72 programmes. *Plos One, 12*(6), e0178954. https://doi.org/10.1371/journal.pone.0178954

Vijayakumar, L., Chandra, P. S., Kumar, M. S., Pathare, S., Banerjee, D., Goswami, T., & Dandona, R. (2022). The national suicide prevention strategy in India: Context and considerations for urgent action. *The Lancet Psychiatry, 9*(2), 160–168. https://doi.org/10.1016/S2215-0366(21)00152-8

Weaver, L. J., Karasz, A., Muralidhar, K., Jaykrishna, P., Krupp, K., & Madhivanan, P. (2023). Will increasing access to mental health treatment close India's mental health gap? *SSM—Mental Health, 3*, 100184. https://doi.org/10.1016/j.ssmmh.2022.100184

Wig, N. N., & Murthy, S. R. (2015). The birth of national mental health program for India. *Indian Journal of Psychiatry, 57*(3), 315–319. https://doi.org/10.4103/0019-5545.166615

World Health Organization. (2017). *Mental Health Atlas 2017 Country Profile: India.* World Health Organization. Retrieved from https://www.who.int/publications/m/item/mental-health-atlas-2017-country-profile-india

World Health Organization. (2019). *Country Cooperation Strategy 2019–2023.* The WHO India Country Cooperation Strategy 2019–2023. Retrieved from https://www.who.int/india/country-cooperation-strategy-2019-2023

World Health Organization. (2021a, September 21). *Comprehensive Mental Health Action Plan 2013–2030.* Retrieved from https://www.who.int/publications-detail-redirect/9789240031029

World Health Organization. (2021b, December 28). *Health workforce in India: Why, where and how to invest?* https://www.who.int/publications-detail-redirect/9789290228813

World Health Organization. (2022, May 13). *Report on evolution of Ayushman Bharat Pradhan Mantri Jan Arogya Yojana.* Retrieved from https://www.who.int/publications-detail-redirect/9789290229438

World Health Organization. (2023a). *Mental health.* Retrieved from https://www.who.int/india/health-topics/mental-health

World Health Organization. (2023b, May 19). *World health statistics 2023: Monitoring health for the SDGs, sustainable development goals.* Retrieved from https://www.who.int/publications-detail-redirect/9789240074323

Access to Mental Health Care in Nepal: Current Status, Potential Challenges, and Ways Out

Pawan Sharma, Kamal Gautam, and Kedar Marahatta

Abstract Nepal is a small Himalayan nation situated between India and China. The history of mental health care development in Nepal is around 60 years. The burden of mental health issues is high and resources are limited. Though there has been steady improvement in mental health care services, Nepal faces challenges similar to other lower middle income countries and some unique ones. The major challenges in mental health care in Nepal are high treatment gap, unregulated help seeking pattern, poor fund and research, inadequate and inequitable manpower, huge out of pocket expense, poor referral system, poor mental health literacy, high stigma, non-judicious prescribing and various administrative difficulties. In this chapter we discuss about the historical aspects, epidemiology, policies and legislations, services, challenges and potential ways out for mental health care in Nepal.

Keywords Nepal · Mental health care · Psychiatry · Mental health challenges · Treatment gap · Ways out

1 Introduction

Nepal with an area of 147,181 km^2 and a population of approximately 30 million, is located in South Asia and shares territorial borders with India and China. It is one of the eleven member states of WHO south East Asian region. Nepal became a republic, federal state after the promulgation of the constitution in 2015. The history of health development in Nepal has been summarized into four periods; 1951–1970:

P. Sharma (✉)
Department of Psychiatry, School of Medicine, Patan Academy of Health Sciences, Lalitpur, Nepal
e-mail: pawan60@gmail.com

K. Gautam
Transcultural Psychosocial Organization, TPO Nepal, Kathmandu, Nepal

K. Marahatta
WHO Country Office for Nepal, Patan, Nepal

© The Author(s), under exclusive license to Springer Nature Singapore Pte Ltd. 2024
S. M. Y. Arafat and S. K. Kar (eds.), *Access to Mental Health Care in South Asia*,
https://doi.org/10.1007/978-981-99-9153-2_6

the early health development programs of disease eradication after the end of the Rana oligarchy; 1970–1990: the turn to primary health care during the Panchayat; 1990–2010: the rise of non-governmental organizations (NGOs) after the People's War; and 2010–present: the return to health systems development in the post-conflict and post-disaster period (Seale-Feldman, 2019; Table 1). Unlike most of the countries, Nepal never had a mental asylum, and mental health services started out in general hospital settings in Nepal. The first out-patient service in psychiatry was started in 1962 and in-patient treatment service was started in 1965 (Upadhyaya, 2015). However, before that patients with severe mental illness would go to Ranchi Mental hospital, Gorakhpur or Lucknow i.e. cities of India for treatment. Male patients having psychosis with or without criminal background were kept in Dhulikhel Jail whereas female patients were kept in the Central Jail of Kathmandu (Upadhyaya, 2015). With time, there was a slow and steady improvement in the mental health sector of Nepal. Community mental health services started in Nepal in the 1980s under the leadership of the NGOs like United Mission to Nepal (UMN) whose main aim was to train health personnel in order to provide mental health services at primary care level. The notable five-year pilot project of 1984 turned out to be successful and the model was replicated by government academic institutions (Singh et al., 2022). Subsequently, several academic courses like Doctor of Medicine (MD) i.e. post graduate in Psychiatry was initiated for the first time at the Institute of Medicine (IOM) in 1997. A 2-year MPhil programme in clinical psychology was started in 1998 and in 2000, a program in psychiatric nursing was started. The National Mental Health Policy was developed and endorsed by Ministry of Health in 1997 (Shyangwa & Jha, 2008).

Table 1 Historical landmarks in mental health in Nepal (Shyangwa & Jha, 2008; Upadhyaya, 2015)

Year	Landmark events
1962	Psychiatric OPD services started
1965	Psychiatric in-patient services started
1976	Narcotic drugs control act was framed
1976	Rehabilitation center for drug abusers started by NGO sector
1984	Central level mental hospital started
1984	Community health development project (CDHP) in Lalitpur by UMN
1989	Mental Health project started at IOM, financial aid of NGO
1997	National mental health policy and plan developed and adopted by the Ministry of Health
1997	MD psychiatry training started
1998	M.Phil in clinical psychology started
2000	Psychiatric nursing courses started

2 Epidemiology and Burden of Mental Illness in Nepal

Mental disorders were ranked as the second leading cause of years of healthy life lost due to disability (YLDs) in Nepal (Mishra et al., 2020). Among the South Asian countries, Nepal ranks second in prevalence rate (307 per 1000) of psychiatric morbidity as per a review (Ranjan & Asthana, 2017). Suicide in Nepal also has become a major public health concern due to increasing rates and high burden (Thapaliya et al., 2018). The first National Mental Health Survey (NMHS) of Nepal was conducted in 2019–2020 with a sample size of 15,088 (9200 adults and 5888 adolescents i.e. 13–17 years) in seven provinces of Nepal. The survey used International Neuropsychiatric Interview (MINI) for psychiatric disorders, version 7.0.2 for Diagnostic and Statistical Manual of Mental Disorders-5 (DSM-5) for both adults and kids. It was translated and adopted in Nepali language (Dhimal et al., 2022). The wards were taken as Primary Sampling Units (PSUs) and were selected from each of the seven provinces of Nepal using a multi-stage Probability Proportionate to Size (PPS) sampling technique. From each PSU, the list of households was obtained and then the individual members from each household were listed. Individual participants from the household who were selected using a systematic sampling technique were taken as Secondary Sampling Units (SSUs). The major findings have been presented in Table 2. Before the main survey, a pilot survey was conducted among 1647 participants including 276 children aged 13–17 years and 1371 adults aged 18 years & above, in three districts of Nepal: Dhanusha, Bhaktapur and Dolakha using the same tool. The three districts taken represented three ecological regions of Nepal. In the pilot survey the prevalence of current mental disorders among adults and children were 13.2% and 11.2% respectively. The prevalence of current suicidality was 10.9% among adults and 8.7% among children (Jha et al., 2019).

A nationwide cross-sectional study among a representative sample of Nepalese adults between the age of 18 and 65 years with a sample size of 2100 selected by multistage random cluster sampling using Hospital Anxiety and Depression Scale (HADS), to detect cases of anxiety (HADS-A), depression (HADS-D) and comorbid anxiety and depression (HADS-cAD) found the age- and gender-adjusted point prevalences of HADS-A, HADS-D and HADS-cAD to be 16.1, 4.2 and 5.9% respectively (Risal et al., 2016). There have also been prevalence studies conducted in different vulnerable populations in Nepal. A systematic review of 26 studies on the prevalence of mental disorders in geriatric population showed a prevalence of depressive symptom in a range of 25.5% to 60.6% in the community. The prevalence ranged from 17.3 to 89.1% in aged-care facilities and it was in the range of 53.2–57.1% in hospital settings. The prevalence of depressive disorders varied between 4.4% in community sample and 53.2% in hospital sample. The prevalence of cases of anxiety symptoms ranged from 21.7 to 32.3%. The other identified disorders in this group were psychosis and alcohol use disorder (Thapa et al., 2018). A review on prevalence of mental disorders among Bhutanese refugees in Nepal showed high incidence of mental disorders including anxiety, depression and post-traumatic stress disorder in both tortured and non-tortured participants (Kane et al.,

Table 2 Findings of National Mental Health Survey, 2019/20 (Dhimal et al., 2022)

Disorders	Lifetime % (95% CL)	Current% (95% CL)
Adults		
Any mental disorder	10.0 (8.5–11.8)	4.3 (3.5–5.2)
Schizophrenia and any psychotic disorders	0.2 (0.1–0.3)	0.1 (0.1–0.3)
Bipolar affective disorders	0.2 (0.1–0.5)	0.1 (0.1–0.3)
Depressive disorders	2.9 (2.3–3.7)	1.0 (0.8–1.4)
Anxiety and stress related disorders	–	3.0 (2.5–3.6)
Suicidality	–	7.2(5.9–8.8)
Adolescents		
Any mental morbidity	–	5.2 (4.2–6.4)
Bipolar affective disorder	–	0.2 (0.1–0.4)
Depressive disorders	–	0.6 (0.4–1.0)
Anxiety and stress related disorder	–	2.8 (2.0–3.8)
Any psychotic disorder	–	0.3 (0.2–0.6)
Behavioural and emotional disorder	–	1.0 (0.7–1.4)
Suicidality	–	4.1(3.3–5.2)

2018; Mills et al., 2008). Among the children population a scoping review showed that the prevalence of emotional and behavioural problems in children going to school was in the range of 12.9 and 17.03%. The prevalence of Autism Spectrum Disorder (ASD) was estimated to be three in every 1000 persons. Similarly, prevalence of anxiety disorders ranged from 18.8 to 24.4% and Attention Deficit Hyperactivity Disorder (ADHD) ranged from 10 to 11.7% in different clinical samples of children and adolescents (Chaulagain et al., 2019). A study among 66 sex trafficking survivor females staying in two NGOs showed that 87%, 85.5% and 29.7% of the sample scored above anxiety, depression and PTSD thresholds, respectively which is very high (Rimal & Papadopoulos, 2016).

Nepal went through a decade long conflict from 1996 to 2006 and experienced a mega earthquake in 2015. It has been seen that this has led to an increase in mental health and psychosocial issues (Tol et al., 2010). A study done among 720 adults in the post conflict scenario using a three-stage sampling following a proportionate stratified random sampling found out that 27.5% of the sample met the threshold for depression. Also 22.9% of sample met the threshold for anxiety, and 9.6% of sample met the threshold for PTSD (Luitel et al., 2013). A study among 513 participants four months after the mega earthquakes using stratified multistage cluster sampling in three earthquake affected districts in Nepal showed that one out of three adults reported of having symptoms of depression and distressing levels of anger, one out of five adults engaged in problem drinking, and one out of ten participants had suicidal thoughts (Kane et al., 2018). Among the children population a prevalence of Post-Traumatic Stress Symptoms (PTSS) ranging from 10.7 to 51% of earthquake-affected areas in the Kathmandu district of Nepal was seen. A study done in former child soldiers during Maoist insurgency reported that 53.2% met the cut-off score for PTSS (Chaulagain et al., 2019).

3 Mental Health Policy and Legislation

The Constitution of Nepal has made a provision for free basic health services and equal access to health services for every citizen under the rights relating to health. The list of basic health services includes Mental health care in Section 4 (e) of Section 3 of the Public Health Services Act, 2075 (2018) (Nepal Law Commission, 2018). Similarly, mental health services have been included in the 'basic and emergency health services' in Schedule 1 and 2 of the Public Health Regulations 2077 (2020), and service arrangements for mental health to be made at the federal, the provincial, and the local levels are in place (Department of Health Services, 2020).

The Government of Nepal's 15th Five-Year Plan (2019/20–2023/24) also includes a plan to expand access to mental health services at all levels. The government has implemented an action plan including mental health initiatives in line with the Multisectoral Action Plan for the Prevention and Control of Non-Communicable Diseases (2014–2020). The action plan emphasizes a concrete mental health strategy that needs to be formulated and implemented in line with the constitution, national health policy, and federal governance system (National Planning Commission, 2023). The National Health Policy, 2076 (2019) allows for the existing policies to be repealed after the issuance of the detailed thematic strategy (Department of Health Services, 2020).

Currently, there is no standalone mental health policy but is governed by the National health policy which is the single over-arching policy with different subsections for different health conditions. Mental health is mentioned in Sect. 17.5. The National Mental Health Strategy and Action Plan (2020) provides a comprehensive description of action plans for mental health care in Nepal. This strategic action plan describes the provision of free mental health services in primary care in all parts of the country. The major aims of this action plan are-integration of mental health in primary care setting, inter-sectoral coordination among government, private and NGO sector and right based all-inclusive mental health provision for all. For achievement of these aims, the following strategies and action plan are made (*WHO*, 2021):

1. Ensure easy, affordable, and equal access to mental health services for all.
2. Arrange the means, resources, human resources, and mechanisms required for the delivery of mental health and psychosocial services.
3. Increase public awareness to promote mental health and eradicate existing superstitions, myths, and misconceptions.
4. Protect the basic human rights of people with mental health problems and psychosocial disabilities.
5. Integrate the information related to mental health services into the existing health information system and promote study and research on mental health.

Regarding substance use disorders, the treatment and rehabilitation are based on the Ministry of Home Affairs' Directive on the Operation of Treatment and Rehabilitation Center for the Users of Narcotic Drugs, 2018 and National Opioid Substitution Therapy Guideline 2013. The national policy documents have envisioned to develop a National Standardized Treatment and Rehabilitation Protocol for alcohol and substance use disorder in Nepal. The Narcotics Drug Prevention and Control National Master Plan 2022–2027 has envisioned to develop a "Accepted Standard Training Curriculum" to train existing service providers (Ministry of Home Affairs, 2022, 2023). Additionally, the "Directive on the operation of treatment and rehabilitation center for the users of narcotic drugs, 2018" also recommends treatment based on "National Treatment Protocol" (Pant et al., 2023).

Though there is a perception of criminality associated with suicide, attempted suicide was never criminalized in Nepal. However, the new Criminal Code (2017) of Nepal criminalizes the abetment of suicide. Section 185 Prohibition on Abetment of Suicide states: (1) "No one should provoke or generate a situation abate anyone to commit suicide or to create circumstances compelling someone to commit the same. (2) Anyone found guilty under the clause is liable to a five-year jail sentence and Rs 50,000 fine" (approx. $405 USD) (Utyasheva et al., 2022).

There is no mental health act in Nepal till now. However, few acts of Nepal are activated regarding the mental illnesses. Chapter 7 of the Act Relating to Rights of Persons with Disabilities, 2074 (2017) provides for every citizen's right to health, rehabilitation, social security, and recreation. Sections 35 and 36 of the Act also ensure additional service facilities for people with mental or psychosocial disabilities (Nepal Law Commission, 2017).

4 Available Mental Health Services and New Avenues in Nepal

4.1 Governance

The Ministry of Health & Population (MoHP) overall leads mental health services in Nepal. Under the MoHP, the Department of Health Services (DoHS) is responsible for coordinating and providing mental health services at a public level. Within the DoHS, the NCD and Mental Health Section of the Epidemiology and Disease Control Division (EDCD) acts as the focal agency for mental health and takes on various responsibilities, including planning and organizing services, collaborating with other government and non-government sectors, and implementing national plans and programs related to mental health. Moreover, the Curative Service Division of DoHS is in charge of managing mental health services at secondary and tertiary care level. On the other hand, the Management Division of DoHS oversees the Health Information System and supply of psychotropic medications. The National Health Training Centre (NHTC) identifies training needs, develops and accredits training curricula accordingly, and organizes training sessions to specific cadres of health care providers based on the accredited training modules. Similarly, the National Health Education Information and Communication Centre (NHEICC) within the DoHS acts as the focal division to prepare and widely disseminate information, education and communication (IEC) materials on mental health in Nepal. The Nursing and Social Security Division of the DoHS acts as a focal division for mobilization of nurses (including the recently introduced school nurse program who are envisioned to conduct school mental health prevention and promotion programmes).

4.2 Help Seeking Behaviour for Mental Illness

The help seeking for mental disorders is varied in Nepal as per geographical location as availability is not equal in all parts of Nepal. The help seeking ranges from faith healers, supernatural role practioners, general practioners, community health workers to mental health professionals. Faith healers are the first contact in most of the cases in comparison to the psychiatrist as they are easily approachable and people have belief in supernatural cause for mental disorders (Pradhan et al., 2013). A 14 center nationwide study found out most of the patients with severe mental illnesses (SMIs) had their first contact with faith healers (49%). 29.8% of patients with common mental disorders (CMDs) had first contact with faith healers and 26% of the patients had first contact with psychiatrists. The duration between the onset of illness and the first carer visit was 30.72 ± 80.34 (median:4) weeks which is higher when compared with the global data (Gupta et al., 2021). The National Mental Health Survey 2020 showed that among the people who had sought for treatment, it was found that non-specialist doctors (8.8%), faith healers (6.7%) and psychiatrists (6.5%) were the service providers sought for treatment (National Mental Health Survey, 2020).

4.3 Mental Health Services

The mental health care delivery system in Nepal is decentralized. It comprises a mix of public health facilities, private sector service providers and the involvement of NGOs at federal, provincial and local levels. Basic and emergency health facilities include basic health service centres, basic hospitals, general hospitals, specialist and specialized hospitals, teaching hospitals under the Institute of Health Sciences, Ayurveda service centres, specialist Ayurveda hospitals and homeopathy hospitals and polyclinics. Mental health care is provided mainly at the secondary or tertiary level, at one specialist public–private psychiatric hospital and four private psychiatric hospitals. Mental health care is also provided for inpatients in many of the 364 private general hospitals and 27 Government hospitals in the country (*WHO*, 2021). There is only one out-patient mental health unit for children and adolescents in Nepal which is at Kanti Children's Hospital, and there is no dedicated inpatient facility (Chaulagain et al., 2019). Majority of mental health services are delivered by specialists.

There are 19 medical colleges in Nepal both public (5) and private (14). All of these academic institutions have the Department of Psychiatry. There are ongoing post graduate courses in Psychiatry (MD psychiatry) in almost all medical colleges. Two academic institutions are running the courses of MPhil in clinical psychology. There are five different post-graduate training programmes of psychiatry as per the affiliation to the universities but the curriculum and evaluation process of the training is not uniform. There are about 45 residents in psychiatry training currently. Also, the undergraduate curriculum of Nepal varies from medical schools in the four Lower and Middle Income Countries (LMICs) of South Asia like Bangladesh, India, and Sri Lanka (Arafat et al., 2021). There are considerable disparities in course content teaching/learning modalities and modalities of assessments for psychiatry curriculum across medical universities in undergraduate level within the country,. Also, the relative proportion of psychiatry as a subject in medical curricula as well as teaching/learning and assessments as a proportion to whole curriculum are far below ideal (Marahatta et al., 2021).

The Government of Nepal aims to fulfil the treatment gap through task sharing approach by training the health care providers as well. Services range from community level case screening and referral by Female Community Health Volunteers (FCHVs) using the Community Informant Detection Tool (CIDT) for basic emotional support by community based psychosocial workers (CPSWs); basic psychosocial support by paraprofessional counsellors; diagnosis and management of common mental disorders by trained government health care workers to Psychiatric services at general hospitals and Psychiatric hospitals (Luitel et al., 2020). The mental health resources have been summarized in Table 3.

Table 3 Mental health resources of Nepal in 2023 (*WHO*, 2021; Rai et al., 2021)

Health budget as a proportion of national budget 2023/24	5.87%
Estimated annual budget for mental health interventions (excluding human resources and hospital operations)	USD 1.5 m
Per capita public funds allocation for mental health	Approx. 0.05 USD
Number of registered psychiatrists	250
Number of child psychiatrists	4
Number of registered clinical psychologists	37
Number of lay counsellors	Approx. 1300
Number of psychiatric nurses	Approx. 75
Number of districts with fund allocation for mhGAP training in 2023	77 (all districts)

4.4 Mental Health Gap Action Program (MhGAP) in Nepal

The World Health Organization (WHO) launched the Mental Health Gap Action Programme (mhGAP) and the mhGAP Intervention Guide (mhGAP-IG) for mental, neurological and substance use disorders with the aim of providing evidence-based clinical guidance to primary healthcare workers (WHO, 2010). The first version of the mhGAP-IG (V1.0) has been translated, adapted and implemented in over 100 countries (Keynejad et al., 2018). An updated version of the mhGAP-IG (i.e. V2.0) was launched by WHO in 2016 (WHO, 2016). WHO mhGAP was first tested by the PRogramme for Improving Mental health carE (PRIME) project (Lund et al., 2012) which included a consortium of five low and middle income countries in Asia and Africa, one of which was Nepal. The evaluation results of mhGAP demonstrated that the detection of depression by mhGAP-IG trained primary healthcare workers increased by 15.7% (from 8.9 to 24.2%) 3-month after the training but these rates again dropped to 10.2% twenty-four months after the training (Jordans et al., 2019).

Later, the mhGAP-IG (V2.0) was translated and adapted under the leadership of National Health Training Centre (NHTC). The adaptation and testing of WHO mhGAP in Nepal opened an avenue for task-sharing approaches on mental health and psychosocial support (MHPSS). Consequently, the following training modules targeting various cadres of medical practitioners and paramedic professionals have been endorsed, accredited and in vogue in the country:

- Module 1: This training module aims to build the capacity of nurses on provision of-psycho-education to disorders included in the adapted Nepali version of WHO mhGAP; basic psychosocial support and behavioural activation for depression. This is a 6-day training but includes an optional module of 2 days on counselling for alcohol problem (CAP) as well.
- Module 2: It has been further splitted into Module 2a (training module for medical doctors) and Module 2b (training module for paramedic professionals). This training module is based on the Nepali adapted version of WHO mhGAP V2 for mental, neurological and substance use disorders in non-specialized settings. This is a 5-day training. Additionally, this module also contains the curriculum for training of trainers (ToT). This training builds the capacity of healthcare providers on assessment, management, treatment, follow up and referral of patients with MNS disorders.
- Module 3: This training module targets medical doctors, nurses and paramedic professionals. This is a 5-day training on assessment, management, follow up and referral of children and adolescents with developmental, behavioural and emotional disorders.
- Module 4: This training module aims to build the capacity of female community health volunteers (FCHVs) on screening and referral of individuals with MNS disorders in the communities. This is a 2-day training and uses standard validated community informant detection tool (CIDT) for screening of mhGAP disorders.
- Module 5: This training module aims to build the capacity of public health professionals including managers and administrators on conceptualization, designing,

implementation and evaluation of community based mental health programmes. This is a 2.5-day training.
- Module 6: This training module is basically derived from the para-professional counsellor training developed and used by several non-government organizations working on MHPSS in Nepal. This training targets health assistants and nurses within the government health care delivery system. It runs in three phases-basis, advance 1 and advance 2, each lasting for 10 days. The participants of the training must appear in online tests and evaluation and must complete the field assignments before accreditation.

4.5 Newer Avenues

Telepsychiatry in Nepal also has gained popularity after the COVID-19 pandemic. Many government hospitals and private sectors seemed motivated, and utilized telepsychiatry as a medium of service in Nepal (Singh et al., 2022) which is being continued in the current context as well. A perspective article from South East Asia involving 52 respondents (medical students, psychiatry trainees and early carrier psychiatrists) showed a lack of theoretical and practical training on newer digital tools and digital health interventions in psychiatry. And a need of implementing psychiatry training programs integrating digital tools properly adapted to the digital era was felt (Orsolini et al., 2021). A study from eastern Nepal among 104 patients (73 follow-ups and 31 new) showed that telepsychiatry is a feasible and viable option for mental health service delivery in Nepal (Shakya, 2021). There are 24 h suicide help lines run by government hospitals like Mental Hospital Lagankhel, Patan Hospital, Tribhuvan University Teaching Hospital and NGOs in Nepal. One of the important example is the crises line "1166" run by the Mental Hospital Lagankhel under the technical and financial support of WHO and Transcultural Psychosocial Organization Nepal (TPO Nepal) (WHO, 2022).

A unique concept implemented considering the treatment gap in Nepal is the 'Satellite Clinic'. These clinics are conducted as outreach clinics in rural parts of the country by Psychiatrists to provide specialized out-patient services to people either monthly or bimonthly. A local pharmacy or a community health center hosts these outpatient services. There is nominal consultation fee of three to five USDs for each patient (Sharma et al., 2020).

The newer neuromodulation techniques like rTMS, HD-tDCS have also been started in Nepal in recent years in both public and private sectors.

5 Challenges in Mental Health Care in Nepal

Challenges faced by Nepal in mental health care almost resemble those faced by other LMICs. These include mental health being kept as a low public-health priority agenda and subsequent minimal funding; resistance to decentralization of services; challenges in integration of mental health care in primary-care settings; the low numbers of workers who have received training and supervision in mental health care; and the frequent scarcity of public-health perspectives in mental health leadership (Saraceno et al., 2007). The following are the major challenges that Nepal faces in mental health care:

5.1 High Treatment Gap

The disease burden of mental illnesses is high and the resources are limited. Though the Government of Nepal aims to fulfil the treatment gap through task sharing approach by training the health care providers, the case detection rates are quite low considering the lack of awareness, inadequate capacity building of health care providers, irregular supply of psychotropic medications, inadequate mental health budget, etc. These have resulted in difficulty with mental health service delivery through the government health care system (Upadhaya et al., 2017). A community based study using three-stage sampling technique among 1,983 adults from 10 Village Development Committees (VDCs) of Chitwan district showed 90% of the participants didn't participate in the treatment for depression and alcohol use disorder; and major barriers to care were fear of being perceived as "weak" for having mental health problems, lack of financial means to afford care,, fear of being perceived as "crazy" and being too unwell to ask for help (Luitel et al., 2017).

5.2 Unregulated Help Seeking Pattern

A scoping review of 86 studies from Nepal covered a wide range of diagnostic and treatment strategies by faith healers like divination, recitals, spoken and non-spoken rituals, pulse checks, offerings, and altered states of consciousness which were all non-medical and not based on any proven intervention. This didn't depend upon exact technique, making this a major challenge in management (Pham et al., 2021). They are an important part of the belief system and may act as barriers at times for evidenced based medical intervention. Most of the patients with severe mental illnesses (SMIs) contact faith healers and have a high duration of undertreated illness ranging from weeks to years (Gupta et al., 2021).

5.3 Poor Fund and Research

The allocation of budget for the health sector in Nepal is 5.87% and the chunk available for Mental health sector is low. The national funding for research is low. The research from developing countries have been criticized for being donor-driven, focused on non-significant problems rather than major psychiatric disorders, catering to the priorities of external donor agencies, being poor quality, not being well documented, not being disseminated and put to use by policy makers at all levels and sectors of society. The same is true for Nepal (Sharma & Subedi, 2019).

5.4 Inadequate and Inequitable Manpower

The resources available to cater the need of whole nation is very less. Around 250 psychiatrists and 37 psychologists for a nation of 30 million populations is inadequate. Also, the psychiatrists are available in the major cities and majority of patients have to travel a long distance to avail the services.

5.5 Huge Out of Pocket Expense

A population based survey of 2040 adults showed that people with symptoms of depression utilize more healthcare and spend greater out of pocket costs compared to people without depression. The major chunk of money was utilized for frequent visits to pharmacists and visits to general and specialist doctors, however, there was minimal use of specialist mental health services (Rajan et al., 2020). As per the National Mental Health Survey, 2020, the patient with mental disorder had an average expenditure of NRs 16,053 for the treatment in the past 12 months. The expense on transport and other costs associated with seeking treatment was NRs 4,146 and NRs 3,460 respectively (1 USD = 130 NRs). These are significant expenditures considering the low per capita of the country. This huge out of pocket expenditure without major achievement acts as a challenge in our context (National Mental Health Survey, 2020).

5.6 Malfunctioning Referral and Reporting System

The referral to mental health services is late either by the faith healers or the general practioners. Also there is lack of a formal referral mechanism from primary to secondary/tertiary care or vice versa (Luitel et al., 2015). Another challenge in mental health care is data keeping and reporting. Though mental disorders are reported on the national HMIS through a web portal from all government health facilities, due to low case detection rate and lack of knowledge among all health workers the reporting is not adequate. This is more pronounced in case of reporting of suicide (Marahatta et al., 2017).

5.7 Poor Mental Health Literacy

Mental health has been described as a 'behind the scenes' issue by public and policy makers. Most of the Nepalese people do not view mental health issues as diseases, disorders or health problems. They view these as spiritual issues that in turn leads to minimal help-seeking behaviour indicating low levels of mental health literacy. The most concerning fact and a challenge is people are not aware of the available treatments for mental disorders as well (Shakya, 2016).

5.8 Lower-Middle Income Status and Income Disparity

Social factors like poverty, internal migration, urbanization, and lifestyle changes, are moderators of the high burden of mental illness in many LMICs and same is true for Nepal too. The high incidence of mental illness and substance abuse disorders Nepal has lead into an economic trap of disease burden. Determinants of mental disorders like poverty and income disparity are common in Nepal and pose as challenges.

5.9 High Stigma

A cross-sectional study among 180 patients with mental illness attending a psychiatric Outpatient Department (OPD) showed a prevalence of self-stigma to be present among 54.44% patients (Maharjan & Panthee, 2019). A qualitative study conducted in a district of Nepal identified stigma as a combination of lack of knowledge (ignorance and misconceptions), negative attitudes (prejudice) and excluding or avoiding behaviors (discriminations). The stigma was prevalent in the community and acted as a barrier for service utilization making it a challenge to mental health care (Devkota et al., 2021).

5.10 Non-judicious Prescribing (Poly Pharmacy)

Non judicious prescribing of psychotropics by other specialists and polypharmacy by the psychiatrist has also been a major challenge in day to day clinical practice in Nepal.

5.11 Administrative Difficulties

Administrative challenges have further complicated the delivery of proper mental health care. To execute the action plans effectively, the provincial and local levels of government require a well-trained and capable civil service workforce which is lacking. There are other administrative problems like corruption, fiscal indiscipline, political instability, lack of good governance etc. (Shrestha, 2019).

5.12 Scarcity of Medications

A qualitative research among primary health care workers identified shortage of psychotropic medicines in primary care setting, high workload, lack of private space for counseling, and grievances of health workers regarding incentives to be major barriers and challenge for the treatment of mental health issues at the primary care level (Upadhaya et al., 2020). Though many psychotropic medications are in free medicine list of government, they are unavailable at places and if available due to lack of trained manpower, have not been used.

5.13 Lack of Collaboration in Non-health Sector

Nepal has very poor mental health integration into non-health sectors. Though some development has been seen like gender-based violence, child protection, and disability management are increasingly including mental health components but still more needs to be done. Migrant worker health programs also have very little involvement of mental health.

6 Potential Ways Out for Nepal

There is a compelling rationale for the government and other stakeholders to consider prioritizing investments in mental health care for the country's population through evidence-based mental health promotion, prevention and treatment through accessible and affordable services. Under the context of ongoing continued efforts on advocacy, implementation and experience in the country around mental health, there is an enabling policy environment and receptivity about the importance of mental health across the stakeholders. To build on this landscape, there are key thematic recommendations that can play catalytic roles in making a substantive contribution to making mental health everyone's business in the country.

6.1 Human Resources Development and Distribution

For this there is a need to increase the capacity of mental health care workforce as well as infrastructures for mental health care. Also the distribution of services should be equitable.

6.2 Awareness Creation Targeting the Mental Health Literacy

One of the ways to reduce stigma and raise awareness is integration of mental health into the school curriculum, conduct awareness-raising programmes and implement the Social Emotional Learning (SEL) interventions modelled in the investment case via the Ministry of Education. The mental health literacy would improve if the people are educated at a younger age. Also, there is a need to educate traditional healers on which cases to refer and when as a part of collaboration.

6.3 Augmented Research and Funding

The research and fund for programmes need an upliftment. Research units need to be established in the academic institutions which can develop culturally contextualized and cost effective interventions and foster scientific evidence generation on mental health,

6.4 Health Insurance

The coverage of health insurance needs to be made in all districts of Nepal and mental disorders need to be covered in them.

6.5 Functioning Referral System and Information Management System

The referral system should be functioning at an optimum level. This would help in decreasing the work pressure at tertiary facilities and would empower lower tier of health system like primary care center and district hospitals. Additionally, creating a well synchronized and centralized information management system for continuous surveillance of data and rigorous monitoring and evaluation of mental health programmes will immensely contribute to quality service delivery and improved outcomes.

6.6 Availability of Psychotropic Medications

To increase the access to psychotropic medications we need to develop an efficient, functional drug procurement and distribution system and ensure regular availability of essential psychotropic medication as outlined in the Essential Medicine List across primary care clinics. This would make mental health care more affordable.

6.7 Inter-Sectoral Collaboration

There is also a need to promote the interface of mental health with other priority public health and social protection programs such as maternal health, TB, HIV, One Stop Crisis Management Centers (OCMC), emergency preparedness and response readiness.

6.8 Protection of Human Rights

As Nepal lacks mental health act, its high time we endorsed mental health act for the protection of rights of mentally ill people.

6.9 Disaster Preparedness

We have realized the toll disasters can have on mental health system in the earthquake of 2015 and COVID-19 pandemic, hence proper disaster preparedness is must in Nepal.

6.10 Suicide Prevention

Regarding the suicide prevention strategy apart from prioritizing implementation of population wide and targeted interventions for suicide prevention there is need to implement the regulatory ban on highly hazardous pesticides and ban other hazardous pesticides via the Ministry of Agriculture. We also need to strengthen school health initiatives to promote socio-emotional learning of adolescents including interventions against bullying and child abuse. There is also a need to develop culturally appropriate interventions for Nepal.

Finally, investing in robust national governance systems for mental health will provide the necessary framework for effective and sustainable mental health care practices. By implementing these strategic recommendations, the government can play a catalytic role in making mental health a shared responsibility and significantly improve the well-being of the nation's population. The way out can only be achieved by ensuring multi-sectoral coordination and community engagement to promote mental health, foster help seeking and reduce stigma and discrimination.

7 Conclusions

Nepal, a small landlocked country in South Asia between China and India, has a large population residing in rural area and are deprived of mental health care. The majority of mental health services is concentrated in major cities. There is increasing awareness and investment in mental health system both from private and government sector especially after the emergencies like the 2015 Nepal earthquake and COVID-19 pandemic. Despite improvement as compared to past, Nepal still faces challenges that a LMIC faces and some specific to the country. With an aim to strengthen mental health services at the all tiers from primary health care centres to tertiary hospitals and academic institutions there is need for training of specialist providers, investing in research for generating local evidence, implementing mhGAP in the primary care setting and making provision of psychosocial services throughout the country.

References

Arafat, S. M. Y., Kar, S. K., Sharma, P., Marahatta, K., & Baminiwatta, A. K. A. B. (2021). A comparative analysis of psychiatry curriculum at undergraduate level of Bangladesh, India, Nepal, and Sri Lanka. *Indian Journal of Psychiatry, 63*(2), 184–188. https://doi.org/10.4103/psychiatry.IndianJPsychiatry_615_20

Chaulagain, A., Kunwar, A., Watts, S., Guerrero, A. P. S., & Skokauskas, N. (2019). Child and adolescent mental health problems in Nepal: A scoping review. *International Journal of Mental Health Systems, 13*(1), 53. https://doi.org/10.1186/s13033-019-0310-y

Department of Health Services. (2020). ACT & REGULATIONS. Retrieved July 29, 2023, from http://dohs.gov.np/info/act-regulations/

Devkota, G., Basnet, P., Thapa, B., & Subedi, M. (2021). Factors affecting utilization of mental health services from Primary Health Care (PHC) facilities of western hilly district of Nepal. *Plos One, 16*(4), e0250694. https://doi.org/10.1371/journal.pone.0250694

Dhimal, M., Dahal, S., Adhikari, K., Koirala, P., Bista, B., Luitel, N., Pant, S., Marahatta, K., Shakya, S., Sharma, P., Ghimire, S., Gyanwali, P., Ojha, S. P., & Jha, A. K. (2022). A nationwide prevalence of common mental disorders and suicidality in Nepal: Evidence from national mental health survey, 2019–2020. *Journal of Nepal Health Research Council, 19*(4), 740–747. https://doi.org/10.33314/jnhrc.v19i04.4017

Gupta, A. K., Joshi, S., Kafle, B., Thapa, R., Chapagai, M., Nepal, S., Niraula, A., Paudyal, S., Sapkota, P., Poudel, R., Gurung, B. S., Pokhrel, P., Jha, R., Pandit, S., Thapaliya, S., Shrestha, S., Volpe, U., & Sartorius, N. (2021). Pathways to mental health care in Nepal: A 14-center nationwide study. *International Journal of Mental Health Systems, 15*(1), 85. https://doi.org/10.1186/s13033-021-00509-4

Jha, A. K., Ojha, S. P., Dahal, S., Sharma, P., Pant, S. B., Labh, S., Marahatta, K., Shakya, S., Adhikari, R. P., Joshi, D., Luitel, N. P., & Dhimal, M. (2019). Prevalence of mental disorders in Nepal: Findings from the Pilot Study. *Journal of Nepal Health Research Council, 17*(2), 141–147. https://doi.org/10.33314/jnhrc.v0i0.1960

Jordans, M. J. D., Luitel, N. P., Kohrt, B. A., Rathod, S. D., Garman, E. C., De Silva, M., Komproe, I. H., Patel, V., & Lund, C. (2019). Community-, facility-, and individual-level outcomes of a district mental healthcare plan in a low-resource setting in Nepal: A population-based evaluation. *PLoS Medicine, 16*(2), e1002748. https://doi.org/10.1371/journal.pmed.1002748

Kane, J. C., Luitel, N. P., Jordans, M. J. D., Kohrt, B. A., Weissbecker, I., & Tol, W. A. (2018). Mental health and psychosocial problems in the aftermath of the Nepal earthquakes: Findings from a representative cluster sample survey. *Epidemiology and Psychiatric Sciences, 27*(3), 301–310. https://doi.org/10.1017/S2045796016001104

Keynejad, R. C., Dua, T., Barbui, C., & Thornicroft, G. (2018). WHO Mental Health Gap Action Programme (mhGAP) Intervention Guide: A systematic review of evidence from low and middle-income countries. *BMJ Ment Health, 21*(1), 30–34. https://doi.org/10.1136/eb-2017-102750

Luitel, N. P., Jordans, M. J. D., Sapkota, R. P., Tol, W. A., Kohrt, B. A., Thapa, S. B., Komproe, I. H., & Sharma, B. (2013). Conflict and mental health: A cross-sectional epidemiological study in Nepal. *Social Psychiatry and Psychiatric Epidemiology, 48*(2), 183–193. https://doi.org/10.1007/s00127-012-0539-0

Luitel, N. P., Jordans, M. J., Adhikari, A., Upadhaya, N., Hanlon, C., Lund, C., & Komproe, I. H. (2015). Mental health care in Nepal: Current situation and challenges for development of a district mental health care plan. *Conflict and Health, 9*, 3. https://doi.org/10.1186/s13031-014-0030-5

Luitel, N. P., Jordans, M. J. D., Kohrt, B. A., Rathod, S. D., & Komproe, I. H. (2017). Treatment gap and barriers for mental health care: A cross-sectional community survey in Nepal. *Plos One, 12*(8), e0183223. https://doi.org/10.1371/journal.pone.0183223

Luitel, N. P., Breuer, E., Adhikari, A., Kohrt, B. A., Lund, C., Komproe, I. H., & Jordans, M. J. D. (2020). Process evaluation of a district mental healthcare plan in Nepal: A mixed-methods case study. *BJPsych Open, 6*(4), e77. https://doi.org/10.1192/bjo.2020.60

Lund, C., Tomlinson, M., De Silva, M., Fekadu, A., Shidhaye, R., Jordans, M., Petersen, I., Bhana, A., Kigozi, F., Prince, M., Thornicroft, G., Hanlon, C., Kakuma, R., McDaid, D., Saxena, S., Chisholm, D., Raja, S., Kippen-Wood, S., Honikman, S., et al. (2012). PRIME: A programme to reduce the treatment gap for mental disorders in five low- and middle-income countries. *PLoS Medicine, 9*(12), e1001359. https://doi.org/10.1371/journal.pmed.1001359

Maharjan, S., & Panthee, B. (2019). Prevalence of self-stigma and its association with self-esteem among psychiatric patients in a Nepalese teaching hospital: A cross-sectional study. *BMC Psychiatry, 19*(1), 347. https://doi.org/10.1186/s12888-019-2344-8

Marahatta, K., Samuel, R., Sharma, P., Dixit, L., & Shrestha, B. R. (2017). Suicide burden and prevention in Nepal: The need for a national strategy. *WHO South-East Asia Journal of Public Health, 6*(1), 45–49.

Marahatta, K., Pant, S. B., Basnet, M., Sharma, P., Risal, A., & Ojha, S. P. (2021). Mental health education in undergraduate medical curricula across Nepalese universities. *BMC Medical Education, 21*(1), 304. https://doi.org/10.1186/s12909-021-02743-3

Mills, E., Singh, S., Roach, B., & Chong, S. (2008). Prevalence of mental disorders and torture among Bhutanese refugees in Nepal: A systemic review and its policy implications. *Medicine, Conflict and Survival, 24*(1), 5–15. https://doi.org/10.1080/13623690701775171

Mishra, S. R., Sthresha, N., Gyawali, B., & Shrestha, A. (2020). Nepal's increasing burden of non communicable diseases and injuries, global burden of disease study 1990–2017. *Journal of the American College of Cardiology, 75*(11_Supplement_1), 3478–3478. https://doi.org/10.1016/S0735-1097(20)34105-X

Ministry of Home Affairs. (2022). *National Master Plan on Prevention and Control of Narcotic Drugs*. Retrieved August 6, 2023, from https://moha.gov.np/en/page/national-master-plan-on-prevention-and-control-of-narcotic-drugs-2

Ministry of Home Affairs. (2023). Retrieved from https://www.moha.gov.np/

National Mental Health Survey. (2020). *Reports, Nepal Health Research Council*. Retrieved August 6, 2023, from https://nhrc.gov.np/wp-content/uploads/2022/10/National-Mental-Health-Survey-Report2020.pdf

National Planning Commission. (2023). *Periodic Plans*. Retrieved July 29, 2023, from https://npc.gov.np/en/category/periodic_plans

Nepal Law Commission. (2017). *The Act Relating to Rights of Persons with Disabilities, 2074 (2017)*. Retrieved July 29, 2023, from https://lawcommission.gov.np/en/?cat=632

Nepal Law Commission (2018). The public *health service act 2075*.

Orsolini, L., Jatchavala, C., Noor, I. M., Ransing, R., Satake, Y., Shoib, S., Shah, B., Ullah, I., & Volpe, U. (2021). Training and education in digital psychiatry: A perspective from Asia-Pacific region. *Asia—Pacific Psychiatry, 13*(4), e12501.

Pant, S. B., Gurung, B., & Howard, J. (2023). Recovery and Rehabilitation from Alcohol, substance use and related disorders in Nepal: Call for Paradigm shift. *Journal of Psychosocial Rehabilitation and Mental Health, 10*(2), 131–134. https://doi.org/10.1007/s40737-023-00337-4

Pham, T. V., Kaiser, B. N., Koirala, R., Maharjan, S. M., Upadhaya, N., Franz, L., & Kohrt, B. A. (2021). Traditional healers and Mental Health in Nepal: A scoping review. *Culture, Medicine, and Psychiatry, 45*(1), 97–140. https://doi.org/10.1007/s11013-020-09676-4

Pradhan, S. N., Sharma, S. C., Malla, D. P., & Sharma, R. (2013). A study of help seeking behavior of psychiatric patients. *Journal of Kathmandu Medical College, 2*(1), Article 1.

Rai, Y., Gurung, D., & Gautam, K. (2021). Insight and challenges: Mental health services in Nepal. *BJPsych International, 18*(2), E5. https://doi.org/10.1192/bji.2020.58

Ranjan, J. K., & Asthana, H. S. (2017). *Prevalence of mental disorders in India and other South Asian countries.*

Rajan, S., Rathod, S. D., Luitel, N. P., Murphy, A., Roberts, T., & Jordans, M. J. D. (2020). Healthcare utilization and out-of-pocket expenditures associated with depression in adults: A cross-sectional analysis in Nepal. *BMC Health Services Research, 20*(1), 250. https://doi.org/10.1186/s12913-020-05094-9

Rimal, R., & Papadopoulos, C. (2016). The mental health of sexually trafficked female survivors in Nepal. *International Journal of Social Psychiatry, 62*(5), 487–495. https://doi.org/10.1177/0020764016651457

Risal, A., Manandhar, K., Linde, M., Steiner, T. J., & Holen, A. (2016). Anxiety and depression in Nepal: Prevalence, comorbidity and associations. *BMC Psychiatry, 16*(1), Article 1. https://doi.org/10.1186/s12888-016-0810-0

Saraceno, B., van Ommeren, M., Batniji, R., Cohen, A., Gureje, O., Mahoney, J., Sridhar, D., & Underhill, C. (2007). Barriers to improvement of mental health services in low-income and middle-income countries. *The Lancet, 370*(9593), 1164–1174. https://doi.org/10.1016/S0140-6736(07)61263-X

Seale-Feldman, A. (2019). Historicizing the Emergence of Global Mental Health in Nepal (1950–2019). *HIMALAYA—The Journal of the Association for Nepal and Himalayan Studies, 39*(2), Article 2. https://doi.org/10.2218/himalaya.2019.7849

Shakya, D. R. (2016). The Nepal earthquake: Use of a disaster to improve mental health literacy. *BJPsych International, 13*(1), 8–9.

Sharma, P., & Subedi, S. (2019). Psychiatric research in Nepal. *Journal of Psychiatrists' Association of Nepal, 8*(1), Article 1. https://doi.org/10.3126/jpan.v8i1.26328

Sharma, P., Joshi, D., & Shrestha, K. (2020). Mental health and COVID-19 in Nepal: A case of a satellite clinic. *Asian Journal of Psychiatry, 53*, 102175. https://doi.org/10.1016/j.ajp.2020.102175

Shakya, D. R. (2021). Observation of telepsychiatry service in a teaching hospital of eastern Nepal during COVID-19 pandemic. *Insights on the Depression and Anxiety, 5*(1), 025–028.

Shrestha, R. (2019). *Governance and Institutional Risks and Challenges in Nepal* (Nepal). Asian Development Bank. Retrieved from https://www.adb.org/publications/governance-institutional-risks-challenges-nepal

Shyangwa, P. M., & Jha, A. (2008). Nepal: Trying to reach out to the community. *International Psychiatry, 5*(2), 36–38. https://doi.org/10.1192/S1749367600005579

Singh, R., Gupta, A. K., Singh, B., Basnet, P., & Arafat, S. M. Y. (2022). History of psychiatry in Nepal. *BJPsych International, 19*(1), 7–9. https://doi.org/10.1192/bji.2021.51

Thapa, D. K., Visentin, D., Kornhaber, R., & Cleary, M. (2018). Prevalence of mental disorders among older people in Nepal: A systematic review. *Kathmandu University Medical Journal (KUMJ), 16*(62), 181–190.

Thapaliya, S., Sharma, P., & Upadhyaya, K. (2018). Suicide and self harm in Nepal: A scoping review. *Asian Journal of Psychiatry, 32*, 20–26. https://doi.org/10.1016/j.ajp.2017.11.018

Tol, W. A., Kohrt, B. A., Jordans, M. J. D., Thapa, S. B., Pettigrew, J., Upadhaya, N., & de Jong, J. T. V. M. (2010). Political violence and mental health: A multi-disciplinary review of the literature on Nepal. *Social Science & Medicine, 70*(1), 35–44. https://doi.org/10.1016/j.socscimed.2009.09.037

Upadhyaya, K. D. (2015). Mental health & community mental health in Nepal: Major milestones in the development of modern mental health care. *Journal of Psychiatrists' Association of Nepal, 4*(1), 60–67.

Upadhaya, N., Jordans, M. J. D., Pokhrel, R., Gurung, D., Adhikari, R. P., Petersen, I., & Komproe, I. H. (2017). Current situations and future directions for mental health system governance in Nepal: Findings from a qualitative study. *International Journal of Mental Health Systems, 11*(1), 37. https://doi.org/10.1186/s13033-017-0145-3

Upadhaya, N., Regmi, U., Gurung, D., Luitel, N. P., Petersen, I., Jordans, M. J. D., & Komproe, I. H. (2020). Mental health and psychosocial support services in primary health care in Nepal: Perceived facilitating factors, barriers and strategies for improvement. *BMC Psychiatry, 20*(1), 64. https://doi.org/10.1186/s12888-020-2476-x

Utyasheva, L., Robertson, G., & Sharma, J. R. (2022). Perception of the criminality of attempted suicide in Nepal and its impact on suicide reporting. *International Journal of Law and Psychiatry, 83*, 101796. https://doi.org/10.1016/j.ijlp.2022.101796

WHO. (2021). *Nepal—WHO Special Initiative for Mental Health*. Retrieved July 2, 2023, from https://www.who.int/publications/m/item/nepal---who-special-initiative-for-mental-health

WHO. (2022). *Nepal's National Suicide Prevention Helpline Service helping save lives*. Retrieved July 23, 2023, from https://www.who.int/nepal/news/detail/09-12-2022-Nepal-National-Suicide-Prevention-Helpline-Service-helping-save-lives

Mental Health Care in Pakistan

Aisha Noorullah[ID], Nargis Asad, Shahina Pirani, Samiya Iqbal, and Murad M. Khan

Abstract The chapter explores the landscape of mental health care in Pakistan, a low- and middle-income country. It sets the stage by providing an overview of Pakistan's geographical and demographic aspects, along with prevailing challenges such as political disputes, violence, terrorism, epidemics, and natural disasters that significantly impact the psychological well-being of the population. The historical evolution of mental health services in Pakistan is explored, tracing the transition from mental asylums to improved psychiatric units affiliated with teaching hospitals. The prevalence and burden of mental illnesses receive attention, underscoring the prevalence of common mental disorders. While comprehensive epidemiological surveys are limited, insights from community-based and health facility-based studies provide substantial evidence. The chapter also highlights various mental health services, encompassing public-funded government hospitals, private healthcare systems, small private psychiatric setups, and non-governmental organizations (NGOs). The absence of a formal referral system for psychiatric disorders leads to individual and familial influences on help-seeking decisions. Emerging trends like telepsychiatry, mental health apps, and helplines are explored. This chapter encapsulates the multifaceted aspects of mental health care in Pakistan, identifying key pathways, challenges, and recommendations to enhance the nation's mental health care infrastructure.

A. Noorullah (✉) · N. Asad · S. Pirani · S. Iqbal
Department of Psychiatry, Aga Khan University, Karachi, Pakistan
e-mail: aisha.noorullah@aku.edu

N. Asad
e-mail: nargis.asad@aku.edu

S. Pirani
e-mail: shahina.pirani@aku.edu

S. Iqbal
e-mail: samiya.iqbal@aku.edu

M. M. Khan
Department of Psychiatry and Brain & Mind Institute, Aga Khan University, Karachi, Pakistan
e-mail: murad.khan@aku.edu

Keywords Mental health care · Pakistan · Pathway of mental health care · Mental health services · Challenges of mental health care

1 Introduction

Pakistan is a multiethnic country in South Asia. It is the world's fifth-most populous country, home to approximately 220 million people (Pakistan Bureau of Statistics, 2020). The predominant religion of the country is Islam, the second-largest Muslim majority. Pakistan has four provinces: Punjab, Sindh, Baluchistan, and the Khyber Pakhtunkhwa (KPK) plus the Islamabad Capital Territory and other administrative areas (Gilgit-Baltistan and Azad Jammu and Kashmir—AJK) (National Institute of Population Studies, 2019). Around 63% of the total population is rural, while 37% is found to be residing in urban areas. The population age structure is 0–14 (38%), 15–64 (58%), and 65 years and over (4%). The life expectancy at birth for women in Pakistan is approximately 65.5 years, while for men is 64.5 years (Pakistan Bureau of Statistics, 2020). Around 50.6% of the population consists of men, while women make up around 49.3%. The literacy rate is around 61% (Pakistan Bureau of Statistics, 2020). As per the latest Household Integrated Economic Survey (HIES), 21.9% of the population is living below the poverty line (Shehzad, 2021).

Pakistan is battling with diverse health challenges and has one of the poorest mental health indicators. Mental health in Pakistan is complicated by a plethora of economic, sociocultural, and religious factors, further deteriorated by the inadequacy of mental health infrastructure (Ali & Gul, 2018). Of the overall health budget, the government invests 0.4% in mental health. Moreover, the shortage of qualified psychiatrists, with less than 500 available in the country, poses a significant barrier to accessible mental health care (Bhatti, 2020).

The nation's experience of long-standing political disputes, violence, terrorism, epidemics, droughts, earthquakes, and issues related to safety and security has profound impacts in various domains (Abbas & Jamil, 2019). These challenges have resulted in economic problems, increased poverty rates, unemployment, and notable economic disparities. All these factors collectively contribute to the emergence of psychological issues in the population. Furthermore, the healthcare system has not adequately responded to the growing mental health needs of individuals, precipitating the existing challenges. To be precise, a paucity of mental health professionals, services, and legislation all lead to an immense treatment gap.

1.1 Historical Aspects of Mental Health Services: The Historical Evolution and Current Context

At the time of Pakistan's independence in 1947, there were three asylum-like hospitals located in Hyderabad, Lahore, and Peshawar. These hospitals were managed by medical officers so were unable to provide quality services to the patients. Patients were often kept in chains, and the facilities were commonly referred to as "Mad Houses." Lahore Mental Hospital is an illustrative example of custodial service to mental health care drawn from the influence of British systems. The primary aim of institutionalization was to separate patients with psychiatric disorders from the community. With time, the evidence became apparent that individuals with psychiatric illnesses could receive better care and management within the community setting. This shift toward community-based care gained recognition in Pakistan during the twentieth century (WHO, 2017), reflecting a growing understanding of the needs of individuals with psychiatric disorders. The government established the first psychiatric units in Karachi and Lahore, attached to the Jinnah Postgraduate Medical Centre and Government Mayo Hospital, respectively. Recognizing the need for psychiatric units in all government hospitals affiliated with medical colleges, additional units were gradually established, although there was a severe shortage of mental health professionals. The private sector also played a role by opening small psychiatric hospitals across the country. Active psychiatric in-patient units have played a crucial role in raising awareness and managing patients. The involvement of the private sector has further enhanced the availability of services, eliminating long waiting times commonly experienced in developed countries. Unfortunately, the dream of establishing psychiatric services at rural health centers and basic health units remains unfulfilled. Improvement in services was witnessed especially in Lahore where the old Lahore Mental Hospital was re-designated as a full institute, Sir Cowasjee Institute at Hyderabad (commonly referred to as Giddu Hospital), was elevated to a teaching hospital, and major teaching hospitals were upgraded. Recently, the Sindh government has taken the decision to grant autonomy to the Sir Cowasjee Jehangir Institute of Psychiatry (SCJIP), a renowned mental health facility with a history of 150 years (The Newspaper's staff reporter, 2019). As part of this process, the hospital will be upgraded to meet international standards and will be affiliated with Liaquat University of Medical and Health Sciences (LUMHS). Several non-governmental organizations (NGOs) have played a significant role in the establishment of psychiatric services, offering them either at nominal or no cost.

2 Epidemiology and Burden of Mental Illness in Pakistan

2.1 Common Mental Disorders

Globally, the burden of psychiatric disorders was substantial in 2019, affecting approximately 970 million individuals, with 82% residing in low- and middle-income countries (WHO, 2022).

In Pakistan, there is a dearth of large-scale epidemiological surveys to estimate the prevalence of various psychiatric disorders. Studies carried out in various cities (both community & hospital facility-based) provide consistent evidence regarding the high prevalence of common mental disorders. It is important to note that the findings cannot be generalized due to the heterogeneity of the study samples and methodologies employed such as various assessment tools and diverse populations. A systematic review of literature conducted in Pakistan revealed valuable insights into the prevalence and risk factors associated with anxiety and depressive disorders. The findings demonstrated that the average overall prevalence of anxiety and depressive disorders in the community population of Pakistan was 34% (Mirza & Jenkins, 2004). Prevalence rates varied, with a range of 29–66% observed among women and 10–33% among men.

Valuable insights from studies shed light on the risk factors associated with common mental disorders such as anxiety and depression. Social adversity has been reported to be a common risk factor. Low education, financial difficulties, female gender, housewife, and lack of confiding relationships have been replicated. The increasing prevalence of mental health issues in Pakistan can be attributed to a combination of factors. These include consanguineous marriages, poor maternal care leading to higher rates of birth injuries, economic decline, widespread unemployment, and the transformation of the traditional family system (joint family system) into a nuclear setup (Taqui et al., 2007). Furthermore, over the past two decades, a significant migration from rural to urban areas has also contributed to a considerable rise in psychological problems.

The occurrence of ongoing disasters such as floods and the aftermath of the COVID-19 pandemic further exacerbate the toll on the mental health of the Pakistani people (Noorullah, 2020) (Table 1).

Table 1 Demonstrates varying levels of anxiety and depression being reported by various studies

Source	Psychiatric disorder	Population	Prevalence	Frequency
Ali et al. (1993)	Depression & anxiety	Ambulatory patients	38.4%	–
Mumford et al. (1996)	Depression & anxiety	Community-based	46% women 15% men	–
Mumford et al. (1997)	^#Depression & anxiety	Community-based	66% 25%	–
Ali and Siraj (2000)	Depression & anxiety	Community-based	30.4%	–
Nisar et al. (2004)	#~Depression	Community-based	7.5%	–
Husain et al. (2000)	*Depression	Community-based	44%	–
Kazi et al. (2006)	@Depression	Community-based	39.4%	–
Ali et al. (2009)	@@ Depression & anxiety	Community-based	28.8%	–
Imam et al. (2007)	*Depression	Health facility-based	–	30.5%
Khan et al. (2007)	#*Anxiety	Health facility-based	28.3%	–
Shaikh et al. (2011)	@Depression	Health facility-based	–	40.9%
Noorullah et al. (2020)	@@, @@@ Paternal post-partum depression		28.3%	–

*More common in females
Point prevalence
^Rural Punjab
@Pregnant Women, @@post-partum
~Women in a fishing community
@@@ Paternal

> **Box # 1. The key findings regarding the Common Mental Disorder**
> 1. Prevalence of depression is higher among females (Ali et al., 1993; Husain et al., 2000; Imam et al., 2007; Mirza & Jenkins, 2004).
> 2. Female gender, being a housewife, having a low level of education, and experiencing financial difficulties (regardless of gender) are associated with an increased risk of common mental disorders (Mirza & Jenkins, 2004).
> 3. Being married does not serve as a protective factor against common mental disorders (Khan et al., 2008).
> 4. Pregnancy is associated with an increased risk of depression (Ali et al., 2009; Kazi et al., 2006; Shaikh et al., 2011).

5. Individuals residing in rural areas face a higher risk of experiencing anxiety and depression (Mumford et al., 1997).
6. Female victims of domestic violence are more susceptible to developing a psychiatric disorder (Haqqi & Faizi, 2010).

2.2 Suicide and Self-harm

Suicide is a serious public health problem (WHO, 2021a). Every year suicide contributes to 700,000 deaths worldwide. 77% of overall suicides occurred in low- and middle-income countries in 2019. According to the WHO Global Health Estimates, 19331 [males:14,771; females:4560] suicides were reported in Pakistan, making a suicide rate of 8.9 per 100,000 population (WHO, 2021b). Self-harm is the most important risk factor for suicide in subsequent years. For each suicide, there are more than 20 suicide attempts (Owens et al., 2002). By this estimate, 200,000–400,000 acts of self-harm occur yearly in Pakistan.

In Pakistan, statistics on suicide are neither collected nationally nor published in the annual national morbidity and mortality surveys. The country does not report its mortality data on suicide to the World Health Organization (WHO). In Pakistan, the reporting of suicide and self-harm cases is significantly limited. This is primarily due to the criminalization of such acts, resulting in potential legal consequences including imprisonment and financial penalties. In our sociocultural context, where stigma is deeply rooted, and religious norms are reinforced by legal measures, the reporting of suicidal behaviors remains constrained. In the last few years, multiple studies have been conducted on suicidal behavior, utilizing diverse sources of information, collectively indicating the escalating nature of this problem.

A study finding revealed that young adults and married women constituted the largest subgroup who attempt self-harm (Khan et al., 1996). The prevailing method was benzodiazepines. Interpersonal conflicts involving the opposite sex were identified as the primary precipitating factor. It is noteworthy that marriage, which holds significant cultural significance in Pakistan, appears to be a major source of stress for women.

Multiple retrospective chart reviews have been conducted across various hospitals involving patients with self-harm (Ahmed & Zuberi, 1981; Khan & Reza, 1998; Patel et al., 2008). The available local literature suggests that self-harm in Pakistan is more commonly observed among females, of younger age and married. The most frequently reported method of self-harm is the ingestion of medication followed by organophosphorus poisoning. Domestic issues, particularly interpersonal conflicts, have emerged as a precipitant for self-harm.

According to a study conducted in Pakistan, a strong association exists between suicide and depression (Khan et al., 2008). The research findings revealed that a significant number of individuals who died by suicide had a psychiatric disorder, but only a minor fraction was receiving psychiatric care at the time of their death. None of the individuals sought medical assistance during the month prior to their suicide. This is strongly in contrast to the developed nations where people are in contact with health services in the month prior to their death.

There are gender differences in the occurrence of suicide and self-harm, more males are involved in completed suicide. The methods commonly used for completed suicide include hanging, ingestion of insecticides, and firearms.

It is important to note that many cases of medically non-serious self-harm or suspected suicides are brought to private clinics and hospitals, where they are not categorized as suicide attempts and are not reported to the police. In Pakistan, under law, all cases of suspected suicides and self-harm must be taken to one of the medicolegal centers (MLCs). Due to the absence of a database, the demographic patterns and means involved in cases of self-harm, which will assist in identifying high-risk individuals cannot be transformed into scientific information.

Recently, suicide has been decriminalized in Pakistan (The Express Tribune, 2022). Patients who present to the hospital for medical intervention due to self-harm and suspected suicide will no longer be required to go through any medicolegal process. The implementation of this change is still pending and awaited.

2.3 Schizophrenia

The exact prevalence of Schizophrenia in Pakistan is unknown. A report indicated that the estimated prevalence of schizophrenia in Pakistan is approximately 1.5% (Nawaz et al., 2020).

2.4 Child and Adolescent Mental Health Issues

Approximately 45% of Pakistan's total population comprises children under the age of 18 (National Institute of Population Studies, 2019). Evidence indicates a substantial prevalence of child and adolescent mental health problems in Pakistan. Multiple studies conducted in both private and public hospital outpatient clinics have revealed a high prevalence of ADHD (Syed et al., 2006, 2007). Additionally, a population-based study focusing on school-going children has also reported a high frequency of ADHD (Syed & Husein, 2007). The prevalence of mental retardation in Pakistan is notably high due to a range of factors. Estimations indicate a prevalence rate of 19.0 per 1,000 children for serious retardation and 65.3 per 1,000 children for mild retardation.

A recent study on caregiver burden has been conducted, revealing that 11.8% of caregivers experienced severe overall strain (both subjective and objective), 47.4% reported moderate strain, and 40.8% reported low strain (Aftab et al., 2023).

2.5 Gender and Mental Health

Women in Pakistan face a complex interplay of psychosocial circumstances that make them more susceptible to psychological issues. Practices such as forced exchange marriage (Watta Satta), early marriages (child brides), Karo Kari (honor killings), dowry, rape, domestic violence (Tinker, 1999), acid attacks, and nose cutting (punishment for acts of unfaithfulness and sexual misconduct in the name of honor) (Frembgen, 2006) impose severe physical and emotional trauma on women. These harmful practices, rooted in societal norms and cultural beliefs, perpetuate a cycle of violence and oppression, further exacerbating the mental health challenges faced by women in Pakistan. Marriage is not considered a protective factor for women in Pakistan precipitating psychological distress and increasing vulnerability to suicidal tendencies (Khan et al., 2008). It is accompanied by various challenges such as demand for dowry before and after marriage, abuse (physical, sexual, and emotional), the extended family system, and the interference of in-laws in women's daily lives, all these factors are detrimental to the psychological well-being of women. Fearfulness of disheartening and upsetting parents prevented many women from overtly discussing their discontent within their marriage. Marriage is often seen as a societal obligation for Pakistani women, requiring adaptability, unlike men who are expected to make fewer adjustments. Some women empowerment campaigns in the last few years have started the conversation but may not adequately bring into light the specific issues faced by rural women.

The cultural expectation in Pakistan that discourages emotional expression in men, reflected in statements like "men don't cry" (Shaharyar, 2014), "man up", and "crying is for the weak", have a profound effect on their emotional well-being. These unrealistic standards lead to internal frustrations, which may manifest in violence, aggression, and a higher risk for suicidal behavior.

2.6 Substance Use Disorders

Substance use disorders are an important concern for the Pakistani population but owing to the stigma associated with it, limited data is available. Few studies have examined the prevalence, patterns, and risk factors for addiction and relapse in Pakistan. Based on the urine samples received from people with suspected substance misuse in a reference laboratory in Rawalpindi, Pakistan, the drug that most frequently tested positive was marijuana, followed by benzodiazepines and opiates (Younas et al., 2022). However, based on the patient's self-reports Opioid use surpasses Cannabis (Mansoori et al., 2018; Jabeen et al., 2017). Young males with low educational attainment were more susceptible to substance misuse. Most begin during the teenage years and twenties. Stress, family disputes, and peer pressure were the most common reasons cited for the initiation of substance abuse. Polysubstance use, withdrawal syndrome, peer pressure, family factors, lack of recreational activities, psychiatric disorders, and financial challenges were among the various risk factors for relapse (Jan et al., 2022).

3 Available Mental Health Services

Currently, mental health services in Pakistan include a mix of public-funded government hospitals, privately-owned healthcare systems, some small private psychiatric setups, and non-governmental organizations (NGOs). Within this landscape, psychiatric services are provided through various channels, outpatient and in-patient services in government, private hospitals, and those run by charitable/welfare organizations. However, some private setups only provide outpatient clinical services. Patients often bear the financial burden personally, covering costs out of their own pockets. Charges in private facilities may vary, limiting access to those who can independently afford them. At present, psychiatric facilities are accessible within teaching hospitals, whether they belong to the private or public sector.

In Pakistan, there is no established formal referral system for psychiatric disorders (Gilani et al., 2005). The resultant void in this system leaves individual and familial inclinations to influence the decision-making process when seeking psychological assistance. In determining this course, a cluster of factors comes into play, where cost emerges as a pivotal consideration, particularly within low and middle-income contexts such as Pakistan (Hussain et al., 2018). Individuals and families who do not have affordability issues predominantly turn to the private sector for mental healthcare and cover expenses directly out-of-pocket (Khan, 2016). Conversely, individuals facing economic limitations tend to opt for mental health support through public sector hospitals.

Notably, psychiatric services in the public sector often have insufficient quality due to limited resources. These services predominantly lean toward custodial care, with a heavy dependency on psychotropic medication that lacks a rehabilitative dimension. Family members commonly accompany patients in these settings, sharing the responsibility for personal care within the wards.

Patients often directly approach specialists or consultants, even for minor concerns, and similarly access tertiary care, including illnesses that could be effectively addressed in the primary healthcare domain. Mental health services in Pakistan have not been integrated within the primary healthcare system (PHC), despite the advocacy within the 2003 national mental health policy (Karim et al., 2004). This integration gap perpetuates the absence of a cost-effective approach to mental health care delivery.

The private and public sector pathways align with modern scientific practices. On the other hand, the cultural fabric of Pakistan is woven from a blend of rituals, traditions, and folk convictions, paving paths beyond the landscape of scientific medicine. The roots of beliefs regarding the origins of psychiatric illness and the method of healing are intricate and multilayered. Interpretations of psychological ailments encompass concepts like jinn possession, spirits, and enchantments, giving rise to a variety of healing methodologies other than contemporary medicine.

In Pakistan, faith healers play a significant role in providing care for individuals dealing with mental health issues (Mansoor et al., 2020), especially among women and those with limited education (Farooqi, 2006). Patients also have often turned to methods such as homeopathy, naturopathy (tibb), Islamic faith healing, and sorcery for their psychological issues (Sehat Kahani, 2023). The utilization of shrines in Pakistan as culturally sanctioned spaces for healing has been documented (Pirani, 2009).

Some of the practices that are integrated into everyday life as part of the treatment offered by shamans include using amulets or talismans, utilizing holy water, performing rituals, and engaging in recitations.

Regarding the different types of specialized psychiatric services, over time, child and adolescent psychiatric services in Pakistan are steadily improving as institutes gain recognition from the College of Physicians and Surgeons Pakistan (CPSP), leading to the provision of better clinical services (Azeem et al., 2015). Forensic psychiatry is almost non-existent (Hassan, 2022). The deficiency of expertise in forensic psychiatry has significant repercussions, as it deprives individuals with psychiatric disorders of mental healthcare care leading to serious outcomes such as capital punishment for those who could be the candidates for treatment rather than punishment. Consultation-liaison psychiatric services are only offered in a limited number of hospitals (Saeed et al., 2020). These services differ from those in developed countries, as they primarily adopt a reactive approach by providing referrals, when necessary, rather than having a psychiatrist integrated as a member of non-psychiatric teams like internal medicine. Moreover, there is no dedicated consultation-liaison psychiatrist available; instead, general adult psychiatrists provide consultations.

4 New Avenues

In remote areas where psychiatry services may not be readily available, coupled with mental health ignorance and stigma being huge barriers to seeking help, alternative innovative means like telepsychiatry and telepsychology-therapy-based programs are needed to bridge the gap. Telepsychiatry can be a useful means of providing a cohesive management plan, especially in resource-poor areas (Dham et al., 2018). There is significant evidence demonstrating the benefits of telepsychiatry treatments and this form of communication can save considerable travel time and cut costs for patients while receiving high-quality care and continuous assessment (Hilty et al., 2013).

Telepsychiatry can not only provide a platform for mental health care delivery in remote and rural areas but it can also be used in metropolitan cities. By linking clients to psychiatrists located in different areas, it can strengthen the currently limited mental health network in the country. In Pakistan, the use of cellular services is heavily rampant which can serve as an enabling factor for pursuing telemental health consultations.

The COVID-19 challenge brought with it some opportunities as well and telemedicine clinics have become more mainstream, in the mental health service sphere also teleclinics have provided a viable option to abridge the physical distance between patients and mental health practitioners.

Aga Khan University Hospital as a leading tertiary care teaching hospital has many success stories in telemedicine. The Department of Psychiatry at AKUH responded to the pandemic by transitioning successfully to teleclinics for psychiatry and psychology consultations (Nadeem et al., 2020). From a feasibility perspective, it may be worthwhile to explore the secondary hospitals of AKUH for establishing Telepsychiatry services. Secondary hospitals are affiliated medical centers in smaller cities or in the downtown areas of a city.

Health facilities also exist in remote geographies such as Northern Pakistan. These facilities are managed by AKUH and Aga Khan Health Services, Pakistan. Recently, Aga Khan Health Service, Pakistan in collaboration with the Brain & Mind Institute, initiated the Taskeen mental health helpline at the Aga Khan Medical Centre in Gilgit. The aim of this helpline is to provide timely, easily accessible, and confidential mental health help to the people of Gilgit. This helpline offers free psychological support and counseling services by trained psychologists efficient in local languages from Gilgit-Baltistan and Chitral (The AKU, 2023).

Recently, a mobile health app named mPareshan, meaning "distress" in English, has been developed for screening and basic counseling for common mental disorders by lady health care workers. (AKDN, 2021).

5 Challenges

The provision of effective mental health care services in Pakistan encounters various barriers resulting from an amalgam of factors. These challenges encompass limited financial resources and research prospects, as well as cultural cognitions influencing individuals' willingness to seek help for their psychological issues.

5.1 Poor Funding and Research

Inadequate financial resources allocated to mental health care from the national budget impede the commencement and implementation of effective patient-centered services. The dearth of investment in research further limits evidence-based practices and impedes the understanding of mental health issues specific to the Pakistani context. Most medical research in mental health is facility-based and is often initiated by individuals rather than being focused on addressing national health needs. As a result, its relevance to the country's requirements is limited.

The lack of effective communication between researchers, potential beneficiaries of research findings, and policymakers undermines the utilization of available evidence. Policymakers often lack awareness of the importance of utilizing evidence-based research to shape their decisions.

5.2 Lack of a National Data Base for Psychiatric Disorders

No national database is available for psychiatric disorders. Different public sector and private sector hospitals across the country handle numerous patients without consolidating data at a national level. Consequently, there is a lack of scientific information concerning the socio-demographic characteristics of patients and relevant clinical information making it difficult to plan and target services and resources.

Despite the World Health Organization's (WHO) goal to reduce suicide rates by 10% (WHO, 2017) by 2030 and the inclusion of suicide reduction in the sustainable development goals (WHO, 2014) progress in developing countries may be hindered by the absence of adequate surveillance systems. The Aga Khan University Hospital Self-Harm Monitoring System (AKUH-SHMS), Pakistan, is one of the few surveillance systems for self-harm in the country exemplifying a cost-effective health facility-based system that routinely collects data (WHO, 2021c).

5.3 Mental Health Taskforce (Inadequacy and Inequity)

The shortage of mental health professionals, including psychiatrists, psychologists, and allied mental health experts along with the uneven distribution of the existing workforce creates significant gaps in service delivery. As a result, individuals in rural and underserved areas face restricted access to timely and appropriate mental health care.

5.4 High Out-of-Pocket Expenses

Individuals seeking treatment for mental health issues often bear out-of-pocket expenses, either by themselves or their families. This financial burden further exacerbates inequalities in accessing quality care, as many individuals are unable to afford the required services. For those who are already struggling to meet the necessities of life, mental health care becomes a luxury option that remains out of reach.

5.5 Poor Mental Health Literacy

The lack of awareness regarding mental health issues is evident at various levels, including the public and non-mental health professionals. Limited public awareness and understanding of mental health contribute to stigma and discrimination. This lack of mental health literacy prevents early identification, timely intervention, and appropriate support for individuals experiencing mental health problems.

5.6 Low Income and Income Disparity

People from diverse socioeconomic statuses have varying income levels, with some experiencing very low incomes. As a result, socioeconomic factors play a crucial role in influencing mental health outcomes.

5.7 Inappropriate Prescription Practices and Self-administration of Medications

Inappropriate prescribing practices, including the overuse and misuse of psychotropic medications, contribute to the problem of polypharmacy. This can lead to adverse effects, drug interactions, and poor treatment outcomes. According to a cross-sectional household survey, the prevalence of benzodiazepine usage was found to be 14%. Of those using benzodiazepines, only 3% were doing so on the advice of a psychiatrist, while the majority had been using these medications based on the advice of general practitioners (40%) or were self-medicating (24%) (Iqbal et al., 2011).

5.8 Delay in the Help-Seeking Process

Cultural beliefs and practices lead individuals to seek help from alternative traditional healing therapies including spiritual healers, clergymen, Hakeem, homeopaths, or even many quacks for psychological problems (Shaikh & Hatcher, 2005). Help-seeking behavior from complementary and alternative medicine is a very complex phenomenon, prevalent in rural and tribal areas, driven by many factors. These include the availability, accessibility, and affordability of the services and approval of such practices within the community. A study conducted in a rural area of Pakistan highlighted the significant role of faith healers in providing care for individuals with psychological issues, particularly for women and those with limited education (Saeed et al., 2000). Beliefs in the evil eye, black magic, and the perception that psychiatric disorder is caused by supernatural forces delay the help-seeking. The belief in supernatural explanations for psychiatric disorders also exists in the educated population (Waqas et al., 2014). As faith healers are not mental health experts, they utilize their own classifications which do not align with scientific diagnostic categories, such as saya (27%), jinn possession (16%), or churail (14%). Another study revealed that patients in public sector hospitals often attempted multiple traditional healing methods before seeking professional help for their psychiatric disorders, including homeopathy, naturopathy, Islamic faith healing, and sorcery (Farooqi, 2006). Individuals experiencing symptoms of depression typically waited an average of 4.5 years before seeking consultation from a psychiatrist (Sadruddin, 2007).

Mental health remains a stigmatized subject in Pakistan, with derogatory terms such as "crazy" (Pagal) and "mentally challenged" (nafsiyati) often used to describe individuals experiencing psychological issues (Sehat Kahani, 2023). The stigma associated with psychiatric disorders remains a significant challenge in Pakistan. Negative societal attitudes and misconceptions contribute to social exclusion, discrimination, and reluctance to seek mental health services. Other than the help-seeking behavior from traditional nonprofessional healers and associated stigma, another factor that leads to delays in timely intervention is the primary healthcare system in Pakistan. It remains ineffective and poorly organized and poses unique challenges for referrals and management of common mental disorders (Shaikh & Rabbani, 2004).

5.9 *Complex Interplay of Various Factors*

A complex interplay of various factors as mentioned above leads to a substantial burden and presents immense challenges in the domain of mental health in Pakistan.

6 Recommendations

Challenges faced in mental health care in Pakistan are multifaceted. Addressing these challenges requires comprehensive and focused efforts from various stakeholders such as government, mental health professionals, non-governmental organizations (NGOs), community leaders and local organizations, educational institutions and schools, healthcare facilities (public and private), researchers, academicians, patients, and caregivers of individuals with psychological issues. This is a comprehensive but not exhaustive list. Patients and caregivers of individuals with psychological issues are vital stakeholders in the realm of mental health. Their experiences, perspectives, and feedback are crucial for shaping supportive and effective mental health interventions, policies, and services. Involving patients and caregivers in discussions and decision-making can contribute to more holistic and responsive approaches to

Mental Health Care in Pakistan

mental healthcare. Collaboration of various stakeholders at multiple levels is the key to tackling mental health challenges in Pakistan.

6.1 Uncovering the Mental Health Burden

Conducting large-scale epidemiological surveys to estimate the prevalence of psychiatric disorders and plan appropriate services.

6.2 Budget Allocation

Allocating more funding to mental health services in the national health budget. Advocating the importance of mental health in overall well-being and the potential long-term cost savings associated with early intervention and prevention is of cardinal importance. A report (Alvi et al., 2023) that extrapolates 2006 data on the economic burden of mental illnesses in Pakistan reveals a substantial estimated burden of £2.97 billion (Rs. 616.9 billion). Given this information, a thorough reconsideration of budget allocation for mental healthcare is strongly advised.

6.3 Investment in Mental Health Research

Encouraging more interventional research in mental health to complement cross-sectional studies. To tackle the challenges posed by poor mental health, it is essential to prioritize comprehensive research focused on creating interventions that are both clinically effective and cost-effective while also being relevant to the local context (Alvi et al., 2023). Adequate allocation of funding and resources is of utmost importance to sustain and bolster initiatives in mental health research. Encourage collaboration between academic institutions (both private & public), government, and non-governmental organizations to conduct comprehensive studies on mental health issues, prevalence, treatment outcomes, and interventions. It is very important to conduct a need assessment in areas where research is required so that findings can inform national needs.

6.4 National Database Establishment

For understanding mental health patterns, needs, vulnerable high-risk groups, disparities, and above all monitoring and evaluation across the country, a national record-keeping system for rich scientific data is very important.

6.5 Bridging the Gap of Task Force

Ensuring equitable distribution of mental health professionals in rural and urban areas. There is no doubt that many challenges are associated with practicing in remote regions. To encourage mental health professionals to work in rural and underserved areas, incentive programs, such as financial incentives, scholarships, and career development opportunities could be of some help. Technology can be used to bridge the gap between urban mental health professionals and rural communities in the form of telepsychiatry.

6.6 Financial Support

There is a great discrepancy in the monthly income of various socioeconomic groups. The cost of mental health treatment needs to be adjusted based on an individual's income level, ensuring that those with limited financial means receive full support (Sliding scale payment system). This method may work for those who earn some income on a regular basis. Providing full coverage for mental health services to individuals who work on daily wages, are unemployed, or lack a proper monthly income is a critical consideration. While offering full coverage may be challenging due to financial constraints, in Pakistan, an alternative could be to improve services in public sector hospitals, so quality services are accessible to the majority.

6.7 Mental Health Awareness

Enhancing mental health literacy through targeted awareness campaigns and educational initiatives (involving the public/patients/caregivers/non-mental health professionals/allied health care professionals). Encouraging open dialog for reducing stigma and promoting help-seeking behaviors is recommended.

6.8 Regulation for Over-the-Counter Medications and Substances, Ensuring Proper Prescriptions for Safe Dispensation

To ensure safe and responsible dispensation and reduce the risk of misuse and abuse, the regulation of over-the-counter medications and substances is essential. Proper prescriptions for medications ensure that individuals receive the right dosage under medical supervision, minimizing the risk of side effects drug interactions, and toxicity.

6.9 Building Bridges for Pathways to Care

Engage complementary alternative medicine healers as important stakeholders, providing them with training and support for referrals.

6.10 Psychological Well-Being for All Genders—A Call for Inclusive Care

To ensure comprehensive care, it's important to consider mental health concerns for both males and females. Encouraging emotional expression and help-seeking behavior among men can be helpful. Creating a supportive environment to safeguard women's psychological well-being, and promoting gender equality and empowerment can help women thrive emotionally and maximize their own potential.

6.11 Leveraging Lady Health Workers for Rural Mental Health Care

Strengthening existing resources by utilizing networks of lady healthcare workers and supervisors to provide mental health care in rural areas (Aftab et al., 2018).

6.12 Empowering Mental Health Awareness in School

Introducing mental health initiatives in schools to enhance learning environments and enhance the early identification and referral of mental health issues (Syed & Hussein, 2010).

6.13 Developing Specialized Psychiatric Services

To improve the overall mental health care landscape, it is essential to develop specialized psychiatric services such as consultation liaisons, forensic psychiatric services, drug rehabilitation services, and geriatric services. Psychiatric facilities that lack child and adolescent units should also put effort to establish such services. Aga Khan University Hospital in Karachi, Pakistan provides 24 h consultation-liaison psychiatric services for the emergency department and all other specialties within the hospital. This serves as a commendable example of how low and middle-income countries can establish effective C-L services by utilizing their available mental health professionals to provide consultations (reactive referrals, no C-L consultant psychiatrist but the consultations are provided by general adult & child and adolescent psychiatrists, and referrals range from urgent to routine based on their severity).

6.14 Strengthening Capacity Building for Professionals and Non-professionals: An Examination of Referral Sources

Enhancing primary health services to enable general physicians to make appropriate referrals and manage common psychiatric disorders effectively has been a long-term conversation that always poses challenges. This has been an old conversation. A work in progress at Aga Khan University Hospital Karachi, regarding the source of referral of patients in outpatient clinics in three months (January–April 2023) clearly indicates that 50% ($n = 542$) were self-referred, by family friends, and other patients, followed by 17% ($n = 187$) referred within the hospital, AKUH (physicians, student counselors, staff). Interestingly only 3.6% ($n = 39$) of the referrals were from outside doctors (general physicians and specialists). These findings answer some questions about the evolving source of the referral pattern in 2023 but it also raises a few questions regarding who is the targeted population for raising awareness regarding early consultations and referrals. In this case, it may be the public so once they suffer from psychological issues, they know early warning signs. Interestingly quality service provided in the health care system can inspire referrals for other patients for positive outcomes.

6.15 Mental Health Legislation and National Health Policy

The Mental Health Ordinance of 2001 is an important step in establishing the legal framework for mental health care in Pakistan. The legislation has a goal to protect the rights of individuals with mental disorders. The ordinance introduced significant changes in various domains, ranging from treatment protocols and care practices to informed consent procedures and matters related to the management of property for those affected by mental illnesses. A critical achievement of this legislation was the eradication of outdated and stigmatizing language from discussions pertaining to mental health.

Subsequently, the National Mental Health Policy of 2003 provided a comprehensive roadmap for the enhancement of mental health services across the nation, emphasizing community-based care, the integration of mental health into primary health services, and the destigmatization of mental illnesses.

Despite these advancements, there remain challenges in putting these policies and legislation into practice. Limited resources, social stigma, and a lack of awareness about mental health continue to hinder the optimal realization of these policies on the ground.

Continued collaborative efforts among government bodies, healthcare institutions, and civil society are required to ensure that mental health legislation and policies translate into effective, accessible, and culturally sensitive services for individuals in Pakistan.

7 Conclusion

Mental health care in Pakistan is struggling with multifaceted challenges within a low- and middle-income country context. The historical evolution of mental health services reflects gradual progress, although the burden of common mental disorders accentuates the urgency of comprehensive interventions. The accessibility of the available diverse mental health services is shaped by financial considerations. The absence of a formal referral system highlights the necessity for organized pathways, where uncomplicated cases are managed through primary and secondary care, while complex cases are directed to specialist consultants. The emergence of telepsychiatry and digital solutions in Pakistan offers a promising aspect for advancing mental health care provision in the country. The persistent challenges such as funding deficits, stigma, and complementary alternative medicine practices call for collective attention. The chapter's recommendations offer a strategic roadmap to bridge gaps in funding, research, awareness, and care infrastructure. By enhancing budget allocation, establishing a national database, enhancing mental health literacy, and promoting an inclusive approach to care, Pakistan has the potential to improve mental health. Collaboration among various stakeholders such as policymakers, healthcare institutions, and the community at large is important for facilitating holistic mental health care. By prioritizing these recommendations and nurturing a collective commitment to the nation's psychological well-being, Pakistan can overcome its challenges and make the way for a more resilient, informed, and compassionate mental healthcare landscape.

References

Abbas, T., & Jamil, S. (2019). Psychological consequences of terrorism: case study of Pakistan. *Margalla Papers, 23*, 71–79.

Aftab, W., Rabbani, F., Sangrasi, K., Perveen, S., Zahidie, A., & Qazi, S. A. (2018). Improving community health worker performance through supportive supervision: A randomised controlled implementation trial in Pakistan. *Acta Paediatrica, 107*, 63–71.

Aftab, R., Pirani, S., Mansoor, M., & Nadeem, T. (2023). Caregiver strain and its associated factors in autism spectrum disorder in Karachi, Pakistan. *Journal of College Physicians Surgeons Pakistan, 33*(07), 784–788.

Aga Khan Development Network (AKDN)-AKU. (2021). mPareshan: Using a mobile app to provide mental health care in rural Sindh. Retrieved from https://the.akdn/en/resources-media/whats-new/spotlights/mpareshan-using-mobile-app-provide-mental-health-care-rural-sindh

Ahmed, S. H., & Zuberi, H. (1981). Changing pattern of suicide and parasuicide in karachi. *The Journal of the Pakistan Medical Association, 31*(4), 76–78.

Ali, B., Saud, A., Mohammad, S. N., Lobo, M., Midhet, F., Ali, S. A., & Saud, M. (1993). Psychiatric morbidity: prevalence, associated factors and significance. *Journal of Pakistan Medical Association, 43*(4), 69.

Ali, B. S., & Siraj, A. (2000). Prevalence of anxiety and depression in an urban squatter settlement of Karachi. *Journal of the College of Physicians and Surgeons-Pakistan, 10*(1), 4–6.

Ali, N. S., Ali, B. S., & Azam, I. S. (2009). Post partum anxiety and depression in peri-urban communities of Karachi, Pakistan: A quasi-experimental study. *BMC Public Health, 9*, 384.

Ali, T. M., & Gul, S. (2018). Community mental health services in Pakistan: Review study from Muslim world 2000–2015. *Psychology, Community & Health, 7*(1), 57–71.

Alvi, M. H., Ashraf, T., Kiran, T., Iqbal, N., Gumber, A., Patel, A., & Husain, N. (2023). Economic burden of mental illness in Pakistan: An estimation for the year 2020 from existing evidence. *BJPsych International*, 1–3.

Azeem, M. W., Rana, M. H., & Stubbe, D. (2015). New Era for child psychiatry in Pakistan. *Journal of Pakistan Psychiatric Association, 12*(1), 6.

Bhatti, M.W. (2020, March 01). Pakistan needs more trained psychiatrists. *International The News*. Retrieved from https://www.thenews.com.pk/print/621912-pakistan-needs-more-trained-psychiatrists

Dham, P., Gupta, N., Alexander, J., Black, W., Rajji, T., & Skinner, E. (2018). Community based telepsychiatry service for older adults residing in a rural and remote region-utilization pattern and satisfaction among stakeholders. *BMC Psychiatry, 18*, 1–13.

Farooqi, Y. N. (2006). Traditional healing practices sought by Muslim psychiatric patients in Lahore, Pakistan. *Int J Disabil Dev Educ, 53*(4), 401–415.

Frembgen, J. W. (2006). Honour, shame, and bodily mutilation. Cutting off the nose among tribal societies in Pakistan. *Journal of the Royal Asiatic Society, 16*(3), 243–260.

Gilani, A. I., Gilani, U. I., Kasi, P. M., & Khan, M. M. (2005). Psychiatric health laws in Pakistan: From lunacy to mental health. *PLoS Med, 2*(11), e317.

Haqqi, S., & Faizi, A. (2010). Prevalence of domestic violence and associated depression in married women at a Tertiary care hospital in Karachi. *Procedia-Social and Behavioral Sciences, 5*, 1090–1097.

Hassan, T. (2022). Forensic psychiatry in Pakistan: Where next following the Supreme Court judgement. *European Psychiatry, 65*(S1), S600–S600.

Hilty, D. M., Ferrer, D. C., Parish, M. B., Johnston, B., Callahan, E. J., & Yellowlees, P. M. (2013). The effectiveness of telemental health: A 2013 review. *Telemedicine and e-Health, 19*(6), 444–454.

Husain, N., Creed, F., & Tomenson, B. (2000). Depression and social stress in Pakistan. *Psychological Medicine, 30*(2), 395–402.

Hussain, S. S., Gul, R. B., & Asad, N. (2018). Integration of mental health into primary healthcare: Perceptions of stakeholders in Pakistan. *East Mediterranean Health Journal, 24*(2), 146.

Imam, S. Z., Hashmi, S. H., Islam, M. G., Hussain, M. A., Iqbal, F., Ilyas, M., Hussain, I., Naqvi, S. H., & Khan, M. M. (2007). Liaison psychiatry and depression in medical inpatients. *Journal of Pakistan Medical Association, 57*(3), 159–162.

Iqbal, S. P., Ahmer, S., Farooq, S., Parpio, Y., Tharani, A., Khan, R. A., & Zaman, M. (2011). Benzodiazepine use among adults residing in the urban settlements of Karachi, Pakistan: A cross sectional study. *Substance Abuse Treatment, Prevention, and Policy, 6*(1), 1–7.

Jabeen, S., Raja, M. S., Saeed, S., Zafar, M. M., Ghani, R. A., Mahmood, A., et al. (2017). Factors influencing vulnerability towards heroin addiction in a Pakistani cohort. *Pakistan Journal of Zoology, 49*(1), 95–99.

Jan, M. M., Akhunzada, U. F., Ahmad, T., Waheed, F., Ehsan, N., Bilal, L. Z., et al. (2022). Assessment of risk factors of relapse in drug addicts in rehabilitation centers in Peshawar city. *Journal of Medical Sciences, 30*(04), 265–269.

Karim, S., Saeed, K., Rana, M. H., Mubbashar, M. H., & Jenkins, R. (2004). Pakistan mental health country profile. *International Review of Psychiatry, 16*(1–2), 83–92.

Kazi, A., Fatmi, Z., Hatcher, J., Kadir, M. M., Niaz, U., & Wasserman, G. A. (2006). Social environment and depression among pregnant women in urban areas of Pakistan: Importance of social relations. *Social Science & Medicine, 63*(6), 1466–1476.

Khan, M. M., Islam, S., & Kundi, A. K. (1996). Parasuicide in Pakistan: Experience at a university hospital. *Acta Psychiatrica Scandinavica, 93*(4), 264–267.

Khan, M. M., & Reza, H. (1998). Gender differences in nonfatal suicidal behavior in Pakistan: Significance of sociocultural factors. *Suicide and Life-Threatening Behavior, 28*(1), 62–68.

Khan, H., Kalia, S., Itrat, A., Khan, A., Kamal, M., Khan, M. A., et al. (2007). Prevalence and demographics of anxiety disorders: A snapshot from a community health centre in Pakistan. *Annals of General Psychiatry, 6*(1), 1–6.

Khan, M. M., Mahmud, S., Karim, M. S., Zaman, M., & Prince, M. (2008). Case-control study of suicide in Karachi, Pakistan. *The British Journal of Psychiatry, 193*(5), 402–405.

Khan, M. M. (2016). Economic burden of mental illnesses in Pakistan. *Journal of Mental Health Policy and Economics, 19*(3), 155.

Mansoori, N., Mubeen, S. M., Mohiuddin, S. M., & Ahsan, S. (2018). Factors associated with substance abuse among male illicit drug users in rehabilitation centres of Pakistan. *Annals of King Edward Medical University, 24*(4).

Mansoor, S., Mansoor, T., & Waseem, A. (2020). Association of socio-demographic factors with first contact and mode of referral to tertiary care psychiatric facility in Islamabad. *Pakistan Armed Forces Medical Journal, 70*(4), 1054–1060.

Mirza, I., & Jenkins, R. (2004). Risk factors, prevalence, and treatment of anxiety and depressive disorders in Pakistan: Systematic review. *BMJ, 328*(7443), 794.

Mumford, D. B., Nazir, M., & Baig, I. Y. (1996). Stress and psychiatric disorder in the Hindu Kush. *The British Journal of Psychiatry, 168*(3), 299–307.

Mumford, D. B., Saeed, K., Ahmad, I., Latif, S., & Mubbashar, M. H. (1997). Stress and psychiatric disorder in rural Punjab: A community survey. *The British Journal of Psychiatry, 170*(5), 473–478.

Nadeem, T., Siddiqui, S., & Asad, N. (2020). Initiating psychiatry teleclinics during the COVID-19 pandemic in a tertiary care hospital in Karachi, Pakistan. *Psychological Trauma: Theory, Research, Practice, and Policy, 12*(7), 807.

National Institute of Population Studies. (2019). Pakistan Demographic and Health Survey 2017–18. NIPS and ICF.

Nawaz, R., Gul, S., Amin, R., Huma, T., & Al Mughairbi, F. (2020). Overview of schizophrenia research and treatment in Pakistan. *Heliyon, 6*(11), e05545.

Nisar, N., Billoo, N., & Gadit, A. A. (2004). Prevalence of depression and the associated risks factors among adult women in a fishing community. *Journal-Pakistan Medical Association, 54*(10), 519–525.

Noorullah, A. (2020). Mounting toll of Coronavirus cases raises concerns for mental health professionals. *Journal of the College of Physicians and Surgeons-Pakistan, 30*(7), 677.

Noorullah, A., Mohsin, Z., Munir, T., Nasir, R., & Malik, M. (2020). Prevalence of paternal postpartum depression. *Pakistan Journal of Neurological Sciences, 15*(3), 11–16.

Owens, D., Horrocks, J., & House, A. (2002). Fatal and non-fatal repetition of self-harm: Systematic review. *The British Journal of Psychiatry, 181*(3), 193–199.

Pakistan Bureau of Statistics. (2022). Pakistan Demographic survey 2020. Government of Pakistan. www.pbs.gov.pk

Patel, M. J., Shahid, M., Riaz, M., Kashif, W., Ayaz, S. I., Khan, M. S., et al. (2008). Drug overdose: a wakeup call! Experience at a tertiary care centre in Karachi, Pakistan. *Journal of the Pakistan Medical Association, 58*(6), 298–301.

Pirani, F. (2009). Therapeutic encounters at a Muslim shrine in Pakistan: an ethnographic study of understandings and explanations of ill health and help-seeking among attenders. Ph.D thesis, Middlesex University.

Sadruddin, S. (2007). *Predictors of treatment delay in depressive disorders in Pakistan.* University of Toronto.

Saeed, K., Gater, R., Hussain, A., & Mubbashar, M. (2000). The prevalence, classification and treatment of mental disorders among attenders of native faith healers in rural Pakistan. *Social Psychiatry and Psychiatric Epidemiology, 35,* 480–485.

Saeed, H., Siddiqui, S. A., Mansoor, M., & Khan, M. M. (2020). Liaison psychiatry in low- & middle-income countries: Experiences at the Aga Khan University Hospital (AKUH), Karachi, Pakistan. *Asian Journal of Psychiatry, 48,* 101889.

Sehat Kahani. (2023). Mental Health & and Why is it Still a Taboo in Pakistan, 2022. Retrieved from https://sehatkahani.com/mental-health-in-pakistan-and-why-is-it-still-a-taboo/

Shaikh, B. T., & Rabbani, F. (2004). The district health system: a challenge that remains. *EMHJ-Eastern Mediterranean Health Journal, 10*(1–2), 208–214.

Shaikh, B. T., & Hatcher, J. (2005). Complementary and alternative medicine in Pakistan: Prospects and limitations. *Evidence-Based Complementary and Alternative Medicine, 2,* 139–142.

Shaikh, K., Premji, S. S., Rose, M. S., Kazi, A., Khowaja, S., & Tough, S. (2011). The association between parity, infant gender, higher level of paternal education and preterm birth in Pakistan: A cohort study. *BMC Pregnancy and Childbirth, 11,* 1–10.

Shaharyar, A. (2014, Nov 2). Parenting: Boys don't cry? *The Express Tribune.* Retrieved from https://tribune.com.pk/story/783576/parenting-boys-dont-cry

Shehzad, R. (2021, Sept 21). 22% Pakistanis living below poverty line. *The Express Tribune.* Retrieved from https://tribune.com.pk/story/2322313/22-pakistanis-living-below-poverty-line-na-told

Syed, E. U., Naqvi, H., & Hussein, S. A. (2006). Frequency, clinical characteristics and co-morbidities of attention deficit hyperactivity disorder presenting to a child psychiatric clinic at a university hospital in Pakistan. *Journal of Pakistan Psychiatry Society, 3*(2), 74–77.

Syed, E., & Hussein, S. A. (2007). Prevalence of parent-rated hyperkineticdisorder and associated risk factors in school going population. *Pakistan Journal of Neurological Sciences, 2*(1), 1–5.

Syed, E. U., Hussein, S. A., & Yousafzai, A. W. (2007). Developing services with limited resources: Establishing a CAMHS in Pakistan. *Child and Adolescent Mental Health, 12*(3), 121–124.

Syed, E. U., & Hussein, S. A. (2010). Increase in teachers' knowledge about ADHD after a week-long training program: A pilot study. *Journal of Attention Disorders, 13*(4), 420–423.

Taqui, A. M., Itrat, A., Qidwai, W., & Qadri, Z. (2007). Depression in the elderly: Does family system play a role? A Cross-Sectional Study. *BMC Psychiatry, 7*(1), 1–12.

The AKU. (2023). New mental health helpline launches in Gilgit. Aga Khan University. Retrieved from https://www.aku.edu/news/Pages/News_Details.aspx?nid=NEWS-003019

The Express Tribune. (2022, Dec 23). Law penalising suicide attempts abolished. Retrieved from https://tribune.com.pk/story/2392477/law-penalising-suicide-attempts-abolished

The Newspaper's staff reporter. (2019, June 22). Govt to make Sir Cowasjee Jehangir Institute of Psychiatry autonomous. *DAWN.* Retrieved from https://www.dawn.com/news/1489606

Tinker, G. A. (1999). Improving women's health in Pakistan. Health, nutrition, and population series Washington, D.C: World Bank Group. Retrieved from http://documents.worldbank.org/curated/en/225041468757537910/Improving-womens-health-in-Pakistan

Waqas, A., Zubair, M., Ghulam, H., Ullah, M. W., & Tariq, M. Z. (2014). Public stigma associated with mental illnesses in Pakistani university students: A cross sectional survey. *PeerJ, 2,* e698.

World Health Organisation. (2014). Preventing suicide: A global imperative. WHO. http://apps.who.int/iris/handle/10665/131056

World Health Organisation. (2017). WHO releases guidance on responsible reporting on suicide. WHO. http://www.who.int/mental_health/suicide-prevention/en/

World Health Organization. (2021a). Suicide. Retrieved from https://www.who.int/news-room/fact-sheets/detail/suicide

World Health Organization. (2021b). *Suicide worldwide in 2019: Global health estimates.* WHO.

World Health Organisation. (2021c). *Live life: An implementation guide for suicide prevention in countries.* World Health Organization.

World Health Organization. (2022). *World mental health report: transforming mental health for all.* WHO.

Younas, A., Aamir, M., Kirmani, S. I., Haroon, Z. H., Bibi, A., & Munir, M. U. (2022). Assessment of pattern of drug abuse from different clinical settings in a reference laboratory of Pakistan during the COVID-19 pandemic. *Pakistan Armed Forces Medical Journal, 72*(5), 1757–1761.

Psychiatric Morbidity and Mental Health Services in Sri Lanka

Sajeewana C. Amarasinghe and Thilini N. Rajapakse

Abstract During the past several decades, Sri Lanka has seen a rapid development of psychiatry services throughout the country. From a single mental health hospital in the early twentieth century, psychiatry services have become decentralized, have extended to all districts of the country, and a multitude of psychiatry specialists, diplomates and other team members have been trained. In the mid-1990s Sri Lanka had one of the highest suicide rates in the world, and yet over the subsequent decades, the country achieved dramatic success in the reduction of suicide rates by banning toxic pesticides. And yet, much still remains to be done. We are facing new challenges, particularly the economic and socio-political upheavals of the past few years, which may be associated with increased rates of psychiatric morbidity such as depression, alcohol misuse on one hand, plus reduced availability of healthcare professionals and services in psychiatry. This chapter describes the development of psychiatry services during the past decades in Sri Lanka, examines the challenges that face us now, and explores strategies regarding the way forward to optimize mental health services in Sri Lanka in forthcoming years.

Keywords Mental health · Sri Lanka · Psychiatric morbidity · Mental health services · Challenges of mental health care

1 Introduction

Sri Lanka is a small tropical island in the Indian Ocean with a multi-ethnic population and a long and diverse history. Archeological remains of a ninth century hospital in Mihintale are likely to be the earliest evidence available of hospitals in Sri Lanka. In the more recent past, the development of mental health services in the country

S. C. Amarasinghe
National Institute of Mental Health, Mulleriyawa New Town, Sri Lanka

T. N. Rajapakse (✉)
Department of Psychiatry, Faculty of Medicine, University of Peradeniya, Peradeniya, Sri Lanka
e-mail: trajapakse@pdn.ac.lk

© The Author(s), under exclusive license to Springer Nature Singapore Pte Ltd. 2024
S. M. Y. Arafat and S. K. Kar (eds.), *Access to Mental Health Care in South Asia*, https://doi.org/10.1007/978-981-99-9153-2_8

has been intertwined with the socio-political backdrop of the island nation. After several decades under Portuguese, Dutch and British rule, Sri Lanka gained independence in 1945. The subsequent postcolonial period too has been fraught with upheaval. A thirty-year ethnic conflict that ended in 2009, the tsunami in 2005, the "Easter bombings" in 2019 and the COVID pandemic followed by a severe economic crisis with political upheaval in 2022, are some of the many challenges that Sri Lanka has experienced in recent times. On the flip side, during the past decades, the country also experienced periods of economic recovery, development and increasing tourism. These socio-cultural and political changes over the past decades have had an inevitable impact on psychiatric morbidity and mental health service development and delivery in the country.

2 Development of Psychiatry Services in Sri Lanka

2.1 The Early Years

The concept of mental illness was included within Ayurvedic medicine in Sri Lanka, going back over 2000 years. Supernatural causes were often attributed to illness, and treatment was based on these premises (Gambheera, 2011).

It was during the time of British rule in Sri Lanka, in the nineteenth century, that the concept of "lunatic asylums" to house people with mental illness was first introduced in this country. Several lunatic asylums were established, including the Lunatic Asylum in Borella in 1847 (Gambheera, 2011). Living conditions in these asylums were extremely poor, and by the early twentieth century, there was severe overcrowding and very poor basic facilities in these established lunatic asylums. In response to this dire situation, the Mental Hospital Angoda was established in 1926, with facilities for 1728 patients (Gambheera, 2011). But even with these measures, the issues of overcrowding, gross lack of sanitation and basic facilities, continued. In this context, the report by British psychiatrist Edward Mapother, issued after his tour of mental health services in India and Sri Lanka (or Ceylon as it was then called), had an important impact on the direction of mental health service provision in this country at that time (Gambheera, 2011; Mills & Jain, 2009). The Mapother Report highlighted the gross deficiencies in standards of care for patients with mental illness at that time. Following Mapother's recommendations, an outpatient psychiatry clinic was started at General Hospital Colombo, and the first acute psychiatry unit outside the Angoda Mental Health Asylum was opened, again at General Hospital Colombo, in 1949 (Gambheera, 2011; Mills & Jain, 2009).

During the nineteenth century, in 1873 to be exact, Sri Lanka's Lunacy Ordinance was first established, and since then the act has undergone several revisions, the last in 1956, when the act was renamed the Mental Diseases Ordinance (Hapangama et al., 2023). However, there are many shortfalls associated with this Ordinance, chief of which is the fact that it only applies to the mental hospital that existed at the time the law was written, i.e., to the National Institute of Mental Health (Hapangama et al., 2023; Mendis, 2004). Thus the Ordinance does not apply to the many other district psychiatry units distributed throughout the rest of Sri Lanka. Guidance on community care provided by the Ordinance is also limited. During the past two decades, concerted efforts have been in process to amend the Ordinance and make it more up-to-date, but progress has been slow. Amending the current Mental Diseases Ordinance is an urgent need that needs to be completed as soon as possible.

2.2 Recent Developments in Mental Health Services

The past four decades have seen a rapid expansion of mental health services, in Sri Lanka. There has been a strong focus away from the asylum-based model, and towards decentralizing mental health services to all parts of the country.

Despite the lack of funding, there has been a concerted effort to improve community psychiatry services. Sri Lanka has a well-developed primary care service that reaches grass-root levels in most parts of the country. One main strategy to improve community-level psychiatry services in Sri Lanka has been to link mental health services with already existing, widespread primary care services. This has been recommended by the World Health Organization as one of the most viable ways to bridge the "mental health gap" in resource limited settings (World Health Organization, 2008).

The Sri Lanka Mental Health Policy, first published in 2005, promoted the development of mental health services in the country, and the most recent Mental Health Policy of 2022 emphasizes the multidisciplinary model of psychiatric care, extending to the community level.

Sri Lanka has a well-developed, free public health care system which consists of at least one General or Teaching Hospital in every district. These are multi-specialty tertiary care centres. In addition, there are smaller Base Hospitals with major specialties. The primary care system consists of District hospitals manned by medical officers. The preventive sector consists of 360 MOH (Medical Officer of Health) divisions. The MOH offices are manned by primary care doctors, public health nurses, public health midwives and public health nursing sisters. This excellent public health care system has been utilized to develop inpatient and outpatient mental health care services. The mental health policy (2005–2015) envisaged that every district should have at least one general hospital psychiatry unit. This has been achieved to a great extent and we have at least one General Hospital Psychiatry Unit in 23 of the 24 districts in the country. Urban centres like Colombo, Kandy and Gampaha have multiple inpatient units.

2.3 Outpatient Services

The outpatient psychiatric services too have seen a rapid expansion. Consultant psychiatrists have been appointed to almost all Teaching/General hospitals as well as most Base hospitals. All General and Base hospitals have outpatient services. In addition, many consultant psychiatrists conduct outreach clinics in the smaller district hospitals in their catchment areas.

2.4 Rehabilitation Services and Long Term-Care

The mental health policy in 2005 proposed that Sri Lanka should have at least one intermediate care rehabilitation unit in every district. This has been achieved to a partial extent, but there are still districts that lack these units. Establishment of rehabilitation units for those with substance use disorders is another priority.

Sri Lanka urgently needs to further develop community-based rehabilitation services, as well as long-term care services to cater to severely mentally ill patients who cannot be looked after in the community. At present, much of the burden of care for such patients falls to the families of patients. Some patients are also housed at the National Institute of Mental Health (former Angoda Mental Hospital) and private sector or NGO-run care homes. There is no clear supervision of these latter institutes.

2.5 The National Institute of Mental Health (NIMH)

The National Institute of Mental Health (NIMH) (formally the Mental Hospital Angoda) has been converted into a tertiary care psychiatric hospital the provides acute and intermediate care general adult psychiatric services. The Institute also provides subspecialties services, including child and adolescent psychiatry, forensic, old age, perinatal and addiction psychiatry. Furthermore, there has been an emphasis on the provision of a wide range of vocational training activities and opportunities for supported employment.

The number of admissions and inpatients to NIMH has drastically reduced after the development of general hospital services as described previously. NIMH currently provides inpatient care for about 500 acute and intermediate care patients. Unfortunately, vestiges of the old asylum remain, and NIMH still provides shelter for 400 homeless, long-term care patients. The NIMH no longer admits long-term patients and concerted efforts are being made to relocate the remaining long-term patients to the community.

2.6 Public Access to Mental Health Services

As described above, hospital-based clinic or ward psychiatry services are available in almost every district of the country, as part of the free healthcare system. Patients are able to directly approach these psychiatry services via the outpatient departments of the relevant hospitals. In addition, if they wish, patients are also able to directly seek treatment from psychiatrists and mental health professionals working in the private sector.

3 Human Resource Development in Psychiatry

Running parallel to the development of infrastructure, there has been a strong emphasis on the development of human resources in the field of psychiatry in Sri Lanka, during the past decades. The Postgraduate Institute of Medicine (PGIM) of the University of Colombo, Sri Lanka, since 1980 has been conducting a five-year postgraduate training leading to the MD in Psychiatry. This includes a mandatory 1–2 year stint at an overseas training centre in UK or Australia. This has given Sri Lankan psychiatrists a perspective of psychiatry in the Western world and helped them develop similar services at home.

Sri Lanka had over 100 consultant psychiatrists working in the Ministry of Health and university psychiatry units in 2021. Unfortunately, most of these psychiatrists are working in general hospitals in major cities. The Ministry of Health has tried its best to ensure that there is at least one consultant psychiatrist in every district. However, it has been difficult to retain psychiatrists in the more distant parts of the country.

In recent years, the PGIM and Ministry of Health have commenced training subspecialists in child and adolescent psychiatry, as well as forensic and old age psychiatry. But despite these efforts, the number of subspecialists in psychiatry in the country remains quite low.

The recent economic crisis has resulted in the emigration of a large number of Sri Lankan Psychiatrists to the UK and Australia, which has led to a further crisis in human resources. At the time of writing, it is estimated that the number of general adult psychiatrists in the country has been reduced to about 80. The subspecialties in psychiatry have been severely impacted by this migration, with only five child and adolescent psychiatrists remaining in the country at the time of writing.

3.1 Medical Officers of Mental Health (MoMH) and the Diploma Programme in Psychiatry

In order to overcome the challenges caused by the shortage of specialists in psychiatry, Sri Lanka started training Medical Officers of Mental Health (MoMH) in the late 1990s. These doctors are given a 3-month training in mental health and sent to work in mental health clinics at the primary care level, under the supervision of the local consultant psychiatrist.

Thereafter the Ministry of Health and the Postgraduate Institute of Medicine (PGIM) went on to develop the one-year Diploma in Psychiatry training programme. This produced a large number of medical officers designated to work in the primary care outpatient services, under the guidance of local consultant psychiatrists.

3.2 Training of Community Psychiatric Nurses (CPNs)

The training of community psychiatric nurses (CPNs) is a key innovation started in Sri Lanka in recent years. Nurses with a 3-year diploma in general nursing were also given a 6-month training in mental health and posted to psychiatry units all over the country, and approximately 150 CPNs have been trained so far.

3.3 Training of Psychiatric Social Workers and Occupational Therapists

The Ministry of Health has also trained several batches of psychiatric social workers and occupational therapists, and they have been deployed to General and Teaching Hospital Psychiatry Units in different parts of the country.

3.4 Training of Clinical Psychologists

Sri Lanka has a huge dearth of clinical psychologists at present. The Graduate Studies Department of the University of Colombo has commenced a 2 year M.Phil in Clinical Psychology. Despite this, currently, there is a significant shortage of clinical psychologists working in the country. The Ministry of Health has made plans to recruit Clinical Psychologists to General hospital psychiatry units.

All these training programmes and subsequent development of human resources have enabled the development of multidisciplinary psychiatry teams in most of the general and teaching hospital units in Sri Lanka. Unfortunately, the economic crisis which dramatically worsened in 2022, and the resultant migration of healthcare professionals might hamper this development. We are likely to experience a loss of human resources in all the above fields in the forthcoming few years, due mostly to migration overseas.

3.5 Psychiatry Training for Medical Undergraduates

In a nod to the importance of psychiatry in general medical practice, psychiatry is now a separate final-year subject in all the university medical faculties in Sri Lanka. All final-year medical students complete a 6–8 week professorial clinical appointment in psychiatry, and face a clinical and theory examination in psychiatry as part of their final MBBS qualification examinations. Therefore, all newly passed out doctors in Sri Lanka are well versed in basic psychiatry and this has a very important positive impact on service provision at a primary care level.

4 The Burden of Psychiatric Illness in Sri Lanka

4.1 Depression

Similar to most other countries, in Sri Lanka too depression is a major psychiatric disorder, and a study from the Western Province of the country found the lifetime-ever prevalence of depression in Sri Lanka to be 6.6% (Ball et al., 2010). A survey of second-year students in three faculties at the University of Jaffna found that 31% screened positive for depression (Abeyasinghe et al., 2012). While depression in Sri Lanka does commonly present with the core features described in the ICD11 and DSM 5, certain features, such as somatic and biological symptoms, are often more commonly seen as presenting complaints (Abeyasinghe et al., 2012; Ball et al., 2010). It is also significant that somatic and other symptoms of depression are often expressed by patients in culturally familiar ways, for example, as a "heaviness of limbs", "head-ache/heaviness" or "burning type-chest pain (literally expressed as *fire in the stomach*") (Abeyasinghe et al., 2012)." Features of depression may also be interpreted and expressed by the sufferer through the lens of cultural and local beliefs, for example, it may be attributed to "past karma" or a "bad astrological time" instead of being identified as a medical problem (Abeyasinghe et al., 2012). Thus, having an awareness of how depression may present in the local context is very important to ensure that the condition is detected by healthcare professionals, particularly by first contact and primary care doctors. Increasing community and public awareness about depression and how it presents, is also important.

4.2 Suicide and Self-harm

During the past several decades, Sri Lanka has achieved a dramatic reduction in rates of suicide island-wide, with the restriction of access to toxic pesticides (Gunnell et al., 2007; Knipe et al., 2017). In the mid-1990s, Sri Lanka had one of the highest suicide rates in the world (Gunnell et al., 2007). At that time, rates of suicide were highest among young men, who were dying by ingesting highly toxic pesticides, and depression and alcohol use disorders were common psychiatric comorbidities (Abeyasinghe & Gunnell, 2008). From a suicide rate of 47/100,000 in 1995, the rates have now fallen to about 15/100,000 population, which is a significant achievement. However, rates of suicide in the country still remain higher than the global average (Ilic & Ilic, 2022). Present-day patterns of suicide resemble trends seen in most other parts of the world—rates of suicide are higher among males compared to females and among older compared to younger people (Moscicki, 2001; Rajapakse et al., 2023).

Since 2016, the most common method of suicide in Sri Lanka has been hanging, with pesticide suicides taking second place—to a large part this is likely due to method substitution (Rajapakse et al., 2023). During the COVID pandemic, there were concerns that rates of suicide and self-harm in the country would increase, but reassuringly levels of suicide and self-harm in Sri Lanka have remained constant during the pandemic period, similar to findings from other parts of the world (Pirkis et al., 2021; Rajapakse et al., 2023). However after the pandemic, towards the end of 2021, Sri Lanka saw a slight upward trend of suicide rates by hanging among males (Rajapakse et al., 2023). And then during the latter part of 2022, the country experienced a severe economic and political crisis. Thus, as we emerge out of the shadow of the pandemic, the country is facing rising unemployment and economic restrictions—all factors which are well-known to be associated with increased rates of suicide. International data reports that every 1% rise in male employment is associated with a 0.9% rise in suicide rates among employment-age males; times of economic crisis go hand-in-hand with increased rates of depression, alcohol misuse and domestic violence—which likely mediate this increased risk of suicide (Bhalotra et al., 2020; Reeves et al., 2015). In this context, it is imperative that we continue to closely monitor suicide rates in the country, continue to prioritize mental health services and actively work to mitigate risk factors as much as possible, such as advocating for labour retraining, active labour market schemes and increasing social capital (Reeves et al., 2015).

Sri Lanka also has a public health problem due to attempted self-harm. Currently, most hospital presenting non-fatal self-poisoning is due to medication overdoses, and ingestion of other household poisons, though pesticide self-poisoning is still common, particularly in more rural agricultural areas (Rajapakse et al., 2013). In contrast to patterns of suicide, attempted self-harm is more common in young people, and is often associated with acute emotional distress associated with interpersonal conflict, which is also seen in other parts of South Asia (Husain et al., 2019; Mohanta et al., 2019; Rajapakse et al., 2013). A large majority of young people who attempt self-poisoning are below the age of 25 years, and particularly for adolescents the precipitating stressors are conflicts with parents, or partners (Attygalle, 2022). A complex interplay of multiple factors, including socio-economic difficulties, parental alcohol misuse, violence within the home while growing up, internet addiction and parenting challenges are likely background issues contributing to self-harm behaviour in young people (Bandara et al., 2022; Rajapakse et al., 2020). A proportion of those who attempt self-poisoning in Sri Lanka do not have psychiatric morbidity; but the risk of self-harm is significantly increased in the context of mental illness such as depression and alcohol use disorders, and a greater association between psychiatric morbidity and self-harm is seen in older age groups (Pushpakumara et al., 2021; Rajapakse et al., 2016).

An important factor to consider, both in suicide and self-harm, is the role of media glamourization of this complex issue (Sorensen et al., 2023). Despite some steps to reduce this phenomenon, the glamourization of suicide and self-harm, particularly via online platforms, is a significant problem that needs to be further reduced.

Despite the relatively high prevalence of attempted self-harm by self-poisoning in Sri Lanka, the rate of repetition of self-harm appears to be much lower than that reported in the West—this again in keeping with other South Asian findings (Pushpakumara et al., 2019). The reasons for the lower repetition rate are not clear.

4.3 Substance Misuse

Sri Lanka is a land of contrasts, and alcohol is no exception—we have a relatively high per capita consumption of alcohol, and yet a large proportion of the population is also completely abstinent, often due to religious beliefs. Alcohol misuse carries with it a significant human, social and economic cost. It was estimated that alcohol-related costs attributed to 1.07% of the Sri Lankan GDP in 2015 (Wang et al., 2018). There is a strong gender bias in the use of alcohol in Sri Lanka, similar to other South Asian countries—a cross-sectional survey of the nine provinces in Sri Lanka found that males were much more likely to be current drinkers compared to females (39.6% vs. 2.4%, respectively) (Somatunga et al., 2014). This gendered pattern of use is likely to reflect the cultural norms of this region, and this may change with time. A national alcohol prevalence survey of 2014 found that current drinking was more common in males with an education level below or up to grade 10, who were also employed. It was also most prevalent among males aged 45–55 years (Somatunga et al., 2014).

Although alcohol use disorders are more male-centred, the problems that go with binge drinking and alcohol dependence impact the males, females and families—it is associated with an increased risk of domestic violence, depression and self-harm within the family as a whole (Ariyasinghe et al., 2015; Bandara et al., 2022; Rajapakse et al., 2020). Many children grow up in households with alcohol-related domestic violence, the cost of which often goes unnoticed, but which contributes to maladaptive behaviours such as self-harm in the younger age groups (Bandara et al.,

2022). Alcohol misuse among men has also been associated with an increased risk of depression in their partners or wives (Ariyasinghe et al., 2015).

Examination of data from the Department of Excise and Department of Census and Statistics of Sri Lanka indicates that recorded per capita consumption of alcohol has increased since the end of the ethnic conflict, from 1.59 L of pure alcohol in 1998, to 2.55 L in 2013 (Nugawela et al., 2017). These findings were based on recorded sales of alcohol from 18 (of 25) districts that were not directly exposed to the conflict, and without considering the use of illicit alcohol, so actual amounts may be higher (Nugawela et al., 2017). The economic development soon after the end of the ethnic conflict, alongside the local development of the alcohol industry and ineffectual strategies to curb alcohol misuse may have contributed to these increasing trends of alcohol use.

Much of the recent increase in alcohol (based on recorded sales) was found to be due to the increased consumption of beer, with some increase in the use of spirits (Nugawela et al., 2017; Somatunga et al., 2014). The increasing use of beer is a clear shift from patterns of use during the previous decades—a study from Colombo in the late 1980s found that arrack and illicit spirits ("kasippu") were commonly used, with beer being hardly ever used (Samarasinghe et al., 1987). The relatively cheaper price of beer, and perhaps the misconception that beer is a "less harmful" alcohol may have promoted this increasing use of beer in recent decades. Illicitly brewed alcohol is also commonly used in Sri Lanka—local brews, namely "kasippu" and "toddy". "Kasippu", in particular, is an illicit brew with high alcohol content. In times when "licit" alcohol sales are restricted or when taxes are increased, there is usually a shift towards the use of illicit alcohol, and a further challenge is that there is no formal record of illicit alcohol use, so it is difficult to accurately gauge prevalence of use.

In recent years, other substance misuse has also become of increasing concern. Cannabis is one of the most common illicit drug misuse, but Sri Lanka is now seeing increasing levels of opioid and stimulant misuse (United Nations Office on Drugs and Crime, 2008).

4.4 Psychiatric Morbidity in Older People

Sri Lanka has an ageing population, and while data on the prevalence of psychiatric morbidity in specific population groups is limited, a survey conducted among all districts among older persons (aged 60 years and over) in 2006 revealed that almost one-third of this population had depressive symptoms (27.8% overall, and 24.0% and 30.8% among males and females, respectively) (Malhotra et al., 2010). A significant association was observed between the presence of depressive symptoms and disability, functional limitations, perceived income inadequacy or living alone (Malhotra et al., 2010). The cross-sectional nature of the survey prevents us from making conclusions about the causality of these associations, but the fact that depressive symptoms are more common in those with disability and financial insecurity indicates the need for more social support for the elderly. Increasing rates of dementia have also been reported by regional studies in the country, indicating the need to develop geriatric psychiatry services (de Silva et al., 2003). At present, community-based support services for elderly people with dementia are minimal, and the burden of long-term care falls almost entirely on the family.

4.5 Children and Adolescents

A cross-sectional study conducted in the Sabaragamuwa Province found concerning levels of psychiatric morbidity among teenagers—36% of adolescents screened positive for depression (19% being severely depressed) and 28% for severe anxiety (Rodrigo et al., 2010). Psychological morbidity was significantly higher in students who were facing barrier examinations at the end of the year, reflecting the relationship between educational pressures and psychiatric morbidity in the teenage population (Rodrigo et al., 2010). Research conducted on schoolchildren in the North Eastern Provinces after the ethnic conflict suggested that up to 30% were experiencing symptoms of PTSD, and 19%, features of depression, indicating the impact of the past conflict on the younger population in the country (Catani et al., 2008).

Another concern is the increasing use of substances among young people. A survey of school children aged 13–17 years has reported that the prevalence of current alcohol use (in the month prior to the survey) was 5.8% among boys and 1.1% among girls—the gender distribution of substance use among teenagers reflecting the overall societal gender distribution of substance use and misuse, in the country (Senanayake et al., 2018). Among teenagers, the prevalence of smoking was 6.4% and 0.7% in boys and girls, respectively, and the prevalence of other substance use was 4.1% and 1.1%, respectively (Senanayake et al., 2018). Of concern is the finding that 42.5% who had taken more than a sip of alcohol had imbibed their first drink before the age of 14 years (Senanayake et al., 2018).

5 Mental Health Services in Sri Lanka

When considering the psychiatry services in Sri Lanka from the time the country gained independence in 1945, there is no doubt that there has been a massive increase in infrastructure and resources in mental health in the country. From a single mental health asylum in Angoda, psychiatry services have now branched out to almost all districts in the country. The PGIM and the Ministry of Health together have facilitated the training of many specialists in psychiatry, as well as MoMHs, diplomates in psychiatry, community psychiatry nurses, psychiatric social workers and occupation therapists. Psychiatry is now a separate final-year subject in all medical faculties in the country, ensuring that all recently qualified doctors also have basic training in psychiatry.

5.1 Challenges in Service Provision

However many challenges still remain. Although services are distributed to most districts in the country, the distribution is still uneven, with more services and psychiatrists being clustered in urban areas, particularly the Western Province that includes the capital of Colombo. Rehabilitation services, for those with major psychiatric disorders and substance use disorders are limited, and provision for long-term residential care for the patients who need this is minimal. While psychiatry clinics and inpatient units have developed considerably, there is still a significant shortfall in psychiatry services extending into the community, with much of the community psychiatry care being placed upon patient families.

5.2 Shortfalls in Human Resources and the "Brain Drain"

There is also still a significant shortfall in human resources in psychiatry, ranging from psychiatrists to clinical psychologists, as described above. This shortage of resources is being greatly exacerbated following the 2022 economic crisis, due to the loss of trained psychiatrists, as well as other members of the psychiatry team, by migration overseas. As a result, some of the more recently established psychiatry units, particularly those in more peripheral areas of the country, have now become significantly short-staffed.

5.3 The Disconnect Between Services and the People—Stigma and Mental Health Literacy

Public awareness about mental illness has been gradually increasing during the past decades. Formal and informal programmes and awareness programmes about mental health issues are often conducted, particularly in urban areas. However, there are still shortfalls in mental health literacy in the community, and common problems such as depression may go undetected. Furthermore, the stigma surrounding mental illness is still marked and widely prevalent (Fernando et al., 2017). The occurrence of a mental illness is associated with a strong sense of shame, not only for the individual, but also for the family, and therefore, concerted efforts are made to "hide" the problem from society (Fernando et al., 2017). The stigma around mental illness may also colour the attitudes of health care professionals and even institutional responses, establishing further barriers against the provision of appropriate help for those in need, and this is similar to challenges described from neighbouring South Asian nations (Fernando et al., 2010; Shidhaye & Kermode, 2013). These are some of the factors that prevent people in need from seeking help from mental health services. Of course, other aspects also contribute—such as difficulty accessing services, and lack of services in distant areas. A further important factor is the faith and belief of the people in the community—people often ascribe to supernatural causes of mental illness. For example, the changes experienced in depression are sometimes ascribed to a "bad astrological time" or "evil spirits" (Abeyasinghe et al., 2012). Based on these belief systems, patients often seek alternate help, seek blessings or resort to traditional rituals to try to deal with the problem. This may be perceived by some as a less-stigmatized, more culturally accepted way of seeking help. Evidence suggests that some of the patients who seek treatment from Ayurveda health services do have high levels of psychological distress (Gunathilaka et al., 2019).

6 The Way Forward

Psychiatry services in Sri Lanka have come a long way indeed, from the days of the single Asylum in Angoda. During the past decades, psychiatry services have become decentralized, have extended to all districts of the country, a multitude of psychiatry specialists, diplomates and other team members have been trained, and mental health literacy is gradually shifting for the better in the community. And yet, much still remains to be done, and there is a long way to go. Listed below are suggested strategies to ease the current issues regarding psychiatry services in Sri Lanka:

- **Advocate with administrators and policy makers to continue to provide funds and support for the development of mental health services throughout Sri Lanka**:
  - In times of economic crisis, there is a risk that funding for mental health services will be sidelined as being of "less priority". Hence ongoing advocacy is essential.
- **Focus on ongoing development/maintenance of these psychiatry services in order to**:
  - Continue functioning psychiatry services in all districts
  - Ensure that essential medications in psychiatry are available in sufficient quantities
  - Develop community psychiatry services as advocated in the Mental Health Policy 2022
  - Focus on the development of services for the rehabilitation of people with substance use disorders and major psychiatric disorders.
- **With regards to the shortage of psychiatrists and trained psychiatry personal**:
  - Increase local training of psychiatrists, psychiatry diplomates, psychiatric nurses, social workers and occupational therapists. Facilitate training of clinical psychologists

- Ongoing psychiatry training and awareness programme for **non-psychiatry** healthcare professionals, particularly primary health care workers
- Promote collaboration with other allied services—such as social services—and enlist their involvement in the care of those with mental illness
- Continue psychiatry as a separate final-year subject for all medical undergraduates
- Promote general adult psychiatrists to also have "special areas of interest/training"—such as training in child and adolescent psychiatry—so that general adult psychiatrists can provide cover for sub-specialty areas until the shortfall of subspecialists becomes less
- Promote responsible alternate methods of providing services to distant areas, for example, via telepsychiatry.

- **Advocate with administrators and policy makers to update the current Mental Health Act as a matter of urgency**
- **Explore innovative ways of increasing public mental health literacy and reducing stigma associated with mental illness**
- **Work with the media to minimize the glamourization of suicide and self-harm**
- **Advocate for mental health support of special groups, for example**:
  - The elderly: Increase healthcare and community awareness about mental illness in the elderly, service provision and provision of social support
  - Adolescents: Work with families and the education sector to reduce exam stress, promote development of life skills and build closer links between schools and vocational pathways.

7 Conclusions

Sri Lanka has made important strides in the development of mental health services during the past decades. This includes the development of psychiatry services throughout the country, training of a multitude of psychiatrists and healthcare workers in psychiatry, development of an updated mental health policy and a dramatic reduction in rates of suicides after the mid-1990s. And yet, now we are facing new challenges, to which the country must adapt and find a way forward. Advocating strongly for the continued prioritization of mental health services in the country, promoting mental health training, especially for non-psychiatry healthcare professionals, and updating the Mental Health Act, are some of the key steps to consider in the next few years. There should also be a focus on developing community mental health services and integrating them with other locally available services to enable the provision of ground level psychosocial support and rehabilitation services. Increasing public health awareness about mental illness and how to seek help, and reducing the stigma around mental illness is another priority. By addressing these key areas, Sri Lanka will be better placed to provide mental health services throughout the country, ensuring that all people receive the mental support and care they need for their psychological well-being.

References

Abeyasinghe, D. R. R., Tennakoon, S., & Rajapakse, T. N. (2012). The development and validation of the Peradeniya depression Scale (PDS)—A culturally relevant tool for screening of depression in Sri Lanka. *Journal of Affective Disorders, 142*(1–3), 143–149. http://www.ncbi.nlm.nih.gov/entrez/query.fcgi?db=pubmed&cmd=Retrieve&dopt=AbstractPlus&list_uids=22877969

Abeyasinghe, R., & Gunnell, D. (2008). Psychological autopsy study of suicide in three rural and semi-rural districts of Sri Lanka. *Social Psychiatr Psychiatr Epidemiology, 43*(4), 280–285. http://www.ncbi.nlm.nih.gov/entrez/query.fcgi?db=pubmed&cmd=Retrieve&dopt=AbstractPlus&list_uids=18253684

Ariyasinghe, D., Abeysinghe, R., Siriwardhana, P., & Dassanayake, T. (2015). Prevalence of major depressive disorder among spouses of men who use Alcohol in a rural community in Central Sri Lanka. *Alcohol and Alcoholism, 50*(3), 328–332. https://doi.org/10.1093/alcalc/agu105

Attygalle, U. R. (2022). A family life cycle perspective on deliberate self-harm among adolescents: An initial qualitative study. *Asia Pacific Journal of Counselling and Psychotherapy, 13*(2), 125–133. https://doi.org/10.1080/21507686.2022.2098349

Ball, H. A., Siribaddana, S. H., Kovas, Y., Glozier, N., McGuffin, P., Sumathipala, A., & Hotopf, M. (2010). Epidemiology and symptomatology of depression in Sri Lanka: A cross-sectional population-based survey in Colombo District. *Journal of Affective Disorders, 123*(1–3), 188–196. https://doi.org/10.1016/j.jad.2009.08.014

Bandara, P., Page, A., Senarathna, L., Kidger, J., Feder, G., Gunnell, D., Rajapakse, T., & Knipe, D. (2022). Domestic violence and self-poisoning in Sri Lanka. *Psychological Medicine, 52*(6), 1183–1191. https://doi.org/10.1017/S0033291720002986

Bhalotra, S., Kambhampati, U., Rawlings, S., Siddique, Z. (2020). *Intimate partner violence. The influence of job opportunities for men and women.* World Bank Policy Research Working Paper, Issue. W. Bank.

Rodrigo, C., Gurusinghe, S. W. J., Wijeratne, T., Jayananda, G., Rajapakse, S. (2010). Symptoms of anxiety and depression in adolescent students; a perspective. *Child and Adolescent Psychiatry and Mental Health, 4*(10).

Catani, C., Jacob, N., Schauer, E., Kohila, M., & Neuner, F. (2008). Family violence, war, and natural disasters: A study of the effect of extreme stress on children's mental health in Sri Lanka. *BMC Psychiatry, 8,* 33. https://doi.org/10.1186/1471-244X-8-33

de Silva, H. A., Gunatilake, S. B., & Smith, A. D. (2003). Prevalence of dementia in a semi-urban population in Sri Lanka: Report from a regional survey. *International Journal of Geriatric Psychiatry, 18*(8), 711–715. https://doi.org/10.1002/gps.909

Fernando, S. M., Deane, F. P., & McLeod, H. J. (2010). Sri Lankan doctors' and medical undergraduates' attitudes towards mental illness. *Social Psychiatry and Psychiatric Epidemiology, 45*(7), 733–739. https://doi.org/10.1007/s00127-009-0113-6

Fernando, S. M., Deane, F. P., McLeod, H. J., & Davis, E. L. (2017). Carer burden and stigma in schizophrenia and affective disorders: Experiences from Sri Lanka. *Asian J Psychiatry, 26,* 77–81.

Gambheera, H. (2011). The evolution of psychiatric services in Sri Lanka. *South Asian Journal of Psychiatry, 2*(1), 25–27.

Gunathilaka, H. J., Vitharana, P., Udayanga, L., & Gunathilaka, N. (2019). Assessment of anxiety, depression, stress, and associated psychological morbidities among patients receiving ayurvedic treatment for different health issues: First study from Sri Lanka. *BioMed Research International, 2019,* 2940836. https://doi.org/10.1155/2019/2940836

Gunnell, D., Fernando, R., Hewagama, M., Priyangika, W. D. D., Konradsen, F., & Eddleston, M. (2007). The impact of pesticide regulations on suicide in Sri Lanka. *International Journal of Epidemiology, 36*(6), 1235–1242. http://www.ncbi.nlm.nih.gov/entrez/query.fcgi?db=pubmed&cmd=Retrieve&dopt=AbstractPlus&list_uids=17726039

Hapangama, A., Mendis, J., & Kuruppuarachchi, K. (2023). Why are we still living in the past? Sri Lanka needs urgent and timely reforms of its archaic mental health laws. *BJPsych International, 20*(1), 4–6. https://doi.org/10.1192/bji.2022.26

Husain, M. O., Umer, M., Taylor, P., Chaudhry, N., Kiran, T., Ansari, S., Chaudhry, I. B., & Husain, N. (2019). Demographic and psychosocial characteristics of self-harm: The Pakistan perspective. *Psychiatry Research, 279*, 201–206. https://doi.org/10.1016/j.psychres.2019.02.070

Ilic, M., & Ilic, I. (2022). Worldwide suicide mortality trends (2000–2019): A joinpoint regression analysis. *World Journal of Psychiatry, 12*(8), 1044–1060. https://doi.org/10.5498/wjp.v12.i8.1044

Knipe, D. W., Chang, S. S., Dawson, A., Eddleston, M., Konradsen, F., Metcalfe, C., & Gunnell, D. (2017). Suicide prevention through means restriction: Impact of the 2008–2011 pesticide restrictions on suicide in Sri Lanka. *Plos One, 12*(3), e0172893. https://doi.org/10.1371/journal.pone.0172893

Somatunga, L. C., Ratnayake, L. V. R., Wijesinghe, W. M. D. N. K., Yapa, Y. M. M. M., & Cooray, M. P. N. S. (2014). National alcohol use prevalence survey in Sri Lanka. *Journal of the Postgraduate Institute of Medicine, 1*(1), 1–12. https://doi.org/jpgim.7858

Malhotra, R., Chan, A., & Ostbye, T. (2010). Prevalence and correlates of clinically significant depressive symptoms among elderly people in Sri Lanka: Findings from a national survey. *International Psychogeriatrics, 22*(2), 227–236. https://doi.org/10.1017/S1041610209990871

Mendis, N. (2004). Mental Health Services in Sri Lanka. *Bulletin of the Board of International Affairs of the Royal College of Psychiatrists* (3).

Mills, J., & Jain, S. (2009). A disgrace to a civilised community': Colonial psychiatry and the visit of Edward Mapother to South Asia, 1937–8. *Clio Medica (Amsterdam, Netherlands), 86*, 223–242.

Mohanta, D., Tabassum, N., Sarker, P. S., Azad, K. A. K., & Karmaker, M. (2019). Pattern and outcome of self-poisoning among adult population admitted in a tertiary care hospital. *Journal of Medicine, 21*(1), 20–25. https://doi.org/10.3329/jom.v21i1.44096

Moscicki, E. K. (2001). Epidemiology of completed and attempted suicide: Toward a framework for prevention. *Clinical Neuroscience Research, 1*, 310–323.

Nugawela, M. D., Lewis, S., Szatkowski, L., & Langley, T. (2017). Rapidly increasing trend of recorded alcohol consumption since the end of the armed conflict in Sri Lanka. *Alcohol and Alcoholism, 52*(5), 550–556. https://doi.org/10.1093/alcalc/agx044

Pirkis, J., John, A., Shin, S., DelPozo-Banos, M., Arya, V., Analuisa-Aguilar, P., Appleby, L., Arensman, E., Bantjes, J., Baran, A., Bertolote, J. M., Borges, G., Brecic, P., Caine, E., Castelpietra, G., Chang, S. S., Colchester, D., Crompton, D., Curkovic, M., et al. (2021). Suicide trends in the early months of the COVID-19 pandemic: an interrupted time-series analysis of preliminary data from 21 countries. *Lancet Psychiatry, 8*(7), 579–588. https://doi.org/10.1016/S2215-0366(21)00091-2

Pushpakumara, P., Thennakoon, S. U. B., Rajapakse, T. N., Abeysinghe, R., & Dawson, A. H. (2019). A prospective study of repetition of self-harm following deliberate self-poisoning in rural Sri Lanka. *Plos One, 14*(2), e0199486. https://doi.org/10.1371/journal.pone.0199486

Pushpakumara, P., Dawson, A. H., Adikari, A. M. P., Thennakoon, S. U. B., Abeysinghe, R., & Rajapakse, T. N. (2021). Exploration of associations between deliberate self-poisoning and psychiatric disorders in rural Sri Lanka: A case-control study. *Plos One, 16*(8), e0255805. https://doi.org/10.1371/journal.pone.0255805

Rajapakse, T., Griffiths, K. M., & Christensen, H. (2013). Characteristics of non-fatal self-poisoning in Sri Lanka: A systematic review. *BMC Public Health, 13*(331).

Rajapakse, T., Christensen, H., Cotton, S., & Griffiths, K. M. (2016). Non-fatal self-poisoning across age groups, in Sri Lanka. *Asian Journal of Psychiatry, 19*, 79–84. https://doi.org/10.1016/j.ajp.2016.01.001

Rajapakse, T., Russell, A. E., Kidger, J., Bandara, P., Lopez-Lopez, J. A., Senarathna, L., Metcalfe, C., Gunnell, D., & Knipe, D. (2020). Childhood adversity and self-poisoning: A hospital case control study in Sri Lanka. *Plos One, 15*(11), e0242437. https://doi.org/10.1371/journal.pone.0242437

Rajapakse, T., Silva, T., Hettiarachchi, N. M., Gunnell, D., Metcalfe, C., Spittal, M. J., & Knipe, D. (2023). The impact of the COVID-19 pandemic and lockdowns on self-poisoning and suicide in sri lanka: An interrupted time series analysis. *International Journal of Environmental Research Public Health, 20*(3). https://doi.org/10.3390/ijerph20031833

Reeves, A., McKee, M., Gunnell, D., Chang, S. S., Basu, S., Barr, B., & Stuckler, D. (2015). Economic shocks, resilience, and male suicides in the great recession: Cross-national analysis of 20 EU countries. *European Journal of Public Health, 25*(3), 404–409. https://doi.org/10.1093/eurpub/cku168

Samarasinghe, D. S., Dissanayake, S. A., & Wijesinghe, C. P. (1987). Alcoholism in Sri Lanka: An epidemiological survey. *British Journal of Addiction, 82*(10), 1149–1153. http://www.ncbi.nlm.nih.gov/entrez/query.fcgi?db=pubmed&cmd=Retrieve&dopt=AbstractPlus&list_uids=3479164

Senanayake, S., Gunawardena, S., Kumbukage, M., Wickramasnghe, C., Gunawardena, N., Lokubalasooriya, A., & Peiris, R. (2018). Smoking, Alcohol consumption, and illegal substance Abuse among Adolescents in Sri Lanka: Results from Sri Lankan Global School-Based Health Survey 2016. *Advances in Public Health, 2018*, 1–7. https://doi.org/10.1155/2018/9724176

Shidhaye, R., & Kermode, M. (2013). Stigma and discrimination as a barrier to mental health service utilization in India. *International Health, 5*(1), 6–8. https://doi.org/10.1093/inthealth/ihs011

Sorensen, J. B., Pearson, M., Pushpakumara, J., Leth-Sorensen, D., Buhl, A., Konradsen, F., & Senarathna, L. (2023). Alcohol use, self-harm and suicide: A scoping review of its portrayal in the Sri Lankan literature. *Heliyon, 9*(7), e17566. https://doi.org/10.1016/j.heliyon.2023.e17566

United Nations Office on Drugs and Crime. (2008). *Rapid situation and response assessment of drugs and HIV in Bangladesh, Bhutan, India, Nepal and Sri Lanka. A Regional Report.*

Wang, W., Ranaweera, S., Amarasinghe, H., Chandraratne, N., Thavorncharoensap, M., Ranasinghe, T., Karunaratna, S., Kumara, D., Santatiwongchai, B., Chaikledkaew, U., Abeykoon, P., & De Silva, A. (2018). Economic costs of alcohol use in Sri Lanka. *Plos One, 13*(6). https://doi.org/10.1371/journal.pone.0198640

World Health Organization. (2008). *Integrating Mental Health Care into primary care: Global perspectives.*

Access to Mental Health Care in South Asia: Variations of Challenges and Ways Forward

Ravi Philip Rajkumar

Abstract The geographical region of South Asia includes eight countries: Afghanistan, Bangladesh, Bhutan, India, the Maldives, Nepal, Pakistan and Sri Lanka. Nearly a quarter of the world's mentally ill persons live in these countries. The countries of the South Asian region share certain common social, cultural and economic factors, but they also encompass a wide range of ethnicities, cultures, languages and religions, and each of them represents a unique socio-ecological system with a distinct profile of challenges and opportunities. This chapter compares the specific profiles of challenges and barriers to mental health care in each of the above countries, based on the most recent available data and literature. Following this, recent research on innovative methods of working around these challenges is summarized and critically reviewed. The information presented in this chapter could serve as a valuable starting point for those interested in addressing country-specific gaps in the available evidence, in developing specific mental health interventions, in evaluating existing services, and in advocating for changes in legislation and policy where acceptable.

Keywords Mental health care · Mental health gap · Mental health policy · Primary health care · Service evaluation · Social psychiatry · Stigma · South Asia

1 Introduction

The geographical region of South Asia includes eight countries: Afghanistan, Bangladesh, Bhutan, India, the Maldives, Nepal, Pakistan and Sri Lanka. This region accounts for nearly a quarter of the world's population or approximately 1.97 billion people (The World Bank, 2022). According to the 2019 Global Burden of Disease Study (GBD, 2019), there are approximately 236 million people suffering from a mental or behavioural disorder in South Asia, out of an estimated total of 970

R. P. Rajkumar (✉)
Department of Psychiatry, Jawaharlal Institute of Postgraduate Medical Education and Research (JIPMER), Puducherry, India
e-mail: ravi.psych@gmail.com

© The Author(s), under exclusive license to Springer Nature Singapore Pte Ltd. 2024
S. M. Y. Arafat and S. K. Kar (eds.), *Access to Mental Health Care in South Asia*,
https://doi.org/10.1007/978-981-99-9153-2_9

million worldwide. In other words, 24% of the world's mentally ill persons live in South Asia (Global Burden of Disease Collaborative Network, 2019). A comparison of GBD estimates over the period 1990–2019 shows that the number of persons living with mental illness in South Asia has increased by around 40% in the past three decades (Liu et al., 2020). These figures are most likely underestimates of the true scope of the problem: a recent umbrella review of South Asian studies found much higher prevalence rates for a wide range of mental disorders, particularly in vulnerable populations or sub-groups (Hossain et al., 2020).

The countries of the South Asian region share certain common social, cultural and economic factors. From an economic perspective, these countries are classified as low- and middle-income countries (LMICs) with low to medium levels of human development, and high levels of inequality in income, gender development, and access to education and basic medical care (United Nations Department of Economic & Social Affairs, 2020; United Nations Development Programme, 2022).

Socially, South Asian countries are characterized by collectivistic cultural values, which privilege the community or group over the individual (Pelham et al., 2022) and by a high cultural power distance, which indicates cultural tolerance of inequality (Hofstede Insights, 2022). These cultural values are associated with higher levels of group cohesion and social support, which can protect against the development of mental illness (Axinn et al., 2015). However, they are also associated with beliefs related to group or family shame and honour, leading to stigmatization and delays in treatment (Abdullah & Brown, 2011; Ran et al., 2021), and difficulties in identifying risk factors for mental illness, such as childhood sexual abuse and intimate partner violence (IPV) (Ahmad et al., 2009; Nadeem et al., 2020). Religion plays an important part in the lives of South Asian peoples. Though it can provide solace, support and a sense of meaning to the mentally ill and their caregivers (Chaudhry, 2008), it can also contribute to stigmatization through adherence to supernaturalistic explanatory models (Gurung et al., 2022; Kuek et al., 2023).

South Asian countries experience a significant burden of both communicable and non-communicable diseases. As a result of this, government funding for mental health is often limited: in countries such as Bangladesh and Nepal, mental health expenditure accounts for less than 1% of total health expenditure (Rajkumar, 2022; Saxena et al., 2003). This low level of investment in mental health is also reflected in a shortage of manpower (World Health Organization, 2021a). A high proportion of the population resides in rural areas where access to mental health care is limited (Bain & Adeagbo, 2022; Jayaram et al., 2011).

South Asian countries also experience vulnerabilities due to the social and economic changes brought about by globalization. Changes in cultural values, which are generally in the direction of greater individualism, have mixed and complex effects. On the one hand, they can encourage greater openness about mental health and illness, reduce stigmatization, and facilitate access to treatment. On the other hand, they can also weaken traditional social support systems and networks, increasing vulnerability to mental illness and suicide (Arnett, 1999; Dorji et al., 2017; Hamamura, 2017; Ogihara & Uchida, 2014). Cultural change can also lead to clashes between "old" and "new" beliefs and practices, some of which can have negative consequences for mental well-being (Sood, 2016). Increased industrialization and urbanization can contribute to social problems such as unemployment, overcrowding, substance abuse and pollution, all of which can have deleterious effects on mental health (Nambiar et al., 2017; Robertson, 2019). Changes in diet and activity levels can lead to an increase in non-communicable diseases, which are a risk factor for common mental disorders (CMD) (Ahmed et al., 2017; Shawon et al., 2022). Increased life expectancy, due to improved nutrition, sanitation, control of communicable diseases and economic development, has led to a concomitant increase in the need for geriatric mental health services (Mazumder et al., 2023).

For all these reasons, there is a substantial treatment gap for mental disorders in South Asia, as well as a vulnerability to increased mental morbidity in the face of large-scale crises. This was vividly illustrated during the recent COVID-19 pandemic, in which the prevalence of depression and anxiety rose to 34% and 40% respectively in South Asia (Hossain et al., 2021) and 5–8% of surveyed individuals reported suicidal ideation (Tanha et al., 2022). In such situations, those individuals most in need of mental health care often experience significant barriers to accessing it (Murphy et al., 2021). To a lesser extent, these "formidable barriers to a rapid and robust mental health response" exist whenever a South Asian country is affected by a natural disaster (Sobowale & Torous, 2016) or an economic or political crisis (World Health Organization, 2022a). Furthermore, experts in public health have identified climate change as a looming threat to mental health in South Asian countries, (Sharpe & Davison, 2021; Tiwari et al., 2022). For all these reasons, it is essential to identify and implement strategies to overcome or circumvent the barriers to effective mental health care in South Asian countries.

The enumeration of shared challenges to mental health care in South Asia is helpful from a conceptual perspective and can be of use when planning cross-national mental health initiatives. However, it should not be allowed to obscure the immense diversity that exists both between and within the individual nations of South Asia. These countries encompass a wide range of ethnicities, cultures, languages and religions, and each of them represents a unique socio-ecological system with a distinct profile of challenges. With this point of view in mind, the current chapter will review the existing literature on specific challenges and barriers to mental health care in each of the nine South Asian countries and construct a brief profile of each country. These profiles are based on the existing literature from each country, as well as on World Health Organization (WHO) statistics and reports. After this evidence is critically examined, specific strategies to surmount these barriers, or "ways forward," will be outlined. These strategies will be discussed using the WHO's guiding principles on mental health care as a conceptual framework, with a focus on recent initiatives and innovations from each individual country.

2 Variations on a Theme: Challenges to Mental Health Care in South Asia

The WHO's World Mental Health Report (World Health Organization, 2022b) specifies four domains that can be used to evaluate the quality of mental health care. These are (a) leadership and governance, (b) community-based services, (c) promotion and prevention, and (d) information, evidence and research. These four categories are heuristically useful in assessing and comparing the quality of mental health care across countries. Each of them can be used to develop indicators of the performance of mental health services, as explained below:

- The status of mental health legislation or governing bodies are indicators of governance,
- the level of integration of mental health care into primary care, or the availability of community-based rehabilitation services, is indicators of community-based service,
- the existence and functioning of specific mental health initiatives, such as suicide prevention programmes, can be used to gauge the efficacy of mental health promotion and prevention services, and
- the availability of data from national mental health surveys, or the availability of published research on mental health services, provides a measure of the level of information, evidence and research available in a given country.

In the following section, each of the eight South Asian countries will be compared in terms of these four categories based on available data from published literature, national mental health reports and WHO profiles. Two additional categories have also been added to provide a more complete picture. The first—pathways to care and stigma—will be used to compare the trajectories of help-seeking behaviour for mental illness in each country, as well as country-specific factors associated with stigmatization of persons with mental illness. The second—country-specific challenges—will examine other specific barriers, adversities or vulnerabilities related to mental health in each country, such as the effects of climate change, natural disasters or civil unrest. These six categories together provide a rough "360°" snapshot of mental health care challenges in South Asian countries.

2.1 *Leadership and Governance*

Effective leadership is required for the planning, implementation and monitoring of mental health services, as well as to safeguard the rights of persons with mental illness and their caregivers. This includes the formulation of a national mental health programme, the constitution and functioning of a governing body or authority for mental health, the enactment of specific laws related to the mentally ill, budgetary allocations for mental health, and the existence of similar policies and supervisory authorities at the regional or state level.

Cross-national assessments of existing mental health policies were published by the WHO in 2006 and in 2020. The 2006 evaluation covered only six South Asian countries, with no data on Bangladesh and Sri Lanka and found that five of these countries had mental health policies that had been developed over the previous two decades, with the earliest being in India in 1982 and the latest in Pakistan in 2003. Maldives did not have a national mental health policy at this point in time. The 2020 assessments, which were part of the WHO's mental health atlas, reported that there were well-defined national policies in all South Asian countries except Pakistan. The quality of these policies with reference to WHO and international human rights standards was rated as high (5 out of 5) in Afghanistan, Bangladesh, India, Maldives and Sri Lanka, and somewhat lower in Bhutan (3 out of 5) and Nepal (4 out of 5). It is important to note that specific allocations in terms of finance and personnel for the implementation of this policy were made only in three countries—Bangladesh, India and Sri Lanka (World Health Organization, 2017, 2020a, 2020b, 2020c, 2020d, 2020e, 2020f, 2020g).

Until the end of the Second World War, mental health legislation in South Asia was based on British colonial laws, such as the Lunacy Acts in India, Pakistan and Sri Lanka (Dey et al., 2019; Hapangama et al., 2023; Raza-ur-Rahman et al., 2015). Initial attempts at post-independence legislation were largely based on these laws and focused primarily on issues of admission, detention and discharge in specific mental health care facilities (Antony, 2000; Raza-ur-Rahman et al., 2015). A survey of existing mental health laws in South Asian countries, conducted as part of the WHO's Mental Health Atlas (2020) found evidence of updated mental health legislation in five South Asian countries—Afghanistan, Bangladesh, India, Pakistan, and Sri Lanka. All these laws received a rating of 5 on 5 with reference to human rights standards. However, Bhutan, Maldives and Nepal were not documented as having a specific mental health-related law. In these countries, some aspects of mental health law, such as the need for admission instead of incarceration for mentally ill offenders, are incorporated into penal laws (World Health Organization, 2022c). The need to formulate a law that is consistent with Nepal's mental health action plan has been emphasized by experts from this country (Rai et al., 2021a; Singh & Khadka, 2022).

Budgetary allocations provide another measure of a national government's commitment to mental health care. The WHO's mental health atlas provides data for six of the eight South Asian countries on this variable. When measured as the percentage of healthcare spending allotted to mental health care, this figure ranges from a minimum of 0.04% in Pakistan to a maximum of 4.2% in Afghanistan. Using the minimum cut-off of 1% suggested by Saxena et al. (2003), only two South Asian countries—Afghanistan and India—invest at least this portion of their health budget in mental health. An independent review found that budgetary allotments for mental health were at an acceptable level in India and Sri Lanka (1.7–2%) but were below the figure of 4–6% seen in two African countries (Raja et al., 2010).

A supervisory or governing body is essential in order to ensure that policies are implemented and enforced and that the rights of the mentally ill are protected. Based on data provided by the WHO, such a regulatory body for mental health exists only in three Asian countries—Afghanistan, Bangladesh and India. The Afghan authority is rated by the WHO as dysfunctional, while the authorities in Bangladesh and India are considered partially functional. Even where central authorities exist, as in India, state- or regional-level mental health authorities are still in the process of being constituted (Hongally et al., 2019).

These measures, by themselves, do not provide a complete picture of the state of mental health governance in each country. It is important that each country periodically assesses the performance of its own mental health care system, and uses this information to address shortcomings and improve service delivery. This has been done in India and Nepal. India's National Mental Health Survey (2015–16) identified specific deficits in governance and implementation, including inadequate infrastructure and personnel, inadequate coverage of certain districts and areas, deficits in allied care facilities such as de-addiction and rehabilitation, a lack of facilities for postgraduate education in psychiatry in some states, and a need for more well-defined state mental health policies (Gururaj et al., 2016b). Nepal's National Mental Health Survey (2020) focused more on individual and familial barriers, but also identified difficulties in accessing care in remote areas and costs of care (due to a lack of publicly-funded treatment) as factors that needed to be addressed at the level of policy and planning (Nepal Health Research Council, 2020).

The perspectives of local and regional policy makers regarding better mental health governance are also important, as they have a keener awareness of local realities and limitations. A qualitative study of respondents from 6 LMICs, including two South Asian countries (India and Nepal), identified certain strategies that were considered to be desirable in the context of good mental health governance. These included empowerment of regional or local policy-makers and managers, development of health infrastructure, accountability, engagement with patients and caregivers, and the development of locally feasible and acceptable strategies to improve mental health literacy (Petersen et al., 2017).

Effective governance can also be assessed by comparing the performance of mental health care systems over time. This can be done by comparing the WHO's older mental health care profiles for South Asian countries, compiled in the period 2006–2009 (WHO & Ministry of Health, 2006, 2006a, 2006b, 2007a, 2007b, 2009), with the more recent Mental Health Atlas data collected in 2017–2020 (World Health Organization, 2017, 2020a, 2020b, 2020c, 2020d, 2020e, 2020f, 2020g). Definite improvements have been noted in some domains for most South Asian countries over this period. Funding for mental health was increased in Afghanistan; mental health regulatory bodies were constituted in Afghanistan and Bangladesh; national mental health programmes were formulated in Maldives and Nepal; postgraduate education in psychiatry was made fully functional in Nepal; and at least one new mental health prevention and promotion programmes was initiated in all of the South Asian countries. However, no improvement was noted in certain other domains, such as the availability of allied mental health professionals, and mental health-related funding decreased over this period in Bhutan and Pakistan. Overall, this suggests that progress in mental health systems has been uneven over the past two decades, underlining the need for better long-term governance.

2.2 Community-Based Service

To be effective, acceptable and accessible, mental health services should not be separated or confined solely to specific hospitals or institutions. Instead, they should be integrated into primary health care at the community and district levels and should exist alongside treatment facilities for communicable and non-communicable diseases (Hanlon et al., 2016; Petersen et al., 2017).

The WHO's Mental Health Atlas provides estimates of the extent to which mental health care is integrated into primary health care for seven of the eight South Asian countries, rated on a scale of 0–5. Scores of 4 or 5 indicate a good level of functional integration. Of these countries, only Bhutan received a score of 5 on 5. Afghanistan, Bangladesh, Nepal and Pakistan received a score of 3, while Sri Lanka and the Maldives received scores below 3 (World Health Organization, 2017, 2020a, 2020b, 2020c, 2020d, 2020e, 2020f, 2020g). This suggests that the availability of adequate community-based mental health care is below par in most of South Asia.

The consequences of this lack of adequate community care have been addressed by researchers from each country. For example, in Afghanistan, many consultations occur in private clinics and involve out-of-pocket expenditure on the part of patients and caregivers (Kovess-Masfety et al., 2021a). A qualitative study from Bangladesh found that most primary care facilities were not equipped to deliver adequate treatment for mental illness or substance use disorder, even though this was identified as a priority by national policy-makers (Islam et al., 2022). Pelzang (2012) examined the situation in Bhutan and found that though integration of mental health into primary care was enshrined in national policy, this goal was not yet fully achieved at the ground level due to a lack of infrastructure; as a result, many patients diagnosed at the primary level actually received treatment from secondary or tertiary-level hospitals. In India, integration of mental health into primary care has been implemented for four decades, following the pioneering District Mental Health initiatives of 1982; however, there is marked variability in service availability and outcomes, particularly in districts or states with low resources (Ramaswamy et al., 2018). A qualitative study from Nepal found that patients and caregivers were generally satisfied with the availability of mental health care at the primary level. Nevertheless, they reported difficulties related to frequent changes in personnel, periodic shortages of medications, and a lack of privacy (Luitel et al., 2020). In contrast to this result, a qualitative study from Pakistan examined the perspectives of health care professionals, including primary care staff, on the integration of mental health care at the community level. Though they recognized the importance of providing integrated care, they also cited several difficulties, including a lack of systemic support, resource shortages, and a difficulty in taking on additional responsibilities due to their current heavy workload (Hussain et al., 2018).

Another measure of the level of integration of mental health into primary health care is the proportion of funding for mental health that is assigned to primary health, as opposed to separate psychiatric hospitals. Based on WHO data (World Health Organization, 2020a, 2020b, 2020c, 2020d, 2020e, 2020f, 2020g), it was found that 100% of mental health funding in Afghanistan and Maldives was allocated to psychiatric hospitals. In contrast, this allocation was only 20% in Nepal, indicating a relatively higher availability of funds for primary mental health care. More flexible allotments were seen in Bangladesh, Bhutan and Pakistan, with no fixed amount allotted for psychiatric hospitals. Though the Mental Health Atlas did not provide any specific data on India, the Centre for Mental Health Law and Policy (CMHLP), a non-governmental organization (NGO) founded in 2007, provides data on the best estimates of budgetary allotment for mental health. The most recent CMHLP report (2022–23) noted that there was a reduction in funding for tertiary-level hospitals, a strengthening of primary and secondary-level care, and a new allotment of funds for a telepsychiatry project that aims to bridge the treatment gap in remote and rural areas (Keshav Desiraju Indian Mental Health Observatory, 2022).

Many mental illnesses are chronic and require rehabilitation and long-term follow-up, which should ideally be provided in the community. Only three countries have published reports on the state of these facilities at the primary care level, and only two of these reports are recent. A joint assessment of the state of mental health in Pakistan, conducted by the national Ministry of Health and the WHO, reported a shortage of rehabilitation facilities at the primary level in 2006 (WHO& Ministry of Health, 2019). The comprehensive survey of mental health systems undertaken during India's National Mental Health Survey identified deficits in both rehabilitation and substance use facilities in primary care (Gururaj et al., 2016b). In a qualitative study of patients and caregivers from Nepal, the level of services for rehabilitation in the community was rated as often inadequate (Koly et al., 2021).

2.3 Promotion and Prevention

Mental health care encompasses both the treatment of specific disorders and programmes or interventions designed to prevent specific outcomes or to promote mental health in individuals and groups. Examples of such programmes include suicide prevention (Borah et al., 2023), school mental health (Kumar, 2021), maternal mental health (Akter et al., 2020) and disaster or emergency mental health readiness (Newnham et al., 2020). Though such preventive and health promotion initiatives are of vital importance, they are often assigned a low priority in South Asian countries due to a lack of resources and investment (Kumar, 2021; Sood et al., 2017).

In the WHO's Mental Health Atlas, the presence of at least two functional programmes was used as an index of the adequacy of mental health promotion and prevention (World Health Organization, 2021a). Based on the available data, three countries (Bangladesh, Bhutan and Sri Lanka) have seven such programmes, Afghanistan and India have four, Nepal has three, and Maldives and Pakistan have only two. When considering the actual functioning of these programmes, Bangladesh, Bhutan, India, Pakistan and Sri Lanka were rated as having fully functional programmes. In Afghanistan, three of the four programmes were functional, but these were being run by NGOs and not the national government. In Nepal, only one of the three programmes, related to early child development, was considered to be running effectively, and there was no data on the status of Maldives' two promotion and prevention programmes (World Health Organization, 2020a, 2020b, 2020c, 2020d, 2020e, 2020f, 2020g).

The WHO provides seven broad categories of mental health promotion and prevention programmes: (i) suicide prevention, (ii) mental health awareness and stigma reduction, (iii) early child mental health, (iv) school mental health, (v) parental or maternal mental health, (vi) occupational mental health, and (vii) disaster and emergency mental health. As mentioned above, only Bangladesh, Bhutan and Sri Lanka have well-defined programmes addressing each of these seven categories.

Suicide prevention programmes are of particular importance from a public health perspective. South Asian suicide rates are higher than global averages, particularly among women. National suicide rates range from 2.7 to 16.5 per 100,000 in these countries, with particularly high rates observed in India (16.5 per 100,000) and Sri Lanka (14.2 per 100,000). Thus, the existence of a functioning national suicide prevention programme is another valuable indicator of mental health promotion and prevention. It is a matter of concern that only three of the eight South Asian countries—Bangladesh, Bhutan and Sri Lanka—were rated as having functioning suicide prevention programmes. No overall programme was identified in Afghanistan, Maldives, Nepal, or Pakistan as of 2020 (World Health Organization, 2020a, 2020b, 2020c, 2020d, 2020e, 2020f, 2020g). A comprehensive suicide prevention strategy was launched in India in 2022 (Ransing et al., 2023), based on surveillance, intersectoral collaboration, and the promotion of positive mental health in youth. Though no such strategy has been implemented in Nepal yet (Marahatta et al., 2017), a suicide prevention helpline was made active in 2021 on a pilot basis (World Health Organization, 2022d).

Similarly, initiatives to increase mental health awareness and reduce the stigma associated with mental illness are an essential part of mental health promotion, particularly in South Asia where mental health literacy is low (Dey et al., 2019; Petersen et al., 2017). On the basis of data collected by the WHO in 2017–2020 (World Health Organization, 2017, 2020a, 2020b, 2020c, 2020d, 2020e, 2020f, 2020g), it was found that four South Asian countries (Afghanistan, Bhutan, India and Sri Lanka) had a broad-based programme aimed at improving mental health awareness and combating stigma. This programme was run by an NGO in Afghanistan and by the national government in the other three countries. In Bangladesh and Nepal, programmes existed but their scope was much narrower—in Bangladesh, the focus was on media sensitization regarding mental illness and suicide reporting, while in Nepal, the focus was on annual Mental Health Day commemorations. Of these two, only the programme in Bangladesh was rated as functional. The limitations of the existing initiatives in Nepal were outlined in a review by Gurung et al. (2022). Maldives and Pakistan did not have any programme addressing this issue, despite the high need for such initiatives (WHO & Ministry of Health, 2006, 2009; Mohamed, 2015; Husain, 2020).

It should also be noted that even where such programmes are implemented and supported by governments, they can encounter significant difficulties at the ground level that lower their efficacy and impact. For example, staff involved in a stigma reduction programme in India reported significant limitations related to logistics, community engagement, and low levels of baseline mental health literacy (Kallakuri et al., 2021).

2.4 *Information, Evidence and Research*

The development, scaling and implementation of mental health care facilities and interventions requires accurate data on service requirements and on the prevalence of specific disorders. Moreover, any interventions provided should be based on the best available evidence and should be evaluated for efficacy in their local context (World Health Organization, 2021a, 2021c).

The best data on the burden of mental illness in a given country can be obtained from national epidemiologic surveys. Such large-scale surveys have been conducted in Afghanistan, Bhutan, India and Nepal.

The Afghan National Mental Health Survey was conducted through a public-private partnership and covered 16 of the country's 34 provinces. The results of this survey showed that the estimated prevalence of mental disorders was around 11% for depression, 5% for post-traumatic stress disorder (PTSD), and 3% for generalized anxiety disorder. The frequency of lifetime suicidal ideation was 7% (Kovess-Masfety et al., 2021a, 2021b; Sabawoon et al., 2022).

The prevalence of common mental disorders in Bhutan was surveyed as part of the Gross National Happiness Study, conducted in 2015. In this survey, the estimated prevalence of CMDs in the general population was 29%. However, this study was based on a single screening tool, the General Health Questionnaire (GHQ-12), and did not cover other types of mental disorder (Sithey et al., 2018).

In India, the National Mental Health Survey (NMHS) was conducted as a joint initiative between the Ministry of Health and Family Welfare and the National Institute of Mental Health and Neuro Sciences (NIMHANS). This survey examined the prevalence, correlates and treatment outcomes of all categories of mental disorder across twelve of India's 28 states, (Gururaj et al., 2016a, 2016b). The NMHS found that the prevalence of mental disorders in India was 10.7%, with CMD accounting for over 85% of this figure. 4.7% had a lifetime alcohol use disorder, and 21% had a lifetime nicotine use disorder. Apart from this survey, the Government of India, in collaboration with the All-India Institute of Medical Science (AIIMS), conducted the National Survey on Extent and Patterns of Substance Use in India in 2019 (Ministry of Social Justice and Empowerment, Government of India and National Drug Dependence Treatment Centre, All India Institute of Medical Sciences, 2019). This study covered all the states of India and found a similar prevalence of alcohol use disorders (4.6%) but also noted high rates of disorders related to the use of cannabis (2.8%) and opioids (2.1%) (Singh, 2020).

The complete results of Nepal's National Mental Health Survey were published in 2020 (Nepal Health Research Council, 2020). This nation-wide initiative surveyed both adults and adolescents. The lifetime prevalence of mental disorders was found to be 10% in adults and 5.2% in adolescents, with CMD accounting for 60–65% of this figure.

As national surveys require significant commitments in terms of manpower, infrastructure and time, local or regional surveys provide an acceptable alternative in terms of estimating the burden of mental illness in a given country. The WHO Mental Health Atlas provides estimates of the number of relevant publications in this field for seven of the eight South Asian countries. Pakistan, Nepal and Bangladesh had a relatively high research output, while Afghanistan and Bhutan had the lowest (World Health Organization, 2020a, 2020b, 2020c, 2020d, 2020e, 2020f, 2020g).

Independent reviews have also examined the mental health research output of South Asian countries. A meta-analysis of the global prevalence of CMDs identified eleven epidemiological studies of good quality that met criteria for inclusion in subsequent analyses—six from India, four from Pakistan and one from Bangladesh (Steel et al., 2014). A later review of studies conducted during the first year of the COVID-19 pandemic, covering both Africa and Asia, retrieved 133 publications of relevance. Of these, 111 (83%) were from three South Asian countries—India, Pakistan and Bangladesh—with India alone accounting for 87 (65%) of published papers (Kar et al., 2020). The findings of both these reviews suggest that these three countries outperform other South Asian countries in terms of actionable mental health research. Apart from these qualitative findings, Roche et al. (2021) examined the limitations related to mental health research in countries from the Asia-Pacific region, including India and Nepal, and identified a lack of specific funding for such research as a key barrier in this regard.

Mental health research also requires the availability of trained investigators with postgraduate or doctoral training in mental health-related disciplines such as psychiatry, clinical psychology, psychiatric social work and psychiatric nursing. Among South Asian countries, Bhutan, and Maldives lack facilities for training doctors and allied professionals in these disciplines, and those who wish to pursue higher education in this field must do so in other countries, particularly in India (WHO & Ministry of Health, 2006, 2007a). In Nepal, postgraduate education in psychiatry has been available only for the last two decades, and training in certain areas or sub-specialties is still in its infancy (Rai et al., 2021b; World Health Organization, 2020e). It is likely that improvements in the quality and quantity of research in these South Asian countries will require further developments in education and training.

2.5 Pathways to Care and Stigma

In order to improve mental health care, it is important not only to provide adequate services, but to ensure that they are utilized by those in need of such care. In order to attain this goal, it is important to identify and quantify factors that impede access to mental health care. This can be done by examining two key factors: the process of help-seeking for mental illness in each country, and negative beliefs and attitudes that hinder help-seeking.

2.5.1 Pathways to Care

The term "pathways to care" refers to the pattern and trajectory of help-seeking behaviour taken by patients and caregivers. It encompasses all help-seeking measures undertaken from the time of the appearance of symptoms to the time care is sought from the mental health system. According to international experts, studying patients' pathways to care is a "valid and cost-effective" measure of assessing both access to mental health treatment and the barriers encountered during the process of help-seeking (Volpe et al., 2015). Among the countries of South Asia, research on pathways to care has been conducted in Bangladesh, India, Nepal, Pakistan and Sri Lanka, with the majority of studies arising from India. There are no studies on pathways to psychiatric care in Afghanistan, Bhutan or Maldives.

Indian studies have been conducted both in patients with mental illness in general, and in special populations such as children and the elderly. On reviewing these studies, it was found that patients with psychosis were often (18–46%) taken to a faith healer before seeking psychiatric treatment. Similar results were observed in patients with bipolar disorder; 33% of these patients' first point of contact was with a faith healer. 44–62% of these patients directly sought treatment from a mental health professional (Khemani et al., 2020; Nebhinani et al., 2022; Sahu et al., 2019; Singh et al., 2023). In contrast, patients with depression were less likely (6%) to receive initial care from a faith healer (Nebhinani et al., 2022). In studies involving more heterogeneous groups of patients with mental illnesses, both common and severe, it was found that around 40% sought help directly from a mental health care facility. However, delays of around six months before contact with a psychiatrist were common, and around 57% had sought help from two or more "other" sources, such as faith healers, general physicians, or practitioners of traditional medicine, prior to this (Goyal et al., 2022; Jain et al., 2012; Prabhu et al., 2015). In children, the most notable finding was a much longer delay in arriving at appropriate care when compared to adults, sometimes extending to as long as five or ten years. Parents' levels of mental health literacy were low, and help was initially sought from relatives, teachers, general physicians or paediatricians. Contacts with traditional or faith healers were relatively less, ranging from 12 to 20% (Anand et al., 2018; Chakraborthy et al., 2014; Joseph et al., 2020). In the elderly, it was found that there was a low awareness of dementia and related conditions among both caregivers and medical professionals, leading to delays in diagnosis. Moreover, there was a shortage of mental health facilities equipped to manage this patient population (Thomas et al., 2023).

Three studies have examined pathways to mental health care in Nepal. Their results suggest that the most common point of first contact is a general physician or doctor in a hospital (30%), with only 26% consulting a psychiatrist directly. Initial contacts with faith healers were relatively less common in patients with CMDs (28%) but were seen in almost half of patients with severe mental illness (Adhikari & Jha, 2021; Gupta et al., 2021; Kisa et al., 2016).

A review of studies from Bangladesh found that only around 16–28% sought help from a psychiatric care provider directly. Most first contacts were with general physicians in hospital or private sector settings (44%), and 22–30% sought help from a traditional medicine practitioner or faith healer. The average number of "steps" along the pathway to care before contacting mental health services was 2.5–3. Referrals from a general medical to a psychiatric setting were made by 70% of hospital physicians, but only 40% of private physicians. There was a wide range of delays in help-seeking. Paradoxically, faith healers or traditional practitioners referred patients for psychiatric care early, after 5–7 weeks, while it took over 20 weeks for private physicians to refer patients to mental health care facilities (Giasuddin et al., 2012; Nuri et al., 2018).

In Pakistan, pathways to care have been studied only in patients with severe mental illness. 43% of patients were directly taken to a psychiatrist, while the rest initially contacted faith healers (15%), general physicians (5%), or did not seek any formal treatment beyond support from others in the community. Psychiatrists were the second point of contact in 47%, while 4% consulted a clinical psychologist (Naqvi et al., 2009). In contrast, a study of patients seeking treatment at an out-patient clinic in Sri Lanka found that over half of patients sought psychiatric care directly. The remainder contacted general physicians (24%), faith healers (19%) or Ayurvedic medicine practitioners (3%). 15% of respondents believed that their illness had a supernatural cause, and 17% thought their symptoms would resolve spontaneously over time: these beliefs were associated with delays in appropriate treatment (Gomez et al., 2017).

2.5.2 Stigma

The term "stigma" is derived from an ancient Greek word meaning a mark or sign and originally referred to the marks inflicted on slaves or criminals. In the context of mental health care, stigma refers to a complex combination of negative beliefs, attitudes and behaviours towards persons with mental illness. Stigma leads to discrimination and violence against the mentally ill, exclusion from society, and is one of the chief barriers to accessing appropriate treatment (Makhmud et al., 2022). Experiences of stigma can also cause persons with mental illness to perceive themselves negatively (e.g., as inferior, dangerous, or incurable), causing low self-esteem, demoralization, and further delays or interruptions in treatment: this is known as "self-stigma" (Lucksted & Drapalski, 2015).

Several studies from South Asian countries have identified stigma as a barrier to timely mental health care. In Bangladesh, both youth and women reported that their willingness to seek such care was negatively influenced by societal attitudes, which were encountered among peers, members of the community, and even family members (Koly et al., 2022; Sifat et al., 2022). In Bhutan, stigma was found to be strongly related to supernaturalistic beliefs about the causes of mental illness, such as black magic, curses, or *karma* (retribution for misdeeds in a past life); this was found to interfere with both mental health care and suicide prevention initiatives (Dorji et al., 2017; Pelzang, 2012). In India, stigma appears to be more of a social phenomenon. For example, students with mental illness face stigmatization from teachers (Raghavan & Sanjana, 2022), patients with mental illness were seen as "unmarriageable" or "unemployable" (Patra et al., 2022; Raghavan et al., 2023) and as bringing shame to the family as a whole (Raghavan et al., 2023). Self-stigma was more evident in respondents from urban areas (Patra et al., 2022). Similar findings about the perceived dangerousness, "incurability", and lack of fitness for marriage or employment of the mentally ill were observed in a survey of respondents from Afghanistan. A novel finding from this country was that formal diagnostic labels for mental illness, such as "depression", were themselves associated with stigma (Nine et al., 2022). A comprehensive review of stigma in Nepal (Gurung et al., 2022) found that it was a complex and multifaceted phenomenon. The core beliefs associated with stigma were similar to those noted in Bhutan (fate, magic, curses), while its social consequences were similar to those noted in India. Besides delays in treatment, stigma was associated with various experiences of discrimination in both India and Nepal, including verbal abuse, rejection, and even forced confinement and physical restraint in some cases (Gupta et al., 2021; Pham et al., 2021; Sathyanath et al., 2023). In Bangladesh, India, and Nepal, it was observed that stigma and discrimination had an intersectional dimension: in other words, persons with mental illness were more likely to experience stigma if they also belonged to a socially disadvantaged or "lower group", in terms of either gender, caste or socioeconomic status (Faruk & Rosenbaum, 2023; Goswami, 2021).

Though stigma has its origins in cultural attitudes, beliefs and values, it can be perpetuated—or attenuated—by the effects of mass media, both conventional and electronic. Two studies from India found that media reports on mental illness echoed the social prejudices associated with stigma: patients with mental illness were portrayed as "dangerous", "unpredictable", "unreliable", "unstable" and even as prone to committing violent crimes, such as sexual assault or homicide (Raj et al., 2021; Arneaud et al., 2023). A survey of media personnel from Bangladesh found that the majority of respondents perceived a need to improve portrayals of mental illness in the media; however, they were less certain about the importance of changing societal beliefs in this regard. Several of these personnel felt that they would benefit from training to improve their knowledge and attitudes towards mental illness, suggesting that this approach could be beneficial in improving the quality of reporting on mental illness (Shalahuddin Qusar et al., 2022).

Stigmatization of persons with mental illness by healthcare professionals is also an important aspect of the phenomenon of stigma, and it is particularly relevant when considering delays or barriers related to mental health care. This aspect of stigma has been studied in India, Pakistan, and Sri Lanka. Research from India found that mental illness-related stigma among healthcare students and professionals was of a low to moderate level, was often covert, and could be noted at both individual and structural levels. Though many of the surveyed respondents were willing to treat persons with mental illness, they were less accepting of such persons regarding marriage, employment, or living together in the same neighbourhood. It was also found that certain diagnoses, such as schizophrenia and substance use disorders, were associated with higher levels of stigma (Challapallisri & Dempster, 2015; Chandramouleeswaran et al., 2017; Munisami et al., 2021; Poreddi et al., 2015; Satyanath et al., 2016). In Pakistan, around half of surveyed students and professionals had negative attitudes towards mental illness, though their attitudes regarding treatment were less negative. Moreover, over one-third of students believed that persons with mental illness should seek help from family members rather than from professionals (Abdullah et al., 2021; Laraib et al., 2018; Naeem et al., 2006). Two studies from Sri Lanka examined mental illness-related stigma in medical students, doctors and nurses. In this setting, it was observed that substance use disorders were more stigmatized than mental illnesses, and that individual psychological factors, such as mindfulness and compassion, were negatively associated with stigma and social rejection (Baminiwatta et al., 2023; Fernando et al., 2010).

2.6 Other Country-Specific Challenges

Certain specific challenges related to mental health care do not fit into the above five categories but have a substantial impact on treatment access, availability and quality. These challenges, and their specific relevance to each South Asian country, are summarized in Table 1.

Some of these problems, such as a shortage of mental health professionals to deliver psychosocial interventions, are common to all South Asian countries, while others are related to geographical, cultural or political factors that are specific to a given country. It is also important to note that problems such as intimate partner violence, disaster preparedness, or a lack of inclusive education for children with mental disorders have a broader social and political context. These challenges cannot be addressed within the mental health care system alone and require effective intersectoral collaboration.

3 Ways Forward: General Principles, Local Solutions

During the Cold War, the president of Finland, Urho Kekkonen, was questioned about his country's foreign policy, which involved cautious diplomatic engagement with both Russia and Western countries. His defence of this policy was expressed in the

Table 1 Other specific challenges related to mental health care in South Asian countries

Category	Country-specific factors and findings
Climate change	• Specific challenges to physical, mental and social well-being are posed by rising sea levels in Maldives (WHO & Ministry of Health, 2006a) • Mental health risks related to flooding may be exacerbated by climate change in Bangladesh (Wahid et al., 2023), India (Pal et al., 2022) and Pakistan (Riaz et al., 2023)
Natural disasters	Regional proneness to specific types of disasters, such as • the 2004 South Asian tsunami affecting India, Maldives and Sri Lanka (Becker, 2007; Ibrahim & Hameed, 2006; Schenk & Bui, 2018) • earthquakes in Afghanistan (Kovess-Masfety et al., 2021a, 2021b) Disaster mental health readiness has been identified as low in Pakistan (Ochani et al., 2022)
Social, political or economic instability	• Civil unrest can be associated with increased mental morbidity and difficulties in help-seeking. This has been documented in Afghanistan (Sabawoon et al., 2022) and Sri Lanka (Doherty et al., 2019; Siriwardhana et al., 2015; Thomas et al., 2022) • Violent conflicts can lead to the destruction of existing health care infrastructure and delay or event completely prevent help-seeking for mental illness (Kovess-Masfety et al., 2021a, 2021b, 2022; Doherty et al., 2019) • An economic crisis, as recently seen in Sri Lanka, may lead to difficulties in sustaining mental health care infrastructure (World Health Organization, 2022a) • Specific challenges in terms of diagnosis, access and continuity of care are posed by forcibly displaced individuals or refugees, as noted in Bangladesh (Mistry et al., 2021) and Sri Lanka (Doherty et al., 2019; Thomas et al., 2022)
Mental health literacy	• Low mental health awareness and literacy is a problem common to all South Asian countries and has been identified as a significant barrier to mental health care in Afghanistan (Kovess-Masfety et al., 2021a, 2021b), Bangladesh (Koly et al., 2022; Sifat et al., 2022), India (Mehrotra et al., 2018), Pakistan (Munawar et al., 2020), Nepal (Devkota et al., 2021) and Sri Lanka (Ediriweera et al., 2012) • This problem is pervasive both in the general population and among the caregivers of persons with mental illness
Mental health awareness in non-psychiatric healthcare workers	• In Pakistan, mental illness makes up around 10% of the case load of general practitioners, but two-thirds were unaware of diagnostic criteria for common mental disorders, and overprescription of benzodiazepines was common (Naqvi et al., 2012)
Shortages of allied mental health professionals	• Low numbers of clinical psychologists, psychiatric social workers, occupational therapists and psychiatric nurses have been reported across all South Asian countries, both in the WHO reports (World Health Organization, 2017, 2020a, 2020b, 2020c, 2020d, 2020e, 2020f, 2020g) and in local reports from Bangladesh (Koly et al., 2021), Bhutan (Pelzang, 2012), India (Gururaj et al., 2016b; Lakshmana et al., 2022), and Pakistan (Jafree & Burhan, 2020) • This leads to deficits in access to psychosocial therapies and rehabilitation

(continued)

Table 1 (continued)

Category	Country-specific factors and findings
Shortages of other key mental health resources	• Shortages of essential psychiatric medications have been noted in Bangladesh (Rahman et al., 2022), Bhutan (Pelzang, 2012), Nepal (Rahman et al., 2022) and Pakistan (WHO & Ministry of Health, 2009) • Deficits in physical infrastructure were flagged as a matter of concern by patients, caregivers and mental health care workers in Afghanistan (Kovess-Masfety et al., 2021a, 2021b), Bhutan (Pelzang, 2012), India (Gururaj et al., 2016b) and Pakistan (Jafar et al., 2022) • Difficulties in maintaining physical records at the community level have been identified in India (Sriramalu et al., 2022) and may lead to problems with treatment adherence and continuity
Issues related to substance use disorders	• Certain countries may be more vulnerable to specific types of substance use disorder—for example, Afghanistan and Pakistan are located in the "Golden Crescent", an area characterized by high illicit opium production (Nafeh et al., 2022; Talpur & George, 2014) • Laws related to substance use have been described as unduly stringent or punitive in Afghanistan (Nafeh et al., 2022), Bangladesh (World Health Organization, 2021b), India (Rao et al., 2019) and Sri Lanka (Dissabandara et al., 2009). This may lead to persons with substance use disorders being incarcerated instead of receiving appropriate treatment • Facilities for the management of substance use are often inadequate. This has been noted in Afghanistan (Nafeh et al., 2022), India (Gururaj et al., 2016b) but has not been systematically studied in other South Asian countries • The medical model of substance use disorders is not widely known or accepted at the community level, leading to delays in seeking appropriate care (Balhara et al., 2016)
Community engagement	• Difficulties in engaging with or obtaining cooperation from local communities has been documented in Bangladesh (Koly et al., 2021), Bhutan (Dorji et al., 2017), India (Kallakuri et al., 2021; Thara et al., 2008) and Maldives (Mohamed, 2015)
Issues related to specific vulnerable populations	• Attitudinal, systemic and intersectoral barriers to mental health care for *children and adolescents* have been reported from India (Raghavan & Sanjana, 2022), Nepal (Atreya et al., 2023; Rai et al., 2021a, 2021b), Pakistan (Jafree & Burhan, 2020) and Sri Lanka (World Health Organization, 2022a). These include stigma, a lack of appropriate facilities and personnel, non-availability of inclusive education, and conflicts of interest with school management • Social and structural factors pose significant barriers to the delivery of *maternal mental health care* in Afghanistan (Tomlinson et al., 2020), India (Goswami, 2021) and Sri Lanka (Hapangama & Kuruppuarachchi, 2021). These include intimate partner violence, a lack of family support, dismissive attitudes from non-psychiatric medical personnel, and difficulties in integrating mental health into existing antenatal or postnatal care systems • A marked *urban-rural discrepancy* in the availability of mental health care facilities and manpower has been observed in several South Asian countries, including Bhutan (WHO & Ministry of Health, 2007a), Nepal (Jackson et al., 2022) and Pakistan (WHO & Ministry of Health, 2009). This leads to a significant mental health gap in persons from rural, remote and hilly areas • Research from India has found that even when *social welfare benefits* for patients with chronic mental illness are available, many patients cannot access them due to stringent eligibility criteria and complex bureaucratic procedures (Raghavan et al., 2021; Reddy et al., 2021)

following phrase: "Finlandization is not for export." By this, he meant that a policy that was effective and safe for Finland could not be blindly transplanted to another country. Though foreign policy and mental health policy are quite different from each other, the general principle holds good: solutions that are feasible and acceptable in one setting may fail in another (Diamond, 2019). A policy or model that is effective in India or Sri Lanka may not be effective in Pakistan or Nepal. Sometimes, it is possible to adapt an existing model to a new setting; at other times, this is not feasible, and indigenous plans and methods should be developed. Likewise, direct transfers of Western models of mental health care to the South Asian context have significant drawbacks, including medicalization, universalization and a neglect of the social roots of mental illness (Doherty et al., 2020; Rodrigo & Wimalasingham, 2006; Sinha, 2023). These factors lead to an over-emphasis on the disease model of mental illness, a neglect of the role of social and cultural factors in symptom formation and in recovery, and missed opportunities for intersectoral collaboration with social justice and welfare agencies. They also pose significant challenges when attempting to adapt Western training models and materials for use in South Asian countries (Kirmayer & Pedersen, 2014). This does not mean that Western models cannot be used in South Asian settings; rather, it implies that they need to be carefully adapted to local needs, strengths and limitations, taking into account the perspectives of both mental health professionals and service users.

The country-specific overview provided above is somewhat akin to the diagnostic evaluation conducted by a medical professional. Its chief purpose is to identify country-specific challenges and barriers to the delivery of accessible, affordable, and acceptable mental health care. Some of these challenges, such as stigma, are common to all countries; however, even here, the specific cultural and religious beliefs contributing to stigma vary from one country to another. Others, such as civil unrest or vulnerability to disasters, differ significantly across countries. It is important to take these factors into account to develop viable and sustainable policies and processes for the improvement of mental health care in each country. In fact, such an analysis needs to be taken further and to consider intra-country differences, both at the geographical level (e.g., across states, or between rural and urban regions) and in particular sections of a given society (e.g., women, the elderly, migrants, or members of ethnic and religious minorities). General principles and plans, outlined at the national and international level, remain important as guides to the development of local plans and initiatives as long as they are not used rigidly.

a. **The WHO's framework for transformation of mental health care**

In 2022, the WHO published its World Mental Health Report, based on the central theme "Transforming mental health for all" (World Health Organization, 2022b). The choice of words in this theme is significant. "Transformation" implies a need to re-imagine and re-orient mental health care along multiple axes rather than simply upgrade or modify existing services. "For all" emphasises that mental health care is a human right to be "valued, promoted and protected," in the words of WHO Director-General Tedros Ghebreyesus. In order to achieve this transformation, the WHO has provided a comprehensive plan which includes a list of six specific principles.

These are a set of six values that should guide the development, implementation and evaluation of mental health services. These are enumerated and explained in Table 2, with references to key WHO documents and relevant literature.

The implementation of these general principles should be tailored to the needs of a specific country. For example, if basic mental health infrastructure or governance is lacking, this should be a priority. If mental health funding is allocated mainly to specific hospitals, it can be redistributed to ensure the functioning of community mental health services. If the integration of mental health care into primary care is poor, this should be addressed through measures such as task-shifting, adequate training of non-specialists, and the development of a functioning referral system. If pharmacological therapies are not available, their supply should be ensured; on the other hand, if they are available and accessible, attention should be paid to the implementation of psychosocial interventions. Finally, if basic structures and programmes are functioning well in the short term, then attention should be paid to vulnerable or neglected populations, as well as to issues of follow-up, continuity of care, rehabilitation and reintegration into a community. If these long-term issues are not addressed, interventions and programmes may have good initial results but poor outcomes over longer periods of time (Thara et al., 2008). The final aim should be to promote recovery rather than to focus exclusively on diagnosis and symptomatic treatment. This is illustrated in Fig. 1.

Their treatment needs are stage-specific, and this should be matched by the availability of mental health care at each stage. Requirements at higher stages presuppose the availability of basic mental health care services and efficient intersectoral collaboration. A deficit at any stage can lead to a relapse.

With these general principles in mind, it is now possible to review some of the country-specific "ways forward" that have shown promise in improving or even "transforming" the quality and coverage of mental health care.

b. **Country-specific initiatives**

A summary of proposed or tested "ways forward" or "solutions" to existing gaps in mental health care is provided in Table 3. This table does not cover editorials or commentaries about mental health requirements in each country, or the various national mental health plans that have already been discussed in each country's profile. Instead, it focuses on recent studies or protocols that are being developed, implemented or are already complete.

These projects and trials cover a wide range of valuable interventions, ranging from the integration of mental health into primary care to the coverage of special or vulnerable populations. A note of caution is necessary when evaluating them, for the following reasons. First, many of these trials have relied on collaboration with researchers or institutes from high-income countries, raising concerns about long-term sustainability and replicability in the public sector. Second, while some projects have provided clear outcome measures such as response rates or cost-effectiveness, others have relied on more subjective indicators of performance, or are

Table 2 Principles and objectives of the WHO's comprehensive mental health action plan (World Health Organization, 2021c)

Principle	Definition
Universal coverage	• Mental health care should be available, accessible, and affordable for all (World Health Organization, 2022b) • Mental health care should be integrated into general/primary health care (World Health Organization and World Organization of Family Doctors, 2008) • Vulnerable and special populations should receive adequate coverage (World Health Organization, 2019)
Human rights	• Mental health care is a basic human right to be promoted and protected (World Health Organization, 2019, 2021c) • The human rights of persons with mental illness should be promoted. They should not be subjected to discrimination or ill-treatment of any sort (Saxena et al., 2007) • Laws and policies should be updated to ensure the above (Dey et al., 2019)
Empowerment of lived experience	• The voices of persons with mental illness and their caregivers should be heard at all levels of mental health care, and they should be actively involved in their own treatment (Funk et al., 2006; Saha, 2021) • Mental health literacy should be enhanced at the community level through inter-sectoral collaboration, and stigma reduction programmes should be implemented (Sequeira et al., 2022; Makhmud et al., 2022) • The specific cultural and spiritual beliefs and practices of patients, caregivers and communities should be respected, as long as they do not act as a barrier to treatment (Raguram et al., 2002; Sithey et al., 2018)
Life-course approach	• The specific mental health needs and concerns of distinct demographic groups should be considered when planning and developing services (Kaku et al., 2022; Mazumder et al., 2023) • Specific and clear plans for these groups should be developed and implemented (e.g., school mental health, maternal mental health, mental health of the elderly) (World Health Organization, 2021a) • Local threats and vulnerability factors should be taken into consideration (e.g., disaster preparedness) (Patel et al., 2011) • Suicide prevention programmes should address vulnerable groups or stages of the life cycle (Borah et al., 2023; O'Connor et al., 2023)

(continued)

Table 2 (continued)

Principle	Definition
Evidence-based practice	• Strategies and treatments should be based on the best available evidence (Papola et al., 2023) • Data on mental health indicators, both at the population level (e.g., suicide rates, prevalence of common mental disorders, mental health literacy) and at the clinic level (e.g., follow-up rates, adherence to treatment) should be collected and analyzed to guide further improvements (Thara et al., 2010; World Health Organization, 2021a, 2021c) • Mental health services should be held to a high standard of accountability (Devkota et al., 2023)
Multisectoral action	• Mental health is not the exclusive province of mental health professionals; it requires the harmonious interaction of all sectors of society (World Health Organization, 2004, 2021c) • Collaboration with various state and non-state actors is necessary at various levels—e.g., school mental health, social welfare, and employment opportunities for persons with mental illness, protection of women and children from abuse or violence, and addressing the broader social determinants of mental health (Nicaise et al., 2021; Okato et al., 2020) • Collaboration with "non-mental" health professionals and programmes is important to integrate mental health into broader healthcare contexts, such as maternal health and non-communicable disease treatment (Atif et al., 2015; Islam et al., 2022) • Public-private partnerships can be used both to improve mental health care services and to address the needs of specific groups (e.g., occupational mental health or women's mental health) (Owais et al., 2023; Patil et al., 2022)

Patient's status	1 Acutely ill, symptomatic, functionally impaired	2 Symptomatically better	3 Stable with residual or no symptoms	4 Long-term
Clinical management	• Risk management • Acute phase pharmacotherapy and brief psychotherapy	• Education of patient and caregiver • Identification of risk and protective factors • Stabilization phase pharmacotherapy and psychotherapy • Ensuring adherence	• Maintenance pharmacotherapy and psychotherapy • Functional assessment • Rehabilitation	• Recovery - achievement of best possible level of functioning in all domains • Reintegration into the community • Protection from abuse or discrimination
Mental health care system requirements	• Availability and accessibility of care • Basic diagnosis • Essential medications • Non-specialist psychological interventions • Referral system	• Continuity of care • Availability of clinical psychologists • Addressing self- and familial stigma • Social welfare measures for risk factors (e.g., IPV) • Psychosocial measures to improve adherence • Community-based support groups	• Community-based rehabilitation programmes • Availability of occupational therapists, psychiatric social workers • Intersectoral collaboration (e.g., for assistance regarding work or education) • Self-employment opportunities	• Stigma reduction and mental health awareness programmes • Community support groups • Intersectoral collaboration (as in stage 3) • Changes in legislation • Disability and other social welfare benefits

Fig. 1 Illustration of the typical course of events in a person with mental illness

Table 3 Proposed initiatives, innovations and "ways forward" to improve mental health in South Asian countries

Country	Programme	Category	Description
Afghanistan	Family resilience program (Haar et al., 2020)	Mental health promotion; child mental health; vulnerable population	Brief (3 weeks) programme effective in improving child behaviour and family functioning in a low-resource/conflict setting
Bangladesh	Psychosocial support and stimulation for pregnant and lactating mothers (Akter et al., 2020)	Maternal mental health; child mental health; community mental health	Continuous (up to 1 year) counselling and education on maternal depression, facilitation of breast feeding and infant stimulation; qualitatively reported as helpful by mothers
	Integration of mental health into primary care alongside non-communicable diseases (Naheed et al., 2022)	Primary care integration	Development of a protocol to assess the perspectives of patients, caregivers and healthcare workers on integration of mental health into primary health centres with good facilities for non-communicable disease management
India	Public-private partnered daycare (Patil et al., 2022)	Public-private partnership; rehabilitation	Development of a public-private partnership daycare centre for stable patients in a tertiary general hospital. 62% of enrolled patients are on regular follow-up, and 38% found some form of employment
	"Doorstep mental care" for severe mental illness (Menon et al., 2022)	Community mental health	Qualitative assessment of needs and challenges of caregivers and healthcare workers in a largely rural area; data used to develop a "doorstep care" model based on home visits, telepsychiatry, a telephonic helpline and development of educational material
	Teacher-delivered interventions for school mental health (Cruz et al., 2022)	Child mental health; adolescent mental health	Pilot study of teacher-delivered mental health care to a small group of school students. Mixed-methods assessment revealed acceptability by teachers and caregivers, but inconsistent responses from students; results confirmed feasibility but could not establish efficacy

(continued)

Table 3 (continued)

Country	Programme	Category	Description
	Pilot study of task-sharing and referral model (Devassy et al., 2022)	Community mental health	Community health workers and students trained in identifying mental illness and referring when necessary. Patients found the screening process acceptable and effective; referrals could be made in a stepped manner for mild and severe cases of depression
	Acceptability and feasibility of mental health care by community health workers (ASHAs) (Varshney et al., 2022)	Community mental health	Qualitative study of 34 ASHAs found a willingness to engage in mental health screening and care. Feasibility established for identification of severe mental illnesses; difficulty in identifying substance use disorders and CMD suggested need for better training and incentives
	Comparison of tele-mentoring with traditional training of primary healthcare workers (Kumar et al., 2020)	Primary care integration; substance use disorder treatment	Two randomized controlled trials planned to compare tele-mentoring with existing training programmes for skill development in primary health care physicians and staff, covering both mental illness and alcohol use disorders
	Mobile phone-based adjuncts to care (Sreejith & Menon, 2019)	Continuity of care; rehabilitation	A survey of 75 patients with severe mental illness found that phone-based approaches were acceptable. Few respondents reported barriers to phone use. Felt needs included medication and appointment reminders, crisis counselling and information about available services
	Training in knowledge, attitudes and practices for medical students (Pal et al., 2022; Praharaj et al., 2021)	Stigma reduction	Educational modules improved knowledge and attitudes towards mental illness in medical students, but effects on stigma and empathy were inconclusive

(continued)

Table 3 (continued)

Country	Programme	Category	Description
Nepal	Collaborative care for depression in a rural area (Rimal et al., 2021)	Primary care integration	The collaborative care model involved primary healthcare workers as the main agents of care, under supervision and with the collaboration of mental health professionals. Model adapted to suit local conditions. 49% of a cohort of patients with moderate to severe depression responded well to treatment under this model
	Stigma reduction among primary care providers (Kaiser et al., 2022)	Stigma reduction	Comparison of standard training based on WHO guidelines with a model involving exposure to photographic narratives and social contact with recovered or treated persons with mental illness. Both interventions reduced stigma, improved interactions between providers and patients, and increased providers' willingness to treat mental illness
	Delivery of psychological interventions by primary care workers (Aldridge et al., 2022)	Primary care integration	Comparison of a psychological intervention based on behavioral activation, implemented by primary care providers, with treatment as usual for depression. Addition of the psychological intervention was found to be cost-effective and improved patients' quality of life
Pakistan	Training of physicians and support staff serving an internally displaced population based on the WHO mhGAP (Humayun et al., 2017)	Primary care integration; vulnerable population	mhGAP training was feasible in primary care personnel in a conflict area, and resulted in a statistically significant increase in knowledge related to mental illness
	Use of peer volunteers in providing maternal mental health care (Atif et al., 2016, 2019)	Community mental health; maternal mental health	Baseline qualitative study indicated high levels of feasibility and community acceptance of peer volunteers in delivering psychosocial interventions. A 5-year follow-up found that 70% of volunteers were still involved in the programme

(continued)

Table 3 (continued)

Country	Programme	Category	Description
	Development of a school mental health programme in rural areas (Hamdani et al., 2021)	Child and adolescent mental health	Three workshops conducted involving 90 stakeholders, including teachers, mental health professionals and policy makers. Using the Theory of Change approach, a package was developed that included counselling skills, life skills training, involvement of parents, teacher wellness, and training and supervision by experts
	Technology-assisted training of women volunteers to conduct parental group skills training for children with developmental disorders (Hamdani et al., 2022)	Child mental health; community mental heath	Tablet-based training was effective and resulted in an acceptable level (63%) of fidelity with the source material. Participation in subsequent group sessions was good (85%), and the intervention was perceived as acceptable by parents after appropriate cultural adaptations
	Integration of depression care into private clinic setting (Owais et al., 2023)	Public-private partnership; maternal mental health	Training of physicians and clinic assistants in 32 private clinics on diagnosis, prescription of antidepressants and referral led to better improvements in maternal depression than in a control group
Sri Lanka	Training of primary care physicians in mental health care based on WHO guidelines (Jenkins et al., 2012)	Primary care integration	40 h training programme delivered to 250 physicians. Pre- and post-tests revealed a statistically significant increase in knowledge related to mental illness. Qualitative feedback revealed that the training was perceived as acceptable and useful
	Development and implementation of a mental health care package for children living in a conflict zone (Tol et al., 2012)	Child mental health; vulnerable population	A package involving community education and sensitization, peer groups, school-based intervention, counselling and referrals was developed. This group intervention was associated with significant improvements in conduct symptoms but inconsistent effects on PTSD symptoms

Abbreviations: CMD, Common mental disorders; mhGAP, Mental Health Gap Action Programme; PTSD, Post-traumatic stress disorder; WHO, World Health Organization yet to publish their results. Third, several studies have reported short-term performance or outcomes, though the management of mental illness requires a more long-term approach, as seen in Fig. 1. Fourth, with few exceptions, these projects have not addressed the key issue of intersectoral collaboration and coordination. Fifth, conducting such research has proved a challenge in smaller South Asian countries, such as Bhutan and Maldives, for which no published reports could be retrieved. Sixth, only a single study addressed the issue of substance use disorders. Finally, most of these studies have themselves reported several barriers and challenges to successful implementation, which are identical to those reported in the respective country profiles (Atif et al., 2016; Varshney et al., 2022). Despite these limitations, the existing evidence is encouraging because it suggests that it is both possible and feasible to develop country-specific, evidence-based, culturally sensitive interventions that could play a transformative role in mental health care. Once such interventions or programmes are developed, it is essential to ensure their sustainability in the community setting through a long-term, systems-based perspective. This would require a multi-pronged approach that includes stigma orientation, cultural adaptation and "fine-tuning" of interventions over time, development and maintenance of manpower and infrastructure, good governance, and attention to broader social and political factors (Greene et al., 2021).

As mentioned in the WHO's Mental Health Action Plan, there is a need to continue and extend this research, to examine if it can be "scaled up" to provide wider coverage of the population, and to collect data on long-term outcomes from all stakeholders (World Health Organization, 2022b). There is also a need to collect data on the implementation and performance of the various mental health initiatives launched by South Asian governments, such as the national mental health plans recently formulated in India. Where recent epidemiological data is available, as in Afghanistan, India, and Nepal, this should be used to guide service planning and delivery; where no such data is available, regional and national surveys should be undertaken.

Measures should be also taken to improve mental health awareness and to sensitize key "actors", including community and religious leaders, local and regional political representatives, and national governments (World Health Organization, 2021c). Collaboration between medical disciplines could be achieved by educating and sensitizing colleagues about the links between mental health and several medical conditions, including both communicable and non-communicable diseases (Fond et al., 2021; Islam et al., 2022). This would facilitate the integration of mental health care into existing health structures and lead to a more holistic approach to medical practice in general. Likewise, where traditional or spiritual modes of healing are employed by persons with mental illness, it may be beneficial—when feasible—to collaborate with the practitioners of these forms of healing, enlist their help as gatekeepers and establish a channel for referrals (Dorji et al., 2017; Raguram et al., 2002). Stigma reduction programmes should be based on a careful assessment of the specific social, cultural and religious beliefs and practices that underlie stigma in a given country, and not just on general principles (Kaiser et al., 2022; Kallakuri et al., 2021).

Finally, it would be valuable to identify those community resources that strengthen individual and group psychological resilience, even in the face of social and economic challenges. These could be identified through community and hospital-based surveys of factors protective against mental illness in those experiencing adversity, or in examining psychological and social predictors of recovery in those receiving mental health care. Leveraging these "resistance resources" (Antonovsky & Sagy, 2017), and integrating them with high-quality mental health care, is an unexplored but potentially far-reaching opportunity for mental health promotion and prevention in South Asian countries.

4 Conclusion: The Road Ahead

The evidence reviewed in this chapter is of two kinds. The first outlines the challenges involved in planning, implementing and sustaining mental health care in each South Asian country. The second describes efforts that have been made in each country to develop innovative responses to these challenges. These two bodies of evidence are complementary: a careful reading of the papers reviewed in Table 3 reveals that many of them arose from the country-specific challenges summarized in this chapter and that many of the programmes they describe continue to encounter these challenges.

Despite the seemingly daunting list of barriers to mental health care that exist in South Asia, the information in this chapter should not be a cause for discouragement. Defining a problem is the first step to effectively solving it and in planning and delivering realistic solutions that navigate the space between undue optimism and pessimism. The information in this chapter could serve as a valuable starting point for those interested in developing specific mental health interventions, in evaluating existing services, and in advocating for changes in legislation and policy where acceptable. In an age where collaboration among South Asian countries is advocated as a solution to the complex ecological, socioeconomic and health challenges of the modern era (Rahman & Alam, 2021), this data could also be of use in the development of cross-national collaborations. For example, in countries lacking autochthonous mental health infrastructure, mentorship from other South Asian countries with more functional systems could help in launching and evaluating educational, preventive and therapeutic measures.

This information is also valuable in identifying gaps in the available data. For example, we have little or no information on patient satisfaction with existing services, on the mental health service needs of special or vulnerable populations, or on the efficacy of existing national mental health plans and programmes. The guidelines provided by the WHO, as well as the lessons learned from existing South Asian initiatives, could help in gathering evidence and planning humane and accessible services for these populations, who often face a "dual" form of stigmatization and discrimination.

In conclusion, substantial challenges and barriers to mental health care exist in South Asian countries and should not be ignored or minimized. Nevertheless, the available evidence suggests that it is possible to surmount or circumvent these barriers through effective listening to stakeholders, advocacy, cultural adaptations of general principles, community involvement, and commitment to long-term care and sustainability of services on the part of both policy-makers and professionals.

References

Abdullah, T., & Brown, T. L. (2011). Mental illness stigma and ethnocultural beliefs, values and norms: An integrative review. *Clinical Psychology Review, 31*, 934–948. https://doi.org/10.1016/j.cpr.2011.05.003

Abdullah, M., Sethi, M. R., & Irfan, M. (2021). Gender differences regarding stigma towards mental illness among medical students of Peshawar. *Journal of Ayub Medical College, Abbottabad, 33*(1), 120–124.

Adhikari, S., & Jha, A. (2021). Pathway to care in patients having mental illness in Eastern Nepal. *Asian Journal of Psychiatry, 55*, 102504. https://doi.org/10.1016/j.ajp.2020.102504

Ahmad, F., Driver, N., McNally, M. J., & Stewart, D. E. (2009). "Why doesn't she seek help for partner abuse?" An exploratory study with South Asian immigrant women. *Social Science and Medicine, 69*(4), 613–622. https://doi.org/10.1016/j.socscimed.2009.06.011

Ahmed, N., Ahmed, S., Carmichael, Z., & Sami, A. S. (2017). Measuring healthy lifestyle and mental health indicators in South Asian women using the "Your Health: Quality of Life and Well-Being" questionnaire. *Annals of Global Health, 83*(3–4), 463–470. https://doi.org/10.1016/j.aogh.2017.09.007

Akter, F., Rahman, M., Pitchik, H. O., Winch, P. J., Fernald, L. C. H., Huda, T. M. N., Jahir, T., Amin, R., Das, J. B., Hossain, K., Shoab, A. K., Khan, R., Yeasmin, F., Sultana, J., Luby, S. P., & Tofail, F. (2020). Adaptation and integration of psychosocial stimulation, maternal mental health and nutritional interventions for pregnant and lactating women in rural Bangladesh. *International Journal of Environmental Research and Public Health, 17*, 6233. https://doi.org/10.3390/ijerph17176233

Aldridge, L. R., Luitel, N. P., Jordans, M. J. D., Bass, J. K., & Patenaude, B. (2022). Cost-effectiveness of psychological intervention within services for depression delivered by primary care workers in Nepal: Economic evaluation of a randomized control trial. *Global Mental Health, 9*, 499–507. https://doi.org/10.1017/gmh.2022.54

Anand, P., Sachdeva, A., & Kumar, V. (2018). Pathway to care and clinical profile of children with attention-deficit hyperactivity disorder in New Delhi, India. *Journal of Family & Community Medicine, 25*(2), 114–119. https://doi.org/10.4103/jfcm.jfcm_142_16

Antonovsky, A., & Sagy, S. (2017). Aaron Antonovsky, the scholar and the man behind salutogenesis. In M. B. Mittelmark, S. Sagy, M. Eriksson, G. F. Bauer, J. M. Pelikan, B. Lindstrom, G. A. Espnes (Eds.), *The handbook of salutogenesis*. Springer. https://doi.org/10.1007/978-3-319-04600-6_3

Antony, J. T. (2000). A decade with the mental health act, 1987. *Indian Journal of Psychiatry, 42*(4), 347–355.

Arneaud, G. J., Kar, A., Majumder, S., Molodynski, A., Lovett, K., & Kar, S. (2023). Mental health disorders in English newspapers of India: A retrospective study. *The International Journal of Social Psychiatry, 69*(3), 646–652. https://doi.org/10.1177/00207640221132426

Arnett, J. J. (1999). Adolescent storm and stress, reconsidered. *The American Psychologist, 54*(5), 317–326. https://doi.org/10.1037//0003-066x.54.5.317

Atif, N., Lovell, K., & Rahman, A. (2015). Maternal mental health: The missing "m" in the global maternal and child health agenda. *Seminars in Perinatology, 39*(5), 345–352. https://doi.org/10.1053/j.semperi.2015.06.007

Atif, N., Lovell, K., Husain, N., Sikander, S., Patel, V., & Rahman, A. (2016). Barefoot therapists: Barriers and facilitators to delivering maternal mental health care through peer volunteers in Pakistan: A qualitative study. *International Journal of Mental Health Systems, 10*, 24. https://doi.org/10.1186/s13033-016-0055-9

Atif, N., Bibi, A., Nisar, A., Zulfiqar, S., Ahmed, I., LeMasters, K., Hagaman, A., Sikander, S., Maselko, J., & Rahman, A. (2019). Delivering maternal mental health through peer volunteers: A 5-year report. *International Journal of Mental Health Systems, 13*, 62. https://doi.org/10.1186/s13033-019-0318-3

Atreya, A., Upreti, M., & Nepal, S. (2023). Barriers to mental health care access in Nepal. *Medico-Legal Journal, 91*(1), 54–55. https://doi.org/10.1177/00258172221141293

Axinn, W. G., Ghimire, D. J., Williams, N. E., & Scott, K. M. (2015). Associations between the social organization of communities and psychiatric disorders in rural Asia. *Social Psychiatry and Psychiatric Epidemiology, 50*(10), 1537–1545. https://doi.org/10.1007/s00127-015-1042-1

Bain, L. E., & Adeagbo, O. A. (2022). There is an urgent need for a global rural health research agenda. *Pan African Medical Journal, 43*, 147. https://doi.org/10.11604/pamj.2022.43.147.38189

Balhara, Y.P.S., Prakash, S., & Gupta, R. (2016). Pathways to care of alcohol-dependent patients: An exploratory study from a tertiary care substance use disorder treatment center. *International Journal of High Risk Behaviors & Addiction, 5*(3), e30342. https://doi.org/10.5812/ijhrba.30342

Baminiwatta, A., Alahakoon, H., Herath, N. C., Kodithuwakku, K. M., & Nanayakkara, T. (2023). Trait mindfulness, compassion, and stigma towards patients with mental illness: A study among nurses in Sri Lanka. *Mindfulness, 14*(4), 979–991. https://doi.org/10.1007/s12671-023-02108-5

Becker, S. M. (2007). Psychosocial care for adult and child survivors of the tsunami disaster in India. *Journal of Child and Adolescent Psychiatric Nursing, 20*(3), 148–155. https://doi.org/10.1111/j.1744-6171.2007.00105.x

Borah, K., Jose, T. T., Mysore Nagaraj, A. K., & Moxham, L. (2023). Suicide prevention program (SPP) in South Asian Countries: A protocol for systematic review. *F1000Research, 12*, 425. https://doi.org/10.12688/f1000research.132215.2

Chakraborthy, S., Kommu, J. V. S., Srinath, S., Seshadri, S. P., & Girimaji, S. C. (2014). A comparative study of pathways to care for children with specific learning disability and mental retardation. *Indian Journal of Psychological Medicine, 36*(1), 27–32. https://doi.org/10.4103/0253-7176.127243

Challapallisri, V., & Dempster, L. V. (2015). Attitude of doctors towards mentally ill in Hyderabad, India: Results of a prospective survey. *Indian Journal of Psychiatry, 57*(2), 190–195. https://doi.org/10.4103/0019-5545.158190

Chandramouleeswaran, S., Rajaleelan, W., Edwin, N. C., & Koshy, I. (2017). Stigma and attitudes toward patients with psychiatric illness among postgraduate Indian physicians. *Indian Journal of Psychological Medicine, 39*(6), 746–749. https://doi.org/10.4103/IJPSYM.IJPSYM_84_17

Chaudhry, H. R. (2008). Psychiatric care in Asia: Spirituality and religious connotations. *International Review of Psychiatry, 20*(5), 477–483. https://doi.org/10.1080/09540260802397602

Cruz, C. M., Dukpa, C., Vanderburg, J. L., Rauniyar, A. K., Giri, P., Bhattarai, S., Thapa, A., Hampanda, K., Gaynes, B. N., Lamb, M. M., & Matergia, M. (2022). Teacher, caregiver, and student acceptability of teachers delivering task-shifted mental health care to students in Darjeeling, India: A mixed methods pilot study. *Discover Mental Health, 2*(1), 21. https://doi.org/10.1007/s44192-022-00024-z

Devassy, S. M., Scaria, L., & Cheguvera, N. (2022). Task sharing and stepped referral model for community mental health promotion in low- and middle-income countries (LMIC): Insights from a feasibility study in India. *Pilot and Feasibility Studies, 8*(1), 192. https://doi.org/10.1186/s40814-022-01159-0

Devkota, G., Basnet, P., Thapa, B., & Subedi, M. (2021). Factors affecting utilization of mental health services from Primary Health Care (PHC) facilities of western hilly district of Nepal. *Plos One, 16*(4), e0250694. https://doi.org/10.1371/journal.pone.0250694

Devkota, H. R., Baral, Y. R., Khanal, B., & Adhikary, P. (2023). How effectively are social accountability mechanisms being applied in mental health services within the newly federalized health system of Nepal? A multi-stakeholder qualitative study. *BMC Health Services Research, 23*(1), 762. https://doi.org/10.1186/s12913-023-09765-1

Dey, S., Mellsop, G., Diesfeld, K., Dharmawardene, V., Mendis, S., Chaudhuri, S., Deb, A., Huq, N., Ahmed, H. U., Shuaib, M., & Khan, F. R. (2019). Comparing legislation for involuntary admission and treatment of mental illness in four South Asian countries. *International Journal of Mental Health Systems, 13*, 67. https://doi.org/10.1186/s13033-019-0322-7

Diamond, J. (2019). *Upheaval: How nations cope with crisis and change.* Penguin Books.

Dissabandara, L. O., Dias, S. R., Dodd, P. R., & Stadlin, A. (2009). Patterns of substance use in male incarcerated drug users in Sri Lanka. *Drug and Alcohol Review, 28*(6), 600–607. https://doi.org/10.1111/j.1465-3362.2009.00062.x

Doherty, S., Hulland, E., Lopes-Cardozo, B., Kirupakaran, S., Surenthirakumaran, R., Cookson, S., & Siriwardhana, C. (2019). Prevalence of mental disorders and epidemiological associations in post-conflict primary care attendees: A cross-sectional study in the Northern Province of Sri Lanka. *BMC Psychiatry, 19*, 83. https://doi.org/10.1186/s12888-019-2064-0

Doherty, S., Dass, G., Edward, A., Manolova, G., & Solomon, M. (2020). Challenges and lessons learned in re-filming the WHO mhGAP training videos for Sri Lankan context—A qualitative study. *Conflict and Health, 14*, 7. https://doi.org/10.1186/s13031-020-00259-z

Dorji, G., Choki, S., Jamphel, K., Wangdi, Y., Chogyel, T., Dorji, C., & Nirola, D. K. (2017). Policy and governance to address depression and suicide in Bhutan: The national suicide-prevention strategy. *WHO South-East Asia Journal of Public Health, 6*(1), 39–44. https://doi.org/10.4103/2224-3151.206163

Ediriweera, H. W., Fernando, S. M., & Pai, N. B. (2012). Mental health literacy survey among Sri Lankan carers of patients with schizophrenia and depression. *Asian Journal of Psychiatry, 5*(3), 246–250. https://doi.org/10.1016/j.ajp.2012.02.016

Faruk, M. O., & Rosenbaum, S. (2023). Mental illness stigma among indigenous communities in Bangladesh: A cross-sectional study. *BMC Psychology, 11*(1), 216. https://doi.org/10.1186/s40359-023-01257-5

Fernando, S. M., Deane, F. P., & McLeod, H. J. (2010). Sri Lankan doctors' and medical undergraduates' attitudes towards mental illness. *Social Psychiatry and Psychiatric Epidemiology, 45*(7), 733–739. https://doi.org/10.1007/s00127-009-0113-6

Fernando, S. M., Deane, F. P., & McLeod, H. J. (2017). The delaying effect of stigma on mental health help-seeking in Sri Lanka. *Asia-Pacific Psychiatry, 9*(1), e12255. https://doi.org/10.1111/appy.12255

Fond, G., Nemani, K., Etchecopar-Etchart, D., Loundou, A., Goff, D. C., Lee, S. W., Lancon, C., Auquier, P., Baumstarck, K., Llorca, P.-M., Yon, D. K., & Boyer, L. (2021). Association between mental health disorders and mortality among patients with COVID-19 in 7 countries: A systematic review and meta-analysis. *JAMA Psychiatry, 78*(11), 1208–1217. https://doi.org/10.1001/jamapsychiatry.2021.2274

Funk, M., Minoletti, A., Drew, N., Taylor, J., & Saraceno, B. (2006). Advocacy for mental health: Roles for consumer and family organizations and governments. *Health Promotion International, 21*(1), 70–75. https://doi.org/10.1093/heapro/dai031

Giasuddin, N. A., Chowdhury, N. F., Hashimoto, N., Fujisawa, D., & Waheed, S. (2012). Pathways to psychiatric care in Bangladesh. *Social Psychiatry and Psychiatric Epidemiology, 47*, 129–136. https://doi.org/10.1007/s00127-010-0315-y

Global Burden of Disease Collaborative Network. (2020). Global Burden of Disease Study 2019 (GBD 2019) Results. Institute for Health Metrics and Evaluation (IHME). Retrieved from https://vizhub.healthdata.org/gbd-results/

Gomez, D. M., Gunarathna, C., Gunarathna, S., Gnanapragasam, K., & Hanwella, R. (2017). Help-seeking behaviour and its impact on patients attending a psychiatry clinic at National Hospital of Sri Lanka. *The Ceylon Medical Journal, 62*(4), 222–227. https://doi.org/10.4038/cmj.v62i4.8571

Goswami, S. (2021). Examining women's health through a psychosocial lens. *Indian Journal of Medical Ethics, 6*(4), 290–293. https://doi.org/10.20529/IJME.2021.077

Goyal, S., Sudhir, P. M., & Sharma, M. P. (2022). Pathways to mental health consultations: A study from a tertiary care setting in India. *The International Journal of Social Psychiatry, 68*(2), 449–456. https://doi.org/10.1177/00207640211003929

Greene, M. C., Huang, T. T. K., Giusto, A., Lovero, K. L., Stockton, M. A., Shelton, R. C., Dos Santos, P., Saúte, F., & Wainberg, M. L. (2021). Leveraging systems science to promote the implementation and sustainability of mental health and psychosocial interventions in low- and middle-income countries. *Harvard Review of Psychiatry, 29*(4), 262–277. https://doi.org/10.1097/HRP.0000000000000306

Gupta, A. K., Joshi, S., Kafle, B., Thapa, R., Chapagai, M., Nepal, S., Niraula, A., Paudyal, S., Sapkota, P., Poudel, R., Gurung, B. S., Pokhrel, P., Jha, R., et al. (2021). Pathways to mental health care in Nepal: A 14-center nationwide study. *International Journal of Mental Health Systems, 15*, 85. https://doi.org/10.1186/s13033-021-00509-4

Gurung, D., Poudyal, A., Wang, X. L., Neupane, M., Bhattarai, A., Wahid, S. S., Aryal, S., Heim, E., Gronholm, P., Thornicroft, G., & Kohrt, B. (2022). Stigma against mental health disorders in Nepal conceptualised with a 'what matters most' framework: A scoping review. *Epidemiology and Psychiatric Sciences, 31*, e11. https://doi.org/10.1017/S2045796021000809

Gururaj, G., Varghese, M., Benegal, V., Rao, G. N., Pathak, K., Singh, L. K., Mehta, R. Y., Ram, D., Shibukumar, T. M., Kokane, A., Lenin Singh, R. K., Chavan, B. S., Sharma, P., Ramasubramanian, C., Dalal, P. K., Saha, P. K., Deuri, S. P., Giri, A. K., Kavishvar, A. B., Sinha, V. K., et al. (2016a). National mental health survey of India, 2015–16: Prevalence, patterns and outcomes. Bengaluru, National Institute of Mental Health and Neuro Sciences, NIMHANS Publication No. 129. Retrieved from https://main.mohfw.gov.in/sites/default/files/National%20Mental%20Health%20Survey%2C%202015-16%20-%20Prevalence%2C%20Pattern%20%26%20Outcomes_0.pdf

Gururaj, G., Varghese, M., Benegal, V., Rao, G. N., Pathak, K., Singh, L. K., Mehta, R. Y., Ram, D., Shibukumar, T. M., Kokane, A., Lenin Singh, R. K., Chavan, B. S., Sharma, P., Ramasubramanian, C., Dalal, P. K., Saha, P. K., Deuri, S. P., Giri, A. K., Kavishvar, A. B., Sinha, V. K., Thavody, J., et al. (2016b). National Mental Health Survey of India, 2015–16: Mental health systems. Bengaluru, National Institute of Mental Health and Neuro Sciences, NIMHANS Publication No. 130. Retrieved from https://main.mohfw.gov.in/sites/default/files/National%20Mental%20Health%20Survey%2C%202015-16%20-%20Mental%20Health%20Systems_0.pdf

Haar, K., El-Khani, A., Molgaard, V., Maalouf, W., & Afghanistan Field Implementation Team. (2020). Strong families: A new family skills training programme for challenged and humanitarian settings: A single-arm intervention tested in Afghanistan. *BMC Public Health, 20*, 634. https://doi.org/10.1186/s12889-020-08701-w

Hamamura, T. (2017). A cultural psychological analysis of cultural change. *Asian Journal of Social Psychology, 21*(1–2), 3–12. https://doi.org/10.1111/ajsp.12194

Hamdani, S. U., Huma, Z. E., Suleman, N., Warraitch, A., Muzzafar, N., Farzeen, M., Minhas, F. A., Rahman, A., & Wissow, L. S. (2021). Scaling-up school mental health services in low resource public schools of rural Pakistan: The Theory of Change (ToC) approach. *International Journal of Mental Health Systems, 15*(1), 8. https://doi.org/10.1186/s13033-021-00435-5

Hamdani, S. U., Huma, Z. E., & Wissow, L. S. (2022). Technology-assisted task-sharing to bridge the treatment gap for childhood developmental disorders in rural Pakistan: An implementation science case study. *Implementation Science Communications, 3*(1), 99. https://doi.org/10.1186/s43058-022-00343-w

Hanlon, C., Fekadu, A., Jordans, M., Kigozi, F., Petersen, I., Shidhaye, R., Honikman, S., Lund, C., Prince, M., Raja, S., Thornicroft, G., Tomlinson, M., & Patel, V. (2016). District mental healthcare plans for five low- and middle-income countries: Commonalities, variations and evidence gaps. *The British Journal of Psychiatry, 208*(Suppl 56), s47–s54. https://doi.org/10.1192/bjp.bp.114.153767

Hapangama, A., & Kuruppuarachchi, K. A. L. A. (2021). Maternal mental health services in Sri Lanka: Challenges and solutions. *BJPsych International, 18*(4), 100–102. https://doi.org/10.1192/bji.2020.52

Hapangama, A., Mendis, J., & Kuruppuarachchi, K. A. L. A. (2023). Why are we still living in the past? Sri Lanka needs urgent and timely reforms of its archaic mental health laws. *BJPsych International, 20*(1), 4–6. https://doi.org/10.1192/bji.2022.26

Humayun, A., Haq, I., Khan, F. R., Azad, N., Khan, M. M., & Weissbecker, I. (2017). Implementing mhGAP training to strengthen existing services for an internally displaced population in Pakistan. *Global Mental Health, 4*, e6. https://doi.org/10.1017/gmh.2017.1

Hofstede Insights. (2022). Country comparison tool. Retrieved July 19, 2023 from https://www.hofstede-insights.com/country-comparison-tool

Hongally, C., Sneha, V., & Archana, G. (2019). How to make rules and regulations for the states in accordance with the Mental Healthcare Act 2017. *Indian Journal of Psychiatry, 61*(Suppl. 4), S827–S831. https://doi.org/10.4103/psychiatry.indianjpsychiatry_156_19

Hossain, M. M., Purohit, N., Sultana, A., Ping, M., McKyer, E. L. J., & Ahmed, H. U. (2020). Prevalence of mental disorders in South Asia: An umbrella review of systematic reviews and meta-analyses. *Asian Journal of Psychiatry, 51*, 102041. https://doi.org/10.1016/j.ajp.2020.102041

Hossain, M. M., Rahman, M., Trisha, N. F., Tasnim, S., Nuzhath, T., Hasan, N. T., Clark, H., Das, A., McKyer, E. L. J., Ahmed, H. U., & Ma, P. (2021). Prevalence of anxiety and depression in South Asia during COVID-19: A systematic review and meta-analysis. *Heliyon, 7*, e06677. https://doi.org/10.1016/j.heliyon.2021.e06677

Husain, W. (2020). Barriers in seeking psychological help: Public perception in Pakistan. *Community Mental Health Journal, 56*(1), 75–78. https://doi.org/10.1007/s10597-019-00464-y

Hussain, S. S., Khan, M., Gul, R., & Asad, N. (2018). Integration of mental health into primary healthcare: Perceptions of stakeholders in Pakistan. *Eastern Mediterranean Health Journal, 24*(2), 146–153.

Ibrahim, A., & Hameed, A. (2006). Mental health and psychosocial response after the worst natural disaster in the history of the Maldives. *International Review of Psychiatry, 18*(6), 567–572. https://doi.org/10.1080/09540260601038431

Islam, K., Huque, R., Saif-Ur-Rahman, K. M., Ehthesam Kabir, A. N. M., & Enayet Hussain, A. H. M. (2022). Implementation status of non-communicable disease control program at primary health care level in Bangladesh: Findings from a qualitative research. *Public Health in Practice, 3*, 100271. https://doi.org/10.1016/j.puhip.2022.100271

Jackson, J., Dangal, R., Dangal, B., Gupta, T., Jirel, S., Khadka, S., Rimal, P., & Acharya, B. (2022). Implementing collaborative care in low-resource Government, research, and academic settings in Rural Nepal. *Psychiatric Services, 73*(9), 1073–1076. https://doi.org/10.1176/appi.ps.202100421

Jafar, D., Nasir, A., & Hussain, A. (2022). Experiences of nurses regarding challenges faced while dealing with psychiatric patients in both public and private tertiary care hospitals of Karachi, Pakistan. *Journal of the Pakistan Medical Association, 73*(4), 776–780. https://doi.org/10.47391/JPMA.5542

Jafree, S. R., & Burhan, S. K. (2020). Health challenges of mothers with special needs children in Pakistan and the importance of integrating health social workers. *Social Work in Health Care, 59*(6), 408–429. https://doi.org/10.1080/00981389.2020.1781738

Jain, N., Gautam, S., Jain, S., Gupta, I. D., Batra, L., Sharma, R., & Singh, H. (2012). Pathway to psychiatric care in a tertiary mental health facility in Jaipur, India. *Asian Journal of Psychiatry, 5*(4), 303–308. https://doi.org/10.1016/j.ajp.2012.04.003

Jayaram, G., Goud, R., & Srinivasan, K. (2011). Overcoming cultural barriers to deliver comprehensive rural community mental health care in Southern India. *Asian Journal of Psychiatry, 4*(4), 261–265. https://doi.org/10.1016/j.ajp.2011.08.005

Jenkins, R., Mendis, J., Cooray, S., & Cooray, M. (2012). Integration of mental health into primary care in Sri Lanka. *Mental Health in Family Medicine, 9*(1), 15–24.

Joseph, R. G., Kallivayalil, R. A., & Rajeev, A. (2020). Pathways to care in children-perspectives from a child guidance clinic in South India. *Asian Journal of Psychiatry, 54*, 102310. https://doi.org/10.1016/j.ajp.2020.102310

Kaiser, B. N., Gurung, D., Rai, S., Bhardwaj, A., Dhakal, M., Cafaro, C. L., Sikkema, K. J., Lund, C., Patel, V., Jordans, M. J. D., Luitel, N. P., & Kohrt, B. A. (2022). Mechanisms of action for stigma reduction among primary care providers following social contact with service users and aspirational figures in Nepal: An explanatory qualitative design. *International Journal of Mental Health Systems, 16*(1), 37. https://doi.org/10.1186/s13033-022-00546-7

Kaku, S. M., Sibeoni, J., Basheer, S., Chang, J. P., Dahanayake, D. M. A., Irarrazaval, M., Lachman, J. M., Mapayi, B. M., Mejia, A., Orri, M., Jui-Goh, T., Uddin, M. S., & Vallance, I. (2022). Global child and adolescent mental health perspectives: Bringing change locally, while thinking globally. *Child and Adolescent Psychiatry and Mental Health, 16*(1), 82. https://doi.org/10.1186/s13034-022-00512-8

Kallakuri, S., Kaur, A., Hackett, M.L., & Maulik, P.K. (2021). Operational challenges in the implementation of an anti-stigma campaign in rural Andhra Pradesh, India. *Journal of Public Health, 43*(S2), ii26–ii34. https://doi.org/10.1093/pubmed/fdab314

Kar, S. K., Oyetunji, T. P., Prakash, A. J., Ogunmola, O. A., Tripathy, S., Lawal, M. M., Sanusi, Z. K., & Arafat, S. M. Y. (2020). Mental health research in the lower-middle-income countries of Africa and Asia during the COVID-19 pandemic: A scoping review. *Neurology, Psychiatry, and Brain Research, 38*, 54–64. https://doi.org/10.1016/j.npbr.2020.10.003

Keshav Desiraju India Mental Health Observatory. (2022). Union Budget for Mental Health 2022–23. Retrieved from https://cmhlp.org/wp-content/uploads/2022/02/IMHO-Union-Budget-for-Mental-Health-2022-23.pdf

Khemani, M. C., Premarajan, K. C., Menon, V., Olickal, J. J., Vijayageetha, M., & Chinnakali, P. (2020). Pathways to care among patients with severe mental disorders attending a tertiary health-care facility in Puducherry, South India. *Indian Journal of Psychiatry, 62*(6), 664–669. https://doi.org/10.4103/psychiatry.IndianJPsychiatry_512_19

Kirmayer, L. J., & Pedersen, D. (2014). Toward a new architecture for global mental health. *Transcultural Psychiatry, 51*(6), 759–776. https://doi.org/10.1177/1363461514557202

Kisa, R., Baingana, F., Kajungu, R., Mangen, P. O., Angdembe, M., Gwaikolo, W., & Cooper, J. (2016). Pathways and access to mental health care services by persons living with severe mental disorders and epilepsy in Uganda, Liberia and Nepal: A qualitative study. *BMC Psychiatry, 16*(1), 305. https://doi.org/10.1186/s12888-016-1008-1

Koly, K. N., Abdullah, R., Shammi, F. A., Akter, T., Hasan, M. T., Eaton, J., & Ryan, G. K. (2021). Mental health and community-based rehabilitation: A qualitative description of the experiences and perspectives of service users and carers in Bangladesh. *Community Mental Health Journal, 58*, 52–66. https://doi.org/10.1007/s10597-021-00790-0

Koly, K. N., Tasnim, Z., Ahmed, S., Saba, J., Mahmood, R., Farin, F. T., Choudhury, S., Ashraf, M. N., Hasan, M. T., Oloniniyi, I., Modasser, R. B., & Redpath, D. D. (2022). Mental healthcare-seeking behavior of women in Bangladesh: Content analysis of a social media platform. *BMC Psychiatry, 22*, 797. https://doi.org/10.1186/s12888-022-04414-z

Kovess-Masfety, V., Karam, E., Keyes, K., Sabawoon, A., & Sarwari, B. A. (2021a). Access to care for mental health problems in Afghanistan: A national challenge. *International Journal of Health Policy and Management, 11*(8), 1442–1450. https://doi.org/10.34172/ijhpm.2021.46

Kovess-Masfety, V., Keyes, K., Karam, E., Sabawoon, A., & Sarwari, B. A. (2021b). A national survey on depressive and anxiety disorders in Afghanistan: A highly traumatized population. *BMC Psychiatry, 21*, 314. https://doi.org/10.1186/s12888-021-03273-4

Kuek, J. H. L., Raeburn, T., & Wand, T. (2023). Asian perspectives on personal recovery in mental health: A scoping review. *Journal of Mental Health, 32*(2), 517–533. https://doi.org/10.1080/09638237.2020.1818709

Kumar, C. N., Chand, P. K., Manjunatha, N., Math, S. B., Shashidhara, H. N., Basavaraju, V., Thirthalli, J., Manjappa, A. A., Parthasarathy, R., Murthy, P., Ibrahim, F. A., Jagtap, N., Jyrwa, S., Reddy, S., Arora, S., Hawk, M., Kumar, S., Egan, J., & Mcdonald, M. (2020). Impact evaluation of VKN-NIMHANS-ECHO model of capacity building for mental health and addiction: Methodology of two randomized controlled trials. *Indian Journal of Psychological Medicine, 42*(6 Suppl), S80–S86. https://doi.org/10.1177/0253717620969066

Kumar, D. (2021). School mental health program in India: Need to shift from a piecemeal approach to a long-term comprehensive approach with strong intersectoral coordination. *Indian Journal of Psychiatry, 63*(1), 91–96. https://doi.org/10.4103/psychiatry.IndianJPsychiatry_204_20

Lakshmana, G., Sangeetha, V., & Pandey, V. (2022). Community perception of accessibility and barriers to utilizing mental health services. *Journal of Education and Health Promotion, 11*, 56. https://doi.org/10.4103/jehp.jehp_342_21

Laraib, A., Sajjad, A., Sardar, A., Wazir, M. S., & Nazneen, Z. (2018). Perspective about mental illnesses: A survey of health care providers of Abbottabad. *Journal of Ayub Medical College, Abbottabad, 30*(1), 97–102.

Liu, Q., He, H., Yang, J., Feng, X., Zhao, F., & Lyu, J. (2020). Changes in the global burden of depression from 1990 to 2017: Findings from the global Burden of disease study. *Journal of Psychiatric Research, 126*, 134–140. https://doi.org/10.1016/j.jpsychires.2019.08.002

Lucksted, A., & Drapalski, A. L. (2015). Self-stigma regarding mental illness: Definition, impact, and relationship to societal stigma. *Psychiatric Rehabilitation Journal, 38*(2), 99–102. https://doi.org/10.1037/prj0000152

Luitel, N. P., Jordans, M. J. D., Subba, P., & Komproe, I. H. (2020). Perception of service users and their caregivers on primary care-based mental health services: A qualitative study in Nepal. *BMC Family Practice, 21*(1), 202. https://doi.org/10.1186/s12875-020-01266-y

Makhmud, A., Thornicroft, G., & Gronholm, P. C. (2022). Indirect social contact interventions to reduce mental health-related stigma in low- and middle-income countries: Systematic review. *Epidemiology and Psychiatric Sciences, 31*, e79. https://doi.org/10.1017/S2045796022000622

Marahatta, K., Samuel, R., Sharma, P., Dixit, L., & Shrestha, B. R. (2017). Suicide burden and prevention in Nepal: The need for a national strategy. *WHO South-East Asia Journal of Public Health, 6*(1), 45–49.

Mazumder, H., Faizah, F., Gain, E. P., Eva, I. S., Mou, K. F., Saha, N., Rahman, F., Das, J., Islam, A. M. K., Nesa, F., & Hossain, M. M. (2023). Effectiveness of mental health interventions for older adults in South Asia: A scoping review. *Plos One, 18*(7), e0287883. https://doi.org/10.1371/journal.pone.0287883

Mehrotra, K., Nautiyal, S., & Raguram, A. (2018). Mental health literacy in family caregivers: A comparative analysis. *Asian Journal of Psychiatry, 31*, 58–62. https://doi.org/10.1016/j.ajp.2018.01.021

Menon, S., Jagannathan, A., Thirthalli, J., Adarsha, A. M., Parthasarathy, R., & Naveen Kumar, C. (2022). Care at doorsteps for persons with severe mental illnesses as a part of district mental health program (DMHP): A qualitative needs assessment and psychosocial framework. *Community Mental Health Journal, 58*(1), 145–153. https://doi.org/10.1007/s10597-021-00803-y

Ministry of Social Justice and Empowerment, Government of India & National Drug Dependence Treatment Centre, All India Institute of Medical Sciences. (2019). Magnitude of Substance Use in India, Retrieved from https://www.aiims.edu/index.php?option=com_content&view=article&id=9244&Itemid=3761&lang=en

Mistry, S. K., Mehrab Ali, A. R. M., Irfan, N. M., Yadav, U. N., Siddique, R. F., Peprah, P., Reza, S., Rahman, Z., Casanelia, L., & O'Callaghan, C. (2021). Prevalence and correlates of depressive symptoms among Rohingya (forcibly displaced Myanmar nationals or FDMNs) older adults in Bangladesh amid the COVID-19 pandemic. *Global Mental Health, 8*, e23. https://doi.org/10.1017/gmh.2021.24

Mohamed, A. (2015). Resuscitating the national mental health policy in the Maldives. *Australasian Psychiatry, 23*(6), S26–S28. https://doi.org/10.1177/1039856215609766

Munawar, K., Abdul Khaiyom, J. H., Bokharey, I. Z., Park, M. S., & Choudhry, F. R. (2020). A systematic review of mental health literacy in Pakistan. *Asia-Pacific Psychiatry, 12*(4), e12408. https://doi.org/10.1111/appy.12408

Munisami, T., Namasivayam, R. K., & Annamalai, A. (2021). Mental-illness-related stigma in health care in South India: Mixed-methods study. *Indian Journal of Psychological Medicine, 43*(1), 58–64. https://doi.org/10.1177/0253717620932244

Murphy, J. K., Khan, A., Sun, Q., Minas, H., Hatcher, S., Ng, C. H., Withers, M., Greenshaw, A., Michalak, E. N., Chakraborty, P. A., Sandanasamy, K. S., Ibrahim, N., Ravindran, A., Chen, J., Nguyen, V. C., & Lam, R. W. (2021). Needs, gaps and opportunities for standard and e-mental health care among at-risk populations in the Asia Pacific in the context of COVID-19: A rapid scoping review. *International Journal for Equity in Health, 20*(1), 161. https://doi.org/10.1186/s12939-021-01484-5

Nadeem, T., Asad, N., & Hamid, S. N. (2020). Cultural considerations in providing trauma care to female, childhood sexual abuse survivors: Experiences from Pakistan. *Asian Journal of Psychiatry, 48*, 101885. https://doi.org/10.1016/j.ajp.2019.101885

Naeem, F., Ayub, M., Javed, Z., Irfan, M., Haral, F., & Kingdon, D. (2006). Stigma and psychiatric illness. A survey of attitude of medical students and doctors in Lahore, Pakistan. *Journal of Ayub Medical College, Abbottabad, 18*(3), 46–49.

Nafeh, F., Fusigboye, S., & Sornpaisarn, B. (2022). Understanding injection drug use in Afghanistan: A scoping review. *Substance Abuse Treatment, Prevention, and Policy, 17*, 65. https://doi.org/10.1186/s13011-022-00491-1

Naheed, A., Ashraf, M. N., Chakma, N., Jennings, H. M., & Nahar, P. (2022). Protocol for integrating mental health services into primary healthcare facilities: A qualitative study of the perspectives of patients, family members and healthcare providers in rural Bangladesh. *British Medical Journal Open, 12*, e052464. https://doi.org/10.1136/bmjopen-2021-052464

Nambiar, D., Razzak, J., Afsana, K., Adams, A. M., Hasan, A., Mohan, D., & Patel, V. (2017). Mental illness and injuries: Emerging health challenges of urbanisation in South Asia. *The British Medical Journal, 357*, j1126. https://doi.org/10.1136/bmj.j1126

Naqvi, H. A., Hussain, S., Zaman, M., & Islam, M. (2009). Pathways to care: Duration of untreated psychosis from Karachi, Pakistan. *Plos One, 4*(10), e7409. https://doi.org/10.1371/journal.pone.0007409

Naqvi, H. A., Sabzwari, S., Hussain, S., Islam, M., & Zaman, M. (2012). General practitioners' awareness and management of common psychiatric disorders: a community-based survey from Karachi, Pakistan. *Eastern Mediterranean Health Journal, 18*(5), 446–453. https://doi.org/10.26719/2012.18.5.446

Nebhinani, N., Pareek, V., Choudhary, S., Tripathi, S., Singh, P., & Kumar, M. (2022). Pathways of care and attitudes toward psychotropics in patients with depressive disorders and psychotic disorders. *Journal of Neurosciences in Rural Practice, 13*(4), 785–790. https://doi.org/10.25259/JNRP-2021-11-39

Nepal Health Research Council. (2020). Report of National Mental Health Survey Nepal 2020. Retrieved from https://nhrc.gov.np/publication/report-of-national-mental-health-survey-2020/

Newnham, E. A., Dzidic, P. L., Mergelsberg, E. L. P., Guragain, B., Chan, E. Y. Y., Kim, Y., Leaning, J., Kayano, R., Wright, M., Kaththiriarachchi, L., Kato, H., Osawa, T., & Gibbs, L. (2020). The Asia Pacific disaster mental health network: Setting a mental health agenda for the region. *International Journal of Environmental Research and Public Health, 17*(17), 6144. https://doi.org/10.3390/ijerph17176144

Nicaise, P., Grard, A., Leys, M., Van Audenhove, C., & Lorant, V. (2021). Key dimensions of collaboration quality in mental health care service networks. *Journal of Interprofessional Care, 35*(1), 28–36. https://doi.org/10.1080/13561820.2019.1709425

Nine, S. B., Najm, A. F., Allan, E. B., & Gronholm, P. C. (2022). Mental health stigma among community members in Afghanistan: A cross-sectional survey. *International Journal of Social Psychiatry, 68*(7), 1470–1485. https://doi.org/10.1177/00207640211036169

Nuri, N. N., Sarker, M., Ahmed, H. U., Hossain, M. D., Beiersmann, C., & Jahn, A. (2018). Pathways to care of patients with mental health problems in Bangladesh. *International Journal of Mental Health Systems, 12*, 39. https://doi.org/10.1186/s13033-018-0218-y

O'Connor, R. C., Worthman, C. M., Abanga, M., Athanassopoulou, N., Boyce, N., Chan, L. F., Christensen, H., Das-Munshi, J., Downs, J., Koenen, K. C., Moutier, C. Y., Templeton, P., Batterham, P., Brakspear, K., Frank, R. G., Gilbody, S., Gureje, O., Henderson, D., John, A., Kabagambe, W., et al. (2023). Gone Too Soon: priorities for action to prevent premature mortality associated with mental illness and mental distress. *The lancet. Psychiatry, 10* (6), 452–464. https://doi.org/10.1016/S2215-0366(23)00058-5

Ochani, S., Aaqil, S. I., Nazir, A., Athar, F. B., Ochani, K., & Ullah, K. (2022). Various health-related challenges amidst recent floods in Pakistan; strategies for future prevention and control. *Annals of Medicine and Surgery, 82*, 104667. https://doi.org/10.1016/j.amsu.2022.104667

Ogihara, Y., & Uchida, Y. (2014). Does individualism bring happiness? Negative effects of individualism on interpersonal relationships and happiness. *Frontiers in Psychology, 5*, 135. https://doi.org/10.3389/fpsyg.2014.00135

Okato, A., Hashimoto, T., Tanaka, M., Saito, N., Endo, M., Okayama, J., Ichihara, A., Eshima, S., Handa, S., Senda, M., Sato, Y., Watanabe, H., Nakazato, M., & Iyo, M. (2020). Inter-agency collaboration factors affecting multidisciplinary workers' ability to identify child maltreatment. *BMC Research Notes, 13*(1), 323. https://doi.org/10.1186/s13104-020-05162-7

Owais, S. S., Horner, R. D., Khan, M. A., Kenison, K., & Probst, J. C. (2023). Integrating maternal depression care at primary private clinics in low-income settings in Pakistan: A secondary analysis. *Frontiers in Global Women's Health, 4*, 1091485. https://doi.org/10.3389/fgwh.2023.1091485

Pal, S. C., Chowdhuri, I., Das, B., Chakrabortty, R., Roy, P., Saha, A., & Shit, M. (2022). Threats of climate change and land use patterns enhance the susceptibility of future floods in India. *Journal of Environmental Management, 305*, 114317. https://doi.org/10.1016/j.jenvman.2021.114317

Papola, D., Ostuzzi, G., Todesco, B., Gastaldon, C., Hanna, F., Chatterjee, S., van Ommeren, M., & Barbui, C. (2023). Updating the WHO Model Lists of Essential Medicines to promote global access to the most cost-effective and safe medicines for mental disorders. *The lancet. Psychiatry, S2215-0366*(23), 00176-1. https://doi.org/10.1016/S2215-0366(23)00176-1

Patel, P. P., Russell, J., Allden, K., Betancourt, T. S., Bolton, P., Galappatti, A., Hijazi, Z., Johnson, K., Jones, K., Kadis, L., Leary, K., Weissbecker, I., & Nakku, J. (2011). Transitioning mental health & psychosocial support: from short-term emergency to sustainable post-disaster development. Humanitarian Action Summit 2011. *Prehospital and Disaster Medicine, 26*(6), 470–481. https://doi.org/10.1017/S1049023X1200012X

Patil, S., Patil, V., Tekkalaki, B., Chate, S., & Patil, N. M. (2022). Public–private partnership (PPP) model of psychiatry day care center in India: Its challenges and opportunities—A 2-year experience. *Journal of Neurosciences in Rural Practice, 13*, 510–514. https://doi.org/10.1055/s-0042-1750708

Patra, B. N., Patil, V., Balhara, Y. P. S., & Khandelwal, S. K. (2022). Self-stigma in patients with major depressive disorder: An exploratory study from India. *International Journal of Social Psychiatry, 68*(1), 147–154. https://doi.org/10.1177/0020764020975811

Pelham, B., Hardin, C., Murray, D., Shimizu, M., & Vandello, J. (2022). A truly global, non-WEIRD examination of collectivism: The Global Collectivism Index (GCI). *Current Research in Ecological and Social Psychology, 3*, 100030. https://doi.org/10.1016/j.cresp.2021.100030

Pelzang, R. (2012). Mental health care in Bhutan: Policy and issues. *WHO South-East Asia Journal of Public Health, 1*(3), 339–346. https://doi.org/10.4103/2224-3151.207030

Petersen, I., Marais, D., Abdulmalik, J., Ahuja, S., Alem, A., Chisholm, D., Egbe, C., Gureje, O., Hanlon, C., Lund, C., Shidhaye, R., Jordans, M., Kigozi, F., Mugisha, J., Upadhaya, N., & Thornicroft, G. (2017). Strengthening mental health system governance in six low- and middle-income countries in Africa and South Asia: Challenges, needs and potential strategies. *Health Policy and Planning, 32*(5), 699–709. https://doi.org/10.1093/heapol/czx014

Pham, T. V., Koirala, R., & Kohrt, B. A. (2021). Traditional and biomedical care pathways for mental well-being in rural Nepal. *International Journal of Mental Health Systems, 15*, 4. https://doi.org/10.1186/s13033-020-00433-z

Poreddi, V., Thimmaiah, R., & Math, S. B. (2015). Attitudes toward people with mental illness among medical students. *Journal of Neurosciences in Rural Practice, 6*(3), 349–354. https://doi.org/10.4103/0976-3147.154564

Prabhu, A., Vishnu Vardhan, G., & Pandit, L. V. (2015). Pathways to tertiary care adopted by individuals with psychiatric illness. *Asian Journal of Psychiatry, 16*, 32–35. https://doi.org/10.1016/j.ajp.2015.06.005

Praharaj, S. K., Salagre, S., & Sharma, P. S. V. N. (2021). Stigma, Empathy, and Attitude (SEA) educational module for medical students to improve the knowledge and attitude towards persons with mental illness. *Asian Journal of Psychiatry, 65*, 102834. https://doi.org/10.1016/j.ajp.2021.102834

Raghavan, V., Kulandesu, A., Karthick, S., Senthilkumar, S., Gunaselvi, T., Rao, K., John, S., & Thara, R. (2021). Challenges faced by community-level workers in delivering mental health services for a rural community in South India. *Indian Journal of Psychiatry, 63*(3), 307–308. https://doi.org/10.4103/psychiatry.IndianJPsychiatry_907_20

Raghavan, V., & Sanjana, G. (2022). Ethical challenges faced by community mental health workers in urban Chennai. *Indian Journal of Medical Ethics, 7*(4), 290–296. https://doi.org/10.20529/ijme.2022.080

Raghavan, R., Brown, B., Horne, F., Kumar, S., Parameswaran, U., Ali, A. B., Raghu, A., Wilson, A., Svirydzenka, N., Venkateswaran, C., Kumar, M., Kamal, S. R., Barrett, A., et al. (2023). Stigma and mental health problems in an Indian context. Perceptions of people with mental disorders in urban, rural and tribal areas of Kerala. *International Journal of Social Psychiatry, 69*(2), 362–369. https://doi.org/10.1177/00207640221091187

Raguram, R., Venkateswaran, V., Ramakrishna, J., & Weiss, M. G. (2002). Traditional community resources for mental health: A report of temple healing from India. *The British Medical Journal, 325*, 38–40. https://doi.org/10.1136/bmj.325.7354.38

Rahman, M. M., & Alam, K. (2021). The nexus between health status and health expenditure, energy consumption and environmental pollution: Empirical evidence from SAARC-BIMSTEC regions. *BMC Public Health, 21*(1), 1694. https://doi.org/10.1186/s12889-021-11534-w

Rahman, M. A., Babaye, Y., Bhat, A., Collins, P. Y., & Kemp, C. G. (2022). Availability of two essential medicines for mental health in Bangladesh, the Democratic Republic of Congo, Haiti, Nepal, Malawi, Senegal, and Tanzania: Evidence from nationally representative samples of 7958 health facilities. *Journal of Global Health, 12*, 04063. https://doi.org/10.7189/jogh.12.04063

Rai, Y., Gurung, D., & Gautam, K. (2021a). Insight and challenges: Mental health services in Nepal. *Bjpsych International, 18*(2), e5. https://doi.org/10.1192/bji.2020.58

Rai, Y., Karki, U., & da Costa, M. (2021b). Psychotherapy training in Nepal: Views of early career psychiatrists. *BJPsych International, 18*(2), e6. https://doi.org/10.1192/bji.2020.50

Raj, S., Ghosh, A., Sharma, B., & Goel, S. (2021). Portrayal of mental illness in Indian newspapers: A cross-sectional analysis of online media reports. *Indian Journal of Psychiatry, 63*(6), 575–583. https://doi.org/10.4103/indianjpsychiatry.indianjpsychiatry_548_21

Raja, S., Wood, S. K., de Menil, V., & Mannarath, S. C. (2010). Mapping mental health finances in Ghana, Uganda, Sri Lanka, India and Lao PDR. *International Journal of Mental Health Systems, 4*, 11. https://doi.org/10.1186/1752-4458-4-11

Rajkumar, R. P. (2022). The correlates of government expenditure on mental health services: An analysis of data from 78 countries and regions. *Cureus, 14*(8), e28284. https://doi.org/10.7759/cureus.28284

Ramaswamy, R., Shidhaye, R., & Nanda, S. (2018). Making complex interventions work in low resource settings: Developing and applying a design focused implementation approach to deliver mental health through primary care in India. *International Journal of Mental Health Systems, 12*, 5. https://doi.org/10.1186/s13033-018-0181-7

Ran, M.-S., Hall, B. J., Su, T. T., Prawira, B., Breth-Petersen, M., Li, X.-H., & Zhang, T.-M. (2021). Stigma of mental illness and cultural factors in Pacific Rim region: A systematic review. *BMC Psychiatry, 21*, 8. https://doi.org/10.1186/s12888-020-02991-5

Ransing, R., Arafat, S. M. Y., Menon, V., & Kar, S. K. (2023). National suicide prevention strategy of India: Implementation challenges and the way forward. *The Lancet Psychiatry, 10*(3), 163–165. https://doi.org/10.1016/s2215-0366(23)00027-5

Rao, R., Varshney, M., Singh, S., Agrawal, A., & Ambekar, A. (2019). Mental Healthcare Act, 2017, and addiction treatment: Potential pitfalls and trepidations. *Indian Journal of Psychiatry, 61*(2), 208–212. https://doi.org/10.4103/psychiatry.IndianJPsychiatry_463_18

Raza-ur-Rahman, Siddiqi, M. N., & Ahmed, S. H. (2015). Implementation of the mental health act: Are we ready? *The Journal of the Pakistan Medical Association, 65*(12), 1339–1343.

Reddy, S. K., Jagnnathan, A., Ashraf, G. H., Naveen Kumar, C., Thirthalli, J., Banerjee, R., & Muralidhar, D. (2021). Barriers in accessing social welfare benefits for families of children with intellectual and developmental disorders in rural Karnataka: A situation analysis. *Indian Journal of Psychological Medicine, 43*(5), 403–409. https://doi.org/10.1177/0253717621994706

Riaz, M. M. A., Nayyer, B., Lal, A., Nawaz, F. A., & Zil-E-Ali, A. (2023). Climate change and mental health: A call to action to include mental health and psychosocial support services (MHPSS) in the Pakistan flood crisis. *Bjpsych International, 20*(3), 56–58. https://doi.org/10.1192/bji.2023.13

Rimal, P., Choudhury, N., Agrawal, P., Basnet, M., Bohara, B., Citrin, D., Dhungana, S. K., Gauchan, B., Gupta, P., Gupta, T. K., Halliday, S., Kadayat, B., Mahar, R., Maru, D., Nguyen, V., Poudel, S., Raut, A., Rawal, J., Sapkota, S., Schwarz, D., et al. (2021). Collaborative care model for depression in rural Nepal: A mixed-methods implementation research study. *British Medical Journal Open, 11*(8), e048481. https://doi.org/10.1136/bmjopen-2020-048481

Roche, G. C., Fung, P., Ransing, R., Noor, I. M., Shalbafan, M., El Hayek, S., Koh, E. B. Y., Gupta, A. K., & Kudva, K. G. (2021). The state of psychiatric research in the Asia Pacific region. *Asia-Pacific Psychiatry, 13*(1), e12432. https://doi.org/10.1111/appy.12432

Robertson, L. J. (2019). The impact of urbanization on mental health service provision: A Brazil, Russia, India, China, South Africa and Africa focus. *Current Opinion in Psychiatry, 32*(3), 224–231. https://doi.org/10.1097/yco.0000000000000495

Rodrigo, A., & Wimalasingham, V. (2006). Western model of community mental health care: Its applicability to Sri Lanka. *Ceylon Medical Journal, 51*(4), 143–144. https://doi.org/10.4038/cmj.v51i4.1143

Sabawoon, A., Keyes, K. M., Karam, E., & Kovess-Masfety, V. (2022). Associations between traumatic event experiences, psychiatric disorders, and suicidal behavior in the general population of Afghanistan: Findings from Afghan National Mental Health Survey. *Injury Epidemiology, 9*, 31. https://doi.org/10.1186/s40621-022-00403-8

Saha, G. (2021). Advocacy in mental health. *Indian Journal of Psychiatry, 63*(6), 523–526. https://doi.org/10.4103/indianjpsychiatry.indianjpsychiatry_901_21

Sahu, A., Patil, V., Purkayastha, S., Pattanayak, R. D., & Sagar, R. (2019). Pathways to care for patients with bipolar-I disorder: An exploratory study from a Tertiary Care Centre of North India. *Indian Journal of Psychological Medicine, 41*(1), 68–74. https://doi.org/10.4103/IJPSYM.IJPSYM_201_18

Saxena, S., Sharan, P., & Saraceno, B. (2003). Budget and financing of mental health services: Baseline information on 89 countries from WHO's Project Atlas. *The Journal of Mental Health Policy and Economics, 6*, 135–143.

Sathyanath, S., Mendonsa, R. D., Thattil, A. M., Chandran, V. M., & Karkal, R. S. (2016). Socially restrictive attitudes towards people with mental illness among the non-psychiatry medical professionals in a university teaching hospital in South India. *The International Journal of Social Psychiatry, 62*(3), 221–226. https://doi.org/10.1177/0020764015623971

Sathyanath, M., Beesanahalli Shanmukhappa, S., Kakunje, A., Nath, S., & Veetil, M. V. (2023). Stigma and discrimination among persons with mental illness in a tertiary care medical institution in Southern India. *Psychiatriki*, https://doi.org/10.22365/jpsych.2023.013. Advance online publication. https://doi.org/10.22365/jpsych.2023.013

Schenk, W. C., & Bui, T. (2018). Sri Lanka's post-tsunami health system recovery: A qualitative analysis of physician perspectives. *International Health, 10*(1), 20–26. https://doi.org/10.1093/inthealth/ihx064

Saxena, S., Thornicroft, G., Knapp, M., & Whiteford, H. (2007). Resources for mental health: Scarcity, inequity, and inefficiency. *Lancet, 370*(9590), 878–889. https://doi.org/10.1016/S0140-6736(07)61239-2

Sequeira, C., Sampaio, F., de Pinho, L. G., Araújo, O., Lluch Canut, T., & Sousa, L. (2022). Editorial: Mental health literacy: How to obtain and maintain positive mental health. *Frontiers in Psychology, 13*, 1036983. https://doi.org/10.3389/fpsyg.2022.1036983

Shalahuddin Qusar, M. M. A., Hossain, R., Sohan, M., Nazir, S., Hossain, M. J., & Islam, M. R. (2022). Attitudes of mental healthcare professionals and media professionals towards each other in reducing social stigma due to mental illness in Bangladesh. *Journal of Community Psychology, 50*(7), 3181–3195. https://doi.org/10.1002/jcop.22823

Sharpe, I., & Davison, C. M. (2021). Climate change, climate-related disasters and mental disorder in low- and middle-income countries: A scoping review. *British Medical Journal Open, 11*, e051908. https://doi.org/10.1136/bmjopen-2021-051908

Shawon, M. S. R., Jahan, E., Rouf, R. R., & Hossain, F. B. (2022). Psychological distress and unhealthy dietary behaviours among adolescents aged 12–15 years in nine South-East Asian countries: A secondary analysis of the global school-based health survey data. *The British Journal of Nutrition*, 1–10. https://doi.org/10.1017/s0007114522002306

Sifat, M. S., Tasnim, N., Hoque, N., Saperstein, S., Shin, R. Q., Feldman, R., Stoebenau, K., & Green, K. M. (2022). Motivations and barriers for clinical mental health help-seeking in Bangladeshi university students: A cross-sectional study. *Global Mental Health, 9*, 211–220. https://doi.org/10.1017/gmh.2022.24

Singh, O. P. (2020). Substance use in India - Policy implications. *Indian Journal of Psychiatry, 62*(2), 111. https://doi.org/10.4103/psychiatry.IndianJPsychiatry_207_20

Singh, R., & Khadka, S. (2022). Mental health law in Nepal. *Bjpsych International, 19*(1), 24–26. https://doi.org/10.1192/bji.2021.52

Singh, S. P., Winsper, C., Mohan, M., Birchwood, M., Chadda, R. K., Furtado, V., Iyer, S. N., Lilford, R. J., Madan, J., Meyer, C., Ramachandran, P., Rangaswamy, T., Shah, J., Sood, M., & WIC Consortium. (2023). Pathways to care in first-episode psychosis in low-resource settings: Implications for policy and practice. *Asian Journal of Psychiatry, 81*, 103463. https://doi.org/10.1016/j.ajp.2023.103463

Sinha, N. (2023). Global Mental Health movement: Need for a cultural perspective. *Indian Journal of Medical Ethics*, 1–5. https://doi.org/10.20529/IJME.2023.025

Siriwardhana, C., Adikari, A., Pannala, G., Roberts, B., Siribaddana, S., Abas, M., Sumathipala, A., & Stewart, R. (2015). Changes in mental disorder prevalence among conflict-affected populations: A prospective study in Sri Lanka (COMRAID-R). *BMC Psychiatry, 15*, 41. https://doi.org/10.1186/s12888-015-0424-y

Sithey, G., Li, M., Wen, L. M., Kelly, P. J., & Clarke, K. (2018). Socioeconomic, religious, spiritual and health factors associated with symptoms of common mental disorders: A cross-sectional secondary analysis of data from Bhutan's Gross National Happiness Study, 2015. *British Medical Journal Open, 8*(2), e018202. https://doi.org/10.1136/bmjopen-2017-018202

Sobowale, K., & Torous, J. (2016). Disaster psychiatry in Asia: The potential of smartphones, mobile, and connected technologies. *Asian Journal of Psychiatry, 22*, 1–5. https://doi.org/10.1016/j.ajp.2016.03.004

Sood, A. (2016). The Global Mental Health movement and its impact on traditional healing in India: A case study of the Balaji temple in Rajasthan. *Transcultural Psychiatry, 53*(6), 766–782. https://doi.org/10.1177/1363461516679352

Sood, M., Chadda, R. K., & Kallivayalil, R. A. (2017). Primary prevention in psychiatry in general hospitals in South Asia. *Indian Journal of Psychiatry, 59*(4), 510–514. https://doi.org/10.4103/psychiatry.IndianJPsychiatry_180_17

Sreejith, G., & Menon, V. (2019). Mobile phones as a medium of mental health care service delivery: Perspectives and barriers among patients with severe mental illness. *Indian Journal of Psychological Medicine, 41*(5), 428–433. https://doi.org/10.4103/IJPSYM.IJPSYM_333_18

Sriramalu, S. B., Elangovan, A. R., Isaac, M., & Kalyanasundaram, J. R. (2022). Challenges in tracing treatment non-adherent persons with mental illness: Experiences from a rural community mental health center, India. *Asian Journal of Psychiatry, 67*, 102944. https://doi.org/10.1016/j.ajp.2021.102944

Steel, Z., Marnane, C., Iranpour, C., Chey, T., Jackson, J. W., Patel, V., & Silove, D. (2014). The global prevalence of common mental disorders: A systematic review and meta-analysis 1980–2013. *International Journal of Epidemiology, 43*(2), 476–493. https://doi.org/10.1093/ije/dyu038

Talpur, A., & George, T. P. (2014). A review of drug policy in the Golden Crescent: Towards the development of more effective solutions. *Asian Journal of Psychiatry, 12*, 31–35. https://doi.org/10.1016/j.ajp.2014.07.001

Tanha, A. F., Sheba, N. H., Islam, M. S., Potenza, M. N., & Islam, M. R. (2022). A review of common mental health problems in the general population during the COVID-19 pandemic in South Asia. *Current psychology*, 1–21. https://doi.org/10.1007/s12144-022-04106-7

Thara, R., Padmavati, R., Aynkran, J. R., & John, S. (2008). Community mental health in India: A rethink. *International Journal of Mental Health Systems, 2*, 11. https://doi.org/10.1186/1752-4458-2-11

Thara, R., Rameshkumar, S., & Mohan, C. G. (2010). Publications on community psychiatry. *Indian Journal of Psychiatry, 52*(Suppl 1), S274–S277. https://doi.org/10.4103/0019-5545.69248

The World Bank. (2022). Population, total | data. Retrieved July 22, 2023 from https://data.worldbank.org/indicator/SP.POP.TOTL

Thomas, F. C., D'Souza, M., Magwood, O., Thilakanathan, D., Sukumar, V., Doherty, S., Dass, G., Hart, T., Sivayokan, S., Wickramage, K., Kirupakaran, S., & McShane, K. (2022). Examining post-conflict stressors in northern Sri Lanka: A qualitative study. *Plos One, 17*(9), e0267018. https://doi.org/10.1371/journal.pone.0267018

Thomas, P. T., Rajagopalan, J., Hurzuk, S., Ramasamy, N., Pattabiraman, M., De Poli, C., Lorenz-Dant, K., Comas-Herrera, A., & Alladi, S. (2023). Pathways to care for people with dementia in India: An exploratory study using case vignettes. *Dementia, 14713012231193081*. Advance online publication. https://doi.org/10.1177/14713012231193081

Tiwari, I., Tilstra, M., Campbell, S. M., Nielsen, C. C., Hodgins, S., Vargas, A. R. O., Whitfield, K., Sapkota, B. P., & Yamamoto, S. S. (2022). Climate change impacts on the health of South Asian children and women subpopulations—A scoping review. *Heliyon, 8*, e10811. https://doi.org/10.1016/j.heliyon.2022.e10811

Tol, W. A., Komproe, I. H., Jordans, M. J., Vallipuram, A., Sipsma, H., Sivayokan, S., Macy, R. D., & DE Jong, J. T. (2012). Outcomes and moderators of a preventive school-based mental health intervention for children affected by war in Sri Lanka: A cluster randomized trial. *World Psychiatry, 11*(2), 114–122. https://doi.org/10.1016/j.wpsyc.2012.05.008

Tomlinson, M., Chaudhery, D., Ahmadzai, H., Rodriguez Gomez, S., Rodriguez Gomez, C., van Heyningen, T., & Chopra, M. (2020). Identifying and treating maternal mental health difficulties in Afghanistan: A feasibility study. *International Journal of Mental Health Systems, 14*, 75. https://doi.org/10.1186/s13033-020-00407-1

United Nations Department of Economic and Social Affairs. (2020). World Social Report 2020: Inequality in a rapidly changing world. United Nations. Retrieved from https://www.un.org/development/desa/dspd/wp-content/uploads/sites/22/2020/01/World-Social-Report-2020-FullReport.pdf

United Nations Development Programme. (2022). Human Development Report 2021/22. Uncertain times, unsettled lives: Shaping our future in a transforming world. United Nations Development Programme. Retrieved from https://hdr.undp.org/content/human-development-report-2021-22

Varshney, P., Malathesh, B. C., Nirisha, P. L., Harshitha, N. R., Kulal, N., Kumar, C. N., Gajera, G., Suhas, S., Rahul, P., Harshitha, H. A., Manjunatha, N., Manjappa, A. A., Math, S. B., & Thirthalli, J. (2022). Stake holder perspectives on the role of accredited social health activists (ASHAs) in Indian public mental healthcare space: A qualitative study. *Journal of Family Medicine and Primary Care, 11*(11), 7308–7315. https://doi.org/10.4103/jfmpc.jfmpc_543_22

Volpe, U., Mihai, A., Jordanova, V., & Sartorius, N. (2015). The pathways to mental healthcare worldwide: A systematic review. *Current Opinion in Psychiatry, 28*(4), 299–306. https://doi.org/10.1097/YCO.0000000000000164

Wahid, S. S., Raza, W. A., Mahmud, I., & Kohrt, B. A. (2023). Climate-related shocks and other stressors associated with depression and anxiety in Bangladesh: A nationally representative panel study. *The Lancet Planetary Health, 7*(2), e137–e146. https://doi.org/10.1016/S2542-5196(22)00315-1

WHO and Ministry of Public Health. (2006). WHO-AIMS Report on Mental Health in Afghanistan.

WHO and Ministry of Health. (2006a). WHO-AIMS Report on Mental Health in Maldives. Male.

WHO and Ministry of Health. (2006b). WHO-AIMS Report on Mental Health System in Nepal. Kathmandu, Nepal.

WHO and Ministry of Health. (2007a). WHO-AIMS Report on Mental Health System in Bhutan. Thimphu, Bhutan.

WHO and Ministry of Health. (2007b). WHO-AIMS Report on mental health system in Bangladesh.

WHO and Ministry of Health. (2009). WHO-AIMS Report on mental health system in Pakistan.

World Health Organization. (2004). Promoting mental health: Concepts, emerging evidence, practice: Summary report/a report from the World Health Organization, Department of Mental Health and Substance Abuse in collaboration with the Victorian Health Promotion Foundation (VicHealth) and the University of Melbourne. World Health Organization. Retrieved from https://apps.who.int/iris/bitstream/handle/10665/42940/9241591595.pdf

World Health Organization & World Organization of Family Doctors. (2008). Integrating mental health into primary care: A global perspective. Geneva: World Health Organization. Retrieved from https://www.who.int/publications/i/item/9789241563680

World Health Organization. (2017). Mental Health Atlas 2017. Member State Profile: India. Retrieved from https://www.who.int/publications/m/item/mental-health-atlas-2017-country-profile-india

World Health Organization. (2019). The WHO special initiative for mental health (2019–2023): Universal health coverage for mental health. Retrieved from https://apps.who.int/iris/bitstream/handle/10665/310981/WHO-MSD-19.1-eng.pdf

World Health Organization. (2020a). Mental Health Atlas 2020. Member State Profile: Afghanistan. Retrieved from at https://www.who.int/publications/m/item/mental-health-atlas-country-profile-afghanistan

World Health Organization. (2020b). Mental Health Atlas 2020. Member State Profile: Bangladesh. Retrieved from https://www.who.int/publications/m/item/mental-health-atlas-bgd-2020-country-profile

World Health Organization. (2020c). Mental Health Atlas 2020. Member State Profile: Bhutan. Retrieved from https://www.who.int/publications/m/item/mental-health-atlas-btn-2020-country-profile

World Health Organization. (2020d). Mental Health Atlas 2020. Member State Profile: Maldives. Retrieved from https://www.who.int/publications/m/item/mental-health-atlas-mdv-2020-country-profile

World Health Organization. (2020e). Mental Health Atlas 2020. Member State Profile: Nepal. Retrieved from https://www.who.int/publications/m/item/mental-health-atlas-npl-2020-country-profile

World Health Organization. (2020f). Mental Health Atlas 2020. Member State Profile: Pakistan. Retrieved from https://www.who.int/publications/m/item/mental-health-atlas-pak-2020-country-profile

World Health Organization. (2020g). Mental Health Atlas 2020. Member State Profile: Sri Lanka. Retrieved from https://www.who.int/publications/m/item/mental-health-atlas-lka-2020-country-profile

World Health Organization. (2021a). Mental Health Atlas 2020. World Health Organization. Retrieved from https://www.who.int/publications/i/item/9789240036703

World Health Organization. (2021b). Bangladesh—WHO Special Initiative for Mental Health: Situational Assessment. Retrieved from https://www.who.int/publications/m/item/bangladesh---who-special-initiative-for-mental-health

World Health Organization. (2021c). Comprehensive mental health action plan 2013–2030. World Health Organization. Retrieved from https://apps.who.int/iris/handle/10665/345301

World Health Organization. (2022a). Addressing mental health in Sri Lanka. World Health Organization, Regional Office for South-East Asia. Retrieved from https://www.who.int/publications/i/item/9789290210221

World Health Organization. (2022b). World Mental Health Report: transforming mental health for all. World Health Organization Retrieved from https://www.who.int/teams/mental-health-and-substance-use/world-mental-health-report

World Health Organization. (2022c). Addressing mental health in Bhutan. World Health Organization, Regional Office for South-East Asia. Retrieved from https://apps.who.int/iris/bitstream/handle/10665/364873/9789290210153-eng.pdf?sequence=1

World Health Organization. (2022d). Nepal's National Suicide Prevention Helpline Service helping save lives. Retrieved from https://www.who.int/nepal/news/detail/09-12-2022-Nepal-National-Suicide-Prevention-Helpline-Service-helping-save-lives

Research, Innovations, and Ideas to Facilitate Mental Healthcare Delivery in South Asia

Nilamadhab Kar

Abstract A large proportion of the general population in the highly populous South Asian region has mental health problems. There are many challenges for their care, such as lack of resources, inadequate mental healthcare workforce, uneven distribution of professional input, large underserved areas, poor affordability, stigma, etc. There are examples of good practice, research-based evidence of effective services in the community, and consistent progress. However, there are still unmet needs for mental health care; it is evident that many patients do not receive appropriate care. There is a need for multilevel efforts to address this service gap, from providing adequate resources, training mental health professionals, supporting primary care healthcare staff for community-level interventions, developing sub-specialization services, and conducting research on the effectiveness of psychiatric services. Supporting informal family caregivers is an important consideration in the process as most of the psychiatric patients in the region are supported by their families. Regional cooperation between the countries sharing developmental ideas, projects, and research would be helpful. Ultimately, the efforts should lead to more patient-centric, evidence-based care, sustaining their rights under appropriate laws.

Keywords Mental health care · South Asia · Research · Innovation · Mental health services delivery

1 Introduction

Around a quarter of the world's population live in South Asia, making it the most populated area in the world (Hossain et al., 2020; Wikipedia, 2023). Ironically, the mental health burden of these areas is considerable (Hossain et al., 2020; Trivedi

N. Kar (✉)
Black Country Healthcare NHS Foundation Trust, Wolverhampton, UK
e-mail: n.kar@nhs.net

University of Wolverhampton, Wolverhampton, UK

Faculty of Contemplative and Behavioural Sciences, Sri Sri University, Cuttack, India et al., 2007), with proportions of the population with common mental disorders such as depression, anxiety, posttraumatic stress disorder, mixed anxiety and depression, tobacco and alcohol abuse, suicidal behaviors are highest in this region (Naveed et al., 2020; Ogbo et al., 2018).

There could be various reasons; a large fraction of the society is economically challenged and lives in rural areas (Thara & Padmavati, 2013). The accessibility and affordability of appropriate mental health care are limited. These regions are vulnerable to catastrophic natural events which cause massive stress in various areas. Besides, in this region, resources for mental health services are scant and do not reach a large proportion of the population adequately and uniformly.

Considering these factors, there is a need to explore options to improve mental health care in this region through examples of the efforts that have been found successful, further innovation, and research. This chapter looks into the challenges, approaches taken to manage mental health issues and the regional initiatives, to summarize possible ways that may help the planning and delivery of mental health care in this region.

1.1 The Challenges

Psychiatric patients in this region have been managed in several ways for centuries, ranging from faith healing (Kar, 2008), and physical restraint by chains, to treatment by systems of medicine such as Ayurveda (Thara & Padmavati, 2013). Asylums or mental hospitals were established more than a century ago. These methods of treatment are still continuing along with evidence-based psychiatric interventions.

One of the major issues to consider in the methods of providing mental health care in the region is the sheer number of people who need this support. Other issues include the situation that most of the people in these countries live in rural areas, where the needs are higher and resources are scarce. Accessing care may be challenging based on geographical location or traveling distance. In addition, most of these people struggle to afford psychiatric treatment. For these kinds of reasons, a large proportion of patients do not receive any psychiatric treatment. The number of vulnerable or affected people who need mental health care goes really high during disasters involving natural events of cyclones, floods, earthquakes (Kar, 2009; Kar et al., 2004a, 2014), pandemics (Hossain et al., 2021; Tanha et al., 2022), accidents and industrial disasters (Murthy, 2014), or deliberate events such as riots or wars.

1.1.1 Lack of Facilities and Inadequate Workforce

Psychiatric care in these countries has been still primarily clinic or hospital-based and is available mostly in cities or larger towns. This leaves larger areas of the countries underserved. Even for common mental disorders, peripheral or primary care services are inadequate or are ill-prepared.

There are no adequate facilities or infrastructure to cater to the mental health needs of such a huge population. One of the major hurdles is the low number of mental health professionals in South Asian countries which include psychiatrists, psychologists, psychiatric nurses, and social workers, (WHO, 2019). It is estimated that because of the inadequacy of the workforce, approximately 85% of people with mental, neurological, and substance-use disorders in low- and middle-income countries do not receive care (Endale et al., 2020). With the available workforce, specifically psychiatrists, the services are provided in clinics rather than in the community where the need is higher. Multidisciplinary mental health teams hardly exist outside the mental health institutions in these countries.

There are faith, religious, and ritualistic healing which are accessed by a larger proportion of patients (Kar, 2008; Sax, 2014). In addition, there are practices by individuals as quacks without any professional training in mental health (Trivedi & Jilani, 2012). The practice of quackery is quite common in sexual dysfunctions and disorders (Chandra, 2021). While most of these can lead to delays in getting appropriate care, sometimes these practices lead to physical and mental harm to the patients.

1.1.2 Stigma of Mental Illness

Similar to other places in the world, stigma related to mental illness is rife in South Asia (Gurung et al., 2022; Shohel et al., 2022). This is one of the major barriers to seeking help and accepting or maintaining treatment, and it is related to social labeling and ostracizing. The reasons behind stigma are manifold. Studies suggest there is a lack of knowledge of mental illness in the population; people are unaware of the causes and symptoms of mental health problems; there are negative attitudes towards psychiatric patients and beliefs that recovery is unlikely. Most people perceive mentally ill persons as dangerous and irresponsible (Gaiha et al., 2020). However, stigma is prevalent in those with higher or even professional education and aware of its cause and available treatment.

1.2 Meeting the Challenges

Providing holistic mental healthcare and developing services in any region is challenging; it is understandably difficult in resource-scarce areas such as South Asia. It may be helpful to explore the current situation, research findings about the effective interventions, innovations that have been tried, examples of good practice, and the suggestions already available.

Based on the multiple areas and levels of approach, this chapter describes the community or primary care level programs, secondary care, training and support of mental healthcare professionals, the role of the mental health institutions, the role of non-governmental organizations (NGOs), and the government. However, these approaches are interdependent, and collaborative actions are warranted. In the end, how all these activities should lead to patient-centric care is described.

2 Community Mental Health Programs

Community mental health support is the core and has been in focus for any service development discussion (Pandya et al., 2020). Currently, mental health services in the South Asia region are scarce outside cities or larger towns. The District Mental Health Programme in India established a long while back has taken the services up to the district level, but there has not been observable progress beyond the district headquarter hospitals (Singh, 2018); Although some smaller towns may have periodic psychiatric clinics by visiting psychiatrists, other facilities are not available, and it is not common to find multidisciplinary teams. Community mental health care is seriously lacking in the mental health service program.

2.1 Local Evidence of the Effectiveness of Community Programs

There are examples of collaborative community care models (psychosocial services, non-specialist care, and specialist services) for making mental health services available at the community and primary healthcare levels. These have been reported to be not only acceptable but also effective in reducing treatment gaps, improving treatment adherence, and quicker rehabilitation of mentally ill patients. These have generally used specialist primary-level workers trained within specialist programs, case managers, rather than doctors; from specialist and non-specialist organizations involving voluntary and government sectors, to provide community support and treatment for those with severe mental disorders (van Ginneken et al., 2017).

The research evidence base from the region e.g. the community care for people with schizophrenia in India (COPSI) trial suggested that both community and facility-based care are modestly more effective than facility-based care, for reducing disability and symptoms of psychosis; and that it can be implemented in resource scare areas such as rural setting (Chatterjee et al., 2014). A post-conflict, community-level social support program in Nepal was associated with reduced adult onset depressive disorder even in a high-risk population compared with a matched control (Axinn et al., 2022).

These studies suggest that community programs are feasible, acceptable, and effective ways of providing mental health care in the region; which need to be explored and utilized. All these examples strengthen the evidence base that community mental health programs are possible in this developing region, with preventive and therapeutic effectiveness.

2.2 Interventions in the Community

2.2.1 Managing Common Mental Disorders

With available infrastructure in the South Asian countries, added by training of frontline healthcare staff, common mental disorders can be treated in the community. In most parts of the developed economies, primary care physicians diagnose and treat these disorders (Anjara et al., 2019); and only a small proportion are referred to secondary care. Trained nurses can provide psychological assessment and support as well. In this way, the majority of anxiety, depression, and stress-related disorders can be managed. It has been observed that both patients and caregivers perceive primary care-based mental health services as easily accessible, acceptable, and effective (Luitel et al., 2020). These approaches may decrease the huge proportion of untreated psychiatric patients in the community.

2.2.2 Community-Based Intervention

Community-based mental health interventions can include psychoeducation, adherence management, psychosocial rehabilitation, support for livelihood, and referral to secondary services. These can be linked with facility-based care for psychiatric medications, or the management of severe or complex cases with comorbidities. The community interventions can be carried out by the primary healthcare staff; and in some instances along with the support of volunteers of local organizations under supervision. This will have the benefits of regular treatment in decreasing the patient's disability, the burden on the family, and the treatment costs (Chatterjee et al., 2009, 2014).

2.2.3 Social Prescribing

Most of the mental health problems have psychosocial underpinnings. Addressing social determinants of ill health, supporting patients with the non-clinical root cause of poor health, or preventing diseases can be a way forward. This may help in dealing with various mental health issues through social methods. Social prescribing is heterogeneous and tends to include targeted lifestyle interventions, recognizing the interconnections between activity levels, social connectivity, and mental health (Husk et al., 2019). At the personal level, social prescribing can give individuals the knowledge, skills, motivation, and confidence to manage their health and well-being (Morse et al., 2022). Although the evidence base on its effectiveness is limited, there is a potentiality of its growth. This may be acceptable in South Asian countries with diverse sociocultural activities embedded in the usual personal and social life.

2.2.4 Psychiatric Rehabilitation in the Community

Psychosocial rehabilitation of patients with severe mental illness should be possible in the general hospital psychiatric units; however, it is often neglected (Sood & Chadda, 2015). Community-based psychiatric rehabilitation program for people with psychotic disorders in low-resource settings has been found feasible and acceptable intervention with a beneficial impact on disability (Chatterjee et al., 2009). However, more examples in the community, and studies are required about their effectiveness.

2.3 Suicide Prevention

Suicide remains a major concern in South Asia with comparatively higher rates varying between 0.43 and 331.0/100,000 with an average rate that is higher than the world (Jordans et al., 2014). Among the South Asian countries in 2019 Sri Lanka (14/100.000) had the highest rate followed by India (12.7/100,000), and the lowest being Maldives (2.7) (World Bank); As it is known, official reported rates vary widely, and the actual rates could be higher (Jordans et al., 2014; Vijayakumar, 2010).

The risk profile of suicides in South Asian countries is different from the other regions of the world in many ways such as the gender ratio closer to one and the prevalence of psychiatric morbidities such as lower depression level (Vijayakumar et al., 2020). The suicidal concerns range from youth to old age (Kar et al., 2021b, 2022), and different identified vulnerable groups such as students and farmers in India. A considerable proportion has depression, the pooled prevalence of depression in suicide was 37.3%, and that with suicide attempts was 32.7% in South Asia (Arafat et al., 2022c). Not all suicides are due to mental illness per se (Arafat et al., 2022a), but all of them are linked to a lack of or inadequate support for the associated stressful situation. It has been highlighted that the absence of a national suicide prevention strategy, inappropriate media reporting (Kar et al., 2021a; Menon et al., 2021), and inadequate multisectoral engagement are major barriers to effective suicide prevention (Vijayakumar et al., 2022).

2.3.1 Multifactorial, Multilevel Intervention

Suicide prevention remains a social responsibility and requires support from all. Public education, early identification of signs and referral to appropriate supportive services, community assessment, and support, availability of such services, national and regional planning and policy, and specific training of frontline people facing services, are helpful. Integrating all these requires appropriate advice to authorities and the government to develop a comprehensive policy.

There are a few suicide prevention-specific resources and organizations in South Asian countries. However, these organizations are far in between and services are not consistent. There is a need for more such dedicated services within government and non-governmental sectors. The portrayal of suicide in newspapers/media has not helped in most instances; and media having a great role to play in public education, should reorganize their reporting (Kar et al., 2021a; Menon et al., 2021).

There is a definitive beneficial effect to consider periodic training of frontline staff, in primary care, Accident & Emergency units, and mental health professionals on suicide risk assessment and management. There have been reports of increased detection of distress and suicidal ideation by General Practitioners following training (Pfaff et al., 2001); however, the evidence related to the outcome of suicidality has been equivocal (Milner et al., 2017).

2.4 Methods of Community Services

2.4.1 Community Outreach Programs

There are many examples of community outreach in psychiatry. Mental health professionals especially psychiatrists visit underserved areas of smaller towns or industrial setups; which is often done as an individual private practice. However there are many organized satellite clinics supported by mental health institutions (Kar et al., 2004b); these are especially helpful in industrial and other occupational settings with higher psychiatric morbidity (Dutta et al., 2007). In these instances, mental health professionals visit the particular area and provide usually outpatient-based services. However, there is the scope of setting these methods in a more organized way and integrating them into the existing mental healthcare facilities both in the governmental and private sectors.

The community outreach clinics may involve or associate with other centers/ clinics managing mental health issues, e.g., faith healers, religious centers, and those following traditional interventions. This will help in improving awareness of medical intervention, public education, and integrating the healthcare systems in the locally accessed systems.

2.4.2 Remote Clinics

Mental health assessment and management remotely has been in existence for a long time and it is a fast and cost-effective method of reaching out to patients in the community. Tele-clinic and online clinics have proliferated and established their importance further during the COVID-19 pandemic, where these methods maintained mental health services in almost all categories of disorders (Sivakumar et al., 2020). Remote clinics save time, effort, travel, and remain cost-effective. This needs to be supported by appropriate policies and procedures and relevant laws if necessary. Tele or mobile technology-based clinics with assessment and intervention facilities are expected to be helpful, (Pandya et al., 2020) in the current situation in South Asia and may need to be facilitated.

2.4.3 Role of Local Volunteers and Health Workers

Involving local communities is a key method of supporting mental health intervention (Rathod et al., 2017); it helps in improving awareness, dispels stigma, and makes the interventions more culturally acceptable, with support from local persons. Members from community-based self-help groups can be trained as mental health champions who can facilitate mental health service delivery in rural areas with lower cost implications. There are many examples. An intervention model titled systematic medical appraisal, referral, and treatment (SMART) mental health project in rural Andhra Pradesh in India was designed to facilitate the identification and treatment of common mental disorders such as stress, depression, anxiety, and suicide risk. It was delivered by lay village health workers (Accredited Social Health Activists—ASHAs) and primary care doctors (Tewari et al., 2017). This project reported facilitating and hindering factors for providing mental health services in the villages, which may help in developing such projects.

Similarly in Maharashtra, India a program involving local volunteers termed *atmiyata* champions (close buddies) and *mitras* (friends), provided support and basic counseling to people with common mental health disorders in the community; and facilitated access to mental healthcare and social benefits, improved community awareness of mental health issues, and promoted well-being (Shields-Zeeman et al., 2017). Following the Odisha Supercyclone in 1999, local volunteers as *sneha-karmi* (affectionate workers) received training and supported cyclone survivors through trauma counseling effectively (Murthy et al., 2003).

2.4.4 Family as Caregiver

Support from family as caregivers is a key ingredient to the success of community-based mental health problems. This is abundantly available for most patients in South Asia, where most patients (almost 90%) live in families (Sood & Chadda, 2015). Families are actively involved in taking care of mentally ill patients, and are an effective resource for mental healthcare delivery (Avasthi, 2010). This is a great asset, which needs to be explored to realize its full therapeutic potential in supporting patient care. Family can support not only the care of the patient but also their rehabilitation to improve their level of functioning, sense of autonomy, and empowerment (Thekkumkara et al., 2020). They have a recognized role in suicide prevention (Arafat et al., 2022b). Traditional joint families can defuse the burden of caring and provide a therapeutic environment that could mediate a better course and outcome of major mental disorders (Avasthi, 2010). However as the family structures are changing, the nuclear families may need more support, and it may have impact on the clinical outcomes.

Family caregivers need support through information, psychological, and even financial to carry on their caring role. It is well known that caregiving is stressful, especially in challenging circumstances, and with continuous caregiving with no respite. There are caregiver skill training programs for various psychiatric disorders;

however, their availability and accessibility remain a concern (Baruah et al., 2021; Sengupta et al., 2023).

3 Secondary Care

In most of the urban areas, psychiatrist-led, secondary care facilities mostly outpatients are available, with some inpatient beds. Large psychiatric hospitals which are basically the remnants of asylums of previous years are still present in many areas. However resource concerns are clearly evident in secondary mental health services in South Asian countries (Rathod et al., 2017).

In inpatient care, there is an inadequate number of beds available based on the requirement and there is clearly a felt need of increasing capacity. One way to decrease dependence on hospital admission is better community care, as early effective care in the community may decrease admission rates (Kar, 2015); however, that is probably a long way ahead. Some long-stay asylum-type facilities urgently need to be modified, improving their intervention approach and care quality.

3.1 Pharmacotherapy

Pharmacotherapy has been the mainstay of treatment as there is a serious paucity of professionals for psychological intervention. In medicinal treatment, although some South Asian countries have practice guidelines, e.g. in India (Indian Psychiatric Society, 2022), its adherence is not known. It is noticed that different medicines are combined, some with no obvious evidence base. Similarly, while rational polypharmacy is being considered, irrational polypharmacy is common in clinical practice (Govaerts et al., 2021; Shenoy et al., 2020). This can be addressed by clinical audits and monitoring the clinical practice which can be done at individual, regional, or national levels; e.g., The Prescribing Observatory for Mental Health (POMH) and national audits in the UK (Royal College of Psychiatrists, 2023a, 2023b).

3.2 Psychological Interventions

In the face of the massive shortage of manpower and the enormous need for psychological services; it is important to look at methods of therapy and how that can be provided. Group and internet-based therapies can reach a lot of people and can be provided easily (Kar, 2011). There are examples of free online cognitive behavioral therapy in different parts of the world which has been effective (Mahoney et al., 2021; Ruwaard et al., 2011). With support, this can be made freely available for the users. This is extremely important during stressful situations that affect the masses.

Providing resources for bibliotherapy, which has been found as an affordable and effective intervention (Gualano et al., 2017; Yuan et al., 2018); as a way of books on prescription (Carty et al., 2016) can be helpful. This can be effectively done through e-books which can be read with electronic devices.

It is also important to develop culture-based interventions; which could be more acceptable and helpful for a diverse culture in South Asia; rather than just following the therapies developed in different cultures. It has been observed that following stressful situations and disasters most people were coping with religious activities and devotional songs (Kar, 2006); and this kind of psychological support mechanism needs further exploration regarding their effectiveness. There are a few examples of cultural adaptations of psychotherapeutic approaches utilizing concepts from the Gita (Bhatia et al., 2013; Kalra et al., 2018; Reddy, 2012). It is important to utilize cultural understanding and philosophies in psychotherapeutic interventions and study the effectiveness of these culture-based interventions.

3.2.1 Remote Psychotherapies

While in-person psychotherapy was the norm in the past, with the development of technology, online, video-delivered psychotherapy has been common. In fact, online psychotherapies are established methods of intervention and are in use for a long period of time. Their use has increased during the COVID-19 pandemic and has been reported to be effective and satisfying for patients (Giordano et al., 2022). Online psychotherapies are no less efficacious than in-person psychotherapy (Fernandez et al., 2021). These are gradually getting embedded in the countries in South Asia; however, they need more support, encouragement, and process to access that care. As internet use is increasing in South Asian nations, and most patients live in faraway rural areas, it can be expected that online psychotherapies may be able to improve the reach of these modes of intervention. Group psychotherapies will be exceptionally useful following disasters where the number of people requiring psychological support is particularly high (Kar, 2011).

3.3 Self-rating Tools

The use of psychiatric rating scales is comparatively less in routine clinical practice in contrast to research. Many short self-rating scales can be used to improve the quality of monitoring (psychopathology, side effects, etc.) and clinical and functional outcomes of the patients. Many of these are available in regional languages of South Asia. The use of locally validated vernacular self-rating scales for screening mental illnesses in general and specific disorders may be helpful; along with the development of some culture-specific scales or adaptations. Some examples of the scales for which regional versions are available include patient health questionnaires (Kroenke et al., 2001), general anxiety questionnaires (Spitzer et al., 2006), etc., along with the quality of life scales, e.g., WHO quality of life scale (Kar et al., 2017; Saxena et al., 1998), recovering quality of life scales (Kar et al., 2023; Satapathy et al., 2022), etc. Using outcome measures would be a positive step in the clinical assessment and management of the patients.

4 Sub-specialty Care

Mental health services in psychiatric sub-specialties are still in the early development stage in most parts of South Asia; with a huge growth potential. Many regions have addiction, liaison, and child and adolescent psychiatry; however, there is much scope to improve these services. Child and adolescent psychiatry services are very sporadic, mostly in tertiary centers; with extremely limited services (Willmot et al., 2022). Considering that most mental illnesses start in the early years of life and a significant proportion of children and adolescents have psychiatric problems, the need for support is enormous.

There are de-addiction centers in various places; however, they are poorly resourced, with inadequate professional input and questionable outcomes. There are suggestions to move away from the deaddiction center model to outpatient drug treatment clinics along with community-based treatment (Dalal, 2020).

Forensic psychiatric services are available, especially as prisons in-reach in many areas of South Asia. In prisons, there is a massive mental health burden (Tripathy et al., 2022). Psychosocial interventions such as motivational intervention, interpersonal therapy, cognitive behavioral therapy, positive psychology intervention, music therapy, and acceptance and commitment therapy have helped improve mental health conditions of prison inmates (Thekkumkara et al., 2022). While mental health support should be available in all prisons, there should be specific mental health centers for patients with criminal history.

While the population is aging and the need for old age psychiatry is growing, there does not appear to be a proportionate increase in old age psychiatry services or facilities. Appropriately trained healthcare professionals are not available for geriatric medicine or psychiatry (Matthews et al., 2023). There is also a need for facilities for intellectual disability, eating disorders, perinatal psychiatry, and medical psychotherapy subspecialties.

One of the felt needs is support for emergency mental health care, starting with accident and emergency services which most of the patients attend following self-harm or suicide attempt. As a part of liaison psychiatry, the patients can be psychologically supported. This could be probably easily arranged in secondary setups.

4.1 Disaster Psychiatry

South Asia is in a climatic zone that is vulnerable to natural events such as cyclones, tsunamis, floods, earthquakes, etc. There are also man-made traumatic events of rape, abduction, human trafficking, ethnic violence, civil unrest, riots, war, and mass displacements which result in unnecessary and avoidable woes. Although these are not specific to South Asia, however, many regions in this area remain unsettled by these events for a long time. These traumatic events often have catastrophic consequences and are associated with anxiety, depression, and post-traumatic stress disorders.

Considering the density of the population in South Asia huge number of people is affected. Most of this population hardly gets any mental health care; and those who receive post-disaster care it is limited to immediate or short-term interventions in the early stages (Kar, 2006). There is a need to specifically look into the trauma-related mental health consequences in South Asia and how to improve post-disaster mental health care in this population.

Post-disaster intervention process for mental health support should be predetermined, starting with first responders, practical support, screening, clinical evaluation, support, and referral to primary or secondary mental health services. From the developing knowledge base in this region, over the years, few generalizations can be made (Murthy et al., 2003). Existing structures such as schools/colleges or primary health centers can be made into respite centers that can be used as mental health triage and crisis intervention. Screening survivors following disasters can help triage and identify people with higher risk (Kumar et al., 2023) and those who require support. Local people or volunteers can be trained as trauma counselors, who can be supervised to work long after the initial responders; and relief workers have left the disaster areas. These counsellors of course would need continued supervision and support from clinicians and authorities.

Intervention work should be culturally acceptable, and accessible. So developing methods that work in this population is better, rather than utilizing methods that have been effective in different populations or cultures. Proactive mental health support for trauma survivors may help them to recover fast and may not lead to disabling chronic mental health problems.

5 Training of Health Workforce in Psychiatry

One of the major impediments to the effective implementation of mental health care is inadequate mental health professionals (Endale et al., 2020; WHO, 2019). The need to train and appoint a mental health task force cannot be overemphasized. There are many ways to tackle this while waiting for the workforce to reach the desired level.

5.1 Training of Frontline Healthcare Staff

Primacy care general practitioners, and many other specialists, e.g., physicians, dermatologists, oncologists, geriatricians, and pediatricians can have refresher courses in detecting symptoms of common mental disorders and initiating medicinal treatment when appropriate. They can also be trained on basic psychotherapeutic principles.

Training of grassroots-level workers at the primary care level is an essential element to increase the reach of mental health services in the community. These can help early detection of symptoms and referral. There are many studies related to the training of community-level workers and its effectiveness in the provision of mental health care. Examples of these include Anganwadi workers, and ASHA (Bansal et al., 2021; Kasturkar et al., 2023; Paramasivam et al., 2022; Rahul et al., 2021; Shah et al., 2019).

The curriculum of medical students should include psychiatric assessment and management. They should have mandatory postings in the psychiatric department and be evaluated on the skills of mental state examination and managing common mental disorders. However, this does not appear to be the case in many medical schools in the region.

In addition to the community health workers, training for general nurses, midwives, pharmacists, and social workers is immensely helpful. All the training should include modules for mental health assessment and general principles of management. Developing independent nurse and pharmacist prescribers following appropriate training and clinical experience may also go a long way (Brimblecombe & Dobel-Ober, 2022; Buist et al., 2019); as an additional support system especially where there is a constraint on the availability of doctors. These non-medical prescribers can work under the supervision of doctors, and this is already an established practice in many developed regions. In the areas where there is no psychiatrist, there are various resources available including a book on that title (Patel & Hanlon, 2018).

5.2 Training Non-clinical Professionals in Mental Health

Not just the healthcare professionals, people in other works of life also come in contact regularly with people who have mental health issues. These commonly include teachers, first responders in traumatic situations, disaster workers or volunteers, managers in work environments, even traditional practitioners and faith healers, etc.

Training of volunteers in local NGOs is extremely helpful to providing mental health support in communities. In a program, authorities in Gujarat tried to improve mental health care with the idea of covering a large number of NGOs and had training workshops on mental healthcare and project management. The workshops enabled many to integrate the mental health component into their ongoing service delivery, especially the health programs. The training programs were developed and designed specifically for community-based mental healthcare and project management issues (Bhat et al., 2007).

Teachers and faculty members from schools to universities come across mental health problems in their students as most of the mental illnesses start in childhood or young adult life; and study or examination-related stress is exponentially high (Kar et al., 2021b; Rath et al., 2021a, 2021b). Anxiety and depression are very common in students and student suicide is a major concern in South Asia (Kar et al., 2021b). For these reasons, training teachers in mental health will help in early identification, school-based counseling, and mitigating the problem at the outset.

It is also relevant to involve practitioners of traditional medicine and faith healers in mental health-related training, the reason being most people with mental health symptoms approach them in the first instance in South Asian countries and belief in supernatural causation is still common (Kar, 2008). Their participation will increase awareness, case identification, and referral for evidence-based medicine early.

Another group of individuals who need mental health-related training based on their occupation are first responders (e.g., firemen, The National Disaster Response Force in India), and disaster volunteers and workers. They would need training specifically on trauma response, stress management, cultural sensitivity, etc. This can also help to identify more vulnerable survivors who would need specialist care.

Along with training, continued supervision, and quality assurance are also important aspects of capacity building for appropriate mental health service delivery (Endale et al., 2020).

5.3 *Continuing Professional Development of Mental Health Professionals*

Regular training for clinicians regarding recent developments and skills is extremely important for better services. Although the continuing medical education program is getting embedded for doctors, it needs to be more robust to evaluate if the new learning is reflected in their clinical practice. There is hardly any practice of evaluating (auditing) actual clinical practice and improvements in the standards of care. Besides psychiatrists, the process is almost non-existent for other mental health professionals. Supporting the clinicians for periodic training, setting up a process of peer review and approval/validation process may help.

5.4 Support for Mental Health Professionals

Like any other clinicians, mental health professionals are also vulnerable to stress working in a clinical environment, especially in situations with limited resources. In addition, they face some unique challenges while dealing with difficult or violent patients (Maslach & Leiter, 2016). There are reports of mental fatigue, and burnout, among psychiatrists (Bykov et al., 2022; Sarma, 2018); which affect their clinical work (Kar, 2022). They should be provided with psychological and other appropriate support which should be easily accessible.

5.5 Tele-Training

There has been great progress in online or remote training of mental health professionals working in different areas. This can be a model to facilitate faster training of up-to-date subjects in a cost-effective way. One such example is the digital training academy at the National Institute of Mental Health and Neurosciences (NIMHANS), Bangalore which is training primary care and mental health professionals using tele, in-person, or both in a blended way covering various areas from general psychiatry to addition (Gajera et al., 2023; Khan et al., 2020; Malathesh et al., 2021). These have been particularly helpful during the COVID-19 pandemic (Sheth et al., 2020) when the need for psychiatric support in the community increased exponentially. The recognized benefits of tele-mentoring were a significant increase in learning and self-confidence of counselors. These models have the potential for capacity-building in mental health and addiction in remote and rural areas by leveraging technology (Mehrotra et al., 2018).

5.6 Training with Expert Patients

It is well known that patients help the medical education and training. Expert patients are individuals living with an illness (experts by experience) who can take care of their health by understanding and managing their condition. Expert patients might be able to help other patients in the self-management; and work with physicians in ensuring the development of comprehensive care and disease management methods (Cordier, 2014). They can support training alongside professionals (Coulthard et al., 2013; Ward et al., 2022), develop mental health information brochures, participate in psychiatric research (Tapsell et al., 2020) and they can be involved in developing mental health services. It is advisable that centers should have expert patients to consult for training, service development, and research.

6 Public Education

Improving mental health care can be facilitated by increasing the awareness of mental illnesses. Health literacy especially mental health awareness is poorer in the population in South Asia like many other regions in the world. In this regard, public education has an extremely important role to play. Mental health education can help in managing stigma, decreasing the myth around mental illnesses, and improving appropriate help-seeking for health care. Mental health professionals and organizations should have responsibility for public education and lead this campaign.

Health education, including mental health education, can be started at school level. Identifying the symptoms, and negative contributing factors such as drugs, and encouraging appropriate help-seeking early are some of the key messages. For the general public, print, electronic, and social media are effective ways as they have greater reach in the community. Developing internet resources online in native languages is a key step.

In this process, stories from patients, depicting symptoms development, and remission following treatment are more effective rather than information regarding diagnoses. Realistic portrayal of mental illness and treatment outcomes in films, dramas, soap operas, and serials is extremely important as the dramatized display of mental illness has maintained various myths and misconceptions regarding them in the community. Similarly, reports of suicides in the media often lack public education component; while providing the details of the method and probable cause, they do not inform about the helpful resources for similar problems and do not follow reporting guidelines (Arafat et al., 2020; Kar et al., 2021a; Menon et al., 2020, 2021). These kinds of presentations in media have probably done more harm than good.

6.1 Mental Health First Aid

Mental Health First Aid training helps people to know about mental health issues, recognize symptoms, and provide support to individuals experiencing mental health problems. It teaches people to listen, reassure, and respond, to prevent a mental health crisis or to deal with posttraumatic stress symptoms. Training can be adapted to the situations, nature of work, and the mental health issues the trainees are expected to face and manage. It can be culturally adapted as well (Chandrasiri et al., 2021). This training improves mental health literacy and knowledge (Liang et al., 2023), response to mental ill health and mental health crisis (Mei & McGorry, 2020), decreases negative attitudes and stigma, and increases supportive behaviors toward individuals with mental health problems (Hadlaczky et al., 2014; Morgan et al., 2018). However, there is a need for more studies about its effectiveness (Forthal et al., 2022) and in different cultures.

6.2 Fighting Stigma Related to Mental Illnesses

Stigma remains a major stumbling block regarding access to mental health care by the patients. Dealing with stigma requires consistent awareness campaigns, which can be used at various levels such as social media, local electronic and paper media, and educational, cultural, and occupational institutions. One of the specific content in public education is dealing with myths and misconceptions associated with mental illness and mentally ill people; such as supernatural causation and management; faith healing, marriage as a cure, and once ill, always ill, etc. Public education through case vignettes describing symptoms rather than diagnoses, through local language and visuals, may be helpful (Gaiha et al., 2020).

There is a stigma among healthcare workers as well, which affects the detection of cases in the community. This even extends to mental health professionals and doctors in other departments (Kar & Sharma, 2012). A project titled Reducing Stigma among Healthcare Providers (RESHAPE) is being undertaken in Nepal; which will be compared with the World Health Organization Mental Health Gap Action Programme Intervention Guide (mhGAP-IG) (Kohrt et al., 2022). This may help in suggesting methods of anti-stigma strategy implementation methods.

One of the ways of dealing with stigma and improving adherence to mental health interventions is to have peer support from patients with lived experiences who can share their stories and influence other patients. This approach of patient–patient interaction helps in clarifying the myths and misconceptions, makes them aware of the possibilities, and provides hope.

7 Mental Health Centers

Mental healthcare centers could be tertiary, regional and central, or national institutions, which will have multiple roles, beyond acting up as a referral center for complex clinical situations. It is expected that these organizations would have responsibilities for training mental health professionals; developing and supporting clinical practice standards in psychiatry and providing accreditations to treatment centers in government and private sectors. They would have an advisory role to governments and policymakers, and be the guardians of mental health care in the region and country.

7.1 Maintaining the Quality of Mental Health Care

One of the major roles of all mental health practitioners and institutions is to see that the quality of care is maintained at a high standard. For example, the professionals have appropriate training, care is of high quality and evidence-based practice. In some countries care can be formally scrutinized through a body, e.g., Care Quality

Commission (CQC) in the UK (Care Quality Commission, 2023). They can grade the care provided and recommend suggestions to improve. The CQC team consists of members from a multidisciplinary background with experience in mental health care. This kind of process is not evident in most South Asian countries, although the government approval process is there for private psychiatric units.

7.2 Measuring and Improving the Quality of Care

There are various ways to measure the quality of care provided to patients at an individual professional level and the institutional level. Quality of care can be evaluated through regular clinical audits assessing the care against set standards. These standards can be set locally or at a national level; or can be based on research findings. Service evaluations or quality improvement projects can assess the effectiveness of interventions to improve services. Research can be another way which can suggest a better quality of clinical care. It has been seen that more research-active sites are conscious of the care they provide to the patients; and higher research activity is associated with better psychiatric care (Arriba-Enriquez et al., 2021). Patient satisfaction, symptomatic and functional outcomes, and quality of life can be examples of measures that can indicate the effectiveness of care. These can be routinely measured in psychiatric care settings.

7.3 Managing Poor Quality of Care

Poor quality of care is a major problem, which although frequently encountered, is not usually realized or reported. It is important to set up a process to identify and rectify these practices. Facilitating the reporting and complaints process, and a responsive, transparent, un-interfered complaints management system can help a lot. Patients should be able to complain and this should be properly investigated. Non-evidence-based practices and poor professionalism need to be investigated and dealt with individually and as an organizational approach. At a very basic level, inhuman and unethical practices, e.g., as observed in many faith-based interventions, need to be prevented to protect patients from harm.

8 Non-governmental Organizations

NGOs, and community organizations have an extensive role in mental health care. There are many international and national professional and non-professional organizations contributing towards this in South Asia. However, at a local level in many instances, the density of NGOs varies widely, with too many to too few on the ground, which does not help, especially when they are nonspecific in their objective and low on resources. A few suggestions about the NGOs can be made.

8.1 Stakeholders' Forum

General mental health-related or diagnosis-specific groups have an important role besides peer support. They should be contacted and remain involved in developing services, and policies for the management and research. Professional mental health organizations should support and facilitate the participation of patients, their family members, and caregivers.

8.2 Peer Support Network

The role of peer support in mental health is well recognized, these are helpful where people affected by similar illness and their family members can share and find ways to deal and cope with this. They can be very influential in getting appropriate support and resources including for appropriate policies from governments. There is a need to develop and support such peer support networks in the countries and to have local branches. Professional bodies and governments should facilitate such an approach by clarifying their roles, training, resourcing, and improving access to a peer network (Ibrahim et al., 2020).

9 Governmental Organizations

Health authorities and governments are responsible for mental health care in a country. However, often if is seen they are not aware of the extent and gravity of the situation, the urgency of the needs, its impact on people and the state (economy, happiness index, etc.), and what needs to be done. While dealing with health-related matters, mental health is not usually given its due importance and resources.

Mental health professionals must inform and advise the governments to establish a robust mental health service delivery. A summary of activities is provided in Table 1 which describes options at various organizational levels. Examples of the activities are non-exhaustive and not exclusive to the level described. Public education, suicide prevention, training, and effectiveness research should be facilitated at all levels.

Although many countries have visions, policies, and relevant laws, poor governance has been identified as a key problem in effectively implementing and integrating mental health services. One of the major challenges identified in South Asia is inadequate resources/financing, others are efficiency and effectiveness of existing

Table 1 Summary of the level, roles, and actions in the process of facilitating mental health care

Level	Workforce	Action to improve mental health care
Community	Community health workers Community mental health workers Social workers Volunteers	Frontline health worker training Detect and treat common mental disorders Organized outreach Tele-psychiatry Mental health first aid Social prescribing Ancillary support
Primary care	General physicians Mental health nurses Nurse prescribers Independent prescribers Psychologists Social workers	Routine and emergency care in outpatient Tele-psychiatry Mental health first aid Social prescribing Ancillary support
Secondary care	Psychiatrists Clinical psychologists Mental health nurses Social workers	Routine and emergency care Inpatient care Psychiatric intensive care units Psychotherapies Tele-psychiatry Supervision of the primary care professionals
Specialist care	Psychiatrists with additional specialization Specialist nurses Clinical psychologists Social workers	Sub-specialty training for professionals Psychotherapies Tele-psychiatry
Mental Health Centers	Clinicians with service development roles	The quality setting Developing treatment guidelines Training Research
Non-governmental organization	Volunteers Expert patients Peer groups members	Peer support group Disease-specific support group Volunteering Training
Government	Health authorities Legislators	Enact laws and policies Support seamless mental health services Quality control

systems, responsiveness, inter-sectoral collaboration/cooperation, lack of strategies to improve mental health literacy, and stigma reduction (Petersen et al., 2017).

9.1 Affordable Mental Health Care

Affordability concerns many patients in this region, and psychiatric treatment can be long-term and costly. It is reported that the average healthcare expenditure in South Asian countries was 2.5–5.5% of GDP, with 48.1–72.0% of healthcare costs covered by the patients themselves (Matthews et al., 2023). Governments and other organizations should explore ways to make the services free at the care delivery level. Health insurance should cover psychiatric care and psychosocial disability. Including mental health in national health insurance reforms in the South Asian countries is an important strategic opportunity (Chisholm et al., 2019). There can be various other ways governments and people can support mental healthcare-related costs, which need to be explored.

9.2 Policies and Laws

Governments should have plans to develop manpower for mental health services, expand training programs, and support the process of employment and retention. A convincing political will is required to bring around necessary changes (Rathod et al., 2017). They should also provide resources for services and research to develop local expertise.

Authorities must be informed and supported by mental health practitioners and organizations while planning mental health care in the country, developing policies, and enacting appropriate laws. Legislations related to mental healthcare delivery, especially involuntary admission, and treatment have been developed in South Asia countries and have their share of challenges and controversies (Dey et al., 2019), and there is a need for further evolution to make it more useful for patients. Mental health acts should promote evidence-based care, protect patients' interests, and be linked to actions related to human rights and the mental capacity to decide.

9.3 Ancillary Support

Extending their role beyond mental health services, governments should link up supporting programs for the mentally ill, e.g., financial support for patient and family caregivers, creating and facilitating job opportunities for the mentally ill. There should also be support for wandering, homeless, and mentally ill people with collaborative intervention in the community from social services, police, and NGOs. These holistic programs will facilitate positive outcome of mental illness.

10 Patient-Centric Care

All the efforts to develop and support mental health care should keep the benefit for the individual patient at the center (Fig. 1). This will help to arrange appropriate services around them. It should highlight what options are available and where there is a gap in the support system and the unmet needs; so that the inadequacies can be addressed quickly. Patients, their caregivers, and related professionals or NGOs should always be consulted for service developments.

Similarly, when managing an individual patient, efforts should be taken to provide the best possible evidence-based care with the available resources, highlighting the treatment gaps. The unmet needs should be consistently focused on for appropriate remedial action from the relevant authorities.

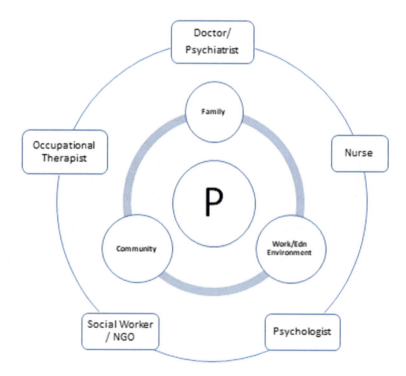

Fig. 1 Patient-centric care provision

11 Conclusion and Recommendations

Considering mental health care, much progress has been made in South Asian countries, and in most places, secondary care is available to a variable degree. However, there is a vast scope for improvement. There are massive unmet needs related to mental health services and systems in these countries, which need to be addressed on a priority basis. Based on the current observations, a few recommendations can be made.

1. Mental health services should be available for patients living in rural areas by making community outreach more robust. Community psychiatry models need to be strengthened.
2. Culturally appropriate and acceptable service delivery models may be developed and tested for their effectiveness.
3. Holistically supporting informal family caregivers is essential to improve the quality of care, as most patients live in their homes in this region.
4. Remote assessment and intervention models using technology can help expertise to benefit patients, and these should be facilitated.
5. There is a need for research about the effectiveness of intervention methods that work for this culturally diverse population rather than just following the care models or systems that work in other regions.
6. Research in mental health needs to be supported and funded at all levels from community to national, especially the outcome research on interventions.
7. As affordability is a concern for most patients in this region of South Asia, healthcare support methods need to be explored to make psychiatric treatment free at the point of care delivery.
8. The importance of developing an adequate mental health workforce with the vision of the service needs, their training, and retention in employment cannot be overemphasized.
9. There is a need to involve patients, and their family members in service development along with clinicians, experts, and authorities.
10. Mental health needs to be prioritized by the authorities and governments related to resource allocation.
11. Regional cooperation between the South Asian countries in developing mental health services would be helpful, sharing good practice and promoting joint research in service delivery, considering the similar sociocultural milieu.

Acknowledgements The Institute of Insight, United Kingdom; and Quality of Life Research and Development Foundation (QoLReF), India; Geriatric Care and Research Organisation (GeriCaRe) for the support in conducting the literature review.

References

Anjara, S. G., Bonetto, C., Ganguli, P., Setiyawati, D., Mahendradhata, Y., Yoga, B. H., Trisnantoro, L., Brayne, C., & Van Bortel, T. (2019). Can general practitioners manage mental disorders in primary care? A partially randomised, pragmatic, cluster trial. *Plos One, 14*, e0224724. https://doi.org/10.1371/journal.pone.0224724

Arafat, S. M. Y., Kar, S. K., Marthoenis, M., Cherian, A. V., Vimala, L., & Kabir, R. (2020). Quality of media reporting of suicidal behaviors in South-East Asia. *Neurology, Psychiatry and Brain Research, 37*, 21–26. https://doi.org/10.1016/j.npbr.2020.05.007

Arafat, S. M. Y., Menon, V., Varadharajan, N., & Kar, S. K. (2022a). Psychological autopsy studies of suicide in South East Asia. *Indian Journal of Psychological Medicine, 44*, 4–9. https://doi.org/10.1177/02537176211033643

Arafat, S. M. Y., Saleem, T., Edwards, T. M., Ali, S.A.-Z., & Khan, M. M. (2022b). Suicide prevention in Bangladesh: The role of family. *Brain and Behavior, 12*, e2562. https://doi.org/10.1002/brb3.2562

Arafat, S. M. Y., Saleem, T., Menon, V., Ali, S.A.-E.-Z., Baminiwatta, A., Kar, S. K., Akter, H., & Singh, R. (2022c). Depression and suicidal behavior in South Asia: A systematic review and meta-analysis. *Glob Ment Health (Camb), 9*, 181–192. https://doi.org/10.1017/gmh.2022.20

Avasthi, A. (2010). Preserve and strengthen family to promote mental health. *Indian J Psychiatry, 52*, 113–126. https://doi.org/10.4103/0019-5545.64582

Axinn, W. G., Choi, K. W., Ghimire, D. J., Cole, F., Hermosilla, S., Benjet, C., Morgenstern, M. C., Lee, Y. H., & Smoller, J. W. (2022). Community-level social support infrastructure and adult onset of major depressive disorder in a South Asian postconflict setting. *JAMA Psychiatry, 79*, 243–249. https://doi.org/10.1001/jamapsychiatry.2021.4052

Bansal, S., Srinivasan, K., & Ekstrand, M. (2021). Perceptions of ASHA workers in the HOPE collaborative care mental health intervention in rural South India: A qualitative analysis. *British Medical Journal Open, 11*, e047365. https://doi.org/10.1136/bmjopen-2020-047365

Baruah, U., Loganathan, S., Shivakumar, P., Pot, A. M., Mehta, K. M., Gallagher-Thompson, D., Dua, T., & Varghese, M. (2021). Adaptation of an online training and support program for caregivers of people with dementia to Indian cultural setting. *Asian Journal of Psychiatry, 59*, 102624. https://doi.org/10.1016/j.ajp.2021.102624

Bhat, R., Maheshwari, S., Rao, K., & Bakshi, R. (2007). *Mental health care pilots in Gujarat: Processes, outcomes and learning*. Indian Institute of Management.

Bhatia, S. C., Madabushi, J., Kolli, V., Bhatia, S. K., & Madaan, V. (2013). The Bhagavad Gita and contemporary psychotherapies. *Indian Journal of Psychiatry, 55*, S315-321. https://doi.org/10.4103/0019-5545.105557

Brimblecombe, N., & Dobel-Ober, D. (2022). The development of nurse prescribing in mental health services: Outcomes from five national surveys 2004–2019. *Journal of Nursing Management, 30*, 1018–1026. https://doi.org/10.1111/jonm.13588

Buist, E., McLelland, R., Rushworth, G. F., Stewart, D., Gibson-Smith, K., MacLure, A., Cunningham, S., & MacLure, K. (2019). An evaluation of mental health clinical pharmacist independent prescribers within general practice in remote and rural Scotland. *International Journal of Clinical Pharmacy, 41*, 1138–1142. https://doi.org/10.1007/s11096-019-00897-1

Bykov, K. V., Zrazhevskaya, I. A., Topka, E. O., Peshkin, V. N., Dobrovolsky, A. P., Isaev, R. N., & Orlov, A. M. (2022). Prevalence of burnout among psychiatrists: A systematic review and meta-analysis. *Journal of Affective Disorders, 308*, 47–64. https://doi.org/10.1016/j.jad.2022.04.005

Care Quality Commission. (2023). Retrieved December 06, 2023 from https://www.cqc.org.uk/

Carty, S., Thompson, L., Berger, S., Jahnke, K., & Llewellyn, R. (2016). Books on prescription—Community-based health initiative to increase access to mental health treatment: An evaluation. *Australian and New Zealand Journal of Public Health, 40*, 276–278. https://doi.org/10.1111/1753-6405.12507

Chandra, A. (2021). Neglected Sexual Health in India's Medical Education and Regulation: Time for a change. *Journal of Psychosexual Health, 3*, 372–374. https://doi.org/10.1177/26318318211050604

Chandrasiri, A., Fernando, M., Dayabandara, M., & Reavley, N. J. (2021). Cultural adaptation of the mental health first aid guidelines for assisting a person at risk of suicide for Sri Lanka: A Delphi expert consensus study. *BMC Psychiatry, 21*, 466. https://doi.org/10.1186/s12888-021-03486-7

Chatterjee, S., Pillai, A., Jain, S., Cohen, A., & Patel, V. (2009). Outcomes of people with psychotic disorders in a community-based rehabilitation programme in rural India. *British Journal of Psychiatry, 195*, 433–439. https://doi.org/10.1192/bjp.bp.108.057596

Chatterjee, S., Naik, S., John, S., Dabholkar, H., Balaji, M., Koschorke, M., Varghese, M., Thara, R., Weiss, H. A., Williams, P., McCrone, P., Patel, V., & Thornicroft, G. (2014). Effectiveness of a community-based intervention for people with schizophrenia and their caregivers in India (COPSI): A randomised controlled trial. *Lancet, 383*, 1385–1394. https://doi.org/10.1016/S0140-6736(13)62629-X

Chisholm, D., Docrat, S., Abdulmalik, J., Alem, A., Gureje, O., Gurung, D., Hanlon, C., Jordans, M. J. D., Kangere, S., Kigozi, F., Mugisha, J., Muke, S., Olayiwola, S., Shidhaye, R., Thornicroft, G., & Lund, C. (2019). Mental health financing challenges, opportunities and strategies in low- and middle-income countries: Findings from the Emerald project. *BJPsych Open, 5*, e68. https://doi.org/10.1192/bjo.2019.24

Cordier, J.-F. (2014). The expert patient: Towards a novel definition. *European Respiratory Journal, 44*, 853–857. https://doi.org/10.1183/09031936.00027414

Coulthard, K., Patel, D., Brizzolara, C., Morriss, R., & Watson, S. (2013). A feasibility study of expert patient and community mental health team led bipolar psychoeducation groups: Implementing an evidence based practice. *BMC Psychiatry, 13*, 301. https://doi.org/10.1186/1471-244X-13-301

Dalal, P. K. (2020). Changing scenario of addiction psychiatry: Challenges and opportunities. *Indian Journal of Psychiatry, 62*, 235–241. https://doi.org/10.4103/psychiatry.IndianJPsychiatry_346_20

de Arriba-Enriquez, J., Sanz-Casado, E., Vieta, E., Rapado-Castro, M., & Arango, C. (2021). Quality of care in psychiatry is related to research activity. *European Psychiatry, 64*, e53. https://doi.org/10.1192/j.eurpsy.2021.16

Dey, S., Mellsop, G., Diesfeld, K., Dharmawardene, V., Mendis, S., Chaudhuri, S., Deb, A., Huq, N., Ahmed, H. U., Shuaib, M., & Khan, F. R. (2019). Comparing legislation for involuntary admission and treatment of mental illness in four South Asian countries. *International Journal of Mental Health Systems, 13*, 67. https://doi.org/10.1186/s13033-019-0322-7

Dutta, S., Kar, N., Thirthalli, J., & Nair, S. (2007). Prevalence and risk factors of psychiatric disorders in an industrial population in India. *Indian Journal of Psychiatry, 49*, 103–108. https://doi.org/10.4103/0019-5545.33256

Endale, T., Qureshi, O., Ryan, G. K., Esponda, G. M., Verhey, R., Eaton, J., De Silva, M., & Murphy, J. (2020). Barriers and drivers to capacity-building in global mental health projects. *International Journal of Mental Health Systems, 14*, 89. https://doi.org/10.1186/s13033-020-00420-4

Fernandez, E., Woldgabreal, Y., Day, A., Pham, T., Gleich, B., & Aboujaoude, E. (2021). Live psychotherapy by video versus in-person: A meta-analysis of efficacy and its relationship to types and targets of treatment. *Clinical Psychology & Psychotherapy, 28*, 1535–1549. https://doi.org/10.1002/cpp.2594

Forthal, S., Sadowska, K., Pike, K. M., Balachander, M., Jacobsson, K., & Hermosilla, S. (2022). Mental health first aid: A systematic review of trainee behavior and recipient mental health outcomes. *Psychiatric Services, 73*, 439–446. https://doi.org/10.1176/appi.ps.202100027

Gaiha, S. M., Taylor Salisbury, T., Koschorke, M., Raman, U., & Petticrew, M. (2020). Stigma associated with mental health problems among young people in India: A systematic review of magnitude, manifestations and recommendations. *BMC Psychiatry, 20*, 538. https://doi.org/10.1186/s12888-020-02937-x

Gajera, G. V., Pandey, P., Malathesh, B. C., Nirisha, P. L., Suchandra, K. H. H., Ibrahim, F. A., Suhas, S., Manjunatha, N., Kumar, C. N., Suresha, B. M., & Jain, S. (2023). Effectiveness of blended versus fully digital training in primary care psychiatry: A retrospective comparison from India. *Journal of Neuroscience in Rural Practice, 14*, 91–97. https://doi.org/10.25259/JNRP-2022-4-20

Giordano, C., Ambrosiano, I., Graffeo, M. T., Di Caro, A., & Gullo, S. (2022). The transition to online psychotherapy during the pandemic: A qualitative study on patients' perspectives. *Research in Psychotherapy, 25*, 638. https://doi.org/10.4081/ripppo.2022.638

Govaerts, J., Boeyckens, J., Lammens, A., Gilis, A., Bouckaert, F., De Hert, M., De Lepeleire, J., Stubbs, B., & Desplenter, F. (2021). Defining polypharmacy: In search of a more comprehensive determination method applied in a tertiary psychiatric hospital. *Therapeutic Advances in Psychopharmacology, 11*, 20451253211000610. https://doi.org/10.1177/20451253211000610

Gualano, M. R., Bert, F., Martorana, M., Voglino, G., Andriolo, V., Thomas, R., Gramaglia, C., Zeppegno, P., & Siliquini, R. (2017). The long-term effects of bibliotherapy in depression treatment: Systematic review of randomized clinical trials. *Clinical Psychology Review, 58*, 49–58. https://doi.org/10.1016/j.cpr.2017.09.006

Gurung, D., Poudyal, A., Wang, Y. L., Neupane, M., Bhattarai, K., Wahid, S. S., Aryal, S., Heim, E., Gronholm, P., Thornicroft, G., & Kohrt, B. (2022). Stigma against mental health disorders in Nepal conceptualised with a 'what matters most' framework: A scoping review. *Epidemiology and Psychiatric Sciences, 31*, e11. https://doi.org/10.1017/S2045796021000809

Hadlaczky, G., Hökby, S., Mkrtchian, A., Carli, V., & Wasserman, D. (2014). Mental Health First Aid is an effective public health intervention for improving knowledge, attitudes, and behaviour: A meta-analysis. *International Review of Psychiatry, 26*, 467–475. https://doi.org/10.3109/09540261.2014.924910

Hossain, M. M., Purohit, N., Sultana, A., Ma, P., McKyer, E. L. J., & Ahmed, H. U. (2020). Prevalence of mental disorders in South Asia: An umbrella review of systematic reviews and meta-analyses. *Asian Journal of Psychiatry, 51*, 102041. https://doi.org/10.1016/j.ajp.2020.102041

Hossain, M. M., Rahman, M., Trisha, N. F., Tasnim, S., Nuzhath, T., Hasan, N. T., Clark, H., Das, A., McKyer, E. L. J., Ahmed, H. U., Ma, P. (2021). Prevalence of anxiety and depression in South Asia during COVID-19: A systematic review and meta-analysis. *Heliyon, 7*. https://doi.org/10.1016/j.heliyon.2021.e06677

Husk, K., Elston, J., Gradinger, F., Callaghan, L., & Asthana, S. (2019). Social prescribing: Where is the evidence? *British Journal of General Practice, 69*, 6–7. https://doi.org/10.3399/bjgp19X700325

Ibrahim, N., Thompson, D., Nixdorf, R., Kalha, J., Mpango, R., Moran, G., Mueller-Stierlin, A., Ryan, G., Mahlke, C., Shamba, D., Puschner, B., Repper, J., & Slade, M. (2020). A systematic review of influences on implementation of peer support work for adults with mental health problems. *Social Psychiatry and Psychiatric Epidemiology, 55*, 285–293. https://doi.org/10.1007/s00127-019-01739-1

Indian Psychiatric Society. (2022). IPS guidelines. Retrieved May 08, 2023 from https://indianpsychiatricsociety.org/ips-guidelines/

Jordans, M. J., Kaufman, A., Brenman, N. F., Adhikari, R. P., Luitel, N. P., Tol, W. A., & Komproe, I. (2014). Suicide in South Asia: A scoping review. *BMC Psychiatry, 14*, 358. https://doi.org/10.1186/s12888-014-0358-9

Kalra, B., Joshi, A., Kalra, S., Shanbhag, V. G., Kunwar, J., Singh Balhara, Y. P., Chaudhary, S., Khandelwal, D., Aggarwal, S., Priya, G., Verma, K., Baruah, M. P., Sahay, R., Bajaj, S., Agrawal, N., Pathmanathan, S., Prasad, I., Chakraborty, A., & Ram, N. (2018). Coping with illness: Insight from the Bhagavad Gita. *Indian Journal of Endocrinology and Metabolism, 22*, 560–564. https://doi.org/10.4103/ijem.IJEM_228_17

Kar, N., Jagadisha, S. P., Murali, N., & Mehrotra, S. (2004a). Mental health consequences of the trauma of super-cyclone 1999 in orissa. *Indian Journal of Psychiatry, 46*, 228–237.

Kar, N., Vishalakshi, Y., & Sharma, P. (2004b). Service utilization in a psychiatric clinic in an industrial set up: Profile of morbidity. *Industrial Psychiatry Journal, 13*, 90–93.

Kar, N. (2006). Psychosocial issues following a natural disaster in a developing country: A qualitative longitudinal observational study. *International Journal of Disaster Medicine, 4*, 169–176.

Kar, N. (2008). Resort to faith-healing practices in the pathway to care for mental illness: A study on psychiatric inpatients in Orissa. *Mental Health, Religion & Culture, 11*, 720–740. https://doi.org/10.1080/13674670802018950

Kar, N. (2009). Natural disasters in developing countries: Mental health issues. *Indian Journal of Medical Sciences, 63*, 327–329. https://doi.org/10.4103/0019-5359.55882

Kar, N. (2011). Cognitive behavioral therapy for the treatment of post-traumatic stress disorder: A review. *Neuropsychiatric Disease and Treatment, 7*, 167–181. https://doi.org/10.2147/NDT.S10389

Kar, N., & Sharma, P. (2012). Attitudinal impediments in the practice of consultation-liaison psychiatry. *Archives of Indian Psychiatry, 14*, 45–50.

Kar, N., Krishnaraaj, R., & Rameshraj, K. (2014). Long-term mental health outcomes following the 2004 Asian tsunami disaster. *Disaster Health, 2*, 35–45. https://doi.org/10.4161/dish.24705

Kar, N. (2015). Lack of community care facilities for older people and increased rate of admission and length of stay in hospitals. *Journal of Geriatric Care and Research, 2*, 28–30.

Kar, N., Swain, S. P., Patra, S., Kar, B. (2017). The WHOQOL-BREF: Translation and validation of the Odia version in a sample of patients with mental illness. *Indian J Soc Psychiatry 33*, 269–273. https://doi.org/10.4103/0971-9962.214599

Kar, S. K., Menon, V., Arafat, S. M. Y., Rai, S., Kaliamoorthy, C., Akter, H., Shukla, S., Sharma, N., Roy, D., & Sridhar, V. K. (2021a). Impact of COVID-19 pandemic related lockdown on Suicide: Analysis of newspaper reports during pre-lockdown and lockdown period in Bangladesh and India. *Asian Journal of Psychiatry, 60*, 102649. https://doi.org/10.1016/j.ajp.2021.102649

Kar, S. K., Rai, S., Sharma, N., & Singh, A. (2021b). Student suicide linked to NEET examination in India: A media report analysis study. *Indian Journal of Psychological Medicine, 43*, 183–185. https://doi.org/10.1177/0253717620978585

Kar, N. (2022). Mental health of the psychiatrists: A need for reflection. *Odisha Journal of Psychiatry, 18*, 67–70. https://doi.org/10.4103/OJP.OJP_3_23

Kar, S. K., Arafat, S. M. Y., Pandey, N. M., Kabir, R., Singh, S. (2022). Suicide in the geriatric population of South East Asia—Contexts and attributes. https://doi.org/10.12688/f1000research.126744.1

Kar, N., ReQoL Translation India Team. (2023). Translation and linguistic validation of recovering quality of life scale in Indian languages: A review of the process and challenges. *Odisha Journal of Psychiatry 19*(1), 3–7. https://doi.org/10.4103/OJP.OJP_20_23

Kasturkar, P., Sebastian, S. T., Gawai, J., Dukare, K. P., Uke, T., & Wanjari, M. B. (2023). Assessing the efficacy of mental health assessment training for accredited social health activists workers in Rural India: A pilot study. *Cureus, 15*, e37855. https://doi.org/10.7759/cureus.37855

Khan, K., Mathur, A., Kaur, S., Ganesh, A., & Chand, P. (2020). Profile of cases discussed in innovative tele-ECHO mentoring program on addiction management. *Asian Journal of Psychiatry, 52*, 102060. https://doi.org/10.1016/j.ajp.2020.102060

Kohrt, B. A., Turner, E. L., Gurung, D., Wang, X., Neupane, M., Luitel, N. P., Kartha, M. R., Poudyal, A., Singh, R., Rai, S., Baral, P. P., McCutchan, S., Gronholm, P. C., Hanlon, C., Lempp, H., Lund, C., Thornicroft, G., Gautam, K., & Jordans, M. J. D. (2022). Implementation strategy in collaboration with people with lived experience of mental illness to reduce stigma among primary care providers in Nepal (RESHAPE): Protocol for a type 3 hybrid implementation effectiveness cluster randomized controlled trial. *Implementation Science, 17*, 39. https://doi.org/10.1186/s13012-022-01202-x

Kroenke, K., Spitzer, R. L., & Williams, J. B. (2001). The PHQ-9: Validity of a brief depression severity measure. *Journal of General Internal Medicine, 16*, 606–613.

Kumar, M. T., Kar, N., Namboodiri, V., Joy, A., Sreeenivasan, D., Kumar, S., & Bortel, T. V. (2023). Post-traumatic stress and depression following a landslide linked to the 2018 floods in Kerala, India: Relevance of screening. *Journal of Emergency Management, 21*, 85–96. https://doi.org/10.5055/jem.0728

Liang, Md. M., Chen, Md. Q., Guo, Md. J., Mei, Ph. D. Z., Wang, Md. J., Zhang, Md. Y., He, Md. L., & Li, Ph. D. Y. (2023). Mental health first aid improves mental health literacy among college students: A meta-analysis. *Journal of American College Health, 71*, 1196–1205. https://doi.org/10.1080/07448481.2021.1925286

Luitel, N. P., Jordans, M. J. D., Subba, P., & Komproe, I. H. (2020). Perception of service users and their caregivers on primary care-based mental health services: A qualitative study in Nepal. *BMC Family Practice, 21*, 202. https://doi.org/10.1186/s12875-020-01266-y

Mahoney, A., Li, I., Haskelberg, H., Millard, M., & Newby, J. M. (2021). The uptake and effectiveness of online cognitive behaviour therapy for symptoms of anxiety and depression during COVID-19. *Journal of Affective Disorders, 292*, 197–203. https://doi.org/10.1016/j.jad.2021.05.116

Malathesh, B. C., Bairy, B. K., Kumar, C. N., Nirisha, P. L., Gajera, G. V., Pandey, P., Manjunatha, N., Ganesh, A., Mehrotra, K., Bhaskarapillai, B., Gunasekaran, D. M., Arora, S., Sinha, N. K., & Math, S. B. (2021). Impact evaluation of technology driven mental health capacity building in Bihar, India. *Psychiatric Quarterly, 92*, 1855–1866. https://doi.org/10.1007/s11126-021-09945-4

Maslach, C., & Leiter, M. P. (2016). Understanding the burnout experience: Recent research and its implications for psychiatry. *World Psychiatry, 15*, 103. https://doi.org/10.1002/wps.20311

Matthews, N. R., Porter, G. J., Varghese, M., Sapkota, N., Khan, M. M., Lukose, A., Paddick, S.-M., Dissanayake, M., Khan, N. Z., & Walker, R. (2023). Health and socioeconomic resource provision for older people in South Asian countries: Bangladesh, India, Nepal, Pakistan and Sri Lanka evidence from NEESAMA. *Global Health Action, 16*, 2110198. https://doi.org/10.1080/16549716.2022.2110198

Mehrotra, K., Chand, P., Bandawar, M., Sagi, M. R., Kaur, S., Aurobind, G., Raj, A., Jain, S., Komaromy, M., Murthy, P., & Arora, S. (2018). Effectiveness of NIMHANS ECHO blended tele-mentoring model on Integrated Mental Health and addiction for counsellors in rural and underserved districts of Chhattisgarh, India. *Asian Journal of Psychiatry, 36*, 123–127. https://doi.org/10.1016/j.ajp.2018.07.010

Mei, C., & McGorry, P. D. (2020). Mental health first aid: Strengthening its impact for aid recipients. *Evidence-Based Mental Health, 23*, 133–134. https://doi.org/10.1136/ebmental-2020-300154

Menon, V., Kaliamoorthy, C., Sridhar, V. K., Varadharajan, N., Joseph, R., Kattimani, S., Kar, S. K., & Arafat, S. Y. (2020). Do tamil newspapers educate the public about suicide? Content analysis from a high suicide Union Territory in India. *International Journal of Social Psychiatry, 66*, 785–791. https://doi.org/10.1177/0020764020933296

Menon, V., Mani, A. M., Kurian, N., Sahadevan, S., Sreekumar, S., Venu, S., Kar, S. K., & Arafat, S. M. Y. (2021). Newspaper reporting of suicide news in a high suicide burden state in India: Is it compliant with international reporting guidelines? *Asian Journal of Psychiatry, 60*, 102647. https://doi.org/10.1016/j.ajp.2021.102647

Milner, A., Witt, K., Pirkis, J., Hetrick, S., Robinson, J., Currier, D., Spittal, M. J., Page, A., & Carter, G. L. (2017). The effectiveness of suicide prevention delivered by GPs: A systematic review and meta-analysis. *Journal of Affective Disorders, 210*, 294–302. https://doi.org/10.1016/j.jad.2016.12.035

Morgan, A. J., Ross, A., & Reavley, N. J. (2018). Systematic review and meta-analysis of Mental Health First Aid training: Effects on knowledge, stigma, and helping behaviour. *Plos One, 13*, e0197102. https://doi.org/10.1371/journal.pone.0197102

Morse, D. F., Sandhu, S., Mulligan, K., Tierney, S., Polley, M., Giurca, B.C., Slade, S., Dias, S., Mahtani, K. R., Wells, L., Wang, H., Zhao, B., Figueiredo, C. E. M. D., Meijs, J. J., Nam, H. K., Lee, K. H., Wallace, C., Elliott, M., Mendive, J. M., Robinson, D., et al. (2022). Global developments in social prescribing. *BMJ Global Health, 7*, e008524. https://doi.org/10.1136/bmjgh-2022-008524

Murthy, S., Kar, N., Sekar, K., Swain, S., Mishra, V., & Daniel, U. (2003). *Evaluation report on psychosocial care of survivors of super-cyclone in Orissa*. NIMHANS.

Murthy, R. S. (2014). Mental health of survivors of 1984 Bhopal disaster: A continuing challenge. *Industrial Psychiatry Journal, 23*, 86–93. https://doi.org/10.4103/0972-6748.151668

Naveed, S., Waqas, A., Chaudhary, A. M. D., Kumar, S., Abbas, N., Amin, R., Jamil, N., & Saleem, S. (2020). Prevalence of common mental disorders in South Asia: A systematic review and meta-regression analysis. *Front Psychiatry, 11*, 573150. https://doi.org/10.3389/fpsyt.2020.573150

Ogbo, F. A., Mathsyaraja, S., Koti, R. K., Perz, J., & Page, A. (2018). The burden of depressive disorders in South Asia, 1990–2016: Findings from the global burden of disease study. *BMC Psychiatry, 18*, 333. https://doi.org/10.1186/s12888-018-1918-1

Pandya, A., Shah, K., Chauhan, A., & Saha, S. (2020). Innovative mental health initiatives in India: A scope for strengthening primary healthcare services. *Journal of Family Medicine and Primary Care, 9*, 502–507. https://doi.org/10.4103/jfmpc.jfmpc_977_19

Paramasivam, R., Elangovan, A. R., Amudhan, S., Kommu, J. V. S., Haridas, H., & Sriramalu, S. B. (2022). Intervention-based mental health training for community level workers in India—A systematic review. *Journal of Family Medicine and Primary Care, 11*, 1237–1243. https://doi.org/10.4103/jfmpc.jfmpc_1134_21

Patel, V., & Hanlon, C. (2018). *Where there is no psychiatrist: A mental health care manual*. Royal College of Psychiatrists.

Petersen, I., Marais, D., Abdulmalik, J., Ahuja, S., Alem, A., Chisholm, D., Egbe, C., Gureje, O., Hanlon, C., Lund, C., Shidhaye, R., Jordans, M., Kigozi, F., Mugisha, J., Upadhaya, N., & Thornicroft, G. (2017). Strengthening mental health system governance in six low- and middle-income countries in Africa and South Asia: Challenges, needs and potential strategies. *Health Policy and Planning, 32*, 699–709. https://doi.org/10.1093/heapol/czx014

Pfaff, J. J., Acres, J. G., & McKelvey, R. S. (2001). Training general practitioners to recognise and respond to psychological distress and suicidal ideation in young people. *Medical Journal of Australia, 174*, 222–226. https://doi.org/10.5694/j.1326-5377.2001.tb143241.x

Rahul, P., Chander, K. R., Murugesan, M., Anjappa, A. A., Parthasarathy, R., Manjunatha, N., Kumar, C. N., & Math, S. B. (2021). Accredited social health activist (ASHA) and her role in district mental health program: Learnings from the COVID 19 pandemic. *Community Mental Health Journal, 57*, 442–445. https://doi.org/10.1007/s10597-021-00773-1

Rath, N., Kar, S., & Kar, N. (2021a). Mental health in the university campus: Emphasizing the need for preventive health actions. *Indian Journal of Social Psychiatry, 37*, 225. https://doi.org/10.4103/ijsp.ijsp_389_20

Rath, N., Kar, S., & Kar, N. (2021b). Personality and mental health factors associated with performance at university level: A study of business administration students. *Industrial Psychiatry Journal, 30*, 323–328. https://doi.org/10.4103/ipj.ipj_34_21

Rathod, S., Pinninti, N., Irfan, M., Gorczynski, P., Rathod, P., Gega, L., & Naeem, F. (2017). Mental health service provision in low- and middle-income countries. *Health Services Insights, 10*, 1178632917694350. https://doi.org/10.1177/1178632917694350

Reddy, M. S. (2012). Psychotherapy—Insights from Bhagavad Gita. *Indian Journal of Psychological Medicine, 34*, 100–104.

Royal College of Psychiatrists. (2023a). National clinical audits. Retrieved March 08, 2023 from https://www.rcpsych.ac.uk/improving-care/ccqi/national-clinical-audits

Royal College of Psychiatrists. (2023b). Prescribing observatory for mental health (POMH). Retrieved March 08, 2023 from https://www.rcpsych.ac.uk/improving-care/ccqi/national-clinical-audits/pomh

Ruwaard, J., Lange, A., Schrieken, B., & Emmelkamp, P. (2011). Efficacy and effectiveness of online cognitive behavioral treatment: A decade of interapy research. *Studies in Health Technology and Informatics, 167*, 9–14.

Sarma, P. G. (2018). Burnout in Indian psychiatrists. *Indian Journal of Psychological Medicine, 40*, 156–160. https://doi.org/10.4103/IJPSYM.IJPSYM_265_17

Satapathy, R., Madhavilatha, K., Annapurna, N., Satapathy, S., Prajwala, M., & Kar, N. (2022). Translation and linguistic validation of recovering quality of life (ReQoL) scale in Telugu: For use in mental health services. *Journal of Geriatric Care and Research, 2022*.

Sax, W. (2014). Ritual healing and mental health in India. *Transcultural Psychiatry, 51*, 829–849. https://doi.org/10.1177/1363461514524472

Saxena, S., Chandiramani, K., & Bhargava, R. (1998). WHOQOL-Hindi: A questionnaire for assessing quality of life in health care settings in India. World Health Organization Quality of Life. *National Medical Journal of India, 11*, 160–165.

Sengupta, K., Shah, H., Ghosh, S., Sanghvi, D., Mahadik, S., Dani, A., Deshmukh, O., Pacione, L., Dixon, P., Salomone, E., WHO-CST team, Servili, C. (2023). World health organisation-caregiver skills training (WHO-CST) program: Feasibility of delivery by non-specialist providers in real-world urban settings in India. *Journal of Autism and Development Disorders, 53*, 1444–1461, https://doi.org/10.1007/s10803-021-05367-0

Shah, Q. N., Dave, P. A., Loh, D. A., Appasani, R. K., & Katz, C. L. (2019). Knowledge of and attitudes towards Mental Illness among ASHA and Anganwadi Workers in Vadodara District, Gujarat State, India. *Psychiatric Quarterly, 90*, 303–309. https://doi.org/10.1007/s11126-019-9625-8

Shenoy, S., Amrtavarshini, R., Bhandary, R. P., & Praharaj, S. K. (2020) Frequency, reasons, and factors associated with antipsychotic polypharmacy in Schizophrenia: A retrospective chart review in a tertiary hospital in India. *Asian Journal of Psychiatry, 51*, 102022. https://doi.org/10.1016/j.ajp.2020.102022

Sheth, S., Ganesh, A., Nagendra, S., Kumar, K., Tejdeepika, R., Likhitha, C., Murthy, P., & Chand, P. (2020). Development of a mobile responsive online learning module on psychosocial and mental health issues related to COVID 19. *Asian Journal of Psychiatry, 54*, 102248. https://doi.org/10.1016/j.ajp.2020.102248

Shields-Zeeman, L., Pathare, S., Walters, B. H., Kapadia-Kundu, N., & Joag, K. (2017). Promoting wellbeing and improving access to mental health care through community champions in rural India: The Atmiyata intervention approach. *International Journal of Mental Health Systems, 11*, 6. https://doi.org/10.1186/s13033-016-0113-3

Shohel, T. A., Nasrin, N., Farjana, F., Shovo, T.-E.-A., Asha, A. R., Heme, M. A., Islam, A., Paul, P., & Hossain, M. T. (2022). 'He was a brilliant student but became mad like his grandfather': An exploratory investigation on the social perception and stigma against individuals living with mental health problems in Bangladesh. *BMC Psychiatry, 22*, 702. https://doi.org/10.1186/s12888-022-04359-3

Singh, O. P. (2018). District Mental Health Program—Need to look into strategies in the era of Mental Health Care Act, 2017 and moving beyond Bellary Model. *Indian Journal of Psychiatry, 60*, 163–164. https://doi.org/10.4103/psychiatry.IndianJPsychiatry_304_18

Sivakumar, P. T., Mukku, S. S. R., Kar, N., Manjunatha, N., Phutane, V. H., Sinha, P., Kumar, C. N., & Math, S. B. (2020). Geriatric telepsychiatry: Promoting access to Geriatric Mental Health Care beyond the physical barriers. *Indian Journal of Psychological Medicine, 42*, 41S-46S. https://doi.org/10.1177/0253717620958380

Sood, M., & Chadda, R. K. (2015). Psychosocial rehabilitation for severe mental illnesses in general hospital psychiatric settings in South Asia. *Bjpsych International, 12*, 47–48.

Spitzer, R. L., Kroenke, K., Williams, J. B. W., & Löwe, B. (2006). A brief measure for assessing generalized anxiety disorder: The GAD-7. *Archives of Internal Medicine, 166*, 1092–1097. https://doi.org/10.1001/archinte.166.10.1092

Tanha, A. F., Sheba, N. H., Islam, Md. S., Potenza, M. N., & Islam, Md. R. (2022). A review of common mental health problems in the general population during the COVID-19 pandemic in South Asia. *Current Psychology*. https://doi.org/10.1007/s12144-022-04106-7

Tapsell, A., Martin, K. M., Moxham, L., Burns, S., Perlman, D., & Patterson, C. (2020). Expert by experience involvement in mental health research: Developing a wellbeing brochure for people with lived experiences of mental illness. *Issues in Mental Health Nursing, 41*, 194–200. https://doi.org/10.1080/01612840.2019.1663566

Tewari, A., Kallakuri, S., Devarapalli, S., Jha, V., Patel, A., & Maulik, P. K. (2017). Process evaluation of the systematic medical appraisal, referral and treatment (SMART) mental health project in rural India. *BMC Psychiatry, 17*, 385. https://doi.org/10.1186/s12888-017-1525-6

Thara, R., & Padmavati, R. (2013). Community mental health care in South Asia. *World Psychiatry, 12*, 176. https://doi.org/10.1002/wps.20042

Thekkumkara, S. N., Jagannathan, A., Jadhav, P., Durgoji, S. K., Muliyala, K. P., Angothu, H., & Reddi, V. S. K. (2020). Family centric rehabilitation' for persons with mental illness in India: Conceptual framework using evidence-based case studies. *Asian Journal of Psychiatry, 54*, 102344. https://doi.org/10.1016/j.ajp.2020.102344

Thekkumkara, S. N., Jagannathan, A., Muliyala, K. P., & Murthy, P. (2022). Psychosocial interventions for prisoners with mental and substance use disorders: A systematic review. *Indian Journal of Psychological Medicine, 44*, 211–217. https://doi.org/10.1177/02537176211061655

Tripathy, S., Behera, D., Negi, S., Tripathy, I., & Behera, M. R. (2022). Burden of depression and its predictors among prisoners in a central jail of Odisha, India. *Indian Journal of Psychiatry, 64*, 295–300. https://doi.org/10.4103/indianjpsychiatry.indianjpsychiatry_668_21

Trivedi, J. K., Goel, D., Kallivayalil, R. A., Isaac, M., Shrestha, D. M., & Gambheera, H. C. (2007). Regional cooperation in South Asia in the field of mental health. *World Psychiatry, 6*, 57–59.

Trivedi, J. K., & Jilani, A. Q. (2012). Reply to queries raised on the article 'the pathway to psychiatric care.' *Indian Journal of Psychiatry, 54*, 398–401. https://doi.org/10.4103/0019-5545.104852

van Ginneken, N., Maheedhariah, M. S., Ghani, S., Ramakrishna, J., Raja, A., & Patel, V. (2017). Human resources and models of mental healthcare integration into primary and community care in India: Case studies of 72 programmes. *Plos One, 12*, e0178954. https://doi.org/10.1371/journal.pone.0178954

Vijayakumar, L. (2010). Indian research on suicide. *Indian Journal of Psychiatry, 52*, S291–S296. https://doi.org/10.4103/0019-5545.69255

Vijayakumar, L., Daly, C., Arafat, Y., & Arensman, E. (2020). Suicide prevention in the Southeast Asia Region. *Crisis, 41*, S21–S29. https://doi.org/10.1027/0227-5910/a000666

Vijayakumar, L., Chandra, P. S., Kumar, M. S., Pathare, S., Banerjee, D., Goswami, T., & Dandona, R. (2022). The national suicide prevention strategy in India: Context and considerations for urgent action. *Lancet Psychiatry, 9*, 160–168. https://doi.org/10.1016/S2215-0366(21)00152-8

Ward, K., Stanyon, M., Ryan, K., & Dave, S. (2022). Power, recovery and doing something worthwhile: A thematic analysis of expert patient perspectives in psychiatry education. *Health Expectations, 25*, 549–557. https://doi.org/10.1111/hex.13375

WHO. (2019). GHO | By category | Mental health workers—Data by country (World Health Organization). Retrieved July 29, 2023 from https://apps.who.int/gho/data/view.main.HWF11v

Wikipedia. (2023). South Asia.

Willmot, R. A., Sharp, R. A., Amir Kassim, A., & Parkinson, J. A. (2022). A scoping review of community-based mental health intervention for children and adolescents in South Asia. *Global Mental Health (Camb), 10*, e1. https://doi.org/10.1017/gmh.2022.49

World Bank World Bank Open Data. Retrieved July 31, 2023 from https://data.worldbank.org

Yuan, S., Zhou, X., Zhang, Y., Zhang, H., Pu, J., Yang, L., Liu, L., Jiang, X., & Xie, P. (2018). Comparative efficacy and acceptability of bibliotherapy for depression and anxiety disorders in children and adolescents: A meta-analysis of randomized clinical trials. *Neuropsychiatric Disease and Treatment, 14*, 353–365. https://doi.org/10.2147/NDT.S152747

Public Mental Health and Access to Mental Health Services in South Asia

Russell Kabir, Sharon Shivuli Isigi, and Catharina Candussi

Abstract Public mental health in South Asia faces several challenges due to a range of socio-economic and cultural factors. In this region, mental health is stigmatized and often not considered a priority health issue. One of the biggest challenges in South Asia is the lack of awareness and understanding of mental health issues. Many people still consider mental illness as a result of personal weakness, and stigma associated with mental illness makes people reluctant to seek treatment. The stigma is often compounded by cultural beliefs and superstitions that lead to individuals and families seeking alternative therapies such as faith healing or traditional medicine instead of evidence-based treatments. Another challenge is the shortage of mental health professionals and resources in the region. Additionally, the lack of investment in mental health services by the government and the private sector further limits access to mental health care. There is often inadequate funding for mental health programmes, and resources are often diverted to other health priorities. Consequently, the formation of legislative initiatives and policies has been approved to address this escalating issue. Therefore, in this chapter, the existing mental health policies and legislation across South Asia are examined.

Keywords South Asia · Public mental health · Services · Legislations · Policies

---

R. Kabir (✉)
School of Allied Health, Faculty of Health, Education, Medicine and Social Care, Anglia Ruskin University, Chelmsford, Essex, UK
e-mail: Russell.kabir@aru.ac.uk

S. S. Isigi
MRC Epidemiology Unit, University of Cambridge, Cambridge, UK
e-mail: Sharon.isigi@mrc-epid.cam.ac.uk

C. Candussi
Department of Nutrition, University of Vienna, Vienna, Austria
e-mail: catharina.candussi@univie.ac.at

© The Author(s), under exclusive license to Springer Nature Singapore Pte Ltd. 2024
S. M. Y. Arafat and S. K. Kar (eds.), *Access to Mental Health Care in South Asia*,
https://doi.org/10.1007/978-981-99-9153-2_11

1 Introduction

Mental health is an important component of a person's overall well-being. The World Health Organization (WHO) defines it "as a state of well-being in which the individual realizes his or her abilities, can cope with the normal stresses of life, can work productively and fruitfully, and can contribute to his or her community state" (World Health Organisation, 2004). In 2019, mental disorders were projected to account for approximately 418 million disability-adjusted life years (DALYs), accounting for 16% of global DALYs. The economic impact of this burden is estimated to be around USD 5 trillion (Arias et al., 2022). According to Steel et al., about 29.2% of the world population will experience a Common Mental Disorder (CMD) during their lifetime (Steel et al., 2014). The term CMD includes specifically depressive disorder, panic disorder, substance use disorders, generalized anxiety, post-traumatic stress, and obsessive-compulsive disorder (National Collaborating Centre for Mental, 2011). Low- and middle-income countries (LMICs) seem more affected by CMD than high-income regions. However, it has been reported depressive symptoms accounting for 26.4%, alcohol abuse 12.9%, anxiety 25.8%, tobacco smoking 18.6%, PTSD 17.2%, mixed anxiety and depression 28.4%, suicidal behaviours 6.4%, misuse of opiates 0.8%, tobacco chewing 21.0%, use of cannabis 3.4%, GAD 2.9%, bipolar disorder 0.6%, IV drug abuse 2.5%, panic disorder 0.01%, stimulant use 0.9%, OCD 1.6%, and phobic disorders 1.8% in SA (Naveed et al., 2020). SA is a geographical zone that includes Afghanistan, Bangladesh, Buthan, India, Maldives, Nepal, Pakistan, and Sri Lanka (The World Bank, 2022).

Characterized by a high population and economic poverty SA faces significant social, economic, and health-related challenges. These challenges include widespread poverty, inequality, violence, political instability, and a heavy burden of communicable diseases (Bhui, 2012). The region is currently undergoing a rapid demographic and epidemiological transition. Population-wise it is one of the fastest-growing regions on earth, with a population growth of 1.41 billion in 2000 to about 1.9 billion in 2021 (The World Bank, 2022). Many areas within the region have underdeveloped public health systems and an expanding yet inadequately regulated private sector, leading to escalating healthcare costs that outpace inflation rates (Bhui, 2012). The prevalence of mental health disorders varies across countries within these regions, with reported rates ranging from 6.5 to 31.0% (Ansari, 2015; Hossain et al., 2019; Sagar et al., 2020). A systematic review and meta-analysis in SA revealed alarming prevalence rates among the population with 26.4% for depressive symptoms, 12.9% for alcohol abuse 25.8% for anxiety, 18.6% for tobacco smoking, 17.2% for post-traumatic stress, 28.4% for mixed anxiety and depression, 0.8% for opiate misuse, 3.4% for cannabis use, 0.6% for bipolar disorder, 0.01% for panic disorder, and 1.6% for OCD (Naveed et al., 2020). Prevalence rates for depression are particularly high in SA, the burden of depressive disorder accounts for 577.8 per 100.000 DALY. Whereby, out of 9.8 million DALYs, 7.8 million years are attributable to major depressive disorders (Ogbo et al., 2018).

Public mental health services attempt to improve mental health and well-being at the population level by enabling and achieving positive mental health (Arafat, 2017). There is very limited recognition of mental health within the public health domain, despite the widespread, increasing burden of mental and behavioural health problems and recent evidence suggests that suicide and other mental health disorder can be prevented with appropriate and timely mental health intervention programmes (Wahlbeck, 2015). Mental health care services are never given high primacy by the governments of different countries from the SA region. There are fewer psychiatrists, and a lack of other mental health professionals such as clinical psychologists, social workers, and trained psychiatric nurses (Arafat & Kar, 2024; Thara & Padmavati, 2013). According to the WHO, only 0.13 (Bangladesh) to 2.3 (Maldives) psychiatrists per 100,000 inhabitants work in this region with a mean of 0.55 per 100.000. Whereas the international goal is a value above 3 per 100,000 inhabitants (WHO, 2019).

Various sociocultural obstacles, such as a lack of awareness and the stigma surrounding mental disorders, frequently result in underreporting or delayed reporting of mental disorders (Trivedi et al., 2007). Social stigmas especially influence one's personality and affect behaviour—leading to either social withdrawal or discrimination (Falk, 2010). Overall, mental health has a high self-stigmatization rate worldwide—around 30% of patients with severe mental illness report a high self-stigmatization. However, across all severe mental disorders, a significant gap in stigmatization between low- and high-income countries can be seen (Dubreucq et al., 2021). Even though the burden of mental health is significant, there is a substantial treatment gap in LMICs, with approximately 76–84% of individuals with mental illness not receiving the necessary treatment (Lund et al., 2012). In low-income regions like Southeast Asia and Africa, patients experience more discrimination and labelling because of their mental illness compared to patients in Europe or North America (Dubreucq et al., 2021). Above all, structural elements are responsible for the lack of treatment options and awareness among the population in SA. This chapter is aimed to review the current public mental health services in South Asian countries.

2 Public Mental Health Programmes and Services in South Asia

Within the last couple of years, policymakers in the SA region seem to recognize the urgent need for mental health programmes. Except for Pakistan, every other nation installed a standalone policy tackling mental health, most of which were introduced within the last five years.

India was the first country who start with its mental health plan in 2014, followed by Bhutan (2015), Maldives (2017), Afghanistan (2019), Nepal (2020), Sri Lanka (2020), and Bangladesh (2020) (WHO, 2017, 2022a, 2022b, 2022c, 2022d, 2022e, 2022f, 2022g). Furthermore, Afghanistan, Bangladesh, India, Pakistan, and Sri Lanka installed legislation within the past couple of years to establish a regulatory framework for mental health services and other treatment and care providers. To safeguard the public and individuals with mental illness from potentially severe consequences of these conditions (Ayano, 2018).

However, as shown in Table 1, topics covered by mental health programmes vary a lot between countries. Nations like Bangladesh, Bhutan, and Sri Lanka follow a comprehensive strategic plan. Contrarily, India and Pakistan only focus on mental health awareness or stigmatization and school-based or psychological first aid programmes. It is striking that only in India and Pakistan is the government fully responsible for managing mental health programmes. Contrarily, in Afghanistan, programmes are only handled by the private sector—in the remaining countries, mixed forms are used. It must be highlighted that external non-government organizations (NGOs), under the supervision of the Ministry of Health, render the health system fragile and hard to control in vast and diverse countries as they are in the SA (Kovess-Masfety et al., 2021). All countries except India set up emergency programmes for disaster preparedness's mental health and psychosocial components.

Furthermore, programmes across countries focus on raising awareness among the population, starting, among other things, in schools. There is a large area of improvement in suicide prevention, early childhood care, and maternal health. This should get more importance because suicide rates among the SA nations can be considered high (WHO, 2021a, 2021b), and the burden of maternal depression is increasing. Recent studies in India showed a perinatal depression rate between 14 and 25% (Badiya et al., 2020; Seshu et al., 2021; Sidhu et al., 2019). Furthermore, ante- and postnatal mental illness is generally very high in LMICs, with a prevalence between 16 and 20% and must be, therefore, adequately addressed in public health policies (Fisher et al., 2012).

Overall, the issue of mental health is poorly prioritized and insufficiently represented at a political level. SA nations mostly do not have effective programmes, legislations, policies, or strategic plans to tackle mental issues across their population (Hossain et al., 2019; Trivedi et al., 2007). One indicator of the poor prioritization is reflected by the amount of government expenditures on mental health with only 0.04% spent in Pakistan, 0.5% in Bangladesh, 0.2% in Bhutan and Nepal, 1.3% in India, and 4.2% in Afghanistan (WHO, 2017, 2022a, 2022b, 2022c, 2022e, 2022f).

3 Overview of Current Legislation and Policies

The escalating concern about mental health disorders in South Asian nations has engendered a rise in public mental health awareness, prompting governments to acknowledge the vital role of mental health in their jurisdictions. Consequently, the formation of legislative initiatives and policies has been approved to address this escalating issue. Therefore, the existing mental health policies and legislation across South Asia are examined.

Table 1 Mental health programmes according to WHO mental health atlas (WHO, 2021b)

Focus of mental health prevention and promotion programme	Programme examples	Area of focus	Management type
Afghanistan (WHO, 2022a)			
Mental health awareness	Peace of mind	National	NGO
School-based	Prevention of mental disorders for young children	District	NGO
Maternal	Positive parental skills training programme	District	NGO
Psychosocial component of disaster preparedness	Psychological first aid and emergency counselling	National	G
Bangladesh (WHO, 2022b)			
Suicide prevention	Integrated into mental health operational plan	National	JM
Mental health awareness	Workshop on responsible reporting of suicide for media professionals	National	JM
Early child development	Bangladesh ECD network	National	JM
School-based	Workshops on "Youth engagement in mental health"	National	JM
Maternal	Supporting maternal mental health of Rohinga refugee women during the perinatal period to promote child health and well-being	District	NGO
Work-related	Seminar on mental health in the workplace	National	JM
Psychosocial component of disaster preparedness	Training on crisis preparedness and management for mental health	National	JM
Bhutan (WHO, 2022c)			
Suicide prevention	National suicide prevention programme	National	G
Mental health awareness	Health promotion division	National	G
Early child development	IMNCI and RH Programme	National	G
School-based	School health and adolescent health programme	National	G
Maternal	Reproductive health programme	National	G
Work-related	Occupational health programme	National	G

(continued)

Table 1 (continued)

Focus of mental health prevention and promotion programme	Programme examples	Area of focus	Management type
Psychosocial component of disaster preparedness	Ministry of home and cultural affairs	National	G
India (WHO, 2017)			
Mental health awareness	National mental health programme	National	G
School-based	District mental health programme	National	G
Maldives (WHO, 2022d)			
School-based	Education Ministry with UNICEF for school-based programme	MI	MI
Psychosocial component of disaster preparedness	Psychosocial support programme	MI	MI
Nepal (WHO, 2022e)			
Mental Health Awareness	Day celebrations	National	G
Early child development	ECD	National	JM
Psychosocial component of disaster preparedness	Integrated into national DRR programmes	National	JM
Pakistan (WHO, 2022f)			
School-based	School Mental Health Programme	District	JM
Psychosocial component of disaster preparedness	Psychological first aid programme	Regional	JM
Sri Lanka (WHO, 2022g)			
Suicide prevention	National suicide prevention programme	Regional	G
Mental health awareness	Mental health promotion programme	National	G
Early child development	Early childhood development and care	National	G
School-based	School health programme	National	G
Maternal	Maternal care programme	National	G

(continued)

Table 1 (continued)

Focus of mental health prevention and promotion programme	Programme examples	Area of focus	Management type
Work-related	Workplace mental well-being	District	G
Psychosocial component of disaster preparedness	MHPSS in emergency	National	JM

G = Government JM = Jointly Managed NGO = Non-Governmental Organization MI = Missing Information

In India, implementing the Mental Healthcare Act 2017 ushered in a momentous shift in the nation's perception of mental health. This Act supersedes the outdated Indian Lunacy Act 1912, which gathered considerable criticism for its archaic terminologies and principles (Basavaraju et al., 2019). An important attribute of the Mental Healthcare Act 2017 is its harmony with the principles expounded in the United Nations Convention on the Rights of Persons with Disabilities (UNCRPD). This boldly declares mental health as an absolute human right and amplifies the importance of honouring inherent dignity, individual autonomy, and the liberty to exercise personal decisions (Watson et al., 2020). Moreover, the Act imposes multiple obligations on the government, notably to construct adequate institutions and offer satisfactory mental health services. Additionally, it emphasizes diminishing the stigma associated with mental illness through public health promotional activities. Notably, this Act mandates insurance providers to broaden their coverage to incorporate treatment for mental health conditions, marking a pivotal development of public mental health in India (Ranade et al., 2022).

Pakistan's approach to mental health is summarized through the Mental Health Act 2001. This Act strives to safeguard the rights of individuals suffering from mental health disorders. However, its execution remains difficult due to resource limitations and insufficient infrastructure. Despite the policy being in effect for nearly two decades, considerable progress is needed to enhance mental health facilities and services in the country (Javed et al., 2020). Conversely, Bangladesh exhibited improvement in its approach towards mental health by implementing the Mental Health Act in 2018. Similar to other regional legislations, this Act protects the rights of mental health service users. However, instituting this legislation is challenging due to systemic limitations, such as insufficiently trained mental health professionals and a lack of public mental health awareness. In Sri Lanka, the evolution of mental health policies has been significant over the years. The National Mental Health Policy 2005, revised in 2013, focuses on decentralizing mental health services and incorporating them into primary care (Kathriarachchi et al., 2019). Additionally, it strives to cultivate a community-based mental health model to assure accessible and efficient care for the population. This policy emphasizes the advancement of human resources dedicated to mental health, promoting research in mental health, and strengthening community mental health services care (Kathriarachchi et al., 2019).

Nepal's Mental Health Policy 1996 emphasizes assimilating mental health into comprehensive health services. This marks a significant step in acknowledging mental health as a critical component of universal health. Nonetheless, the approval of this policy has been significantly disrupted due to a lack of adequate prioritization of mental health issues, political instability, and a lack of funding (Singh & Khadka, 2021). Despite their relatively small population sizes when compared to other South Asian nations, both the Maldives and Bhutan have manifested significant steps towards addressing mental health. These countries have made substantial efforts to frame policies focusing on mental health.

The government of Maldives, acknowledging the escalating prevalence of mental health disorders in the country, has collaborated with international organizations to develop comprehensive mental health strategies. The aim is to enable early detection, effective intervention, and necessary support services for mental health conditions. However, a shortage of specialized professionals and inadequate infrastructure pose significant challenges to the implementation of these policies effectively (Kola et al., 2021). Similarly, Bhutan's government has prioritized mental health, establishing policies to ensure the welfare of those with mental health disorders. Bhutan's strategy is primarily preventive, promoting mental well-being through early intervention and public awareness campaigns.

Their mental health strategy also includes providing continuous training for healthcare professionals, improving the mental health knowledge base through research, and reducing the stigma associated with mental illness. Despite the clear strategy, Bhutan faces resource limitations similar to the Maldives, particularly a shortage of mental health specialists. These limitations challenge implementing the mental health policy objectives (Tsheten et al., 2023). Therefore, while the progress made in formulating mental health policies in South Asian nations is worthy, the region continues to face significant challenges. These encompass a considerable treatment gap, a lack of mental health awareness, and a stigma associated with mental health conditions. These issues emphasize the necessity for these policies to be supplemented by robust infrastructure, enhanced investment, trained human resources, and widespread sensitization efforts.

4 Critical Appraisal of Current Legislation and Policies

The journey of South Asian nations towards formulating mental health policies has indeed been significant and the statuses of the mental health programmes in SA are shown in Table 2. Additionally, the practical efficiency of these policies calls for intensive research. This necessity cuts across the boundaries of the largest nations, such as India and Pakistan, reaching the smaller states like the Maldives and Bhutan, with numerous limitations obstructing the implementation of these mental health policies.

Table 2 Status of mental health programmes in South Asian countries

Country	Mental health programme	Policy	Action plan	Legislation	% Of budget spent on mental health
India (WHO, 2017)	National mental health programme	Mental health awareness, prevention, and anti-stigma	Creating a national focus on mental health issues	Mental Health Care Act 2017	1.3%
Pakistan (WHO, 2022f)	Psychological first aid programme	Disaster preparedness and disaster risk reduction	Community-based mental health services	Mental Health Ordinance 2001	0.4%
Bangladesh (WHO, 2021b)	Workshop on responsible reporting of suicide for media professionals	Mental health awareness	Increasing awareness of mental health issues and where to find assistance	Mental Health Act 2018	0.5%
Nepal (WHO, 2022e)	Day celebrations	Mental health awareness	Increasing awareness of mental health issues and where to find assistance	Mental Health Treatment and Protection Act	0.2%
Bhutan (WHO, 2022c)	National suicide prevention programme	Suicide prevention	Creating awareness to prevent adverse outcomes	No significant mental health legislation	0.2%
Maldives (WHO, 2022d)	Education Ministry and UNICEF school-based programme	School-based mental health prevention and promotion	Developing well-rounded learners and able teachers	Disability Act of the Maldives 2010	–

The Mental Healthcare Act 2017 of India boasts of its progression, striving to enhance the standards of mental health services by adopting a human rights approach to therapy. Nonetheless, the nation struggles with significant challenges when it comes to implementation. A lack of proficient mental health professionals, mainly psychiatrists and clinical psychologists, leads to a treatment gap in the country (Basavaraju et al., 2019). In addition, the scarcity of mental health services in rural territories, combined with the stigma surrounding mental illness, further hinders the Act's practical application. A lack of public consciousness concerning mental health disorders poses a considerable challenge to policy implementation, emphasizing the necessity for vigorous mental health literacy drives (Basavaraju et al., 2019).

Pakistan struggles with the implementation of mental health legislation which remains largely elusive. The challenges faced are similar to those in India which include a crucial treatment gap due to deficient trained personnel and scarce financial resources. Additionally, mental health remains settled at a lower priority level at the policy level, decreasing its inclusion in mainstream health services (Javed et al., 2020, pp. 6–10). Similar challenges are experienced in Bangladesh, Nepal, Bhutan, and the Maldives. Despite their reduced population sizes, the Maldives and Bhutan are no strangers to these challenges. They struggle with similar issues, mainly a shortage of mental health specialists, causing service gaps. Without systematic revisions, mental health legislation are unable to be effective in these territories. With its National Mental Health Policy, Sri Lanka portrays a promising decentralized approach. However, despite this admirable strategy, the country battles similar challenges like deficient mental health services, scarce resources, and an expanding burden of mental health issues among adolescents. Moreover, the stigma connected with mental health disorders remains a recurrent barrier to accessing care (Kathriarachchi et al., 2019).

Additionally, these nations wrestle with geographical limitations that further complicate the delivery of mental health services (Kola et al., 2021; Tsheten et al., 2023). A rigorous investigation explains that while South Asian countries have progressed in formulating mental health policies, considerable gaps remain in their implementation. Areas of uppermost concern surround infrastructure, human resources, and accessibility. These countries must channel a greater investment towards mental health, engage in advocacy, and adopt a multidimensional approach. This approach must combine healthcare, education, and community involvement to ensure the effectiveness of mental health legislation in addressing the region's needs.

Many researchers have explored ways through which governments and other stakeholders in the mental health industry can improve the implementation of legislation and resolve systematic challenges that hamper effectiveness. According to Pandya et al. (2020), South Asian countries can introduce innovations like mobile tele-mental healthcare services and use mobile phones for mental health risk identification, referral, follow-up, and data management. The health gap in rural areas can be bridged by installing essential psychotropic drugs, teleconferencing, and video conferencing equipment for specialist consultation by psychiatrists and psychologists at primary health centres. State mental health agencies can also train community health workers and medical officers on mental health while initiating continuous education and training to sustain non-specialist healthcare professionals in attending to mental health issues (Pandya et al., 2020). While non-specialist care providers cannot prescribe medication, they can facilitate access to mental health care services while linking high-risk cases to specialized professionals.

Conclusively, it is essential to understand and critically appraise South Asia's public mental health state to identify the strengths and shortcomings of these policies and practices. While steps have been taken in the mental health legislation, their practical implementation demands concentrated efforts. South Asia must strive to render mental healthcare accessible, affordable, and stigma-free. The ultimate objective should be to ensure that those with mental health disorders receive the quality care they need and deserve. Consequently, mental health must become a top priority at all levels, from policy formulation to implementation. The region's progress towards this objective will play a vital role in shaping its public mental health outcomes in the years to come.

5 Future Implications and Measures

According to the WHO Mental Health Action Plan "interventions for treatment, prevention and promotion need to be based on scientific evidence and/or best practice, taking cultural considerations into account" (WHO, 2021a). It is striking that there is almost no or insufficient research on SA nations in mental health. Area-wide research would be needed to illustrate the validation of existing strategies or a need for specific programmes. Furthermore, it would be important to take a holistic approach to implementing services, policies, and plans for mental needs that account for different stages in life, including infancy, early childhood, school age, adulthood, maternal period, and older age. The implementation of mental health initiatives faces two primary challenges, as identified by the Movement for Global Mental Health.

Firstly, there is the issue of stigma associated with mental illness. Secondly, the intended recipients often do not seek psychiatric assistance due to their alternative explanatory models, such as perceiving their difficulties as social distress or attributing them to moral weakness or spiritual or religious misfortune (Patel et al., 2011). Although some countries in the SA region have become aware of stigmatization, it must remain an integral part of policymaking. Destigmatization and creating awareness of mental illness are prerequisites for programmes to be accepted. Persons with mental illness must be empowered and involved in future strategic plans to tackle mental health. Integrating biomedical knowledge with culturally appropriate understandings and messages in educational programmes for healthcare workers and communities can contribute to improved detection of common mental disorders and increased demand for healthcare services. A well-trained healthcare workforce is a vital aspect of healthcare systems, yet developing countries often face shortages, inequitable distribution, and inefficiencies in their health human resources. This includes insufficient mental health training for primary healthcare workers, a lack of mental health specialists, and an inadequate mix of skills. These factors collectively impact the care pathways for diagnosing, treating, and preventing mental illness field (Ayano, 2018; Trivedi et al., 2007). Furthermore, resources available at every nation's individual and sociocultural levels must be considered. It is important to not only implement Western ideas on the issue of mental illness but also account for existing methods to cope with mental health issues (Sax et al., 2021).

6 Conclusion

The public mental health determines the occurrence and prevention of mental health-related problems in the community by promoting mental health and well-being. Using a multidisciplinary approach, it primarily focuses on the experience, event, distribution, and determinants of mental health problems. SA countries are facing enormous challenges in providing appropriate public mental health services due to a lack of knowledge among people on mental health-related matters, low coverage of mental health management programmes, lack of proper policy and legislation in place and weak infrastructure, and lack of qualified manpower and resources to provide appropriate and accurate mental health care support. The governments and other relevant stakeholders of SA countries should integrate mental health services as part of the primary health care services. The importance of mental health-related care and services should be promoted at urban and rural levels, and proper allocation of funds to improve mental health services.

References

Ansari, I. (2015). Mental health Pakistan: Optimizing brains. *International Journal Emerging Mental Health, 17*, 288. https://doi.org/10.4172/1522-4821.1000160

Arafat, S. M. Y. (2017). Mental health promotion or public mental health: The time demanded area. *Journal of Behavioral Health, 6*(1), 1–3. https://doi.org/10.3389/978-2-83250-599-1

Arafat, S. M. Y., & Kar, S. K. (2024). Epidemiology of psychiatric disorders and overview of access to Mental Health Care in South Asia. In S. M. Y. Arafat, S. K. Kar (Eds.), *Access to Mental Health Care in South Asia—Current status, potential challenges, and ways out*. Springer Nature. https://doi.org/10.1007/978-981-99-9153-2_1

Arias, D., Saxena, S., & Verguet, S. (2022). Quantifying the global burden of mental disorders and their economic value. *eClinicalMedicine, 54*. https://doi.org/10.1016/j.eclinm.2022.101675

Ayano, G. (2018). Significance of mental health legislation for successful primary care for mental health and community mental health services: A review. *African Journal of Primary Health Care Family Medicine, 10*, e1–e4. https://doi.org/10.4102/phcfm.v10i1.1429

Badiya, P. K., Siddabattuni, S., Dey, D., Javvaji, S. K., Nayak, S. P., Hiremath, A. C., Upadhyaya, R., Madras, L., Nalam, R. L., Prabhakar, Y., Vaitheswaran, S., Manjjuri, A. R., Jk, K. K., Subramaniyan, M., Raghunatha Sarma, R., & Ramamurthy, S. S. (2020). Identification of clinical and psychosocial characteristics associated with perinatal depression in the south Indian population. *General Hospital Psychiatry, 66*, 161–170. https://doi.org/10.1016/j.genhosppsych.2020.08.002

Basavaraju, V., Enara, A., Gowda, G. S., Harihara, S. N., Manjunatha, N., Kumar, C. N., & Math, S. B (2019). Psychiatrist in court: Indian scenario. *Indian Journal of Psychological Medicine, 41*(2), 126–134

Bhui, K. (2012). *Culture and mental health: A comprehensive textbook*. CRC Press. https://doi.org/10.1192/bjp.bp.107.042101

Dubreucq, J., Plasse, J., & Franck, N. (2021). Self-stigma in serious Mental Illness: A systematic review of frequency, correlates, and consequences. *Schizophrenia Bulletin, 47*, 1261–1287. https://doi.org/10.1093/schbul/sbaa181

Falk, G. (2010). *Stigma: How we treat outsiders*. Prometheus Books.

Fisher, J., Cabral De Mello, M., Patel, V., Rahman, A., Tran, T., Holton, S., & Holmes, W. (2012). Prevalence and determinants of common perinatal mental disorders in women in low- and lower-middle-income countries: A systematic review. *Bulletin of World Health Organization, 90*, 139g–149g. https://doi.org/10.2471/BLT.11.091850

Hossain, M. M., Hasan, M. T., Sultana, A., & Faizah, F. (2019). New Mental Health act in Bangladesh: Unfinished agendas. *Lancet Psychiatry, 6*, e1. https://doi.org/10.1016/S2215-0366(18)30472-3

Javed, A., Khan, M. N. S., Nasar, A., & Rasheed, A. (2020). Mental Healthcare in Pakistan. *Taiwanese Journal of Psychiatry, 34*(1), 6. https://doi.org/10.4103/TPSY.TPSY_8_20

Kathriarachchi, S., Seneviratne, V., & Amarakoon, L. (2019). Development of mental health care in Sri Lanka: Lessons learned. *Taiwanese Journal of Psychiatry, 33*(2), 55. https://doi.org/10.4103/TPSY.TPSY_15_19

Kola, L., Kohrt, B. A., Hanlon, C., Naslund, J. A., Sikander, S., Balaji, M., Benjet, C., Cheung, E. Y. L., Eaton, J., Gonsalves, P., & Hailemariam, M. (2021). Covid-19 mental health impact and responses in low-income and middle-income countries: Reimagining global mental health. *The Lancet Psychiatry, 8*(6), 535–550. https://doi.org/10.1016/S2215-0366(21)00025-0

Kovess-Masfety, V., Karam, E., Keyes, K., Sabawoon, A. & Sarwari, B. A. (2021). Access to Care for Mental Health problems in Afghanistan: A National Challenge. *International Journal of Health Policy Management, 11*, 1442–50. https://doi.org/.34172/ijhpm.2021.46

Lund, C., Tomlinson, M., De Silva, M., Fekadu, A., Shidhaye, R., Jordans, M., Petersen, I., Bhana, A., Kigozi, F., & Prince, M. (2012). PRIME: A programme to reduce the treatment gap for mental disorders in five low-and middle-income countries. *PLoS Medicine, 9*, e1001359. https://doi.org/10.1371/journal.pmed.1001359

National Collaborating Centre For Mental, H. (2011). National Institute for Health and Care excellence: Guidelines. In *Common Mental Health disorders: Identification and pathways to care*. British Psychological Society (UK) Copyright © 2011, The British Psychological Society & The Royal College of Psychiatrists.

Naveed, S., Waqas, A., Chaudhary, A. M. D., Kumar, S., Abbas, N., Amin, R., Jamil, N., & Saleem, S. (2020). Prevalence of common mental disorders in South Asia: A systematic review and meta-regression analysis. *Frontiers in Psychiatry, 11*, 573150. https://doi.org/10.3389/fpsyt.2020.573150

Ogbo, F. A., Mathsyaraja, S., Koti, R. K., Perz, J., & Page, A. (2018). The burden of depressive disorders in South Asia, 1990–2016: Findings from the global burden of disease study. *BMC psychiatry, 18*(1), 1–11

Pandya, A., Shah, K., Chauhan, A., & Saha, S. (2020). Innovative mental health initiatives in India: A scope for strengthening primary healthcare services. *Journal of Family Medicine and Primary Care, 9*(2), 502. https://doi.org/10.4103/jfmpc.jfmpc_977_19

Patel, V., Boyce, N., Collins, P.Y., Saxena, S., & Horton, R (2011). A renewed agenda for global mental health. *The Lancet, 378*(9801), 1441–1442

Ranade, K., Kapoor, A., & Fernandes, T. N. (2022). Mental health law, policy & program in India—A fragmented narrative of change, contradictions and possibilities. *SSM—Mental Health, 2*, 100174. https://doi.org/10.1016/j.ssmmh.2022.100174

Sagar, R., Dandona, R., Gururaj, G., Dhaliwal, R. S., Singh, A., Ferrari, A., Dua, T., Ganguli, A., Varghese, M., Chakma, J. K., & Kumar, G. A. (2020). The burden of mental disorders across the states of India: The global burden of disease study 1990–2017. *The Lancet Psychiatry, 7*(2), 148–161

Sax, W. S., Lang, C., Sax, W., & Lang, C. (2021). *The movement for global mental health: Critical views from South and Southeast Asia*. Amsterdam University Press.

Seshu, U., Khan, H. A., Bhardwaj, M., Sangeetha, C., Aarthi, G., John, S., Thara, R., & Raghavan, V. (2021). A qualitative study on the use of mobile-based intervention for perinatal depression among perinatal mothers in rural Bihar, India. *International Journal of Social Psychiatry, 67*, 467–471. https://doi.org/10.1177/0020764020966003

Sidhu, G. S., Sidhu, T. K., Kaur, P., Lal, D., & Sangha, N. K. (2019). Evaluation of peripartum depression in females. *International Journal Applied Basic Medical Research, 9*, 201–205. https://doi.org/10.4103/ijabmr.IJABMR_23_19

Singh, R., & Khadka, S. (2021). Mental health law in Nepal'. *BJPsych International, 19*(1), 24–26. https://doi.org/10.1192/bji.2021.52

Steel, Z., Marnane, C., Iranpour, C., Chey, T., Jackson, J. W., Patel, V., & Silove, D. (2014). The global prevalence of common mental disorders: A systematic review and meta-analysis 1980–2013. *International Jouranl of Epidemiology, 43*, 476–493. https://doi.org/10.1093/ije/dyu038

Thara, R., & Padmavati, R. (2013). Community mental health care in South Asia. *World Psychiatry: Official Journal of the World Psychiatric Association (WPA), 12*(2), 176–177. https://doi.org/10.1002/wps.20042

The World Bank. (2022). *Population, total—South Asia*. World Bank Group. Retrieved June 04, 2023 from https://data.worldbank.org/indicator/SP.POP.TOTL?locations=8S

Trivedi, J. K., Goel, D., Kallivayalil, R. A., Isaac, M., Shrestha, D. M., & Gambheera, H. C. (2007). Regional cooperation in South Asia in the field of mental health. *World Psychiatry, 6*, 57–59.

Tsheten, T., Chateau, D., Dorji, N., Pokhrel, H. P., Clements, A. C., Gray, D. J., & Wangdi, K. (2023). Impact of covid-19 on Mental Health in Bhutan: A way forward for action. *The Lancet Regional Health—Southeast Asia, 11*, 100179. https://doi.org/10.1016/j.lansea.2023.100179

Wahlbeck, K. (2015). Public mental health: The time is ripe for translation of evidence into practice. *World Psychiatry, 14*(1), 36–42. https://doi.org/10.1002/wps.20178

Watson, J., Anderson, J., Wilson, E., & Anderson, K. L. (2020). The impact of the United Nations Convention on the rights of persons with disabilities (CRPD) on Victorian guardianship practice. *Disability and Rehabilitation, 44*(12), 2806–2814. https://doi.org/10.1080/09638288.2020.1836680

WHO. (2004). *Promoting mental health: Concepts, emerging evidence, practice (Summary Report)*. World Health Organization. Retrieved from https://apps.who.int/iris/bitstream/handle/10665/42940/9241591595.pdf

WHO. (2017). *Mental health atlas 2017 country profile: India*. World Health Organization. Retrieved June 05, 2023 from https://cdn.who.int/media/docs/default-source/mental-health/mental-health-atlas-2017-country-profiles/ind.pdf?sfvrsn=2afad897_1&download=true

WHO. (2019). *Psychiatrists working in mental health sector (per 100,000)*. World Health Organization. Retrieved June 04, 2023 from https://www.who.int/data/gho/data/indicators/indicator-details/GHO/psychiatrists-working-in-mental-health-sector-(per-100-000

WHO. (2021a). Comprehensive mental health action plan 2013–2030.

WHO. (2021b). *Mental health atlas 2020*. World Health Organization.

WHO. (2022a). *Mental health atlas 2020 country profile: Afghanistan*. World Health Organization. Retrieved June 05, 2023 from https://cdn.who.int/media/docs/default-source/mental-health/mental-health-atlas-2020-country-profiles/afg.pdf?sfvrsn=d701faec_6&download=true

WHO. (2022b). *Mental health atlas 2020 country profile: Bangladesh*. World Health Organization. Retrieved June 05, 2023 from https://cdn.who.int/media/docs/default-source/mental-health/mental-health-atlas-2020-country-profiles/bgd.pdf?sfvrsn=e8b5a1fb_4&download=true

WHO. (2022c). *Mental health atlas 2020 country profile: Bhutan*. World Health Organization. Retrieved June 05, 2023 from https://cdn.who.int/media/docs/default-source/mental-health/mental-health-atlas-2020-country-profiles/btn.pdf?sfvrsn=2bdf0456_4&download=true

WHO. (2022d). *Mental health atlas 2020 country profile: Maldives*. World Health Organization. Retrieved June 05, 2023 from https://cdn.who.int/media/docs/default-source/mental-health/mental-health-atlas-2020-country-profiles/mdv.pdf?sfvrsn=a19c3014_4&download=true

WHO. (2022e). *Mental health atlas 2020 country profile: Nepal*. World Health Organization. Retrieved June 05, 2023 from https://cdn.who.int/media/docs/default-source/mental-health/mental-health-atlas-2020-country-profiles/npl.pdf?sfvrsn=809a5794_4&download=true

WHO. (2022f). *Mental health atlas 2020 country profile: Pakistan.* World Health Organization. Retrieved June 05, 2023 from https://cdn.who.int/media/docs/default-source/mental-health/mental-health-atlas-2020-country-profiles/pak.pdf?sfvrsn=62378896_6&download=true

WHO. (2022g). *Mental health atlas 2020 country profile: Sri Lanka.* World Health Organization. Retrieved June 05, 2023 from https://cdn.who.int/media/docs/default-source/mental-health/mental-health-atlas-2020-country-profiles/lka.pdf?sfvrsn=3ff2ba8a_6&download=true

Printed in the United States
by Baker & Taylor Publisher Services